KU-169-932

# Contents

# Boxes

# Tables

# Figures

# Acronyms

ABS       Australian Bureau of Statistics
AIC       Australian Institute of Criminology
AIHW       Australian Institute of Health and Welfare
ASOC       Australian Standard Offence Classification
EPA       Environmental Protection Authority (or Agency)
CASA       Centre Against Sexual Assault
HREOC       Human Rights and Equal Opportunity Commission
NCJSF       National Criminal Justice Statistical Framework
RCIADIC       Royal Commission into Aboriginal deaths in Custody

# Acknowledgments

A number of people have been of great assistance in the production of this book. We are grateful to Kevin Tomkins and Nick Hookway for their help with tracking down relevant literature and references on various topics. Our thanks also go to Della Clark, Lyn Devereaux, and Kellie Brandenburg who have contributed to the book's completion through wonderful administrative support. The ongoing enthusiasm and expertise provided by Debra James, Pete Cruttenden, and many others at Oxford University Press is also gratefully acknowledged.

# CHAPTER 1

# Introduction

Crime is one of those topics that people have always found fascinating. It is widely covered in our newspapers and magazines, and is one of the main forms of fiction. Films, television programs, novels, biographies, and games frequently focus on the issue of crime and the law. Most people enjoy a good 'whodunnit' story, while police serials on television are one of the most popular types of shows.

Yet, in many ways our attitude to crime is contradictory. It entertains us as drama but is also a source of revulsion and fear. This does not simply reflect our desire for voyeuristic titillation, but may also be because we all experience crime directly in some way. Fear of crime influences our day-to-day behaviour. We watch our bags and wallets through fear of theft, and worry that our cars will be stolen or vandalised. Some women fear going out alone at night. Often our fears seem justified if we have been a victim of crime ourselves or know someone who has been a victim.

Our interest in crime is due not only to being a victim or potential victim, but also stems from the likelihood that in some areas of our behaviour we are on the wrong side of the law. Most people commit a crime during their lifetime, whether it is the use of an illicit drug such as cannabis, drinking under-age, tax evasion, driving while over the legal limit, or stealing office stationery. In engaging in these acts, we do so in the knowledge that we could end up in court. Many people therefore have the potential to be affected by the punitive sanctions of the criminal justice system even if they do not see themselves as 'criminals'.

How then are we to understand crime? Is the image of crime on our TV screens and video players an accurate representation of crime? Which crimes are not talked about very much, and why not? Should we be afraid of certain types of crimes more than others? Who commits crimes anyway, and who suffers the most from crime? What do present patterns of crime tell us about the nature of our society and the operation of our institutions of criminal justice? It is these kinds of questions that this book is designed to address.

This book is about crime in Australian society. It describes and analyses various kinds of harm, most of which are deemed to be 'criminal' in the eyes of the law. In doing so, the book traces the general trends and patterns of these crimes—from property crime to state crime—and explores their social dynamics and consequences. An important theme of the book is the critical influence of social difference in determining who commits which kinds of crime and how this influences the response of both the state and other social groups.

The book thus has two major strands. Part 1 of the book provides a survey of distinct types of crimes: property crime, violent crime, public order offences, drugs and crime, corporate crime, environmental crime, and state crime. The emphasis in this section is on tracing the contours of social harm associated with particular acts. We want to know the prevalence of certain types of behaviour, who engages in this behaviour, and how we might best explain particular crimes as social phenomena.

Part 2 shifts the focus away from harm to address the social differences influencing offending behaviour and the victimisation process. The question of who is a perpetrator and who is a victim of crime is inextricably bound up with social processes. Crime is not socially neutral. For example, men are more likely than women to engage in violent crimes. Working class people are more likely than middle class people to be prosecuted for offending behaviour, especially in regard to street offences. In other words, social divisions—based upon class, gender, ethnicity, indigenous status, and age—have major influences on who does what to whom and why. Inequalities and social differences must be taken into account if we are to understand fully the social nature of crime and its control in Australian society.

## AMBIGUITIES OF CRIME

The meaning of the word 'crime' is not as straightforward as it first appears. How **crime** is defined and viewed varies depending on how we answer the question 'what is crime?'

From a strictly legal perspective, the answer to 'what is crime' is simply what the law says it is (see White & Haines 2004). In this view, the state has a central place in defining what is criminal and what is not. For an act to be criminal it must be legally condemned by the state and sanctions must apply. This is the bottom line when it comes to how most criminal justice institutions operate, regardless of other perspectives that might also shape official reactions to behaviour that could also be seen as harmful but not legally criminal. One of the key limitations of this definition of crime, however, is that it provides a narrow conception of harm. Furthermore, it often leaves begging the issue of state acts that may themselves be sources of considerable harm, but which are not criminalised by that same state (for example, acts of genocide or torture).

Most sociologists and criminologists adopt a much wider definition of crime, so as to include notions of 'harm' and 'deviance' that are not necessarily acknowledged as criminal by the state. For some, the key emphasis is on a human rights approach to harm, in which various social ills are deemed to be 'criminal' from the point of view of negative social impacts (see, for example, Schwendinger & Schwendinger 1975). In many cases, harmful actions are ignored by agencies of criminal justice, even though things such as price fixing, tax evasion, or preventable workplace deaths cause great social harm. For others, the emphasis is less on defining certain acts as bad or good than on examining the social processes by which an act comes to be seen as a crime. Here the concern is to explore the group interactions and institutional procedures that make certain people and certain actions more liable to be labelled criminal than others (see, for example, Rubington & Weinberg 1978).

From an historical and cross-cultural perspective we find that crime definitions are transitory and relative. What is 'crime' varies greatly depending upon the period and the social context. In medieval Europe, for example, when the Christian Church was the arbiter of what was deemed to be right and wrong, the key crimes included heresy (that is, going against Church doctrine and beliefs) and usury (charging interest on money lent to another person). With the advent of more secular systems of law, crime began to be defined less in religious terms than in respect to property rights (for example, theft) and acts against the state (for example, treason). Comparative analysis shows us that what is a crime in some countries (for example, bigamy) is not so in others (for example, men having up to four wives at the same time). The use of drugs, such as alcohol or cannabis, is subject to widely varying rules and sanctions depending upon the country. At the international or global level, there continue to be disputes and negotiations over how to define war crimes, terrorism, and environmental crimes. Conflicts between states may stem, in part, from disagreements over what is considered a crime (for example, bulldozing residential buildings in an occupied territory) or simply national security (for example, preventing terrorist attacks).

We could also consider the question of 'what is crime' from the perspective of mass media portrayals. Certainly the popular image of crime is that of street crime, involving assaults, murder, theft, and car theft. These images are bolstered by advertising that explicitly uses the 'fear of crime' as a means to sell security devices and private policing as the answer to the presumed problem. The media emphasis tends to be on certain types of predatory crime, and such crime tends to be sensationalised. Moreover, much emphasis is given to the distinctiveness of the criminal, and the appropriateness of the victim; hence, criminality and victimhood is frequently based on stereotype and caricature. Complex crimes and crimes of the powerful tend not to be dealt with in either mainstream or fictional accounts of crime.

Finally, if we ask the question 'what is crime' from a commonsense and everyday perspective, we might find that it operates as a loose notion based upon morality. Most people break the law at some stage in their lives, but common crimes (such as the use of 'soft' illegal drugs) do not always translate into the offenders being perceived or responded to as a criminal by members of the society at large. Crime is frowned upon, but certain types of crime are nevertheless seen as 'acceptable' (for example, victimless crimes, or crimes committed by teenagers as they explore adult activities). In the end it is the state that assigns a criminal status to individuals, regardless of general public opinion or sentiment. Over time, the latter may lead to changes in the criminal law and thus a shift in what is considered a criminal, or a health or moral problem.

## CRIME AND CRIMINAL LAW

The **criminal law** identifies those behaviours deemed by lawmakers to be deserving of punishment and control. Which acts are considered wrongful reflects an historical process, in which various acts over time are prohibited (or conversely, not prohibited) into the future because of the precedents set by the past. This can make law reform slow and difficult. Such was the case, for example, with making rape in marriage a recognised criminal offence. Under the law of coverture, women were seen to be fused into the legal identity of men upon marriage. In such a (fictional) legal unity, there could be no concept of rape, and furthermore it was assumed that women granted consent to sexual relations upon entering the marriage contract. It took a concerted struggle before harm within the marriage contract was socially and legally acknowledged.

Which acts are considered harmful is also a political process, in which the contemporary tenor of law-and-order politics sets the parameters and tone of legislation relating to crime and crime control. To put it differently, criminal laws are a human product, forged in historical and social circumstances that put their unique stamp upon what is considered to be harmful enough to be criminalised at any point in time. Not all harmful acts are criminalised either. This alone makes it clear that decisions about the criminal law are contested rather than technical. The overall aim of criminal law is to prevent certain kinds of behaviour regarded as harmful or potentially harmful, and to do so through a rational system of adjudication and punishment. The challenge for lawmakers is to choose which harms to criminalise and which to deal with through other types of social regulation (for example, such as civil proceedings).

Box 1.1 provides a summary of the key purposes of criminal law. Importantly, the different reasons or purposes are frequently in conflict with each other. The rationale behind any particular criminal law, therefore, can be framed in relation to specific purposes that, in turn, reflect specific ideological or philosophical differences. For instance, conservative versions of New Right thinking about law and order see the upholding of certain moral standards as a crucial aspect of criminal law. Libertarian perspectives within the broad New Right framework, however, see such legislation as an encroachment upon individual rights and liberty. The first favours criminalisation of activity deemed to be immoral; the second wishes keep out of the criminal court those activities freely chosen by individuals, which appear to do no real harm to others around them (White & Haines 2004).

Generally speaking, there tends to be broad agreement that certain types of activities are harmful and represent significant enough wrongdoing to warrant state sanctions. These include, for instance, crimes

## Box 1.1

## PURPOSES OF CRIMINAL LAW

### Moral wrongness

- Morality is seen as underpinning the social fabric of society. Criminal law is a vital instrument in deterring 'immoral' behaviour.
- This perspective is closely allied to Conservative social philosophy in which the point of intervention is to uphold certain morals.
- There is a tendency to expand laws relating to 'moral' issues, such as pornography, to enact harsher penalties in order to enforce the legal and moral code, and for concerns about order and conformity to take priority over concerns about justice.

### Individual autonomy

- Individual autonomy and freedom are the most important social values.
- The criminal law should only be used against behaviour that injures the rights and interests of other people ('harms to others' approach).
- This perspective is closely allied to 'libertarianism', in which the point of intervention is to facilitate freedom and to minimise the restrictions to which people are subjected.
- There is a tendency to restrict the number and use of laws, reduce laws relating to 'victimless' crime, and emphasise individual liberty as the basis for justice.

### Community welfare

- Community interests are the most important social values to the extent that individual autonomy may be sacrificed for the greater good of the community.
- The principal purpose of criminal law is to protect the physical well-being of members of a community.
- Community welfare is the key principle in deciding which behaviour should or should not be criminalised in respect of a full range of 'anti-social' behaviour.

Source: drawn from Findlay et al. (1994).

involving death (homicide, manslaughter, infanticide), crimes involving bodily injury (physical assaults, sexual assaults), and a number of property offences (robbery, theft, damaging property). More contentious is how best to deal with social harms relating to things such as occupational health and public safety offences (physical injury in workplace, injury from consumption of goods), offences against public order (rioting, offensive language), and environmental offences (pollution, toxic and hazardous waste). Particularly volatile areas of dispute are those dealing with 'paternalistic' offences (gambling, prostitution, obscene literature), as these tend to highlight major philosophical differences regarding the place and role of the criminal law in society.

In most cases, according to criminal law, the intent and the act must both concur to constitute the crime:

> All crimes comprise some form of prohibited conduct which may be an act or (in rare cases) an omission. This conduct element denotes the external or physical component of a crime. Another element found in many (but not all) crimes is the mental state of the person at the time when the prohibited conduct was performed. This may take several forms such as intention, recklessness or knowledge in relation to the prohibited conduct. ...However, there are many crimes, known as offences of strict liability and of absolute liability, which do not require any such awareness at all (Findlay et al. 1994: 20).

Conduct elements of a crime refer to the accused's conduct *(actus reus)* that caused the crime. The prohibited conduct must have been performed voluntarily (for example, not being forced to do it, not doing it while sleepwalking). The mental element of a crime refers to a determination that the accused's conduct was accompanied by a prescribed state of mind *(mens rea)*. This reflects the idea that people ought to be judged by their free choice of action.

In some instances the law will ignore the subjective approach (which focuses on the mental element) in favour of arguments based on the community welfare grounds of 'public interest' (particularly if future crime is to be prevented or reduced).

The issue of legal personhood is wrapped around the notion that all adults have the necessary mental capacity to make judgments and take responsibility for their actions. Exceptions to this have to be proven in court, as in the case of those who can show that they were insane (within certain defined legal prescriptions) at the time when the prohibited behaviour took place. In law, children under the age of 10 are treated as being incapable of committing criminal offences in most Australian states. Furthermore, until a child reaches the age of 14 it is presumed that they are incapable of wrong-doing (this is known as the legal doctrine of **doli incapax**), and this presumption must be rebutted before criminal proceedings can be brought against them (that is, prosecution must prove beyond a reasonable doubt that the child knew that the act was wrong 'as distinct from an act of mere naughtiness or childish mischief'; see Schetzer 2000). The issue of criminal responsibility can, however, be problematic. This is especially true in relation to corporations where the concept of *mens rea* is difficult to apply. After all, where do we find the state of mind of a company and, even if we could, how could or should this be represented in juridical practice?

## THE CRIMINALISATION PROCESS

Issues surrounding how best to assess the conduct and mental elements of crime provide some inkling into the social dynamics that underpin criminality. What is formally deemed to be 'criminal' and who is defined as an 'offender' involves a social process, in which officials of the state formally intervene and designate certain acts and certain actors as warranting a criminal label. Until an act, or actor, has been processed in particular ways by the state, there is no 'crime' as such. This is regardless of actual behaviour that takes place. In other words, crime does not 'exist' until there has been an official social reaction to the event.

To become a 'criminal' is to be labelled so by the criminal justice system. Consider the following observation:

> Social groups create deviance by making the rules whose infraction constitutes deviance, and by applying those rules to particular people and labeling them as outsiders. From this point of view, deviance is not a quality of the act the person commits, but rather a consequence of the application by others of rules and sanctions to an 'offender'. The deviant is one to whom the label has been successfully applied; deviant behavior is behavior that people so label (Becker 1963: 9).

This perspective shifts the focus away from the discussion of varying *definitions of crime* (and arguments about the nature of different types of social harm, and whether or not to criminalise these) to an analysis of the ways in which something or someone becomes *institutionally recognised* as being criminal. In this processual account, the emphasis is on the factors that determine the social status of an event or person.

What is important, for present purposes, is that how criminal justice officials (especially the police) intervene in any given situation has a direct impact on whether or not any particular event, or any particular individual, will be 'officially' criminalised. The criminalisation process is contingent upon how discretion is used throughout the criminal justice system. Our attention is thus drawn to the role of the criminal justice institutions in constituting crime, rather than to the actual act or conduct itself.

To illustrate this, we can consider how the process of becoming a young offender has a number of steps and dimensions. The pathways into, and diversions from, juvenile justice go something like this:

- Someone reports an event, or the police see a young person doing something that they feel the young person should not be doing.
- The police officer intervenes, and may simply tell the young person to go on home or move along.
- Depending on the nature of the offensive behaviour, and the attitude and cooperation shown by the young person, the police officer may decide to issue a formal caution (this entails taking the young person to the police station, recording the offence, and having a chat with the young person's parents about the incident).
- If the incident is a bit more serious, the police officer may decide to charge the young person (to formally proceed against the young person).
- If a young person is formally charged with an offence, they will generally be issued with a summons (which outlines when they have to come to court and why).
- If the incident or alleged offence is serious, then the young person may be required to apply for bail (some kind of money and behaviour guarantee that they will show up in court at the required time).
- In some instances, bail will not be offered, and the young person will be placed in detention on remand (that is, in secure custody until the court case goes forward).
- Instead of going to court, the young person may be offered the option of either doing police-assigned community work (as is possible in South Australia), or more likely will be asked to participate in a juvenile conference (or equivalent) where they will be required to meet with any victims as well as others affected by the offence in order to work out some kind of reparation for the harm they have caused.

- If they go to court (usually a Children's Court, which has special rules and procedures to take into account the special needs and circumstances of children), the guilt or non-guilt of the young person is legally determined.
- If found guilty of an offence, the judge or magistrate can assign a range of sanctions (alternative penalties or dispositions), which range from simply giving a warning, imposing a fine, or placing the young person on some kind of community-based behaviour order (which restricts their activity, or which demands that they attend special training or drug and alcohol sessions), through to incarcerating a young person in a youth detention centre.

This story of progress through the system will vary greatly in practice depending upon a wide range of factors. Some of these factors are described in box 1.2.

For any crime to be officially recognised and recorded as a crime, the gatekeepers of the system—the police—have to make initial assessments regarding the nature of the offence, the status of the reporter, the status of the offender, and the status of the victim. When the assessment concludes that the event is worth dealing with officially, then it will be considered worthy of recording officially. The crime then becomes a 'fact'.

## MEASURING CRIME

Crime is ambiguous and complex. It is socially constructed through the imposition of particular definitions, different types of publicity and media coverage, and through management of the data collection process. The ways in which we 'measure crime' are thus intertwined with both 'how crime is defined' (and what is deemed to be serious and harmful) and 'how it is responded to by institutions of criminal justice' (through specific campaigns, programs, and interventions). To take one example of the complexities of crime measurement, the sources of criminal law vary around the country as there is no single body of criminal law governing the whole of Australia. Each state and territory has its own set of criminal laws, and there is also Commonwealth criminal law. Major differences can thus exist in relation to things such as definitions of offences, their range of seriousness, the definitions of defences, and prescribed punishments.

## SOCIAL FACTORS AFFECTING THE CRIMINALISATION PROCESS

Box 1.2

- whether or not the incident was a crime and, if so, how serious it is
- how visible the crime was
- who reported the incident, and whether they were taken seriously by the police
- whether the police have the resources to deal with particular kinds of crimes, and whether it was serious enough in the light of existing resources to respond to it
- the nature of the evidence available to police
- the characteristics and behaviour of the young person
- if and how well the police know the young person, and their family and friends
- the statutory options available for processing the young person, such as police cautioning schemes or juvenile conferencing options
- the influence of reports by social workers and other professionals on how best to deal with the young person
- the 'acting' skills of the young person in court and in the police station
- the attitude of the magistrate or judge, in relation to the appearance and demeanour of the young person in court
- the quality of legal representation
- the previous criminal record of the young person

From the point of view of analysis, social scientists also have their differences when it comes to crime and crime statistics (see Nettler 1984; Jupp 1989; Jupp et al. 2000). Three broad strands within criminology that deal with measurement issues can be identified (White & Haines 2004: 9–10):

- The *realist approach* adopts the view that crime exists 'out there' in society and that the **'dark figure' of crime** needs to be uncovered and recorded. The 'dark figure' of crime refers to crimes that are unreported. There are limitations to the gathering of official statistics (such as reliance solely on police records of reported offences), and one of the roles of criminology is to supplement official statistics (those generated by the police, courts, and prison authorities) through a range of informal or alternative measures. The emphasis is on the problem of omission—to uncover the true or real extent of crime by methods such as victim surveys, self-report surveys, test situations, hidden cameras, and so on.

- The *institutionalist approach* adopts the view that crime is a 'social process', and it rejects the notion that we can unproblematically gain a sense of the real extent of crime by improving our measuring devices and techniques. This approach concentrates instead on the manner in which official institutions of crime control actually process suspects and thus define certain individuals and certain types of behaviour as being 'criminal'. The emphasis is on the problem of bias—to show how some people and events are designated by the criminal justice system as being criminal, while others are not.

- The *critical realist approach* argues that crime measurement can be characterised as having elements of both 'social process' and a grounded 'reality'. The task of measurement from this perspective is to uncover the processes whereby the crimes against the most vulnerable and least powerful sections of the population have been ignored or under-represented. The emphasis is on the problem of victimisation—to demonstrate empirically how certain groups are especially vulnerable to crime and to the fear of crime, and conceptually to criticise the agencies of crime control for their lack of action in protecting these groups.

There are, then, debates within criminology over how and what to measure, and often these debates reflect basic divisions within the field regarding the definition of crime itself.

Even given these debates, however, it is nevertheless a truism that most criminologists still have to rely upon some type of crime statistics in order to interpret or make sense of crime (however defined). With respect to this, researchers and policy-makers frequently refer to official sources of data in their work. Even with limitations, official crime data does provide some sense of overall communal well-being and some indication of broad crime patterns.

Statistical information is collected by police services (including the Australian Federal Police), courts (lower and supreme courts), correctional services (including community corrections), crime prevention units, and regulatory agencies (such as the Australian Competition & Consumer Commission). Some key sources of official crime data in Australia include:

- police offence information systems
- police records on apprehensions and juvenile cautioning
- court 'criminal case management systems'
- correctional services, including community service orders
- juvenile conferencing teams
- fine enforcement registers or systems
- family incident reports or equivalent.

Published statistical information comes in a variety of forms and is available from a diverse range of agencies. Some of the better-known agencies include:

- Australian Institute of Criminology
- Australian Bureau of Statistics (ABS) National Crime and Justice Statistical Centre
- New South Wales Bureau of Crime Statistics
- Western Australia Crime Research Centre
- South Australia Office of Crime Statistics
- Queensland Crime and Misconduct Commission.

Information about victims, crimes, and criminal justice issues is also available from sources such as centres against sexual assault (CASAs), the Human Rights and Equal Opportunity Commission (HREOC), and State and Commonwealth Ombudsman offices.

There are a number of technical problems in trying to compare crime statistics across different jurisdictions. The ABS National Crime and Justice Statistics Centre, through the National Criminal Justice Statistical Framework (NCJSF), attempts to build connections across the main sectors of the criminal justice system nationally. For example, it has developed the Australian Standard Offence Classification (ASOC) as a means to provide a uniform national statistical framework for classifying offences for use by justice agencies and other persons and agencies with an interest in crime and justice issues. Although defined differently according to local state laws, distinct crimes nevertheless can be grouped in such as way as to make comparisons between states possible.

Another issue that makes statistical comparison difficult relates to the fact that the incidents that make up a crime event may involve a number of offenders, a number of victims, different offences, and/or multiple incidents of a single offence type. Hence 'counting rules' have been established, as well as different ways in which to measure different aspects of the criminal event.

For example, individuals may have more than one arrest, conviction, or prison reception during the recording period, so counting only individuals would substantially under-count the *number of offences* (the incidence of crime) dealt with by the criminal justice system. Similarly, counting only charges or convictions or prison receptions would not show the number of distinct persons actually involved in crime, and in fact would over-count the *number of offenders* (the prevalence of crime). The NCJSF is designed to deal with these kinds of matters in a coherent manner that allows for standardised methods of collecting and compiling criminal justice data across the country.

For these reasons considerable care must be taken in interpreting comparisons and trend analyses (see box 1.3). This is especially the case when talking about cross-national statistics. For instance, the nature of record keeping, definitions of juveniles/adults and specific types of crimes, and data-processing techniques varies greatly. Some countries record all arrests and court appearances; others only record convictions. This is important because in many jurisdictions today there is a major emphasis on pre-court diversion programs, and court-ordered diversion programs, which will affect the officially recorded number of convictions. A lower

**Box 1.3**

## WHAT ARE THE BEST WAYS TO INTERPRET CRIME STATISTICS?

Several years of statistics should be examined in order to gauge *trends*, not year-to-year fluctuations, as exceptional events can occur in a given year. For example, homicide figures are quite static, but one singular event can skew the figures in any given year.

Trends should normally be expressed in *rates* rather than absolute figures in order to obtain a more accurate measure of changes in crime (for example, number of incidents per 100,000 people, or car theft in terms of number of vehicles per 100,000 vehicles).

It is important to ensure that *'like is being compared with like'*, since changes can occur in the way in which statistics are compiled over time (for example, variance in counting rules, legal definitions and changes).

conviction rate, therefore, is no guarantee that crime is declining, or that the number of people coming into contact with the criminal justice system is likewise going down. Another area of concern is the nature of the offences that may come to court notice, and that may result in a conviction. In some jurisdictions this may include such things as failure to pay a train fare. In others, there may be a more rigid distinction between minor or trivial offences, which may be proceeded against without involvement of the court, and more serious criminal justice matters, which do end up in court.

A number of social factors can also affect the production of crime statistics. These include:

- the use of extra police in relation to specific offences, which will result in an apparent increase in that offence (for example, traffic offences)
- the under-reporting of some crimes, such as sexual assault
- the influence of media attention on public perceptions about levels of crime, which can increase the attention given by law enforcement agencies to certain crimes, thereby increasing arrest rates (for example, possession of knives or guns)
- the effects of public recognition of a social harm and increased professional intervention, as has occurred in relation to child abuse
- the way harmful events are classified, such as whether preventable workplace death is seen as homicide or a regulatory offence
- changing opportunities for crime (for example, the advent of home computers, television, and videos has created greater opportunities for crime)
- the over-representation of working class crime and the under-representation of corporate crime
- the effect of political pressure on the way in which crime is reported.

For social scientists, it is important to utilise a wide variety of methods and techniques in order to gauge the nature and frequency of many different types of social harm (see Jupp et al. 2000). A critical perspective that acknowledges the limitations of official statistics needs to be matched by the development of systematic and alternative forms of data collection.

## CONCLUSION

One of the main themes of this chapter has been that the study of crime and social harm is a complex exercise that requires sensitivity to the social processes that underpin the definitions, purposes, and applications of criminal law. Cross-cultural and historical analyses reveal that crime varies greatly from society to society. Measuring crime is likewise complicated by social, technical, and political factors that shape popular understandings of crime.

Who is deemed a criminal, or a victim, is always contingent upon how the state, via law enforcement officials such as the police, intervenes in the social worlds of its citizens. Similarly, what is considered to be a serious social problem, and comes to be defined as a crime, depends very much upon value judgments and the ability to mobilise public sentiment in particular ways. This will vary over time, and from place to place.

The causes of crime are as complicated to explain as the concept itself (see White & Haines 2004). What we see as the reasons why crime takes place determines what is perceived to be the best way of responding to it.

Perspectives on crime are also influenced by the work of criminologists and other social scientists in the area of criminal justice. Mainstream criminology generally accepts narrowly defined administrative definitions of 'crime' and social harm at face value, and engages in public debate and the formation of public policy within conventional understandings of the problem and what to do about it. Alternative or critical criminology offers a critique of existing definitions, examines how criminal justice institutions themselves influence the criminalisation process, and challenges conventional thinking in the light of concerns about human rights and social justice. Thinking about crime is never a neutral process politically or conceptually.

That 'crime' is a product of society thus needs to be understood multidimensionally, from how it is defined to causal factors, types of offences, and the objects of state intervention. To appreciate and understand fully the nature of crime and criminal law, therefore, it is essential to examine the nature of society, and our place within it.

## DISCUSSION QUESTIONS

1 The nature of what is 'a criminal act', and how the 'criminal' is socially and legally portrayed, shifts according to particular socio-economic circumstances. Discuss.

2 What is deemed to be a serious social problem changes over time. Why is this the case?
3 Why is crime ambiguous to define?
4 What is the 'mental element' of crime?
5 Who compiles crime statistics, and what are some of the limitations of official crime statistics?

## GLOSSARY OF TERMS

*actus reus*
> the conduct of the accused at the time of the crime

**crime**
> those acts that are legally condemned by the state and deemed to be deserving of punishment and control

**criminal law**
> those behaviours deemed by lawmakers to be deserving of punishment and control

**'dark figure' of crime**
> those criminal acts that are not reported to the police and therefore do not get recorded in officially recorded crime

*doli incapax*
> the common law presumption that children are incapable of wrongdoing because they are unable to understand the concepts of right and wrong

*mens rea*
> a concept in criminal law that focuses on whether the accused's mental state included an intention to commit harm.

## FURTHER READING

Jupp, V. (1989) *Methods of Criminological Research*, Routledge, London.
Jupp, V., Davies, P. & Francis, P. (eds) (2000) *Doing Criminological Research*, Sage, London.
Schwendinger, H. & Schwendinger, J. (1975) 'Defenders of Order or Guardians of Human Rights', in I. Taylor, P. Walton & J. Young (eds) *Critical Criminology*, Routledge and Kegan Paul, London.
White, R. & Haines, F. (2004) *Crime and Criminology* (3rd edn), Oxford University Press, Melbourne.

## WEBSITES

**www.aic.gov.au**

Australian Institute of Criminology—Provides links to various publications from Australia's leading criminologists that include research, conference papers, publications, and statistics many of which are full text.

**www.homeoffice.gov.uk/rds/pubsintro1.html**

Home Office, UK—Provides access to publications on research conducted by the Research and Statistics Directive on crime in the UK.

**www.ojp.usdoj.gov/nij**

National Institute of Justice—Provides reports on research, development, evaluation, and publications covering all areas of criminal justice in the USA.

**http://canada.justice.gc.ca/en/dept/pub/index.html**

Canadian Justice Department—Provides reports on research, development, evaluation, and publications covering all areas of criminal justice issues in Canada.

# PART 1

# Crime and Social Harm

# CHAPTER 2

# Property Crime

## INTRODUCTION

Most people, at some time, have been or will be the victim of a property crime. The theft of a wallet, damage to our car or the disappearance of the car itself, the burglary of our home—these are events that we accept as a seemingly inevitable part of life. At some time in our lives we may also be a perpetrator of a property crime, such as shoplifting an item of clothing, or the illegal downloading of an MP3 file. It is, therefore, not surprising that property offences make up about 87 per cent of the seven major recorded crimes in Australia (AIC 2002a). In 2001 there were 1,274,729 property crimes reported to the police, compared with 197,219 violent crimes, a ratio of 6.5:1 (ABS 2002b).

Property crimes are unlawful acts that have the intent of gaining property and that generally do not involve the use of force against a person. They form one of two major divisions of crime, the other being violent crimes. Property crimes not only refer to physical property, such as burglary of items from an office, but also to intellectual property, such as theft of ideas and information.

## HISTORY OF PROPERTY CRIME

Laws relating to the protection of property are a modern phenomenon and are closely tied to the evolution of capitalism as a political and economic system. Before the seventeenth century there were few goods to steal and most wealth was held in the form of land. In Europe the class that owned the wealth also controlled the administration of justice and the formulation of law. Its members employed servants to protect them and their goods. Consequently, they had little interest in developing property laws even though groups lower down the social scale would have benefited from this, especially those in trade, manufacturing, and farming.

The industrial revolution changed this by creating a new class of industrialists for whom legal protection of property was essential. Machinery production made portable goods available in large numbers and expanded the opportunities for theft. A succession of laws designed to protect private ownership was gradually enacted (Hall 1952). Over time the notion of individual ownership was extended to information and ideas, so that knowledge and ideas could be owned. Today intellectual property crime is regarded as a major problem. Even knowledge about genetic material has been turned into a commodity that can be stolen.

## MEASURING PROPERTY CRIME

The measurement of property crime tends to be based upon selected categories, such as:

1 *burglary*—the unlawful entry of a dwelling/house or any other premises such as a business, school, shop etc. with or without force, with the intent to steal (in some states, burglary is referred to in the statutes as 'break, enter and steal')
2 *larceny*—the unlawful taking of property other than a motor vehicle without force and without deceit
3 *motor vehicle theft*—the unlawful using or attempted using of a motor vehicle without the consent of the owner
4 *fraud and forgery*—unlawful acts committed or attempted, involving deception, misappropriation, forgery, uttering or counterfeiting etc.

Property crimes constitute the largest category of crime. As mentioned above, in a society where 'private property' is at the heart of the economic system (that is, class societies such as capitalism), the main 'crimes' will revolve around this fact, as do the many different laws (including for example, corporations law, *Trade Practices Act*, equity and trusts, tax law, etc.). The measurement of such crimes, however, tends to be biased towards certain types of property offences, particularly for the purposes of criminal law as such. For example, most recorded property crimes:

**a** involve no violence

**b** involve little or no contact with victims

**c** involve relatively small personal loss.

The reporting of property crime is contingent upon a number of factors, of which *insurance* is a big one, as in the case of house insurance and car insurance, which means that in the case of a theft there is a chance to recover some of the costs of the theft. However, a large proportion of property crime is unreported, due to factors such as the lack of knowledge of the theft, the trivial amount stolen, a lack of confidence in getting the stolen goods back, and so on.

Most definitions and measurements of property crime deal with 'street crime' types of categories that involve a direct and transparent 'gaining of property' rather than corporate crime and theft on a grand scale.

## TRENDS IN PROPERTY CRIME

It is difficult to establish accurately long-term trends in patterns of crime in white Australia's history because of poor record keeping in the eighteenth and nineteenth centuries. However, accurate statistics on appearances at the Magistrates' Courts in all the colonies from 1861 are available (Muhkerjee 1981; see figure 2.1). According to Muhkerjee the upward trend that characterises the period 1861 to 1899 was primarily due to increases in good order and other petty offences. Only 2 per cent of all offences charged in Magistrates' Courts went to trial in higher courts.

The drastic decline in offences that occurred in the 1890s is likely to be related to the recession that occurred at this time. Trends stabilised in the first half of the twentieth century, dipping only during World War I and II, and the Depression of the 1930s. These dips, largely due to declines in offences against the person, good order, and other petty offences, mask the increase in property offences that occurred during these periods. The end of World War II saw a steep incline in offences due to many factors, including demographic changes and the widespread availability of consumer goods. This upward trend continued through the second half of the twentieth century, but towards the end of the century most categories of property crime stabilised.

Between 1993 and 2001 the number of crimes reported to the police reveal that although there have been years when the crime rate has

**Figure 2.1**   All offences heard and determined at Magistrate's Courts in Australia 1859–1971

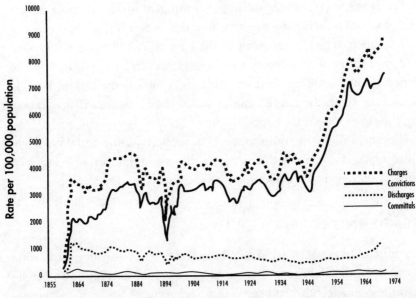

Source: Mukherjee (2000: 45–62).

increased, there have also been years when it has declined or remained stable, particularly since 1998 (see table 2.1). Unlawful entry with intent has declined from a peak rate of 2319.5 per 100,000 persons in 1998 to 2246.9 per 100,000 persons in 2001. Motor vehicle theft also appears to have stabilised, occurring within a range of 636.6 and 725.2 per 100,000 persons. The exception to this is 'other theft', which has shown a small but steady increase every year.

Victim surveys suggest a similar pattern. Every two years the ABS conducts a national survey of crime victims (ABS 2003a). These surveys are generally perceived as more accurate than crimes recorded by the police because the dark figure (that is, unreported crime) is smaller. Police reporting rates, on which official data are based, are high where insurance claims are involved, as is the case with motor vehicle theft. For many crimes, such as attempted break-in, they are very low (see table 2.2).

**Table 2.1** Recorded crime: Victims of property crime 1993–2001 (by number and rate per 100,000 persons)

| | 1993 | | 1994 | | 1995 | | 1996 | | 1997 | | 1998 | | 1999 | | 2000 | | 2001 | |
|---|---|---|---|---|---|---|---|---|---|---|---|---|---|---|---|---|---|---|
| | Number | Rate | Number | Rate | Number | Rate | Number | Rate | Number | Rate | Number | Rate | Number | Rate | Number | Rate | Number | Rate |
| Unlawful entry with intent | 381,783 | 2161.0 | 379,505 | 2125.9 | 385,162 | 2131.7 | 402,079 | 2196.2 | 421,569 | 2276.2 | 434,376 | 2319.5 | 415,735 | 2195.7 | 429,374[r] | 2241.7[r] | 435,524 | 2246.9 |
| Property theft[a] | na | na | na | na | 303,227 | 1678.2 | 313,902 | 1714.6 | 332,525 | 1795.4 | 339,512 | 1812.9 | 322,983 | 1705.8 | na | na | 325,180 | 1677.6 |
| Other[b] | na | na | na | na | 81,935 | 453.5 | 88,177 | 481.6 | 89,044 | 480.9 | 94,864 | 506.6 | 92,752 | 489.9 | na | na | 110,344 | 569.3 |
| Motor vehicle[b] | 112,472 | 636.6 | 119,469 | 669.2 | 127,094 | 703.4 | 122,914 | 671.4 | 130,138 | 702.7 | 131,587 | 702.7 | 129,552 | 684.2 | 138,912[r] | 725.2[r] | 139,943 | 722.0 |
| Other theft | na | na | na | na | 490,158 | 2714.7 | 521,762 | 2850.0 | 530,881 | 2866.4 | 563,482 | 3008.9 | 612,559 | 3235.2 | 681,268[r] | 3556.8[r] | 699,262 | 3607.5 |

na not available
r revised
a A change in the legislation related to unlawful entry with intent (UEWI) offences in South Australia resulted in an inability to provide UEWI disaggregated into property theft and other for 2000.
b Counts for motor vehicle theft prior to 1997 are not directly comparable to other years as Western Australia included the theft of caravans and trailers in addition to motor vehicle theft.

Source: ABS (2002b: 15).

**Table 2.2**  Victims of crime: Reporting rates 2002

| Type of Crime | % |
| --- | --- |
| Motor Vehicle Theft | 95.0 |
| Break-in | 75.1 |
| Attempted Break-in | 31.1 |

Source: ABS (2003a: 15).

However, the data must still be treated with caution.

- Crime victim surveys rely on memory, which is often selective with more trivial criminal incidents being forgotten more easily than serious or dramatic ones.
- They only record crimes that people are aware of. Crimes such as fraud or employee theft will be under-reported because they are often undetected.
- They are affected by the different way in which people define crime. What to one person is an attempted burglary may be regarded as trivial and not worth reporting by someone else.

The methodological rigour with which the surveys are conducted by the ABS means that they are an important source of information about national crime patterns and trends.

The Crime and Safety April 2002 survey (ABS 2003a) provides comparisons of the number of people who identify as being a victim of crime

**Table 2.3**  Victimisation prevalence rates per 100,000 population

| Type of Crime | 1993 | 1998 | 2002 |
| --- | --- | --- | --- |
| | % | % | % |
| Break-in | 4.4 | 5.0 | 4.7 |
| Attempted Break-in | 3.1 | 3.2 | 3.4 |
| Break-in/Attempted Break-in[a] | 6.8 | 7.6 | 7.4 |
| Motor Vehicle Theft | 1.7 | 1.7 | 1.8 |

a   Break-in/attempted break-in includes households that were victims of either a break-in or an attempted break-in, or both. Therefore the figures for break-in/attempted break-in are less than the sum of break-in and attempted break-in figures.

Source: ABS (2003a: 13).

during the years 1993, 1998, and 2002. These show that while the victimisation prevalence rate for break-ins increased from 4.4 per cent in 1993 to 4.7 per cent in 2002, there was a decrease of 0.3 per cent between 1998 and 2002. Although there has been some increase in attempted break-ins and motor vehicle theft, these are quite small (see table 2.3). The idea that Australia is in the grip of an ever-spiralling rise in property crime is therefore not supported by either of these sources.

When considering the extent of property crime it is important to be aware of the trivial nature of many of the incidents. Although property crimes such as theft appear in Annual Police Reports as 'serious crimes', as pointed out earlier these events usually involve no violence and often involve no contact with victims. They also involve relatively small personal loss (see Case Study 2.1). In 2001 the estimated average cost of each incident of shop-theft was $110, yet it accounted for over 50 per cent of crimes committed that year. This compares with the estimated average cost of $1800 for each incident of assault, $2500 for sexual assault, and $1.6 million for homicide. Yet together these violent crimes accounted for less than 10 per cent of all crimes. This is not to suggest that the costs of all property crime are trivial. Motor vehicle theft costs an estimated $6000 per incident while burglary costs an estimated $2400 per incident (see figure 2.2).

**Figure 2.2**  Different crimes as a proportion of total costs

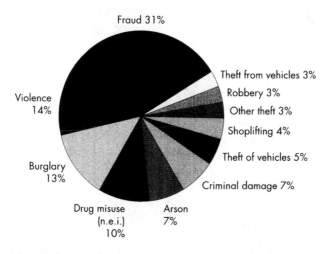

Fraud 31%

Theft from vehicles 3%

Robbery 3%

Other theft 3%

Shoplifting 4%

Theft of vehicles 5%

Criminal damage 7%

Arson 7%

Drug misuse (n.e.i.) 10%

Burglary 13%

Violence 14%

n.e.i.    not elsewhere included

Source: Mayhew (2003: 5).

## EXPLAINING PROPERTY CRIME

Property crime includes so many different kinds of crime that explaining it is akin to explaining why crime itself occurs. As with all crime, however, the pattern that occurs in a given time and place is strongly influenced by factors such as levels of affluence, social attitudes, levels of urbanisation, and the opportunities created by lifestyles.

### Levels of affluence

Australia is an affluent country with a high level of consumption. Most people own many portable goods—from motor vehicles to DVDs and mobile phones. The sharp rise in property crime that occurred after World War II is partly explained by the emergence of a consumer society in which most people own motor vehicles, televisions, and other easily removed electrical goods. Patterns of property crime are therefore closely related to these patterns of consumption. Bicycle theft is common in Belgium where the flat landscape has created a tradition of bike riding, but in Australia, where most families own one or two cars, car theft is high and bike theft is low.

### Attitudes towards property

Patterns of consumption also influence our attitude to property. Although a great deal of attention is paid to property crime by both the media and law enforcement agencies, Western culture is characterised by high levels of expenditure and waste, so the loss of small amounts of property is accepted as normal. The loss might be irritating, but often it is covered by insurance or can be cheaply replaced. Conversely, however, theft of goods from poor households (for example, where people are reliant upon fixed incomes in the form of pensions) can have a dramatic and devastating impact. This can make people especially fearful of crime, especially when the means is not readily available to take suitable crime prevention measures (such as security doors and window locks).

### Levels of urbanisation

In general, higher levels of urbanisation are associated with higher rates of property crime. However, the relationship is a complex one and varies according to the type of crime, as well as population density and patterns of urbanisation. Walker argues that if the level of urbanisation in Australia is taken into account, the level of city crime is significantly less than in the USA (Walker 1994: 14). Studies examining the relationship between crime and population density reveal that cities with high densities have the highest levels of crime, while rural areas with low population densities have the lowest (Walker 1994: 12).

## Opportunity

Australia's hot climate is associated with an outdoor lifestyle so that people spend a considerable amount of time out on the streets or in public places of entertainment. This, together with the high percentage of women in the workforce, means that opportunities for crime are high. Empty houses are more easily broken into than occupied ones, theft is most likely to occur in a public place, and cars left unattended on the street for long periods of time while owners are at work or at the pub are more easily stolen than when locked in a private garage (Walker 1994; Weatherburn 2001).

## SOCIAL CHARACTERISTICS OF PROPERTY OFFENDERS

The dominant image of property offenders is that they are young, disadvantaged males, often Indigenous, and often stealing to support a drug habit. How true is this stereotype?

According to police records, the great majority of property crime is committed by men. In 2001 females were responsible for only about 12 per cent of motor vehicle thefts, just over 10 per cent of unlawful entry with intent, and just under 30 per cent of other thefts. Juvenile males are over-represented in arrests made, as well as those cleared for property offences. In 2001–02 the offender rate for persons aged 15 to 19 years was more than four times the offender rate for the remainder of the population (AIC 2003).

There is no evidence to suggest that overseas-born Australians are more likely to engage in property crime than people born in Australia. In fact, the evidence suggests that the Australian-born population has a higher rate of involvement in property crime (Eastel 1996a: 90–1). The picture for Indigenous Australians is more complex. They are over-represented in petty theft and burglary, but not in other forms of property crime (Lincoln & Wilson 1994: 65; Hayes 1996: 321; Biles 1992).

While there does appear to be a link between drug use and property crime, it is not a simple matter of drug use leading otherwise law-abiding people into crime. Current research suggests that while using drugs in itself does not cause people to engage in crime, it does lead people already committing crimes to increase their criminal activity (Weatherburn 2001).

There is some evidence that disadvantaged groups are over-represented in 'street' crimes such as burglary and motor vehicle theft. A study of burglary conducted by Devery (1991) in Sydney found that the largest number of break, enter, and steal offenders came from districts of low socio-economic status. Devery's study supports overseas data that also suggests a strong inverse relationship between social status and participation in conventional crimes (Box 1987; Visher & Roth 1986; Chiricos 1987). In his analysis of the correlation between social disadvantage and involvement in property crime, Weatherburn also argues that there is 'a strong relationship between the level of social disadvantage in an area and the proportion of its residents actively engaged in some form of property crime' (1996: 213). Along with overseas criminologists he also suggests that poor school performance is linked to involvement in property crime (1996: 222). Neighbourhood-level dynamics, related to economic and social stress on parenting, also has an impact on offending rates (Weatherburn et al. 2001).

While this picture of the property offender provides some support for popular stereotypes, it needs to be challenged for the following reasons:

- We do not know who commits most property crimes. Official crime data are based on offences cleared or on police arrest rates, but in the great majority of property crimes no one is charged (see table 2.4).

**Table 2.4** Clearance rates for selected property crimes 2001

| Offences not finalised at 30 days | % |
| --- | --- |
| Unlawful entry with intent | 93.0 |
| Motor vehicle theft | 90.4 |
| Other theft | 87.8 |

Source: ABS (2002b: 14).

- Unlike most violent crimes, many property crimes are repeated by the same individual over a period of time. Whereas a homicide is usually a one-off incident, the same individual may be responsible for a disproportionate number of property crimes. It is therefore essential to distinguish between who participates in property crime and the *frequency* of their engagement in it.

- Official criminal justice records tell us as much about how the system operates as it does about who is responsible for crime. Certain groups are targeted by the police more frequently than others. Many studies have demonstrated that the police focus their attention on young, disadvantaged males rather than older people, middle class people, and women (Blagg & Wilkie 1995; White & Alder 1994; Youth Justice Coalition et al. 1994).

- Some types of offenders are more easily caught than others. Juveniles in particular are more likely to be caught than, for example, professional thieves. The inexperience of juveniles makes them more vulnerable to detection, as does the fact they are more likely to work in groups. The crimes they engage in, such as motor vehicle theft and burglary, occur in public places and are therefore highly visible (see Cunneen & White 2002).

- In contrast, white collar and corporate crimes have very low levels of visibility. This is just one of many reasons why official crime data provide little information about crimes by 'men in suits'. Other reasons include low levels of reporting, arrest, and clearance rates, despite the high level of social harm they cause.

So, while the popular image of the property criminal may have an element of truth, the full picture is more complex. Instead, property criminals are a varied group and there is no 'typical' property criminal (Tarling 1993).

## TRADITIONAL PROPERTY CRIMES

Theft, burglary, and motor vehicle theft are 'street crimes'; that is, they are highly visible crimes that occur in public spaces and usually involve little technical skill on the part of perpetrators. Other street crimes include assault and robbery. Street crimes are commonly reported in the media and create most public fear. Images of home invasions or of young people on wild joyrides in stolen cars create a perception in the community that social order is breaking down and that 'something must be done' about it. Yet such fears need to be qualified with the recognition that many street crimes

**Figure 2.3** Property crimes by type of location 2001

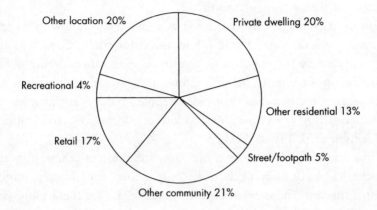

Source: AIC (2002a: 12).

actually take place in locations away from the street or other public places. In 2001, only 26 per cent of all property crimes occurred on the street or in a community location such as car parks and transport facilities (figure 2.3). In fact, most property crimes take place in the office or in a residential setting rather than on the street.

## Theft

Theft can be defined as 'the taking of another person's property with the intention of permanently depriving the owner of the property illegally and without permission, but without force, threat of force, use of coercive measures, deceit or having gained unlawful entry to any structure even if the intent was to gain theft'. It includes offences such as pickpocketing, shoplifting, bag snatching, theft from a motor vehicle, and stealing of animals. It accounts for nearly 50 per cent of the seven major recorded crimes (AIC 2002a: 34).

Although the value of items shoplifted tends to be small, the sheer volume of shoplifting that is believed to occur, as well as its economic value, warrants close attention. It particularly affects small businesses, which lack the security measures available to large stores. A survey of small businesses conducted in 1999 found that there were 674 incidents experienced per 100 businesses (Taylor & Mayhew 2002). A 2 to 3 per cent loss of sales to shoplifters can amount to a 25 per cent loss in profit and can seriously affect the financial viability of the business (Nelson & Perrone 2000). Costs are also passed on to consumers.

How accurate is the perception that young people are responsible for most shoplifting? While official data reveal that young people under the age of 20 are the most common offenders, other groups are also implicated. Professional thieves represent a minority of shoplifters, but steal high volumes. Employees are responsible for a substantial proportion of the stock lost to retailers. Figures are not available for Australia, but the 1994 National Survey of Retail Crime and Security conducted in the UK found that staff theft accounted for 30 per cent of 'stock shrinkage' (Nelson & Perrone 2000).

Most shoplifters are men rather than women (Farrington 1999). However, the gender ratio may vary with age. One study conducted in New South Wales found that while proven male offenders were the majority in the under-29-years age group, women dominated among the 30 to 65-year-olds (Salmelainen 1992). In the past it was believed that elderly people were responsible for significant amounts of shoplifting, but more recent work has challenged this finding (Farrington 1999).

Studies into the motivation of shoplifters suggest the two main motivations are economic gain and psychological and social stress (see case study 2.1). Often these motives are intertwined. For example, a high percentage of offenders are unemployed, which may be a source of psychological and social stress. For young shoplifters, the excitement is also a motivation (Klemke 1982).

## CASE STUDY 2.1

In 1991 in South Australia, a 32-year-old Australian woman pleaded guilty in the Magistrate's Court to the larceny of lemon essence and garlic salt from a supermarket, to the value of $1.98. She was convicted and released on a bond of $200 to be of good behaviour for a period of two years. In 1992 she was again charged with larceny from the same supermarket, this time in relation to a deodorant valued at $2.35. She pleaded not guilty, but was found guilty and convicted. She was also alleged to be in breach of her bond. She was sentenced to seven days' imprisonment for the breach of the bond and fourteen days' imprisonment for the offence to be served cumulatively. She was also ordered to pay the amount of the bond within three months. She appealed against the sentences on the grounds that they were excessive and that the magistrate had failed to exercise his discretion to suspend the sentence of imprisonment.

The defendant had a significant record of prior offending. She had been found guilty of shoplifting on four prior occasions. In sentencing her, the magistrate placed considerable emphasis on the need for deterrence. He said: 'Offences of larceny of the shop stealing variety I regard as quite serious having regard firstly to their prevalence, they are absolutely rife, and having regard secondly to the fact that they affect most members of the community in that shopkeepers find themselves forced to increase the price of everyday items in order to cover the outrageous incidence of such offending.'

Pre-sentence and medical reports presented to the magistrate included the following information:

- Her father was an alcoholic and she had run away from home on many occasions, leaving home for the last time when she was aged 17 years.
- She left school at the age of 15 years and had only been employed for relatively brief periods.
- She was in a de facto relationship with a man who had abused her on many occasions. On one occasion she had reported his conduct and he had been charged with assault occasioning actual bodily harm and was given a suspended sentence. She had a five-year-old daughter.
- She had a 'long history' of abuse of alcohol and prescription drugs, although in recent times she had sought expert assistance and ended this.
- She had a number of serious medical conditions.
- A forensic psychologist suggested that she had poor coping skills under conditions of stress and her intellectual functioning was within the Lower Average range. He also suggested she had suffered from 'battered woman's syndrome'.
- She had previously responded extremely well to community service work and had remained at one place as a voluntary worker.

At the appeal in the Supreme Court of South Australia the Judge rejected the argument that the sentence was excessive, but argued that the magistrate had given too much emphasis on the need for general deterrence and too little emphasis on the personal circumstances of the appellant and the possibilities for rehabilitation. He concluded that while the sentence should be upheld, it should be suspended, a bond imposed, and she should be placed on probation and required to undertake 75 hours of community service.

Source: *Christine Ann Scott v. SA Police* [1993: 589].

As well, opportunity is an important determinant, with self-service stores being particularly soft targets for casual shoplifters (Nelson & Perrone 2000). Retail outlets could take some responsibility for the level of shoplifting, as the way merchandise is displayed is designed to entice the shopper to take it.

## Burglary

The term 'burglary' is one of a number used to describe 'the unlawful entry of a structure with the intent to commit an offence' (AIC 2002a: 29). Closely associated terms are 'unlawful entry with intent', 'break and enter', and 'attempted burglary'. The absence of the use or threat of force is what distinguishes burglaries from residential robberies. The prevalence rate for burglaries in Australia is very high with one third of all property crimes being burglaries (ABS 2002b). Grabosky suggests that 'the odds are that most residents of Australia's urban areas will become the victim of a burglary at least once in their lives' (1995a: 1). In 2002, 64 per cent of unlawful entries occurred in residential settings, with 54 per cent being private dwellings (AIC 2002a: 30–1).

Although classified as a property crime, burglary is similar to violent crime in that it engenders fear among potential victims, especially when private homes are burgled. The invasion of privacy and the lost sense of security can have a psychological impact on victims that can be as devastating as the loss or destruction of property. Burglary is also an issue for businesses. The burglary of shops, warehouses, and offices causes stress, financial loss, and practical problems to managers, employers, and employees. The 1999 Small Business Crime Survey found that 27 per cent of small businesses had experienced a burglary in the preceding financial year (Taylor & Mayhew 2002). Burglaries are also very costly.

According to the ABS, in 2000–01 one in every two offenders involved in unlawful entry with intent was less than 20 years of age, with most being in the range 15–19 years. Just under 90 per cent of offenders were male, although female involvement in burglary is increasing (ABS 2002b: 40–50). However, Ratcliffe (2001) argues that young, 'opportunistic' offenders may be over-represented in official records, while professional burglars are likely to be under-represented.

Most residential burglaries occur on weekdays in the daytime when people are at work. The reverse is true for businesses, with most occurring on weekends and in the evenings (Ratcliffe 2001). Physical geography plays an important part in the distribution of burglaries. Burglars often select targets from locations they observe in their daily activity. This, together with the need to physically travel to and from their home to the crime site, means they tend to choose targets that are physically close to their homes and which offer known escape routes (Brantingham & Brantingham 1981). Ratcliffe found that in Canberra, the average journey from the offender's home to residential targets was five kilometres and that one third of burglaries were committed by offenders who travelled less than 1500 metres from their home (2001: 3). The term '**distance decay**' has been used to describe the way in which the commission of crimes reduces with distance from the perpetrator's home (Rengert et al. 1999).

Felson (1998) suggests that three factors influence the spatial pattern of burglary: the location of motivated offenders, the availability of suitable targets, and the presence or absence of guardians. For example, a CBD located near a slum area with a high concentration of offenders will experience a high level of burglaries. Homes in affluent suburban areas with a high level of security and offenders living distant from them will be relatively unaffected.

## Motor vehicle theft

Motor vehicle theft is regarded as a serious problem by law enforcement agencies partly because of the high rate of theft—in every four minutes a registered vehicle is stolen—and partly because of the financial cost to the community (AIC 2002a; Mayhew 2003). Politicians are also sensitive to community concerns that cars are stolen by young joyriders who then are a risk to both themselves and to others.

But there are aspects of motor vehicle theft that are less understood. Consider the following:

- Professional and petty thieves are responsible for about a half of all motor vehicle thefts. It is theft by these groups, as well as theft from motor vehicles, that costs the community the most because apprehension and recovery rates are lower (Higgins 1997).
- Between 10 and 15 per cent of reported car thefts are intentionally disposed of by their owners in order to claim insurance.

- The recovery rate for motor vehicle theft is generally high. In 2000–01 80 per cent of vehicles were recovered, many very quickly. Forty three per cent are recovered after one day, and 83 per cent are recovered after one week (AIC 2002a). However, around 30 per cent of vehicles have had parts or other items removed from them (Higgins 1997).

Motor vehicle theft is widely understood as a crime committed by young, disadvantaged people who are probably breaking the law in other areas and who lack discipline. This view is enhanced by the media, which is quick to label young car stealers as 'hoons' who threaten the moral fabric of society and thus should be locked up.

It has been argued, however, that insofar as young people are implicated in motor vehicle theft, their behaviour can be explained in terms of three overarching structural factors (see White 1990: 111–35): spatial relations, gender relations, and economic relations.

### Spatial relations

In the past, young people were integrated into social life through the institutions of marriage, work, and school. Today this is no longer the case, especially for young, working class people who have a high rate of unemployment, are early school leavers, and whose lack of money often forces them to remain living with, and dependent on, their parents until well past their teens. They have lots of time but little money to do anything, including paying for transport, which can even preclude 'hanging out' in the local shopping centre or mall.

### Gender relations

Car theft is predominantly a male activity. Cars are a central part of the consumer culture and as well as providing transport they offer essential practical and cultural benefits that are especially significant to males (see Forrester 1999; Walker 1999). They provide a potent status symbol; an expression of male power and aggression; and a means for developing and demonstrating mastery over technical and mechanical skills.

### Economic relations

Many young males are impoverished and unable to establish themselves away from the family home, both physically and psychologically. Car theft is attractive because it offers them an alternative source of money which may not get them away from home, but at least provides them with a form of leisure activity outside it; a sense of control over their environment; and an attractive form of work in the informal economy.

The phenomenon of juvenile car theft needs to be placed in the context of young people's experiences of economic and social exclusion from mainstream society, and in relation to broader cultural dynamics. Car theft helps young working class men establish their masculine identity. It offers excitement, transport, and status. The physical space inside the car has both a symbolic and practical dimension. The young occupants can escape the intrusion of adults, and they can go where they want, when they want, and with whom they want. They are free to create their own social world (White 1990). This analysis is supported by Salmelainen's study of young offenders in detention centres who identified the need for transport (49.6 per cent), and excitement, thrills, and fun (24.1 per cent) as the two most frequently given reasons for motor vehicle theft (1995).

## DIGITAL CRIME

**Digital crime** is the use of information technology for the commission of illegal acts. The term 'digital' refers to the way information is transmitted over telecommunications networks in the form of repeated combinations of the numbers 0 and 1. While a great deal of digital crime involves the use of computers, some involves other forms of digital technology such as 'smart cards' or phone lines. Although digital technology can be used to commit threatening and degrading types of crimes, such as cyberstalking or internet pornography, most digital crime involves fraudulent access to property. As the use of computers and other digital technologies has grown, so have the ways in which people commit property crime (see Grabosky et al. 2001).

Digital crime presents law enforcement agencies with a serious challenge because its transnational nature, its anonymity, and the speed of transactions make it difficult to control.

Computers are used to commit a wide and expanding range of crimes. These include:

- *Theft of telecommunication services*—The illegal acquisition of telecommunication services has become a serious problem involving large sums of money. It involves the illegal accessing of telecommunication services for personal use, such as a counterfeit phone card, or the establishment of a telecommunication business, such as a phone service, through illegal access to an organisation's PBX system. It may be some time before these activities are discovered—if they are discovered at all—and, like many other 'cyber-crimes', it is often difficult to identify who, or even where, offenders are.

- *Copyright infringement*—**Intellectual properties** are mental products that are protected by legal safeguards including copyright law, patents, and trademarks, the aim of which is to ensure that the profits of a creative work are returned to its legal owners. Information technology challenges the principle of 'ownership' of knowledge insofar as artistic creations such as music, films, and multimedia combinations are easily copied, and disseminated more cheaply or even free. These developments are difficult to prevent and seriously threaten the viability of some industries. Between 2000 and 2003, illegal downloading of music from internet sites cost the music industry an estimated 20 per cent of the $44 billion worldwide market, forcing partnerships and takeovers between music giants such as Sony and EMI (Dodd 2003).

- *Electronic sales and business fraud*—The public availability of electronic media for financial transactions has made buying and selling products (as well as the transfer of funds) quick and easy, but it has also made possible new types of fraud. Funds can be siphoned off in transit from one account to another, false accounts can be set up, sums of money altered, and credit cards counterfeited. Email can be used to reach millions of potential victims at the tap of an electronic key. The Nigerian advance fee scam involved unsolicited emails being sent to individuals in Western countries with the request they assist in the transfer of a large sum of money that allegedly belonged to no one and needed to be transferred from a bank in Nigeria. Email recipients were told that in return for an advance fee they would receive a large commission. Investment scams use similar techniques and can provide convincing information about the potential value of their 'product', although in reality it may only exist in cyberspace.

- *Money laundering and tax evasion*—Criminal activity that reaps large sums of money faces the problem of how it can be spent without its illegal origins being exposed. The same difficulty is faced by wealthy individuals or businesses that engage in tax avoidance. Before the availability of electronic technologies, this problem was overcome through means such as the creation of false businesses or the physical transfer of money from one location to another. Electronic transfer, together with the use of encryption technology, has meant that today the transfer of illegally gained or undeclared money is easier than it was in the past.

■ *Identity crime*—Identity crime is the creation of a false identity in order to obtain illegally a benefit of some kind. Whereas in the past identity crime required a high level of skills in forgery, today it has become widespread because of the ease with which electronic media can be used to create false identities. A survey of 1800 of Australia's largest businesses by KPMG in 1999 found that 57 per cent of respondents reported at least one incident (KPMG 1999). In the USA it has been estimated that 95 per cent of financial crimes involve stolen identities (cited in Smith 1999: 1).

■ *Electronic vandalism*—The creation of computer viruses that have the potential to disrupt or destroy computer systems is now a perennial problem. In some cases, such as the 'blaster worm', the aim of the attack appears to be purely mischievous, and sometimes it might be related to attempts at extortion, to gain payment in relation to a threat (Grabosky et al. 2001). In other cases it has a political intent, and may serve as a form of protest. The term 'information warfare' has been coined to describe the way in which defence forces have recognised the potential harm that can be inflicted by disabling or maiming the 'enemy's' computer systems (Institute for the Advanced Study of Information Warfare 2003).

The costs of computer crime are virtually impossible to calculate accurately, but are certainly enormous. The Insurance Council of Australia estimates that cyber-crime costs companies worldwide about $3 trillion each year, with around 67 per cent of computer users affected in some way. The areas of greatest impact are laptop theft, data or network sabotage, virus and Trojan infection, computer fraud, denial of service attacks, and excessive network resource consumption through external scams (James & Murray 2003).

## The prevention and control of digital crime

Digital crime is difficult to control for a number of reasons. The capacity of internet users to disguise their location and identity makes it difficult for law enforcement agencies to identify who the perpetrator is, or even in what country they are located. An offender can be sitting in front of the computer on one continent with the intended victims thousands of miles away on another. This not only leads to problems of identification but also to difficulties of extradition. Some countries have no extradition treaties and may not be willing to cooperate with overseas law enforcement agencies.

The transnational nature of digital crime also creates problems of legal jurisdiction. If the offender is in one country but affects victims in one or more other countries it raises the question of where the offence was actually committed.

Digital crime is difficult to detect and, even if it is known that an offence has occurred, proving it may involve searching through quantities of data. This is usually time-consuming and expensive, especially if sophisticated encryption technology has been used.

Given the difficulties of locating and extraditing offenders, plus the sometimes technical nature of the offence and the time and expense involved for an often uncertain result, it is not surprising that law enforcement agencies can be reluctant to follow up all but the most serious offences.

The principal means of preventing digital crime is through the development and use of sophisticated technologies that prevent illegitimate intrusion and counterfeiting, such as the silicon chip used in 'Smart cards'. Although these can never be foolproof, they can limit the ease with which some crimes can be committed. In addition, businesses can introduce security procedures that prevent information that would allow access to their computer systems from falling into the wrong hands.

For law enforcement agencies, the key requirement is for the significance and extent of digital crime to be recognised and the necessary technology and skills developed to respond to it. This may involve the establishment of special units that employ staff with the highly specialised skills required.

Greater public awareness of digital crime is also important so that people are alert to the possibility of phoney emails or the illegal use of their credit card or phone line.

Increased international cooperation between many agencies—such as employers, government agencies, and law enforcement agencies from different nation states—is also required. This may involve the sharing of information and the establishment of protocols between agencies.

Finally, the development of personal identification systems will also assist in the reduction of digital crime. The Australian government is already some way down this track with proposals for biometric microchip technology to be introduced into Australian passports by the end of 2004. These translate patterns in a person's fingerprints, irises, face, voice, or other characteristics into digital information that can be stored on a chip or machine-readable strip (Colgan 2004). While these developments may enhance national security, they carry with them a level of intrusion into, and potential control of, private citizens that is of considerable concern to civil libertarians.

## CONCLUSION

This review of property crime raises numerous issues, only some of which can be explored here. The most significant relate to the need to understand the social factors that shape the incidence of property crime and social reaction to it. Most importantly, there is a need to go behind taken-for-granted assumptions about the 'problem' of property crime and who is responsible for it.

Writing in the nineteenth century, the socialist anarchist Proudhon answered the question 'What is property?' with the pronouncement that 'Property is theft'. This claim draws attention to the now-rarely acknowledged fact that for property to be stolen it must first be privately owned. As capitalism developed in the eighteenth and nineteenth centuries, the claims of the ascendant capitalist classes—the bourgeoisie and petty bourgeoisie—to private ownership of property in its various guises were met with counterclaims from socialists of various hues that property should not be privatised, but belonged to the people.

Today, one of the few areas in which debates about the universal nature of property exist are in relation to genetic material, in response to attempts by companies such as *Celera* to patent genetic information. Nonetheless, when considering the fact that Australian jails are full of property offenders who are drawn from the unpropertied classes, it is useful to remember Proudhon's challenge.

The question of who is the criminal is central to a critical approach to the study of crime. While official data suggest that property offenders are overwhelmingly young, male, and working class, closer analysis reveals the limitations of this picture. Later chapters will make it clear, for example, that while crime occurs across the social classes, some groups have far more power than others to resist being identified as criminal. In particular, professional criminals and white collar and corporate criminals are far less likely to face the force of the law than are the under-privileged and disadvantaged. The most financially harmful 'property' crimes are, in fact, those committed at the top end of town, rather than those associated with the streets.

The study of property crime reveals many features about how society works. Importantly, it highlights the extent to which property crimes are influenced by structural factors, such as the availability of portable property and levels of urbanisation. It also highlights how different types of property crime tend to be committed by different groups of people. Thus, the motivation to steal property varies greatly depending upon the social and economic circumstances of the participants.

## DISCUSSION QUESTIONS

1  In what ways is the concept of property crime a social construct?
2  What factors should be taken into account when considering trends in levels of property crime?
3  Outline the argument that car theft helps young working class men to establish their masculine identity.
4  The emergence of digital crime as a global phenomenon is leading to increased cooperation between agencies as well as increased surveillance of individuals. What concerns does this raise about the erosion of civil liberties, especially when they are occurring in the context of the war on terror?
5  Is 'SPAM' a form of digital crime?

## GLOSSARY OF TERMS

**burglary**
the unlawful entry of a dwelling, house, or any other premises such as a business, school, shop etc. with or without force, with the intent to steal—in some states, burglary is referred to in the statutes as 'break, enter, and steal' (AIC 2002a: 19)

**digital crime**

the use of information technology for the commission of illegal acts

**distance decay**

the way in which the commission of crimes reduces with distance from the perpetrator's home

**fraud and forgery**

unlawful acts committed or attempted, involving deception, misappropriation, forgery, uttering, or counterfeiting etc.

**intellectual properties**

mental products that are protected by legal safeguards including copyright law, patents, and trademarks, the aim of which is to ensure that the profits of a creative work are returned to its legal owners

**larceny**

the unlawful taking of property other than a motor vehicle without force and without deceit

**motor vehicle theft**

the unlawful using or attempted using of a motor vehicle without the consent of the owner

**street crime**

highly visible crimes that occur in public spaces and usually involve little skill on the part of perpetrators

**theft**

the taking of another person's property with the intention of permanently depriving the owner of the property illegally and without permission, but without force, threat of force, use of coercive measures, deceit, or having gained unlawful entry to any structure even if the intent was to gain theft (AIC 2002a: 34).

## FURTHER READING

Australian Bureau of Statistics (2003d) *Recorded Crime 2002*, Catalogue No. 4510.0, Canberra.

Australian Bureau of Statistics (2003a) *Crime and Safety Australia April 2002*, Catalogue No. 4509.0, Canberra.

Felson, M. (1998). *Crime and Everyday Life* (3rd edn), Sage, Thousand Oaks.

Grabosky, P., Smith, R. & Dempsey, G. (2001) *Electronic Theft: Crimes of Acquisition in Cyberspace*, Cambridge University Press, Cambridge.

May, D. & Headley, J. (2003) *Identity Theft*, Studies in Crime and Punishment No. 13, Peter Lang, New York.

## WEBSITES

**www.aic.gov.au**

Australian Institute of Criminology—Links to various publications from Australia's leading criminologists, including research, conference papers, publications and statistics, many of which are full text.

**www.ncp.gov.au**

National Crime Prevention Programs, Commonwealth Attorney-General's Department—Provides research on ways of reducing and preventing crime and the fear of crime. Most of the reports are available in full text.

**www.ojp.usdoj.gov/nij**

National Institute of Justice—Provides reports on research, development, evaluation, and publications covering all areas of criminal justice in the USA.

# CHAPTER 3

# Violent Crime

## INTRODUCTION

Murder, rape, assault, and robbery—there is little doubt that these violent crimes are the most widely feared criminal offences, and the most readily sensationalised by the media. Violent crime is high on the list of concerns that people have about the quality of life in Australia (Indermaur 1996). Surveys of public attitudes towards the seriousness of different types of crime regularly reveal that crimes such as homicide and armed robbery are regarded more seriously than property crimes (Weatherburn et al. 1996). For most people, fear of physical or emotional harm is greater than concern about material loss.

Public concern with violent crime is not only reflected in the amount of media space that is routinely devoted to it, but also in the regular 'moral panics' about the perceived rising spiral of violence in Australian society. In such panics it is common to hear fears that, unless we crack down on violence now, Australia will become 'like America' in its levels of violence. Despite concern about street violence the media still conveys the impression that Australia is a safer society than the US since terrorism is rare, there are few serial killers, and there are no entrenched ghettos of marginalised ethnic or racial minorities. When this image is shattered by horrific acts like the gang rapes that took place in Sydney in 2001 or the 'bodies in barrels' discovered at Snowtown in South Australia, the innocence and security of the nation is felt to be under attack.

This chapter explores the issue of violent crime by first exploring what is meant by the term and then considering rates and trends. Homicide, hate crime, robbery, assault, and sexual assault are then examined in more detail.

The chapter concludes with a review of explanations for the occurrence of violence and its relationship with social and economic conditions.

## DEFINING VIOLENT CRIME

When we think of violent crime, we tend to think of crimes such as murder, rape, and assault. In one sense we are correct. As far as the criminal justice system is concerned, violent crime refers to the following crimes against the person:

- homicide
- assault
- serious sexual assault
- sexual assault
- kidnapping and abduction
- armed hold-ups
- robbery
- extortion.

This understanding of violent crime is largely supported, and generated, by the media. Both entertainment and news media focus on these types of violence as the ones most likely to threaten citizens in their daily lives. Following the events of September 11 in the United States, terrorism has also been added to the list of threats about which ordinary people must be ever vigilant. This is so even though the likelihood of harm from either terrorists or violent criminals is statistically very low.

There are other violent crimes that are just as heinous as those listed above, but which rarely receive the same kind of treatment in the media and by criminal justice officials. For example, business corporations and white collar criminals also engage in acts that threaten the physical safety of people. Illegal or negligent occupational health and safety practices or the release of unsafe products can be more damaging, and indeed more common, than crimes such as assault.

The state itself is also a major source of violence. While in democratic countries the capacity for physical coercion invested in the state is legitimated on the grounds that it is only used with the consent of its citizens and is for their benefit, there are limitations to this claim. We only have to think of the atrocities committed by armies around the world in Aceh, for example, or Chechnya, Tibet, and Bosnia. State violence is often institutionalised; for example, the razing of Palestinian homes by the Israeli army in the West Bank, the use of napalm by the US Army in Vietnam, the torture of members of the IRA by the British Army, and the incarceration of political dissidents in asylums by successive governments of the former Soviet Union. Even in Australia the state has engaged in systematic violence against its people—if not always recognised as its citizens. For instance, the removal of children from Indigenous Australian parents, while legal, is now recognised as a serious violation of human rights that disrupted and damaged lives.

So although the rest of this chapter concerns conventional constructions of violent crime, it is important to understand that this is only a limited understanding of the violence that occurs in society. As Indermaur (2000: 288) observes, it is important to acknowledge that acts coming under definitions of violence constitute a continuum from less serious or harmful to the more serious, and that what is defined as 'violent crime' varies over time and from place to place. A precise definition of violence is required for the purposes of comparing similar acts, but there is no one standard definition as such.

## RATES AND TRENDS

Official records provide quite a lot of information about how often, when, and where serious crimes such as homicide, assault, and robbery take place. We also appear to know a great deal about the victims and perpetrators of violent crime. This information provides the basis for the control and prevention of crime but, like all crime data, is subject to limitations. Most violent crime is not reported to the police with reporting rates for assault, sexual assault, and robbery particularly low (Indermaur 1996, 2000).

In addition, crime data is never neutral but is subject to interpretation and political manipulation. This is particularly true of violent crime where images of home invasion or assault provide fertile ground for politicians on either side of the political spectrum to promote their policies and attack those of the opposition. Crime is always a key electoral issue (see, especially, Indermaur 2000). In the 1993 national elections, for example, the Liberal party distributed a leaflet with a picture of a frail-looking older woman peering out from behind a security grille, in a blatant attempt to tap popular fears that the then Labor government was not doing enough on law and order (Toohey 2004: 14).

## Long-term trends in violent crime

Assessing arguments about long-term trends in violent crime is difficult because of the paucity of reliable data. What evidence there is suggests that life in nineteenth century Australia was considerably more violent than it is today. One study estimated the homicide rate in Victoria between 1871 and 1875 to be well over double its current rate (Mukherjee et al. 1986).

For a number of reasons, homicide rates are widely regarded as the most reliable indicator of crime trends. The definition of homicide is fairly stable, public records on homicide go back a long way, and the dark figure is believed to be low. Indermaur describes it as the 'gold standard' of the level of violent crime (1996: 3). His analysis of police records of long-term trends in homicide suggest that levels of homicide today are similar to those in 1915 (see figure 3.1).

After 1915 the rate trended downwards, remaining relatively low until after World War II when it moved upwards until plateauing at about 1.9 per 100,000 in the 1970s and 1980s. At its peak, in 1988, the rate was 2.4 per 100,000, more than double the rate observed in 1950. Indermaur argues that this is probably the result of demographic factors. The proportion of young people in the population in the middle of the century was at an historically low ebb, whereas the baby boomers born at that time were just entering their teenage years. It is a well-established fact that young people are over-represented among all groups of offenders.

**Figure 3.1**  Trends in the homicide rate, Australia 1915–94

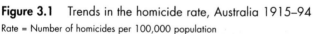
Rate = Number of homicides per 100,000 population

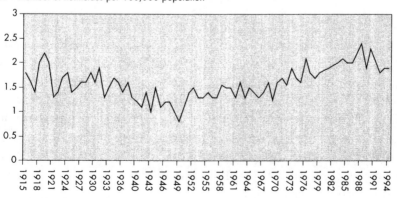

Source: Indermaur (1996).

Indermaur therefore argues that 'rather than seeing increases, we should perhaps see the graph as one of long-term stability with a two-decade respite made possible by the relative depletion of young men in the 1950s and 1960s' (1996: 6).

## Contemporary crime trends

According to official crime data, it would seem that violence in Australia in recent years is much greater than it was in the early 1970s. Police records show that in the eighteen years between 1973–74 and 1991–92 rates for most violent offences increased dramatically:

- violent offences increased 311 per cent from 51.9 per 100,000 persons to 213.4
- serious assault increased by 452 per cent from 20.75 per 100,000 persons to 114.52
- robbery increased by 288 per cent from 23.35 per 100,000 persons to 67.20 (Walker 1994: 4–7).

These trends have continued into the new century. In the nine-year period between 1993 and 2001:

- sexual assault increased from 69.0 per 100,000 persons to 86.4
- robbery increased from 72.3 per 100,000 persons to 137.1.

In the seven-year period between 1995 and 2001:

- assault increased from 562.9 per 100,000 persons to 782.9
- homicide, however, remained relatively stable, increasing slightly from 5.2 per 100,000 persons to 5.4 (AIC 2002a).

Before concluding that we are in the grip of a crime wave it is important to see what victims surveys reveal, as these are not subject to the effects of changes in levels of reporting or police productivity. These reveal less dramatic changes. In the twenty-year period to 1991, robbery and serious assault actually decreased (Walker 1994: 9) while more recent victim surveys show much smaller increases than suggested by police records.

According to the 2002 Crime and Safety Survey (ABS 2003a: 18), in the four-year period between 1998 and 2002 the victimisation rate for personal crimes increased only slightly from 4.8 per cent to 5.3 per cent. For assault, the increase was from 4.3 per cent to 4.7 per cent, and for robbery the increase was from 0.5 per cent to 0.6 per cent. In an analysis that took into account the findings of various victim surveys, Indermaur (2000: 290) found that there was no substantial evidence of an increase in the level of assaults between 1975 and 1997.

Such contradictory evidence means that claims that 'violence is on the increase', and that law and order is breaking down, must be treated cautiously, especially considering that crimes against the person only amount to about 13 per cent of all serious crimes (AIC 2002a: 6). At the same time, there does seem to be a consensus that the incidence of robbery has increased and that this is associated with rising levels of serious drug use (Polk & Warren 1996; Muhkerjee 1996).

## International comparisons

Because of variations in legal statutes and methods of data collection, international comparisons of officially recorded crime are problematic. However, standardised victim surveys have been undertaken in a number of countries. Seventeen industrialised countries participated in the 2000 International Crime Victims Survey (ICVS), which collected data on property and personal offences (see table 3.1). Personal offences included robbery, assault, and sexual offences.

Contrary to public perceptions that the USA has a higher level of contact crime than Australia, the survey suggests that Australia outranks the USA and, in fact, has the highest rate of all countries surveyed. However, the authors of the survey caution against comparing countries that are closely ranked, as the survey's relatively small sample size means that differences between countries are likely to be the result of statistical chance. On the other hand, countries with the highest rates of victimisation usually have a statistically significant higher rate than those with the lowest rates.

For robbery, the ICVS reported that the risk of victimisation was comparatively low in all countries. Poland was highest with a prevalence rate of 1.8 per cent, followed by Australia (1.2 per cent), England and Wales (1.2 per cent), Portugal (1.1 per cent), and France (1.1 per cent). Countries with the lowest risks were Japan and Northern Ireland (0.1 per cent). For sexual assault, prevalence rates were about 1 per cent in Sweden, Finland, Australia, and England and Wales. Women in Japan, Northern Ireland, Poland, and Portugal were least at risk. For assaults

**Table 3.1** International comparison of selected contact crime (robbery, sexual assault, and assault with force) 1999

| Country | %[a] | Country | %[a] |
|---|---|---|---|
| Australia | 29 | Netherlands | 19 |
| Belgium | 19 | Northern Ireland | 22 |
| Canada | 27 | Poland | 20 |
| Catalonia (Spain) | 14 | Portugal | 14 |
| Denmark | 21 | Scotland | 28 |
| England and Wales | 30 | Sweden | 24 |
| Finland | 36 | USA | 20 |
| France | 24 | | |
| Japan | 11 | **Average** | **22** |

a   per cent victimised once or more

Source: van Kesteren et al. (2001).

with force, the countries with highest risks were Scotland and England and Wales (about 3 per cent of respondents reported having been victimised once or more). Australia, Canada, Finland, and Northern Ireland followed closely behind. Risks were lowest in Japan, Portugal, and Catalonia (0.5 per cent or less) (van Kesteren et al. 2001). Overall, it appears that, compared with most other countries, Australia has more contact crime. Contact crime comprised 30 per cent of all crimes surveyed, compared with an average figure of 22 per cent.

A comparison of trends in crime from 1988 for those countries that participated in the ICVSs suggests that in most countries, including Australia, the trend is down rather than up. It must be noted, however, that this is for all crimes, not just violent crimes. The report, in fact, notes that while there has been a consistent fall in property crime, violent crime has risen marginally more than property crime in four out of seven countries.

In general, the data in the ICVS is consistent with national victim surveys in Australia, which suggest that violent crime has risen far less than suggested by police records. The authors of the ICVS note that this discrepancy is true for many countries. They suggest that the higher levels reported in official data result from increased reporting levels rather than a genuine increase in the incidence of violent crime.

International comparisons of homicide rates also suggest that Australia has no need for alarm as it is in the middle range—well below the average rates for the USA, but above that for many countries in the European Union, as well as England and Wales (see table 3.2).

**Table 3.2**   International comparison of homicide rates (per 100,000 population)

| Country | Average per year 1999–2001 | Country | Average per year 1999–2001 |
|---|---|---|---|
| Australia | 1.87 | Italy[8] | 1.50[10] |
| England & Wales[1] | 1.61 | Netherlands[7] | 1.51 |
| Northern Ireland[1] | 2.65 | Norway | 0.95 |
| Scotland[2] | 2.16 | Poland[4] | 2.05 |
| Austria | 1.23 | Portugal | 1.17 |
| Belgium | 1.79[10] | Russia[8] | 22.05 |
| Bulgaria | 3.87 | Spain | 1.12 |
| Czech Republic | 2.52 | Sweden[3] | 1.11[10] |
| Denmark[3] | 1.02 | Switzerland | 1.12 |
| Finland | 2.86 | Turkey[8] | 2.67 |
| France | 1.73 | Canada[6] | 1.77 |
| Germany[5] | 1.15 | Japan[8] | 1.05 |
| Greece | 1.38 | New Zealand | 2.50 |
| Hungary | 2.34 | South Africa | 55.86[10] |
| Ireland (Eire) | 1.42 | USA[9] | 5.56 |

1   by financial year from 1997 (that is, 1997 = 1 April 1997 to 31 March 1998)
2   currently (as at 7 November 2002) recorded as homicide victims
3   includes all deaths initially reported as homicide to the police
4   excludes assault leading to death
5   includes homicides recorded by the ZERV (Central Group for the investigation of crime associated with the government and reunification), which were committed in former East Germany or at the border before reunification of the country
6   includes murder, manslaughter, and infanticide
7   excludes euthanasia
8   includes attempts
9   excludes the murder and non-negligent homicides that occurred as a result of the attacks on 11 September 2001
10   1998–2000

Source: Barclay & Tavares (2003: 10).

## SPECIFIC VIOLENT CRIMES

### Homicide

**Homicide** is unlawfully causing the death of another person. A broader definition provided by Daly and Wilson is that it refers to 'those interpersonal assaults and other acts directed against another person (for example, poisonings) that occur outside the context of warfare, and that prove fatal' (1988: 14). Australian law recognises that the death of a person at the hands of another may take a variety of forms. It may be deliberate and planned, thus constituting culpable homicide, or it may be the unintentional consequence of a lawful act, such as the administration of a drug by a suitably qualified person that accidentally and non-negligently results in the death of the patient. This form of homicide is termed 'excusable homicide'. Justifiable homicides are also exempt from prosecution and cover homicides that occur as the result of the legal demands placed on an individual, such as the police shooting of an armed suspect. While culpable homicides meet the full force of the law, excusable and justifiable homicides do not.

Culpable homicides are divided into **murder** and **manslaughter**. Murder is the intentional killing of another by a person who is sane and who is old enough to be legally responsible for the act. Manslaughter covers a range of culpable homicides where intentionality is more in question. These include:

- significant provocation
- where the death is the involuntary consequence of some other dangerous and illegal action, such as speeding in a car or assault
- gross negligence
- the omission of an action to care for a dependent, such as an infirm elderly person or a child (Polk & Warren 1996: 183–5).

In 2001, the 333 offenders of homicide in Australia were overwhelmingly male (89 per cent) with an offending rate of 3.1 per 100,000 compared with a rate of 0.4 for females. Female offenders were usually older than male offenders, peaking at between 35 and 39 years, whereas the rate of offending for males peaked in the early to mid 20s (20 to 24 years). In general, violence rises steeply towards the end of the male offender's teenage years, peaks in the early to mid 20s, and then falls rapidly (James & Carcach 1998: 27).

Most victims of homicide were also male (see case study 3.1), although 39 per cent were female. Individuals aged 30 to 34 had the greatest risk of victimisation. Whereas males were most likely to be killed with a knife or other sharp instrument (30 per cent), females were more likely to be killed with the offender's hands or feet (34 per cent).

## CASE STUDY 3.1

In 1998 a 19-year-old man was visited by his workmate in his flat in Moonee Ponds. The two men, later described in the courts as 'good friends', spent the afternoon drinking large quantities of beer and whisky. In the early evening the friendly mood between them changed when the visitor described having been accused of acts of child molestation within his own family. According to evidence presented in the court later on, the man's friend became furious upon learning this and embarked on a violent attack against him, biting, punching, and kicking him, and attacking him with a bottle as well as stabbing him repeatedly with two knives. The man died.

The offender attempted to destroy evidence of his crime by setting fire to the flat and disposing of the dead man's body by the side of the Western Highway near Gordon in Victoria. Although he left the state, he was later apprehended by the police and charged with murder.

The offender had had numerous previous offences. Between 1993 and 1997 he had appeared in the Children's Court on fifteen occasions. In 1997 he was convicted in the County Court of twelve counts of burglary, twenty-six counts of theft, two counts of incitement to commit armed robbery, two counts of being in possession of cannabis, and one count of being a prohibited person in possession of a firearm.

Reports presented in Court revealed that the offender had never met his natural father and had been emotionally and physically abused by his mother and various partners. When he was 13 years old he was admitted into the care of Health and Community Services, Victoria, together with his identical twin brother. Although the two boys were allegedly close, they were placed in separate locations and permitted only limited supervised contact. The offender became unsettled in his placements and experienced problems at school.

In sentencing, the judge acknowledged the 'unfortunate circumstances' of the offender's background and acknowledged the importance of his youth and prospects of eventual rehabilitation. He handed down a sentence of imprisonment for a period of 14 years with a non-parole period of 10 years.

Source: *R v Lander* [1999] VSC 554.

Children are often overlooked as victims of homicide, but tragically, on average 25 children a year are killed by a parent, with children under the age of one year experiencing the highest rate of victimisation.

Most homicides occurred after work—on Fridays (21 per cent), Saturdays (12 per cent), and Sundays (16 per cent), and between 6pm and 6am (70.8 per cent) with few incidents occurring between 6am and midday. The majority of incidents occurred in a residential setting (57 per cent), with 28 per cent occurring in a street or open area. Seventeen per cent of incidents occurred in the course of another crime, such as robbery or theft. Most homicides occur between people who know one another (see box 3.1). About half of all homicides occurred between friends or acquaintances (47 per cent); 22 per cent occurred between intimates and 11 per cent between other family members. Only 15 per cent occurred between strangers (Mouzos 2002: 12–13). These patterns are broadly similar to those occurring in previous years. When strangers are killed, the perpetrator is almost invariably male. In a 10-year analysis

**Box 3.1**

## HOMICIDE: OFFENDER–VICTIM RELATIONSHIPS

- homicide involving 'intimates' (spouses and ex-spouses, de factos and former de factos, current or former boyfriends/girlfriends, extra-marital lovers, and partners/former partners of same sex relationships)—over 20 per cent of homicide victims
- family homicide (sons, daughters, parents, grandparents, siblings, and other family relationships, including step relationships)—over 14 per cent of homicide victims
- homicide involving friends and acquaintances (including neighbours)—over 27 per cent of homicide victims
- homicide between strangers (where the victim is 'relatively unknown' to the offender)—over 19 per cent of homicide victims
- homicide involving other relationships (including sex rivals, gang members, business relationships, and situations where the victim and offender are known to each other but the type of relationship is unknown)—nearly 10 per cent of homicide victims
- relationship unknown—nearly 8 per cent of homicide victims

Source: Mouzos (2000).

of patterns of homicide by females, only 8 per cent occurred between strangers (Mouzos 2002: 31).

Although they attract the greatest public attention, multiple homicides in public settings and serial murders are relatively rare in Australia.

### Hate crime

**Hate crime**, sometimes described as bias crime, is violence that is directed at individuals or groups on the basis of their actual or perceived sexuality, disability, or membership of a racial, ethnic, or religious group. Often the motive behind the violence is the intimidation of the group as a whole (Cunneen et al. 1997). Violence includes assault, homicide, vilification, harassment, and/or attacks on property. In Australia, most hate crimes have been directed against gay men, Indigenous Australians, and non–English-speaking background (NESB) migrants.

The pattern of hate crime is quite distinct from other forms of violence:

- Unlike most violence, which occurs between people who have some form of relationship with one another, hate crime often involves the targeting of people who are strangers to the assailant and have had no engagement of any kind with them. It is the perception that the victim belongs to a particular group that leads to the violence, rather than their individual characteristics or behaviour (HREOC 1991a). At the same time, hate crimes also include attacks on individuals who are known to perpetrators, but the motive for their attack is their perceived membership of a particular group (Tomsen 2001: 3).
- Hate crimes, particularly homicide, are characterised by the use of excessive force and brutality. Victims may be taunted and tortured before being murdered, frenzied stabbing is common, injuries may have sexual overtones, and sexual organs may be mutilated and dismembered (see box 3.2; Mouzos & Thompson 2000: 2; Martin 1996).
- The perpetrators of hate crimes often work in groups.
- Victims of hate crime homicides are often older than most homicide victims, while perpetrators are often younger and often unemployed (Mouzos & Thompson 2000: 3).

In the ten years between 1989 and 1999 some thirty-seven men have been identified as being victims of hate-related homicide in New South

**Box 3.2**

## FEATURES OF GAY-RELATED HOMICIDE

- Incidents are highly likely to involve multiple offenders, and highly unlikely to involve multiple victims.
- The victim is most likely to be killed in the privacy of their own home.
- The victim is more likely to be older than the offender.
- The victim is more likely to be brutally beaten to death (with hands or feet or some blunt instrument), or repeatedly stabbed to death with a knife or some other sharp instrument.
- The victim is more likely to be killed by a stranger.
- The offender is more likely to be aged between fifteen and seventeen years, and on average is five years younger than the offender of a non-gay-hate homicide.
- Victims and offenders are more likely to be 'white'.
- Victims are more likely to be in the workforce than are their killers.

Source: Mouzos & Thompson (2000).

Wales alone (Mouzos & Thompson 2000: 2) although the real figure is probably higher.

The occurrence of hate crime challenges Australia's commitment to human rights and has been the subject of some types of action on the part of federal and state governments. Attacks on Muslim women or gay men have led to calls by pressure groups for public condemnation of the intimidation, and the implementation of government measures to ensure the safety of all of its citizens, regardless of sexual preference, race, ethnic background, or religion. In New South Wales, the level of violence experienced by gay men in particular has resulted in special initiatives to deal with hate crime, including the creation of a gay/lesbian client consultant located within the police force and monitoring of male gay–hate homicides. More broadly, the strong links between hate crime and broader social and cultural values has led to arguments that community education should be a central plank of any hate crime prevention strategy (Golden et al. 1999: 270).

### Robbery

Robbery is defined by the Australian Bureau of Statistics (ABS) as 'the unlawful taking of property, with intent to permanently deprive the owner of the property, from the immediate possession of a person or an organisation, or control, custody or care of a person, accompanied by the use and/or threatened use of immediate force or violence' (ABS 2002b: 36).

According to this definition, purse snatching is theft rather than robbery because the act occurs so swiftly that fear of violence is minimal, unlike breaking into a house and confronting the owner. The law also distinguishes between robberies with and without a weapon, with robbery with a firearm forming a category of its own. Most robberies are committed without a weapon and only a small percentage involves the use of a firearm.

The prevalence rate for robbery varies considerably from state to state, with New South Wales having the highest rate of 233.2 per 100,000 people—more than double that of any other state. Most of these incidents occurred in Sydney. The prevalence rate for Australia as a whole is 137 per 100,000 (ABS 2002b). Males are twice as likely as females to be the victims of armed robbery. As with other violent crimes, younger age groups were most vulnerable to robbery, with males aged fifteen to twenty-four being twice as likely to be a victim of armed robbery than persons in any other age category (AIC 2002a: 24–6).

The type of robbery that occurs varies with the location. While most robbery occurs in a non-residential setting, unarmed robberies usually take place in community locations with just under half occurring on streets and 14 per cent in a transport location. Armed robberies are more likely to occur in retail premises, with 38 per cent occurring in banks and chemists (AIC 2002a: 24–6; Salmelainen 1996: 5). Despite media reporting to the contrary, armed robberies in the home are relatively infrequent; in 2002 only 5 per cent took place in a private dwelling.

An analysis of robberies in Sydney found that factors influencing an offender's selection of a target included:

- ease of get-away
- familiarity with the area
- knowledge about the target
- beliefs about the money held by the target (Salmelainen 1996: 1).

About 85 per cent of offenders were male, with offending peaking between the ages of 15 and 19 years. In recent years the age of offenders has increased, so that in 2000–01 the offender prevalence rate among males aged 20 to 24 was more than double the 1995–96 rate. Among females, official data suggest that the rate of offending has increased slightly for females aged 15 to 24 over the same period (AIC 2002a: 49).

Studies suggest that the most frequent motive for robbery is the need for money to support a drug habit (Nugent et al. 1989). Mugford (1992) argues that rising rates of substance use is partly behind the rise in robbery rates that both official and unofficial data suggests is occurring. Many robberies are also conducted under the influence of a drug (National Committee on Violence 1990: 92).

While the popular image of bank robbers is that they are professional criminals often working in gangs, a recent study found that the profile of bank robbers has changed since the 1980s (Borzycki 2003). Since that time the number of bank robberies has declined and offenders have become deskilled. They plan less, use fewer weapons, and rely on sheer numbers to intimidate bank staff. As a result they fail more often than previously. Nonetheless, the level of violence and intimidation used by offenders has increased because they do not carry a weapon, and so rely on other forms of aggression to intimidate bank staff. It is therefore not surprising that of all types of robberies, unarmed gangs are most likely to inflict violence. In contrast, armed offenders working alone or in pairs are less likely to inflict injuries than two decades ago (Borzycki 2003).

If bank robberies are on the decline, how is it that both official and unofficial criminal justice data suggest that robbery is increasing? The answer is that offenders are selecting softer targets because the level of security in banks has increased. Service stations, in particular, have borne the brunt of the increase. The reasons for this are fairly obvious—they have fewer security measures, are often staffed by only one individual, have cash on the premises, allow easy access, are physically distant from other retailers, and are open late when few people are present to resist or witness the crime. Robberies of service stations saw the highest increase in recorded robbery in the nine years between 1993 and 2002, with four out of five being armed robberies. In the four-year period between 1998 and 2002 the risk of robbery to service stations increased threefold, with 24-hour service stations operated by one staff member having the highest degree of vulnerability (Taylor 2002).

## Assault

**Assault** is the direct infliction of force, injury, or violence upon a person, including attempts or threats, providing the attempts/threats are in the form of face-to-face direct confrontation and there is reason to believe that the attempts/threats can be immediately enacted (ABS 2002a: 35). It covers a range of crimes including grievous bodily harm, assault and battery, malicious wounding, and aggravated assault. Serious assault is the most frequent violent crime recorded, although the great majority of victims do not require hospitalisation.

Although it is sometimes said that most victims of assault are male, in reality the gender distribution is fairly even since both police records and victim surveys suggest that males are victims of about 55 per cent of all assaults. Assault, like homicide, can be divided into two major categories: men who assault men in a public setting, and men who assault women in their home. In both types of assault alcohol is often involved, with many male-on-male assaults occurring in close proximity to hotels and clubs.

Assaults occur most frequently in a residential location (42 per cent) and, in these settings, the situation is usually one of domestic violence with female partners, ex-partners, and children the victims. In contrast, the victims of the 38 per cent of assaults occurring in community locations are much more likely to be male, with 40 per cent of male victims being assaulted by strangers (AIC 2002a: 16–18). As with homicide, women are much more likely than men to be threatened or injured by someone they know (ABS 2002a: 7).

## Sexual assault

**Sexual assault** is defined by the ABS as 'physical assault of a sexual nature, directed towards another person where that person:

- does not give consent; or
- gives consent as a result of intimidation or fraud; or
- is legally deemed incapable of giving consent because of youth or temporary/permanent incapacity' (AIC 2003: 20).

It covers a wide range of sexual acts, including rape, sexual assault, oral sex, incest, unlawful sexual intercourse, and indecent assault.

Its legal definition has been subject to considerable change in recent years and is more inclusive than formerly. For example, until relatively recently the law did not recognise marital rape as a criminal offence. As with other violent crimes, offenders of sexual assault are overwhelmingly male. In 2002 the ABS Crime and Safety Survey found that 93 per cent of perpetrators were men.

Sexual assault has one of the lowest levels of reporting. According to the ABS Crime and Safety Survey (2003a: 8), only 20 per cent of female victims report it to the police. For this reason it is unclear whether the rise in sexual assault that has occurred in recent years is the result of a higher incidence or a decline in the dark figure (related to reporting). In a phone-in conducted in Victoria, women who had been victims of sexual assault identified the following reasons for not reporting it:

- doubt that 'any good' would come from reporting it
- a sense of guilt that it had happened
- concern that they would not be believed by the police
- concern about the response of families and friends
- fear of retaliation from the perpetrator (Polk & Warren 1996: 195).

As males and females in the 10 to 14 age range are most at risk of being sexually assaulted (AIC 2002a: 22), the vulnerability and immaturity of victims may also be a factor.

Women victims of assault are more likely to be assaulted by someone they know in their own homes than by a stranger in a public place. Nearly 40 per cent of assaults occurred in the victims' home, although 37 per cent occurred in a public place. Fifty-eight per cent were assaulted by someone they knew and, of these, 33 per cent were a family member, friend, or ex-partner.

As with other crimes against women, feminists argue that female victims of sexual assault experience a range of problems in obtaining social justice. These include:

- their invisibility (failure to report the crime; disregarding their testimony in court)
- blaming them for the incident (by the media, the local community, and the criminal justice system, including police and prosecution)
- the exclusion of 'unworthy' women such as prostitutes from the protection of the law (Naffine 1997; Scutt 1990).

While feminists have drawn attention to women as invisible victims of crime, when it comes to sexual assault male victims are even more invisible. According to the ABS Crime and Safety Survey, 14 per cent of victims of sexual assault are men (2003a: 7). Stanko argues that when men experience sexual assault they are doubly victimised, because as well as being a physical attack the assault is also an attack on the victim's identity as a man. This is one of the reasons why the level of reporting for male sexual assault is even lower than the level of reporting for females.

## EXPLAINING VIOLENT CRIME

In its investigation into violence in Australia, the National Committee on Violence argued that violence was fundamentally multidimensional (1990: 61). While biological, psychological, and social factors all contribute to the occurrence of violence, each on their own is insufficient as an explanation. For example, higher levels of the hormone testosterone may be implicated in men's greater willingness to use force compared with women, but to explain male violence as the result of this is inadequate. It ignores women's capacity for violence and the extent to which levels of violence vary in different social formations. The fact that some communities have very low levels of violence, such as the Semai of Malaysia, or French settlers in colonial Illinois (Ekberg 1998), suggests that whatever biological and psychological factors are found to be associated with violence, the social context in which they occur is critical to their manifestation. So while the dominance of males as offenders suggests that something about male biology may be significant, this is only a partial explanation.

Whereas in the past explanations of violence relied on notions of social pathology and psychology, today the role of culture in the aetiology of violence is understood to be central. With the exception of some abnormal biological conditions, when and where aggression is used is something that is learned through social interaction with others. Norms, values, and beliefs are therefore central to the incidence of violence. Many of the factors identified by the National Committee on Violence have a strong cultural component (1990: 61–3). The most significant factor identified by the Committee was child development and the influence of the family. Culture was specifically identified by the Committee as the second-most important factor, with norms, economic inequality, and cultural disintegration described as key variables. Many of the other factors identified by the Committee have a strong cultural element, including substance abuse, mental illness, media influences, and peers and schooling.

The third-most significant factor identified by the Committee was gender, and it is in this direction, together with economic inequality, that much current research is directed. Although violence occurs across the entire socio-economic spectrum, the observation that conventional criminal violence is concentrated among young, underprivileged men has led to explanations that identify masculinity and marginalisation as critical to the explanation of violence.

## The family and socialisation

According to the National Committee on Violence (1990: 61) 'families constitute the training ground for aggression'. The research and submissions reviewed by the Committee suggested that violence is first learned in the home, and the greater the exposure to violence in the home, the greater the risk that children will grow into adults who regard violent behaviour as normal and acceptable. One of the points made by the Committee was that 'abusive parents themselves tend to have been abused'. This point, has, however, been challenged. Although there has been considerable research into the effects of domestic violence on children who witness it, Mullender and Morley (cited in Patton 2003) argue that many of these studies have methodological flaws. While there does appear to be a higher risk that people reared in violent families will be violent towards their partners (35 per cent compared with 10.7 per cent), most children reared in these environments are well adjusted. Mullender and Morley also point out that the majority of men who assault their wives come from non-violent backgrounds.

## Masculinity

In considering masculinity as a key variable in the explanation of violence, it is important first to acknowledge that, like all explanations, it should be understood as a contributory variable only. For example, it cannot explain female violence, and while we can be confident that men do appear to be responsible for more violent crime than women, there is probably some under-reporting of the involvement of women in violent crime (Ogilvie 1996). In addition, the complexity of masculinity as a social phenomenon needs to be understood, particularly in terms of its intersection with class and ethnicity. While sociologists have attempted to identify a range of masculinities associated with particular classes, ethnic groups, and sexual preference (Connell 1995, 2000), these are necessarily limited in their capacity to capture the wide variation of ways in which men establish and maintain their sense of sexual identity.

Despite these qualifications, the concept of masculinity has provided a powerful analytical tool. Polk's analysis of homicide, for example, draws on it in his characterisation of male-on-male violence in public settings. In his study of homicides that took place in Victoria between 1985 and 1989, Polk identifies four scenarios of lethal violence, three of which involve male-on-male violence (Polk 1994). In one type of violence, homicide is an unintended outcome of engagement in another crime, such as robbery. In another, homicide is a deliberate and premeditated act undertaken to resolve a personal conflict, such as non-payment of a debt. Together these two forms of homicide amounted to 26 per cent of the homicides in Polk's sample (16 and 10 per cent respectively). Confrontational homicide accounted for a further 22 per cent and was the form in which cultural constructions of masculinity, in terms of defence of honour, played a critical role.

Polk points out that as well as being male, perpetrators of homicide are also drawn from low-income social groups. He argues that this is because it is in these groups that traditional constructions of masculinity involving the defence of honour, through a demonstrated willingness to engage in extreme violence, are common. The scenario painted by Polk is one in which a group of young, working class men gather together in a public place such as a party, pub, or barbecue (and in venues close by such as the street, transport venue, and parks) where consumption of alcohol is common (alcohol featured in just under 90 per cent of these incidents). The homicide is unpremeditated and spontaneous, often starting with a relatively trivial exchange of words between groups of people, which is taken by one or more individuals as a challenge to their honour, so they respond with a counter-challenge. A fight breaks out and someone is killed. Polk stresses the social nature of these incidents. Confrontational homicide is public in nature and can involve an audience that takes sides. In some cases it is an innocent bystander who interferes who is killed. But, argues Polk, 'the joint themes of masculinity and lower social class position' resound through it all (1994: 91).

This analysis of the relationship between traditional, working class masculinity and homicide also helps to explain assault involving males in public settings such as pubs, clubs, or transport venues, since the unpremeditated nature of confrontational homicide means that whether such incidents result in homicide is more a matter of chance than deliberate choice.

Despite the power of this explanation of violence, it is still subject to criticism. At the theoretical level, the explanation of crime as a result of the social construction of masculinity is fundamentally tautological, or circular. The features that explain crime (crime is the result of men establishing their masculine identity) are also the features that result from it (men achieve masculinity through doing crime; Collier 1998: 21). The argument also fails to explain why it is that only some men choose to express their masculinity through the use of force.

## Economic marginalisation

The extent to which violence occurs in socially disadvantaged groups is partially explained by the masculinity argument, since it is among these groups that this form of aggressive masculinity is prized. However, recently this argument has been linked to a broader argument about the link between economic marginalisation and violent crime. Writers such as Polk and White (1999) suggest that insofar as there has been an increase in robbery and assault, it is explained by the increasing economic marginalisation of young, working class males that took place in the 1980s and 1990s.

Violence involving marginalised young men has also been explained in terms of the combination of economic disadvantage, racial vilification, and oppressive social environments. Here it is argued that processes of economic and social exclusion provide for a context within which certain groups of young people band together for protection against real and perceived threats. It is also about finding alternative means of social valorisation in an environment hostile to their needs, rights, and, indeed, very presence (Collins et al. 2000). Group dynamics, an emphasis on 'being tough', and the aggressive assertion of social identity frequently find expression in violent behaviour (White & Perrone 2001). To be poor and alienated provides the ground for potential street conflict with other young people and with authority figures such as police and security guards.

## Culture and socialisation

Although it is difficult to prove empirically, there is indirect evidence that cultural values are closely implicated in the occurrence of violence. The most obvious argument is the extent to which levels of violence differ between nations. For example, both Switzerland and the USA have high levels of gun ownership, yet the homicide rate in the USA is five times that of Switzerland.

The influence of the social and political environment is particularly evident in relation to hate crime. Gay bashing in Sydney, or the assault of long grassers in Darwin, only makes sense within a culture that to some degree nurtures these forms of prejudice. Even the judiciary, which is supposed to be impartial, has demonstrated a double standard when it comes to violence against certain groups. In some cases of homophobic homicide, judges have accepted the offender's defence that the victim 'came on' to him, even where excessive and brutal violence has been used. It is hard to imagine this defence being accepted if a man 'came on' to a woman and she responded by stabbing him sixty times. It can only be understood in terms of cultural values that denigrate sexual difference and normalise violence against gay men as an appropriate masculine response to sexual difference (Golden et al. 1999). From this perspective perpetrators of hate crime are acting out mainstream values and norms. To some degree this intersects with dimensions of gender and class, since hate crime can also be understood as an outcome of cultural constructions of masculinity in which marginalised young men, who are excluded from conventional pathways, affirm an exaggerated sense of masculinity through the use of violence (Tomsen 2002).

The role of the social and political environment in the incidence of violence is evident in the proliferation of hate crimes against Muslims and various Asian communities that accompanied the rise of the One Nation party in the late 1990s (see Cunneen et al. 1997). Pauline Hanson promoted a white supremacism that portrayed white, Anglo-Celtic Australians as 'normal' and non-English speaking migrants and Indigenous Australians as 'others' who were to blame for many of the country's social problems. Her antagonism to multiculturalism was clearly on display when she declared, in her maiden speech to Parliament: 'I believe we are in danger of being swamped by Asians ... They have their own culture and religion, form ghettos and do not assimilate' (Hanson 1996). That she was not alone in these views was clear from the significant support generated by One Nation.

Cultural values also have been used to explain domestic violence. Drawing on notions of patriarchy (or male domination), writers such as

Weeks (2002) argue that it is the unequal power relations between men and women that explain why male violence against women is so tragically common. Feminists argue that domestic violence, sexual assault, and homicide arise out of ideological constructions of the family in which men are dominant and women are subservient (Stanko 1985). More broadly, feminists argue that cultural norms assume that men control women and that violence is an acceptable way of achieving this (National Committee on Violence 1990).

Just over half of all female victims of homicide are killed following a domestic altercation, with 55 per cent of these involving termination of a relationship (Mouzos 2002: 14). For feminists, these figures only make sense in terms of men's sense of entitlement to control women. It is this that explains why the cry, 'If I can't have her no one else will', resounds tragically around cases of male homicide of women (Polk 1994). Lees (1997) points out how social norms around how 'normal' men and women behave create a double standard of justice. While the defence of 'provocation' in the case of male perpetrators is often accepted by the judiciary, this rarely applies to female perpetrators. There are many cases in which men have had the charge of murder reduced to manslaughter on the grounds of provocation because their female partner threatened to leave them. However, such a defence is rarely accepted in women. On the contrary, women who have been the victims of assault by their male partners for years, and kill their partners in self-defence, are still jailed (Lees 1997).

At a more general level, it is helpful to acknowledge the extent to which violence is expected and valued in some situations. Violence in sport, in entertainment, within schools, and within the family are all tolerated to some degree within Australian society (National Committee on Violence 1990: 61; Cameron 2000). We should not be surprised if sometimes this gets out of control and spills over into aggression in the home and on the streets, especially among those who are shut out of conventional pathways to self-esteem.

## CONTEMPORARY ISSUES

There are a number of points raised by this review of levels and patterns of violence: the social construction of violence; the role of culture, politics, and the media; the under-reporting of men as victims of violence; and trends in levels of violence.

## The social construction of violence

Like every other social phenomenon, the way we perceive and respond to violence is intimately connected with relationships of domination and subordination. Public perceptions of violence do not occur in a social vacuum but are shaped by institutions such as the media and the criminal justice system. These tend to focus on street crimes as the primary threat to social order and point to young, working class males as the problem. This perspective fails to acknowledge the extent to which street crime is only one of many forms of violence. White collar crime, state crime, and domestic violence are 'hidden' forms of violence that arguably cause more social harm, yet have only become public issues in recent years.

## Culture, politics, and the media

Despite evidence that violent behaviour has a biological and psychological component, the actual manifestation of violent behaviour is most powerfully shaped by culture. This has numerous dimensions to it. Attitudes towards violence within the community, the social construction of masculinity, the legal system and its implementation, and the availability of weapons are just some of the ways in which cultural factors are integral to the expression of violence.

The broader political and social climate also plays a critical role. When law and order is a hot political issue and popular feelings about public safety are inflamed, politicians will be under pressure to 'do something' about perceived rising levels of violence, even if the perception is false. A classic study by Hall et al. (1978) argued that media coverage of bashings were used by a Conservative government in Britain to increase police powers and push a right-wing industrial relations agenda. Although the moral panic about the bashings had little empirical foundation, the growth in police powers in itself led to an increase in police arrests, thereby justifying the alarm. Although they do not link their argument to the media, a number of researchers argue that the rise in levels of crime recorded by the police in Australia since the 1970s are not caused by a real increase in levels of violence but from increased resourcing and improved productivity of the police (Bonney & Kery 1991; Indermaur 1996; Walker 1994).

## Men as victims of violence

The high levels of under-reporting of violence disguise the extent to which males are victims of violence. The same factors that influence men's involvement in violence also prevent them from identifying themselves as victims. For different reasons, the victimisation of men and women has been a hidden social issue. While feminism has lifted the veil on female victims of domestic violence and sexual assault, the extent to which males are also victims of males remains an issue that is worthy of much greater attention, especially in relation to sexual assault.

## Trends in levels of violence

Trends in levels of violence need to be understood as arising out of the complex interplay of social, political, and economic forces that occurs within nations at any point in time (Indermaur 1996). To a great extent, these are played out at a level outside the control of individuals. They include changes in factors such as the demographic distribution of the population, the availability of weapons or drugs, police resources, cultural sensitivities towards violence, and levels of inequality. These forces do not all operate in the same direction. For example, a decline in the number of young males will normally be associated with a decline in levels of violence, but if the job availability for this group is in decline then this is likely to be associated with higher levels of violence. The complexity of these forces necessitates a measured response to claims that violence is increasing, and a resistance to explanations that simply attempt to pathologise particular social groups.

## CONCLUSION

The level of violence that occurs within a community is a critical social issue that strikes at fundamental feelings of individual safety and security. This makes criminal violence particularly sensitive to political manipulation. The complex causes of violent crime, together with the difficulties of establishing accurate data, make it vulnerable to misleading or dubious claims and counterclaims. While it is always difficult to make firm judgements about levels of any kind of crime, the wide range of factors that influence both the occurrence and level of reporting of violent crime make it particularly challenging.

For example, sexual assault, domestic violence, and child abuse have all shown significant increases in recent years. Because these changes have occurred against a backdrop of increased levels of reporting, as a result of changing social attitudes towards violence in the home, as well as rising divorce rates and the widespread entrance of women into the workforce, it is hard to ascertain whether the increase is real or stems from increases in levels of reporting. One of the key roles of criminology is to draw attention to the complex social interactions that lie behind the data in order to avoid the impulsive, knee-jerk political responses so often associated with crime and criminal justice.

A second major theme of this chapter is the relationship between masculinity and crime. Mainstream social constructions of men as tough, virile, and assertive are mediated through class and ethnicity to create a range of ways of 'doing masculinity'. Among working class men this may be expressed in pride in physical strength and a willingness to use violence as a means of establishing power. Understanding this process makes an important contribution to the explanation of violence by men against other men and by men against women. At the same time, this insight needs to be placed in the context of a broader understanding of violence that recognises that it is not limited to the working class, but occurs in different forms across all social classes. It could be argued that the difference lies not in the occurrence of violence between different social groups, but in their capacity to shape public perceptions and political agendas about where the problem lies.

## DISCUSSION QUESTIONS

1 Outline the arguments for and against the view that Australia has become a more violent society since World War I.

2 What is hate crime? How does it differ from conventional violent crime?

3 Identify three social factors that appear to be linked to the incidence of violent crime. How do you explain this association?

4 Why should the media be criticised for regarding the behaviour of young people as the cause of violent crime?

## GLOSSARY OF TERMS

**assault**
the direct infliction of force, injury, or violence upon a person, including attempts or threats, providing the attempts/threats are in the form of face-to-face direct confrontation and there is reason to believe that the attempts/threats can be immediately enacted (ABS 2002b: 35).

**hate crime**
violence that is directed at individuals or groups on the basis of their actual or perceived sexuality, disability, or membership of a racial, ethnic, or religious group

**homicide**
those interpersonal assaults and other acts directed against another person (for example, poisonings) that occur outside the context of warfare, and that prove fatal (Daly & Wilson 1988: 14)

**manslaughter**
culpable homicides in which intentionality is in question; for example, as a result of gross negligence or dangerous and illegal action

**murder**
the intentional killing of another by a person who is sane and who is old enough to be legally responsible for the act

**robbery**
the unlawful taking of property, with intent to permanently deprive the owner of the property, from the immediate possession of a person or an organisation, or control, custody or care of a person, accompanied by the use and/or threatened use of immediate force or violence' (ABS 2002b: 36)

**sexual assault**
physical assault of a sexual nature, directed towards another person where that person does not give consent or gives consent as a result of intimidation or fraud or is legally deemed incapable of giving consent because of youth or temporary/permanent incapacity (ABS cited in AIC 2003: 20).

## FURTHER READING

Bessant, J., Carrington, C. & Cook, J. (eds) (1995) *Cultures of Crime and Violence: The Australian Experience*, La Trobe University Press in association with the Victorian Law Foundation, Bundoora.

Chappell, D. & Egger, S. (eds) (1995) *Australian Violence: Contemporary Perspectives II*, Australian Institute of Criminology, Canberra.

Cook, S. & Bessant, J. (eds) (1997) *Women's Encounters with Violence*, Sage, Thousand Oaks.

Mouzos, J. (2000) *Homicidal Encounters: A Study of Homicide in Australia, 1989–1999* Research and Public Policy Series No. 28, Australian Institute of Criminology, Canberra.

Polk, K. (1994) *When Men Kill: Scenarios of Masculine Violence*, Cambridge University Press, Cambridge.

## WEBSITES

**www.austdvclearinghouse.unsw.edu.au**
Australian Domestic and Family Violence Clearinghouse—Links to many full text newsletters and issues papers, and also has searchable databases on research and best practice.

**www.aic.gov.au**
Australian Institute of Criminology—Links to various publications from Australia's leading criminologists, including research, conference papers, publications, and statistics, many of which are full text.

**www.lawlink.nsw.gov.au/bocsar1.nsf/pages/index**
New South Wales Bureau of Crime Statistics and Research—Links to statistical and research reports from the New South Wales Attorney-General's Department. This site provides access to a comprehensive range of crime and court statistics, fact sheets, and full text crime reports.

**www.abs.gov.au**
Australian Bureau of Statistics—Statistics on crime and prisons in Australia. Most reports are available in html and PDF downloads.

# CHAPTER 4

# Public Order Offences

## INTRODUCTION

Public order offences can be variously described as 'public order offences', 'street offences', 'police offences', and 'summary offences'. If we take New South Wales as a case in point, public order offences in that state include:

- *offensive, indecent, or obscene behaviour*—offensive language, racial vilification, blasphemy, indecency, obscenity
- *presence in public places*—vagrancy, consorting, public drunkenness, loitering, public assemblies
- *trespass*—on private or public land
- *property damage*—vandalism, sabotage, graffiti
- *prostitution*—soliciting, living on the earnings of prostitution.

This chapter provides an examination of public order offences in general, followed by a more detailed discussion of vandalism and graffiti and the policing of public disorder. The chapter begins with a brief history of laws relating to vagabondage in order to explore the social dynamics that shape how public order is construed and policed.

There are three main features to public order offences (Brown et al. 2001: 942):

- the *centrality of the police* (and police discretion) in initiating and prosecuting such charges
- the regulation of *behaviour in public places* (the policing of 'public order' and public spaces)
- the processing of most charges *summarily in the lower courts* (or in some cases, 'on-the-spot' fines).

It is useful to bear these elements in mind when specific types of offence are being considered. There are major issues surrounding who gets targeted under public order offence provisions, and what the punishment process entails.

## HISTORIES OF DISORDER: THE VAGABONDS

The commonsense notion that public order offences exist for the common good is challenged by an analysis of the socio-economic context behind the history of vagrancy laws in England from their emergence in medieval times until the nineteenth century.

In medieval England, religious houses, such as monasteries, were one of the main sources of charity. They played an important role in providing food and shelter to travellers. In 1274, a law was passed to relieve the church of the financial strain associated with this by limiting the number of people demanding charity (Chambliss 1970: 44–5). But the key philosophy of provision of alms by religious houses to the poor, the sick, and the feeble still remained.

By the middle of the fourteenth century, feudal England was experiencing a severe labour shortage. Bubonic plague, known as the Black Death, had decimated the population causing the death of at least 50 per cent of the people. Simultaneously, early industrial development had created a demand for labour in the towns. This conflicted with the labour demands of the rural aristocracy who relied on their serfs, who were tied to the land to work on their properties. At the same time, the costs of the crusades and various wars meant the aristocracy had been willing to sell some serfs their freedom. Together, these changes resulted in a labour shortage in the countryside with landowners facing wage demands from freed serfs, which they could not meet.

To solve their problem the gentry class, who controlled the legislative bodies, passed a law in 1349 limiting the movement of working people by making it a crime to give alms to anyone who was unemployed while being of sound mind and body. The statute provided that:

> Because that many valiant beggars, as long as they may live of begging, do refuse to labour, giving themselves to idleness and vice, and sometimes to theft and other abominations; it is ordained, that none, upon pain of imprisonment shall, under the colour of pity or alms, give

anything to such which may labour, or presume to favour them towards their desires; so that thereby they may be compelled to labour for their necessary living (cited in Chambliss 1970: 45).

The effect of this was to force labourers to accept employment at a low wage, thereby ensuring landowners had an adequate supply of labour at a price they could afford.

By the sixteenth century, the development of commerce and industry was increasing opportunities for crime. Robbery became a major problem and any transportation was hazardous. The result was the enactment of legislation in 1530 that was designed to control persons preying upon merchants transporting goods. The category 'vagrant' was also expanded to include any able bodied person not legally employed:

> If any person, being whole and mighty in body, and able to labour, be taken in begging, or be vagrant and can give no reckoning how he lawfully gets his living; ...and all other idle persons going about, some of them using divers and subtle crafty and unlawful games and plays, and some of them feigning themselves to have knowledge of...craft sciences...shall be punished as provided (cited in Chambliss 1970: 49).

By the nineteenth century the 'problem' of vagrants had taken a new form (see box 4.1). Soldiers returning from the Napoleonic Wars, prolonged periods of economic depression, mass migrations from Ireland as a result of famine, and changes in production methods had created a large number of impoverished people wandering both the towns and countryside. To the respectable and ruling classes these people were both a physical and a moral danger (see Jones 1982). Not only were they seen as carriers of crime and disease from the town to the country, but their apparent unwillingness to work for a low wage also was regarded as a 'moral pestilence' that threatened social order.

It was in this period that the criminal law refined its definition of the vagrant into three categories. An Act passed in 1824 recognised:

- idle and disorderly persons
- rogues and vagabonds
- incorrigible rogues (persistent offenders).

The Act could be used against anyone not in full-time or respectable employment, and also attempted to distinguish between the 'deserving' and 'undeserving' poor through measures such as refusing relief to young, able-bodied people.

While the public discourse that surrounded vagrants presented them as dangerous and a source of social evil, Jones's (1982) analysis suggests there is little evidence to support this. While vagrants did appear to engage in some crime, most of it was of a relatively petty nature and related to survival. Theft of food and clothing made up most of the offences. His research also suggests that many of the criminal charges laid

---

**TYPES OF WAYFARERS, EARLY 1800S TO 1900**

Box 4.1

- men and women *whose work entailed travelling* (includes tailors, painters, sailors looking for a ship, seasonal workers, market gardeners, building workers, miners, etc.)
- *unemployed* males (that is, remnants of decaying trades, victims of recessions and strikes) and unemployed females (who faced especial difficulties and fewer choices):

    'We are willing to work, but it ain't to be had', was the message of these periods and of the depressions of the late nineteenth and early twentieth centuries, and those who demanded greater mobility from the underemployed sections of the population were among the first to cry 'wolf' when it was provided on a large scale (Jones 1982: 185).

- The *'deserving poor'* (that is, a considerable number under 17 years of age, including children of trampers and Irish immigrants who died of cholera, and those who had been pushed out of slum houses; a large number of people over 50 years of age, including workmen who had become physically and mentally sick; and many abandoned women who had been battered, deserted, or widowed)
- *'habitual vagrants'* or tramps (many of whom were casual labourers who, in times of depression, gave up the struggle to find another job; those who left armed forces; and those who rebelled against poorly paid jobs. Without money, references, decent clothes, and regular lodgings it was difficult to get work, or access to charity).

Source: Jones (1982: 183–6).

against vagrants were trumped up, since nearly half of those arrested for offences such as theft, trespass, and damage to property were found not guilty. Charges of drunkenness and disorderly conduct were also probably used as a way of keeping the poor off the street.

The work of Jones (1982) and Chambliss (1970) suggests that, ultimately, vagrants were criminals because they were vagrants. Their 'crimes' were acts of survival such as begging, and sleeping in the open or in unauthorised premises. The most common workhouse offences were refusal to work and the destruction of property. Unemployed workers were hounded, penalised, and removed for 'frequenting' and 'having no visible means of subsistence'. From this perspective the laws of vagrancy were about social order, but it was the social order of the dominant class that demanded adherence to the capitalist work ethic and the requirement that all persons provide for themselves. While such treatment of the poor seems to belong to another era, there remain disturbing parallels with the way in which contemporary laws relating to public order are used against specific social groups.

## Vagrancy laws in Australia

The English *Vagrancy Act* 1824 was widely copied in the Australian colonies. In some parts of Australia vagrancy remains a criminal offence (see, for example, Tasmania's *Police Offences Act* 1935, s. 5). There are, however, important differences between the way vagrancy laws have been used in England and colonial Australia. Whereas in England the laws were concerned with the control of the 'disreputable classes', in Australia they have sometimes been racist in design and enforcement (see Brown et al. 2001 and case study 4.1).

## CASE STUDY 4.1

The Northern Territory has the highest level of homelessness in Australia with Indigenous people making up to 50 per cent of those in the 'primary homelessness' category. Many of these are 'long-grassers', itinerants who live on the streets of Darwin and, during the Wet season, in the long grass around the city and in camps along the beaches. Most have been displaced from tribal areas in northern Australia.

As far as the law is concerned they are a public nuisance. In recent years old policies that had fallen into disuse have been resurrected and used to control Indigenous homelessness. The Northern Territory has a number of public order laws that make illegal certain activities in public spaces. Examples include:

- sleeping in a public space between sunset and sunrise
- storing personal belongings in a public space
- urinating or defecating in a public space
- failing to cease to loiter
- trespassing on Crown land.

Such laws criminalise homelessness because homeless people have little choice but to engage in these activities on the streets. The law specifically states that it is not a defence to show that you had a reasonable justification or excuse for committing the offence, such as having nowhere else to go.

Although no studies have been done on the impact of these laws on long-grassers in Darwin, it is likely that there are indirect links between these laws and the fact that the Northern Territory has the highest level of imprisonment of Indigenous people, if only because they increase the level of contact and surveillance of their lives by authorities.

Although it is sometimes argued that the 'homelessness' of Indigenous people forms part of their normal cultural practice, recently there have been attempts by traditional leaders to encourage them to return to their traditional lands. In May 2003 a group of Elders from across the Top End came to Darwin to encourage the long-grassers to go home. The program had significant success with 200 agreeing to go back to their communities.

One Elder commented that they may be seen as long-grassers in Darwin, but when they go back home they are traditional people. At the same time, the Elders point to the need for follow-up and assistance from the government to set up appropriate infrastructure to assist those who do return.

Source: Churchman (2003) & Goldie (2004).

For example, in New South Wales the Vagrancy Acts of 1835, 1851, and 1901 included a statutory presumption that any non–Indigenous person found 'lodging or wandering in company' with Indigenous Australians was a vagrant, while in Victoria vagrancy laws were used against the Chinese to enforce indentured labour arrangements. Chinese labourers who were unable to work through sickness were imprisoned as vagrants until they recovered. The effect was not only to enforce the labour arrangements, but also to maintain the separation of people of colour from the white population. As well as controlling the Chinese it also reinforced negative images of them as untrustworthy.

Queensland's *Vagrants Act* has remained relatively unchanged since its enactment in 1931. Even out-dated provisions such as 'insufficient lawful means of support', however, are still used today to charge and convict people for eating out of garbage bins and sleeping in public places (Walsh 2004). The use of vagrancy laws to police and harass marginalised public-space users, particularly homeless people, recently prompted the formation of the 'Rights in Public Space Action Group'. Research and action taken by members of this group have highlighted how many of the homeless are treated differently from other public space users, whose behaviour is identical to theirs but is nonetheless tolerated. Among the many criticisms of how the vagrancy laws are constructed and used, therefore, is the discriminatory operation of such laws—particularly against homeless people and Indigenous people (see Walsh 2004).

Understanding the development of laws relating to vagrancy provides important insights into the social processes that underpin how such laws are defined, constructed, and enforced. They highlight the way these laws have been used by dominant social groups to control marginalised populations whose behaviour threatens the prevailing social and economic arrangements.

## PUBLIC ORDER OFFENCES

For comparative statistical purposes, the Australian Bureau of Statistics (ABS) groups **public order offences** into the subdivisions of 'disorderly conduct' and 'regulated public order activities'. Public order offences are defined as:

> Offences involving personal conduct that involves or may lead to a breach of public order and decency, or that is indicative of criminal intent, or that is otherwise regulated or prohibited on moral or ethical grounds. The 'victim' of these offences is generally the public at large. However, some offences such as offensive language and offensive behaviour may be directed towards a single victim (ABS 2003b: 78).

Most public order offences are dealt with in the lower courts, such as Magistrate's Courts. However, in 2001–02 there were 195 cases heard in Australian Higher Courts (ABS 2003b: 13). Table 4.1 shows the breakdown

**Table 4.1** Public order offences by age and sex

Total higher courts adjudicated defendants; principal offence by age and sex

| | Under 20 | 20–24 | 25–34 | 35–44 | 45+ | Unknown | Total | Mean age (years) | Median age (years) |
|---|---|---|---|---|---|---|---|---|---|
| **MALES** | | | | | | | | | |
| Number | 30 | 36 | 35 | 33 | 35 | 5 | 174 | 33.6 | 31.6 |
| Proportion (%) | 1.9 | 1.2 | 0.8 | 1.4 | 2.1 | 0.9 | 1.3 | – | – |
| **FEMALES** | | | | | | | | | |
| Number | 2 | 5 | 6 | 2 | 4 | 2 | 21 | 31.1 | 26.5 |
| Proportion (%) | 1.1 | 1.2 | 0.9 | 0.6 | 2.3 | 1.9 | 1.1 | – | – |
| **PERSONS** | | | | | | | | | |
| Number | 32 | 41 | 41 | 35 | 39 | 7 | 195 | 33.4 | 30.4 |
| Proportion (%) | 1.9 | 1.2 | 0.9 | 1.3 | 2.1 | 1.1 | 1.3 | – | – |

of who is charged with public order offences by age and sex, as a proportion of all offences heard in the Higher Courts.

As mentioned, the vast majority of public order offences are dealt with by Magistrate's Courts. Some indication of the number of cases processed each year in Australia is provided in table 4.2 (ABS 2003b: 46). This table shows the number of public order offences, and the proportion of these offences in relation to the total number of offences heard in these Courts.

Victim surveys suggest that public order offences are taken seriously by the community, affecting perceptions of safety as well as levels of crime and disorder (see ABS 2003a). The most recent ABS victim survey found that overall three-quarters of persons aged 15 years and over perceived that there were problems with crime and/or public nuisance issues in their neighbourhoods (ABS 2003a: 9–10). Dangerous/noisy driving

**Table 4.2** Public order offences by jurisdiction

Experimental Magistrates' Courts data; adjudicated defendants, principal offence

| | NSW | Vic | Qld | SA | WA | Tas[a] | NT | ACT | Aust |
|---|---|---|---|---|---|---|---|---|---|
| Number | na | 12,594 | 10,822 | 3205 | 4589 | 180 | 347 | na | na |
| Proportion (%) | na | 12.6 | 9.5 | 9.5 | 7.9 | 4.0 | 4.6 | na | na |

a  Restricted to Southern Tasmanian Magistrates' Courts for the reference period 1 March 2002 to 30 June 2002

na  not available

(39 per cent); vandalism, **graffiti**, and damage to property (37 per cent); and louts, youth gangs, illegal drugs, and drunkenness (10 to 20 per cent) were identified by respondents as problems.

## PUBLIC ORDER AND THE SOCIAL FABRIC

While public order offences are often relatively trivial, they are taken seriously by community leaders and the police since they are often seen as an indicator of the strength of **social capital** within a community (Forrest & Kearns 2001). The concept of social capital refers to the idea of the reciprocal relations between people that underlie the social fabric (Bourdieu 1986; Coleman 1988; Putnam 1993, 1995). It has been widely used in the analysis of communities on the grounds that strong social capital is a feature of strong communities. Such communities are characterised as having high levels of civic involvement and a corresponding capacity to achieve collective goals. In contrast, neighbourhoods with little social capital are characterised as socially disorganised with high levels of crime, with the result that the local population feels unsafe and lacking in social support.

The idea that neighbourhoods with high levels of crime are socially disorganised was first put forward by members of the Chicago School of criminology (Shaw & McKay 1942). In the 1980s, American criminologists Wilson and Kelling (1982) developed this idea into an influential theory known as the 'broken windows' thesis. This theory about the relationship between crime and social disorder argued that public order offences such as vandalism, graffiti, and vagrancy create a spiral of decline. Visible evidence of decay, such as broken windows, sends a signal to the local community that the neighbourhood is an easy target for criminals because it lacks social control. As criminal activity increases, a sense of fear pervades the district causing the wealthier, more mobile residents to depart, leaving the more vulnerable ones behind. A corresponding influx of criminals, drug addicts, and sex workers then causes further deterioration. Wilson and Kelling argued that the solution to this problem lay in increasing levels of control through the aggressive policing of public disorder, surveillance of the environment, and other forms of control.

These ideas fed into a climate of political conservatism that saw the solution to crime in heightened social control. In the USA the theory was used to support the introduction of 'zero tolerance' policing in the 1990s, in which minor incivilities were treated as serious crimes on the grounds that controlling such crimes would prevent the development of more serious offences. In fact, research on the effectiveness of such forms of social control is mixed (Grabosky 1998), and writers such as Crawford (1998: 133) point out that the groups that need most help, such as the poor and drug addicts, are the ones that tend to be criminalised. Although zero-tolerance policing is not common in Australia, the 'broken window' thesis remains an influential theory informing both policy makers and law enforcement agencies.

## Young people and public order

Many public order types of offences—and, correspondingly, many state responses to public disorders of various kinds—revolve around the activities of young people (those under the age of 25 years). Especially for teenagers, the media perceptions of youth criminality and police interventions in juvenile justice are shaped by the specific features of juvenile offending itself. For example, the following aspects of juvenile offending relate directly to how young people use public space (see Cunneen & White 1995):

- young people tend to hang around in groups, and youth crime tends to be committed in groups
- the public congregation of young people makes them particularly visible, and thus youth crime tends to be more readily apparent and detectable
- young people tend to commit crime in their own neighbourhoods, where there is greater likelihood that they will be recognised and identified by observers
- the social dynamics of the offence means it is often public, gregarious, and attention-seeking
- youth crime is often episodic, unplanned, and opportunistic, and related to the use of public space in areas such as shopping centres and public transport where there is more surveillance.

In summary, the public visibility and group behaviour of young people makes them more prone to arrest for certain types of crimes than their adult counterparts.

Simultaneously, non-criminal behaviour and less serious offending by young people are also subject to routine scrutiny by authority figures and other adults. Again, this is mainly due to the visibility of young people in public spaces, which is enhanced by the fact that they generally hang around in groups. Further to this, large congregations of young people may be disruptive to the flow of pedestrian traffic, and may be accompanied by the making of noise that may be disturbing to some bystanders and shopkeepers. In addition, the adoption of particular unconventional youth cultural 'styles' can mark some teenagers out from the crowd and bring them to the notice of other users of public space. The very presence of young people, much less what they are actually doing, can therefore be perceived as unsettling and problematic.

An important aspect of public order concerns relates to conflicts within and between young people themselves. The congregation of many different groups of young people, from diverse social and cultural backgrounds, occasionally flares into street conflicts. These range from name-calling through to more serious instances of personal harm. Antagonisms between groups of young people on the basis of race and ethnicity have been noted around Australia, and is reflected to some extent in moral panics over 'ethnic youth gangs' (Daniel & Cornwall 1993; White et al. 1999; White & Perrone 2001). Violence against gay men and lesbians by groups of young men is also a significant social problem (Mason & Tomsen 1997). Young women often feel intimidated or threatened by young men (and older men) when they use public spaces (White & Wyn 2004). There is also evidence of intra-group fighting and violence, both in relation to so-called 'gangs' (Aumair & Warren 1994) and particular Indigenous or ethnic minority groups. Street violence of this nature can make young people, in general, feel unsafe and in need of protection when they venture out of their own homes and neighbourhoods.

Another area worthy of greater attention is how the growth in the entertainment economy in Western cities is influencing youth leisure activities and their relationships to each other, and to authority figures. For instance, Chatterton and Hollands (2003) provide a sophisticated analysis of the new night-time economies and cityscapes. An important part of this analysis is the emergent social divisions between various youth based upon money and different forms of enjoyment. Public order is variously defined in the night-time economy, as are offenders of this order.

## VANDALISM AND GRAFFITI

### Vandalism

In addition to issues such as minor assaults and public visibility, considerable public attention has been given to the problem of youth vandalism. **Vandalism** involves the wilful and deliberate destruction or defacement of property. Although few vandals actually get caught (Geason & Wilson 1989), the evidence of such activity permeates the urban environment in the form of wall graffiti, broken windows and street lights, damage to playground equipment, smashed telephone boxes, and carving on park benches.

The legal term given to vandalism is **'criminal damage'**. It refers to a wide range of offences against property where the objective is damage of the property rather than financial gain. Malicious damage to property is one of the most numerous offences recorded by the police. Mayhew estimates that in 2001 there were 1.9 million incidents of criminal damage (2003: 4). Although many incidents are relatively trivial, they are a source of concern to the community. In the 2001 Crime and Safety Survey, 27.2 per cent of respondents identified vandalism, graffiti, and damage to property as a neighbourhood problem (ABS 2002a: 33). The damage can also be expensive, costing an estimated $700 per incident and a total of $1.34 million in 2001 (Mayhew 2003: 4), although La Grange (1996) argues its costs are often overstated.

Research on the nature of vandalism indicates that it is distributed evenly among young people generally. LaGrange argues that while 'some vandals may be antisocial youths who deliberately seek ways to express themselves in costly rampages of destruction—as is believed by the public and portrayed by the media—many are ordinary youths who do their damage spontaneously and with little thought of its costs or consequences' (1996: 140). This is consistent with self-report data on juvenile offending, which suggests that such offending is more uniformly spread across the youth population than arrest figures may indicate (Cunneen & White 1995; Mukherjee 1997a).

The issue of vandalism is intrinsically related to that of public space. It is highly visible and ubiquitous across the urban landscape, and appears to confirm the worst fears of adult society that young people are 'out of control'. Its incidence tends to reinforce the idea that how and why young people use public space requires close monitoring. Hollands (1995: 65) found that only 13 per cent of the young people interviewed in his study in Newcastle, England, admitted to ever personally being involved in any kind of vandalism, with the vast majority of acts being petty in nature (such as stealing street signs or traffic cones).

## Graffiti

**Graffiti** comes in many forms, from scribblings on public toilet walls to murals in the CBD. It can involve offensive words or phrases, creative self-expression, or political protest. But whether written by pen, spray can, or paintbrush, it is always public and displayed on someone else's property. A study in New South Wales found that most graffiti occurred at educational institutions (40.4 per cent), followed by residential (15.5 per cent) and transport locations (14.8 per cent; Fitzgerald 2000: 1).

Graffiti has become part of the normal urban landscape and is rarely reported to the police. In 1999 New South Wales police recorded 6870 incidents of graffiti, but this is probably a small proportion of the actual amount (Fitzgerald 2000: 1). The British Crime Survey found that only 26 per cent of incidents of residential vandalism, including graffiti, were reported to police (Mirrlees-Black et al. 1998). According to Fitzgerald the level of graffiti occurring in recent years has remained stable (2000: 1).

Type the word 'graffiti' into a library catalogue and the results are overwhelmingly drawn from the fine arts literature. Since the 1970s graffiti has been recognised as a creative act. Graffiti writers are described as 'artists' and sometimes sign their work with a 'tag' that identifies it as their creation. Yet many communities are outspoken in their opposition to it and associate it with urban social decline and high crime rates (Bandaranaike 2001).

Graffiti offenders who become known to police are predominantly juvenile males often operating in 'crews' (Bandaranaike 2001; Fitzgerald 2000: 1). In New South Wales in 1999, 75 per cent of all recorded offences were committed by individuals under the age of 18. Only 18.2 per cent were by women (Fitzgerald 2000: 4). However, low clearance rates for malicious damage mean that it is not known who commits most offences. In the New South Wales study, clear-up rates were only 14.1 per cent six months after the incident (Fitzgerald 2000: 4).

## Types of graffiti

Graffiti varies greatly in the message being conveyed and the style of its presentation (see, for example, Forrester 1993; United States Bureau of Justice Assistance 1998; Ferrell 1996; Iveson 2000). Understanding how and why it occurs involves asking what is the cultural meaning of its various forms and who determines this. In what circumstances is it legitimate and for which groups? What are the politics behind perceptions and social responses to different types of graffiti? Such distinctions have an important influence on crime prevention strategies in this area (see White 2001).

Even a cursory review of different graffiti forms reveals the following types of graffiti work:

- *Political graffiti*—This is graffiti with an explicit political message of some kind. Mostly this kind of graffiti originates from the grassroots, from individuals and groups who wish to challenge the legitimacy of the present political economic order or specific government policies. It might include anarchist graffiti (with the anarchist circle around an 'A'), socialist graffiti ('Down with the IMF and World Bank'), feminist graffiti ('Wimmin Take Back The Night') and national liberation graffiti ('Free East Timor'; 'English out of Ireland'). It can be racist or homophobic. Political graffiti can also occasionally reflect the efforts of the powerful to claim legitimacy, in the form of top-down propaganda designed to look like grassroots activity. For example, when the United States invaded the small Caribbean island of Grenada in the 1980s, US troops allegedly spray painted 'welcome' slogans in the main town centres.
- *Protest graffiti*—This graffiti is also political in nature, but targets the form and content of commercial signs. It includes the activities of the BUGAUP (Billboard Utilising Graffitists Against Unhealthy Promotions) organisation, as well as spontaneous actions of individual citizens against racist, sexist, and violent billboards and advertising. This graffiti is designed to highlight the offensive nature of mainstream commercial visual objects in our cityscapes and public spaces.
- *Graffiti art*—This form of graffiti tends to be a well-organised, skilled activity that has a strong aesthetic dimension. It involves the crafting of 'pieces' in which artistic effort is the major consideration. It is informed by defined techniques, learning strategies, evaluation, and group

forums. It is a socially organised activity with subcultural elements of association, group deliberation, initiation processes, and development of mastery of execution.

- *Tagger graffiti*—This form of graffiti is often, but need not be, linked to graffiti art. In some cases, it is seen to represent the first stages of a 'career' in graffiti art, in which novices begin by simply applying themselves to low-level 'tagging' of city sites. The emphasis is on being 'seen' in as many places as possible. It often takes the form of peculiar forms of writing, with distinctive signatures being developed to establish individual and/or group identity. The message is simply one of, 'I'm here', and 'This, too, is my space'.

- *Gang graffiti*—This graffiti is not simply about establishing a presence, but to claim territory. The intent is to communicate claims about gang identity and prowess, and to establish, often in a threatening manner, that this or that 'gang' rules a particular neighbourhood. Whether or not a group of youth is in fact a 'gang' as such, is irrelevant. Middle class suburbs may be targeted even though the members of the group do not engage in criminal gang activity. The connotation of the graffiti is that particular territory is the preserve of certain young people.

- *Toilet and other public graffiti*—This type of graffiti may contain a wide range of messages. It is intended to communicate certain points of view, to be part of a 'discussion', to 'gossip', to establish ascendancy of some writers over others, or to simply have fun by stirring the pot. The precise character and content of the graffiti will tend to vary according to location (for example, train stations, bus shelters, or university student toilet blocks).

### Social differences in graffiti production

The location of graffiti provides insight into the circumstances of its production (see, for example, Carrington 1989). Where the graffiti is located can imply different protagonists, with different messages, and different dynamics underpinning the graffiti production. There are differences between boys and girls toilet graffiti, the substantive content of train graffiti, and the types of wall graffiti in particular urban sites. The physical place of graffiti implies different types of audiences (for example, girls only), and different types of messages (for example, emphasis on sexuality and social relationships).

Some locations are considered 'safe' places for graffiti production (for example, toilets), while others are 'dangerous' in terms of the risks accompanying the production process (for example, moving trains). This influences who does what type of graffiti and why. These factors can be linked to particular conceptions of social identity, such as male bravado stemming from certain notions of masculinity, which, in turn, may be associated with particular kinds of risk-taking behaviour on the part of young men.

Graffiti may also reflect the assertion of ethnic identities. In Adelaide in the mid 1980s, for example, bus shelters began to feature the slogan 'Wogs Rule OK', an assertion of a unique and empowered identity by ethnic minority youth in a poly-ethnic but monocultural society. Conversely, the heightened attention given to the 'race debate' in recent years has been accompanied by various kinds of racist graffiti, as a statement of perceived disempowerment and disillusionment on the part of some sections of the white, Anglo Australian majority.

Graffiti is meaningful activity. That is, it is undertaken for a reason. But how and why it takes places varies enormously (see, for example, Carrington 1989; Ferrell 1996; Farley & Sewell 1976). Vandalism implies destruction, whereas graffiti is generally creative and intended not to destroy existing surfaces but, if anything, to preserve them—in order that there be spaces to comment, protest, demonstrate artistic skill, or identify territory. How vandalism is defined has a major bearing on general perceptions of graffiti. As a broad category, however, it does little to illuminate the substantive and varied nature of graffiti work. In the end, graffiti writing, in its many forms, can be seen basically as a fairly normal, rather than exceptional, part of everyday social life.

From another point of view graffiti can be seen as vandalism, insofar as it affects the preservation of property in a particular way, namely its appearance. Nevertheless, specific types of vandalism do warrant close attention. For example, the incidence of graffiti varies according to whether or not it is organised, whether it is tied to a particular graffiti art culture, or whether it is linked to certain locations such as toilet blocks or bus shelters. So, too, the motivations behind particular kinds of graffiti work or vandalism vary. For instance, graffiti artists may partake in their activity as part of a collective creative endeavour; others do so in a less artistic fashion (through the use of tags or slogans) in order to mark out territory or convey social messages. Some Indigenous young people engage in vandalism as a form of resistance to colonialism, as indicated in vandalism directed in some communities at school buildings, European staff houses, and the store (Brady 1992).

What is seen by young people as an attempt to carve out some social space is regarded by many politicians and town planners as a law and order problem that needs to be controlled. This perspective is, however, changing as people begin to realise the importance of incorporating youth concerns into any program or service response to perceived graffiti problems (see White 2001; Collins 1998). Recent attempts to control graffiti have focused on cleaning it up, educating young people through school programs, surveillance, and channelling the energy of the young people into legitimate areas such as skateboard parks. Bandaranaike argues that while these can be effective short-term strategies, unless they address the underlying causes they will fail (2001). His study of Townsville City Council's 1999 'Graffiti Action Plan', which implemented a 'zero tolerance' approach to graffiti, demonstrated that the plan appeared to be successful, but in reality merely shifted the location of the graffiti artists from centrally located areas, such as the CBD and sporting grounds, to less easily controlled locations such as parks, shopping complexes, culverts, and footpaths (2001: 9). Bandaranaike is one of a number of criminologists who argue that unless the needs of young people to assert their identity and to win space are addressed, the 'problem' of graffiti will remain.

## OFFENSIVE LANGUAGE

Perceptions of 'bad behaviour' and 'bad people' are important to consider when it comes to how and why police carry out their duties in relation to specific groups. Leaving aside for the moment the ongoing climate of distrust and disrespect characterising many local police–youth relations, it is significant that the 'justification' for particular kinds of police action is provided by the apparent attitudes of 'the general public'. This type of regulatory environment thus reflects particular concerns with, and conceptions of, 'acceptable' and 'unacceptable' behaviour in public places on the part of authority figures and other users of these spaces.

For instance, in a recent study of public space issues, a number of older residents in Mildura, a country town in Victoria, were interviewed (see White 1999a). Certain types of behaviour—such as being loud, rude, shouting, and swearing—were identified by older people as being the most annoying or disturbing. Most of the older people felt that there were particular groups of young people who were not using public space in a suitable manner, including (and especially) Indigenous young people. Concern about behaviour such as being loud, shouting, being rude, and swearing was also expressed by older people interviewed in Darwin and Alice Springs.

Perceptions of a 'problem' require some form of police 'solution'. In many cases, intervention is premised upon use of legislation that allows police to charge (usually young) people with offensive behaviour and/or offensive language. For example, the *Summary Offences Act* 1988 of New South Wales (as amended) has a separate provision for 'offensive language'. This provision is actively used by police in dealing with public order matters. The problem with reliance upon such legislation, however, is that such provisions are 'inevitably vague and open-ended, with the characterisation of the behaviour left to the discretion of the police in the first instance, and subsequently to the discretion of magistrates' (Brown et al. 2001). Case law in this area has been uneven, with decisions about what constitutes 'offensive language' varying greatly depending upon the predilections of the judge or magistrate, the specific circumstances, and the parties involved (see Brown et al. 2001).

Public consternation and media attention given to street behaviour (usually focusing on antisocial activity, 'youth gangs', public drunkenness, drug use, visible minorities, and Indigenous people) have been reflected in discussions of 'zero tolerance' policing and new public order legislation (as in the Northern Territory) that expressly targets particular groups and particular types of social behaviour as being offensive. The use of offensive language and offensive behaviour offences is thus generally highly targeted, and socially patterned (White 2002). That is, some groups of people are charged more than others, and this is reflected in overall distributions of charges.

For example, a New South Wales study (Jochelson 1997) found that local government areas with high percentages of Indigenous people tended to have higher rates of court appearances for public order offences such as 'offensive behaviour' and 'offensive language'. This over-representation also occurred in local government areas with low proportions of Indigenous people in their population. More recent data from 1999 recorded crime statistics suggests a continuation of this pattern (Brown et al. 2001). Data also show that Indigenous people account for 15 times as many offensive language offences as would be expected by their population in the community (cited in Heilpern 1999: 241).

Similarly, a study (Mackay & Munro 1996: 6) found that in Victoria during 1993–94: 'Aborigines were 10.3 times more likely to be processed for "resist police", 11.8 times for "hinder police", 14.8 times for "indecent language", and 5.5 times for "offensive behaviour".' The use of local government ordinances in relation to public drinking, particularly as this affects Indigenous people, has also been questioned in the Victorian context (see Allas & James 1997). It appears to generally be the case that Indigenous young people brought before the courts are more likely to come from rural backgrounds (NISATSIC 1997).

It has been noted in many studies that very often people charged with offensive language are also charged with other offences. This is known in Australia as the 'trifecta' and usually involves offensive language, resisting arrest, and assaulting police (see Cunneen 2001; Jochelson 1997). In other words, not only are Indigenous people over-represented in offensive language offences, but they are also frequently charged with multiple offences. Very often these arise out of simple incidents, and are reflective of social processes relating to the nature of the contact in the first place (see Heilpern 1999).

There are several issues that need to be highlighted here. First, the offences are very often precipitated by the intervention of the police in the first place; that is, the police approach Indigenous people for some reason and then become the victim of the offences (Cunneen 2001: 97). Second, except for a notional 'community', the victim of the offence is almost invariably the police officer (Cunneen 2001: 29). Third, the language in question has variable usages and meanings, and it is questionable whether or not the police would themselves be genuinely offended by it. As Jochelson (1997: 15) observes: 'In many of the cases involving Aboriginal people the legislation would appear to provide a trigger for detention for an Aboriginal person who has abusively challenged police authority rather than as a means of protecting members of the community at large from conduct which is patently offensive.'

When we consider broad public perceptions of civility—which often hinge upon the use of certain words, and patterns of police intervention in dealing with 'offensive language'—then the dilemma for young Indigenous people becomes clear. They are being penalised for behaviour that in their cultural universe is part of routine, everyday communication. It is not defined or experienced by them as 'swearing'. For many, it is a normal, and ingrained, part of how young people converse with their family and with each other. As pointed out in an Aboriginal submission to the Royal Commission into Deaths in Custody, what constitutes 'swearing' in some communities is that which is specifically forbidden by Aboriginal law; that is, swearing to certain kinds of 'poison relations'— in-laws, or a sister swearing in front of a brother (Johnston 1991: 352).

Work that has investigated the nature, style, and dynamics of swearing specifically within Indigenous communities has found that its cultural meaning is highly contextual and variable (Langton 1988). For example, there is no sanction on children swearing at or in front of their mothers in some communities, and there is no public sanction on swearing by women (contrast this with traditional conventions in 'Western' society). Significantly, swearing may be an integral part of 'making everybody happy', in that it is part of good-natured banter in the context of formally defined joking relationships. It can also be used aggressively, in order to precipitate a fight within a community or to exercise resistance against the dominant forces outside of it. The specific nature of swearing will differ according to the particular individuals and communities in question. Indigenous people are heterogeneous in composition. There are differences within the varying communities, and between individuals, in terms of political and spiritual beliefs, regional and family ties, traditional and contemporary lifestyles, class and occupational position, and social identity. How people swear is shaped by situational factors in particular social settings. The dynamics of swearing in relation to the police, in particular, can only be fully comprehended in the light of the historical relationship and ongoing conflicts between the police and Indigenous people (see Cunneen 2001).

## RESPONDING TO PUBLIC DISORDER

The policing of behaviour perceived to be disorderly, and of groups of street-present people perceived to be engaged in such behaviour can take many different forms. For instance, while the legislative basis for action varies from state to state, the general trend around Australia has been for police services to be granted extensive powers in relation to young people (see, for example, Blagg & Wilkie 1995; Mukherjee et al. 1997). These range from casual use of 'name-checks', 'move-on' powers, and the search for prohibited implements through to enhanced ability to take fingerprints and bodily samples of alleged young offenders.

The removal of young people from public spaces has also been accomplished through specific legislative measures. In 1997, the *Children (Protection and Parental Responsibility) Act* was proclaimed in New South Wales. The Act allows the police to remove young people under 16 years of age from public places without charge, if the police believe that the young people are 'at risk' of committing an offence or of being affected by a crime, are not under the supervision or control of a responsible adult, or if it is believed the young person is in danger of being physically harmed or injured, or abused. The Act does not specify the sort of offences that might be committed, but if an offence were actually committed, the police would not be picking the young person up under this Act.

In the first six months of 1999, 145 young people were removed from public places in the four local government areas where the legislation was operational. Of these, 90 per cent were Aboriginal children (Chan & Cunneen 2000: 53). The question these figures raise is whether the removal powers ought to target people on the basis of apparently racially discriminatory criteria.

The enforcement of anti-weapons laws also has implications for public order policing. It likewise can also affect large groups of young people in negative ways. For instance, the *Crimes Legislation Amendment (Police and Public Safety) Act* 1998 commenced in July 1998 in New South Wales. The Act made amendments to the *Summary Offences Act* 1988, so as to make the custody of a knife in a public place an offence, to permit police to conduct searches for knives and other dangerous implements, and to enable police to give reasonable directions in public places to deal with persons whose behaviour or presence constitutes an obstruction, harassment, or intimidation, or causes fear. The New South Wales Ombudsman (2000) found that people from 15 to 19 years of age were much more likely to be stopped and searched for knives than any other age group. Significantly, it was pointed out that 'the proportion of persons aged 17 years or younger affected by the directions power is higher than for the knife searches. The police data indicates that 48 per cent of persons 'moved on' were aged 17 years or younger, while 42 per cent of persons searched were juveniles' (New South Wales Ombudsman 2000: 37). The Ombudsman recommended that the police service closely monitor the use of these powers, and be aware of the adverse impact this activity might have on police relations with the community in general or sections of the community subject to such activity.

Another measure of 'public order' policing is the use of offensive language provisions as a means to clear the streets. As noted above, in places such as New South Wales, legislation has been devised that expressly targets particular groups and particular types of social behaviour as being offensive. It is significant in this regard that, since the restoration of the crime of offensive language in 1988 under the *Summary Offences Act*, prosecutions have risen greatly and have overtaken prosecution for offensive behaviour. For example, in 1999 there were 3187 appearances in New South Wales Local Courts for offensive behaviour and 5461 appearances for offensive language (Brown et al. 2001: 956). And, as also seen earlier, research has demonstrated that Indigenous young people are especially likely to be charged with offensive language and offensive behaviour offences, at a level far disproportionate to population size.

Another area in which public order offences surface is that of the policing of political protests. McCulloch (2001a) provides a sustained analysis of how police in states such as Victoria have been highly influenced by a 'paramilitary' model of policing. She argues that this represents a fundamental shift in the nature of policing. Traditionally, the police and the military have had separate roles, marked by differences in objectives and in the use of force. Police are meant to use minimum force against individual suspects and are bound by considerations of due process and judicial oversight. The military operate under a philosophy of maximum force aimed at killing and defeating an enemy. However, in recent years these roles and practices have increasingly been blurred, as the police adopt new technologies (such as protective riot gear), enhance their firepower (including army weaponry), and engage in specialist military training (in areas such as 'counter terrorism'). According to McCulloch (2001a), this trend has had major consequences for dealing with instances of public 'disorder' such as protest marches, demonstrations, and mass mobilisations of concerned citizens.

When it comes to protest-related 'public order offences' McCulloch (2001a, 2001b) indicates that 'justice' is less a matter of the police charging protesters or demonstrators with specific offences (although a small number may be charged with minor offences) than the police, literally, charging *at* protesters. This represents the meting out of new forms of summary violence, as indicated in allegations relating to the policing of the S11 protest against globalisation and the World Economic Forum held in Melbourne in 2000:

> Individual protesters and protest organisers have complained to the Ombudsman about the police tactics and a public interest inquiry is currently being conducted into allegations including excessive use of force, the use of pressure point neck holds, failure to wear name tags, and alleged assaults on members of the media engaged in filming or photographing the baton charge and other instances of police use of force (McCulloch 2001b: 24).

According to McCulloch (2001b, 2002), excessive use of force by police is increasingly justified through the ideological lens of 'counter terrorism'. Insofar as police action is linked to attempts to deal with public events that can, at some level, be associated with 'dissident' groups, then state violence can be blamed on the victims of this violence. As with other measures designed to deal with public disorder, the objective seems to be one of 'cleaning the streets'—whether this be in relation to anti-social behaviour, criminal acts, or political protest.

## CONCLUSION

While all crime is socially patterned, the analysis of laws relating to public order throws into particularly sharp relief the issues of power and control that underlie all criminal justice issues. This may be because the social harm caused by behaviour such as public drinking is generally perceived to be relatively small compared with more serious offences such as assault or burglary. Consequently, the subjective nature of the application of the law—that is, whose behaviour is defined as 'offensive'—is more visible.

Examining the way laws relating to public order have been used in different times and places reveals that their application is far from neutral. Whether acts such as swearing, sleeping in public places, or social protest are defined as 'offensive' or a 'public nuisance' is always a matter for interpretation. Policing public order is, therefore, fundamentally political in nature. This understanding challenges assumptions that in liberal democracies the law always serves the public good. Instead it points to a more subtle understanding that while the law may serve as a safeguard of civil liberty it can simultaneously be used as an instrument of oppression.

## DISCUSSION QUESTIONS

1 What does the history of laws of vagrancy reveal about the way in which the policing of public order has been used to protect the work ethic?
2 What is the 'broken window' thesis? What does the thesis suggest about the relationship between crime and social order?
3 Why does the policing of Indigenous Australians in public spaces reflect both political conflict and cultural difference?
4 What are the arguments for and against viewing graffiti as offensive?
5 Where do protests fit in when it comes to public order offences?

## GLOSSARY OF TERMS

**criminal damage**
a wide range of offences against property where the objective is damage of the property rather than financial gain
**graffiti**
the public display of drawings, words, or other marks in a setting that is usually considered illegal
**public order offences**
offences involving personal conduct that involves or may lead to a breach of public order and decency, or that is indicative of criminal intent, or that is otherwise regulated or prohibited on moral or ethical grounds. The 'victim' of these offences is generally the public at large. However, some offences such as offensive language and offensive behaviour may be directed towards a single victim (ABS 2003b: 78).
**social capital**
the reciprocal relations between people that underlie the social fabric
**vandalism**
the wilful and deliberate destruction of property.

## FURTHER READING

Brown, D., Farrier, D., Egger, S. & McNamara, L. (2001) *Criminal Laws: Materials and Commentary on Criminal Law and Process in New South Wales*, The Federation Press, Sydney.
Cunneen, C. (2001) *Conflict, Politics and Crime: Aboriginal Communities and the Police*, Allen & Unwin, Crows Nest.

Jones, D. (1982) *Crime, Protest, Community and Police in Nineteenth Century Britain*, Routledge & Kegan Paul, London.

McCulloch, J. (2001a) *Blue Army: Paramilitary Policing in Australia*, Melbourne University Press, Carlton.

Wilson, J.Q. & Kelling, G. (1982) 'The Police and Neighborhood Safety: Broken Windows', *Atlantic*, 127: 29–38

## WEBSITES

**www.aic.gov.au**
Australian Institute of Criminology—Provides links to various publications from Australian criminologists, including research, conference papers, publications, and statistics, many of which are full text.

**www.lawlink.nsw.gov.au/bocsar1.nsf/pages/index**
The New South Wales Bureau of Crime Statistics and Research—Provides links to statistical and research reports from the New South Wales Attorney-General's Department, plus access to a comprehensive range of crime and court statistics, fact sheets, and full text crime reports.

**www.cpu.sa.gov.au/sa_indproj.htm**
South Australian Governments Indigenous Crime Prevention Programs—Has access to various reports on addressing public order issues in Aboriginal communities, with most reports in full text.

# CHAPTER 5

# Drugs and Crime

## INTRODUCTION

This chapter explores the relationship between drugs and crime, and in particular examines drug-related crime. At one level, there is nothing new about human beings using drugs. Most cultures in history have some kind of relationship with a psychoactive substance of some kind. That is, they incorporate the taking of substances that alter consciousness in some way—whether it be through drinking wine or beer, smoking hashish, drinking kava, or snorting special powders. In most cases, there are rules and rituals that guide who, when, where, and why substances may be ingested, and how to behave once this has occurred. Drug use is about altering the mind in some way. In general, then, drug use is a 'natural' part of life, historically and in contemporary times.

However, drug use is never a simple affair. There are conventions, regulations, and laws that dictate which drugs are legitimate, and which are not, and that shape the patterns of private and public use of drugs. This chapter examines issues such as possession of illegal drugs, and how drug abuse influences criminal and antisocial behaviour. The concern of the chapter is not to judge whether or not drug taking is good or bad, but to consider how drug use fits into the everyday life patterns of society.

## THE EXTENT OF DRUG USE

The use of psychoactive drugs of various kinds has both a legitimate and non-legitimate character. There are some drugs, such as alcohol, that are legal, and some drugs, such as heroin, that are illegal. However, even with legal drugs there are social and legal guidelines regarding use. Binge drinking, for example, is not seen as socially acceptable according to mainstream definitions of appropriate behaviour. An age of responsibility (usually 18 years) legally demarcates when a person is eligible to publicly buy or drink alcohol. Similarly, if one is intoxicated, this is seen to be problematic, especially if it is associated with social harm of some kind (such as fighting or urinating in public). A significant part of the criminalisation of drug use stems from drug abuse, not simply access to a prohibited substance.

Which substances are deemed to be legal, and which illegal, is determined by specific social and historical processes. For example, alcohol was temporarily outlawed in the United States during the Prohibition era in the 1920s and early 1930s. It is similarly banned today in a number of countries. The reasons why alcohol consumption may be prohibited range from concerns relating to social welfare and public order to religious proscriptions on use of such drugs (for example, the temperance movement in North America and Australia was largely headed by Christian activists, while some Muslim countries ban alcohol use outright).

A history of drug laws in Australia shows that very often which drugs are considered to be 'bad' and which to be 'good' is decided politically rather than through some sort of neutral, technical exercise. In his book, *From Mr Sin to Mr Big*, Manderson (1993) provides a detailed history of Australian drug laws. An important part of Manderson's argument is that moral panics over drug use—for example, relating to opium, heroin, and cannabis—tend to be associated with racism and powerful international pressures rather than genuine concerns about the welfare of users. The banning of opium in places like Australia and the United States, for instance, was directed at Chinese workers. The proponents of a 'White Australia' led particularly vicious racist campaigns against Chinese residents throughout the 1880s and, as part of these anti-Chinese crusades, opium use was especially targeted and vilified. Yet for the Chinese the place of opium was an important part of everyday life:

> The Chinese did not drink their opium, or take it in tablet form or sub-
> cutaneously as White Australians did; although occasionally chewed, it
> was the most invariable custom of the Chinese to smoke it, especially
> prepared in pipes, often in 'dens' fitted out for the purpose. Smoking
> was at once a private and absorbing reverie and a social activity. For the
> Chinese, opium functioned as a recreational drug, like alcohol or

tobacco. Like any such drug, therefore, there were occasional users, regular users, abusers and addicts; there were houses in which the smoking of an opium pipe was regarded as a social courtesy, and others in which it was a serious business. Opium was, in short, as entrenched in the social life of the Chinese as ethyl alcohol is in that of Anglo-Australians (Manderson 1993: 20).

While a personage (fictional though he was) such as Sherlock Holmes might have been portrayed as an occasional needle-user of similar type drugs, the Chinese 'style' of drug use was closely linked to their very presence in the country. The prohibition of opium smoking was, in effect, another form of discrimination against the Chinese, alongside other government measures such as special taxes and exclusion from welfare provisions.

Much of the concern about drug use is about how best to manage drug use, rather than to ban it altogether. To take a couple of examples, first consider the case of driving and alcohol use. While it is legal to drink alcohol if one is of legal age, it is not legal to drink alcohol and then drive a car. In other words, alcohol use is invariably regulated in relation to other kinds of activities in which we might engage. There are also strong links between certain legal drugs, such as cigarettes, and public health campaigns. Again, recent years have seen increased regulatory activity in relation to smoking. Whereas it was previously acceptable to smoke cigarettes in movie theatres, restaurants, public foyers, and even university classrooms, smoking is now confined to very particular areas. Most workplaces, restaurants, public transport, taxis, and so on have been declared 'smoke-free' areas. Smoking itself is still legal (once you've reached the legal age), but the last two decades have seen a dramatic increase in the regulation of where it is permitted to occur.

While popular conceptions of the 'problem' of drug use relate to illegal drugs, in fact most drug use involves legal substances. Nationally, annual spending on illicit drugs, tobacco, medical/legal drugs, and alcohol has been estimated to comprise the following proportions (Parliament of Victoria 1997: 18):

- *alcohol*—43.4 per cent of all spending
- *illicit drugs*—22.7 per cent of all spending
- *tobacco*—20 per cent of all spending
- *medical/legal drugs*—13.7 per cent of all spending

It is clear from these estimates, however, that the main drug of choice (as measured in dollar terms) is alcohol (wine, spirits, and beer). This is followed by illicit drugs, such as cannabis, heroin, and amphetamines, followed by tobacco. Finally, medical and legal drugs make up the last category. Importantly, this category would also include prescription drugs, the use and abuse of which has raised some concern in recent years.

Most discussion of drugs, however, tends to concentrate on illicit or illegal drugs. From a global perspective, table 5.1 provides an indication of drug use patterns for different types of substance. The table provides an estimate of the number of drug abusers (defined narrowly as those who take illicit drugs) annually in the world in the 1990s. What is significant about the table is not so much the percentages, but the actual numbers of people estimated to partake in such drug use.

**Table 5.1** Estimated number of drug abusers (annually) in the world 1990s

|  | Estimated total (million people) | % of total population |
|---|---|---|
| Heroin | 8.0 | 0.14 |
| Cocaine | 13.3 | 0.23 |
| Cannabis | 141.2 | 2.45 |
| Hallucinogens | 25.5 | 0.44 |
| Amphetamines | 30.2 | 0.52 |
| Sedative-type substances | 227.4 | 3.92 |

Source: Parliament of Victoria (1997).

If one were to analyse drug use data in more detail, then we would also have to take into account national and regional differences in all kinds of drug use. For example, France and Italy are known as 'wine-drinking' nations, while in several Middle Eastern countries any kind of alcohol is prohibited. In India 'bhang', derived from the leaves of the hemp plant, is widely consumed by both Muslims and Hindus. During religious festivals street sellers even sell bhang-laced sweets named after the most popular cricketers (Das 2004).

The global perspective also may misrepresent or fail to acknowledge the peculiarities of drug use within particular national contexts. For example, the patterns of cannabis use by age in Australia show a significant rise in the percentage of people who have used cannabis. Between 1977 and 1991, for instance, the proportion of people aged 30 years and over who used cannabis rose from around 5 per cent in 1977 to over 20 per cent in 1991. By 1991, some 55 per cent of 20 to 29 year olds, and over 30 per cent of 14 to 19 year olds, had tried cannabis (Makkai et al. 1994).

The more recent picture is complicated, however, by changes in patterns of drug use, with the use of some types of drug increasing while others are decreasing. According to the National Drug Strategy Household Surveys of people aged 14 years and over, the proportion of the population who had ever used an illicit drug dropped from 46 per cent in 1998 to 38 per cent in 2001. Most of this reduction can be attributed to a drop in cannabis use, as well as in the use of hallucinogens. Conversely, there were reported increases in the proportion of people who said that they had ever used amphetamines, cocaine, and designer drugs (AIC 2003).

In some cases it is not the drug itself that is necessarily seen as the main problem; rather, it might be the dangers associated with how the drug is administered. This applies to both licit and illicit drugs. For example, there was a dramatic rise in the opioid (for example, heroin) overdose mortality rate between 1979 and 1995 with the rate increasing from 10 deaths per million people to almost 70 deaths per million people (Parliament of Victoria 1997). To explain the huge change in mortality rates it is necessary to look at factors such as the nature of the drugs sold on the street, the difficulties of gauging the purity or strength of the drug, the use of 'clean' equipment, and so on. Health problems may also be related to the relationship between substance use and needle-craft. Dirty needles can be contaminated. They can also convey illnesses such as hepatitis C or HIV/AIDS. Injecting drug users, therefore, have to consider the possibility and threat of communicable diseases, especially when needles are shared.

## OFFENDING AND DRUGS

Of the five principal offence categories that account for the majority of the adjudicated defendants in Australia's Higher Criminal Courts during 2001–02, 13 per cent involved illicit drug offences (ABS 2003b: 5). As defined by the Australian Bureau of Statistics (ABS 2003b: 75), **illicit drug offences** include the possession, sale, deal or trafficking, importing or exporting, manufacture, or cultivation of drugs or other substances prohibited under legislation. Specific categories of offence include: import or export illicit drugs; deal or traffic in illicit drugs; manufacture or cultivate illicit drugs; possess and/or use illicit drugs; and other illicit drug offences.

Drug offences feature prominently in both the Higher Courts and the Magistrate's Courts. Table 5.2 shows the breakdown of who is charged with illicit drug offences by age and sex, and drug offences as a proportion of all offences. According to this data, men are far more likely to be charged than women and both groups are predominantly mature adults.

**Table 5.2**   Illicit drug offences by age and sex

Total higher courts adjudicated defendants; principal offence by age and sex

|  | Under 20 | 20–24 | 25–34 | 35–44 | 45+ | Unknown | Total | Mean age (years) | Median age (years) |
|---|---|---|---|---|---|---|---|---|---|
| **MALES** | | | | | | | | | |
| Number | 47 | 250 | 582 | 467 | 341 | 32 | 1719 | 35.7 | 34.2 |
| Proportion (%) | 3.0 | 8.1 | 14.0 | 20.3 | 20.0 | 5.8 | 12.9 | – | – |
| **FEMALES** | | | | | | | | | |
| Number | 7 | 64 | 102 | 78 | 42 | 3 | 296 | 33.8 | 32.4 |
| Proportion (%) | 3.9 | 15.0 | 15.7 | 22.9 | 23.7 | 2.9 | 15.8 | – | – |
| **PERSONS** | | | | | | | | | |
| Number | 54 | 314 | 684 | 545 | 383 | 35 | 2015 | 35.4 | 33.9 |
| Proportion (%) | 3.1 | 8.9 | 14.2 | 20.7 | 20.4 | 5.3 | 13.2 | – | – |

A large number of illicit drug offences are dealt with by Magistrate's Courts. Some indication of the number of cases processed each year in Australia is provided in table 5.3 (ABS 2003b: 46). This table shows the number of offences brought before the Court, and drug offences as a proportion of all offences before the Court.

**Table 5.3**   Illicit drug offences by jurisdiction

Experimental Magistrate's Courts' data; adjudicated defendants, principal offence

|  | NSW | Vic | Qld | SA | WA | Tas[a] | NT | ACT | Aust |
|---|---|---|---|---|---|---|---|---|---|
| Number | na | 5079 | 8978 | 1673 | 4772 | 37 | 202 | na | na |
| Proportion (%) | na | 5.1 | 7.9 | 5.0 | 8.2 | 0.8 | 2.7 | na | na |

a   Restricted to Southern Tasmanian Magistrates' Courts for the reference period 1 March 2002 to 30 June 2002

na   not available

People end up in lower or higher courts depending upon the nature of the offence and how extensive is their involvement with certain drugs. Offenders involved in drug arrests can be divided into two categories (AIC 2003):

- *consumers*—persons charged with user-type offences (for example, possessing or administering drugs for their own personal use)
- *providers*—persons charged with supply-type offences (for example, importation, trafficking, selling, cultivation, and manufacture).

The Australian Bureau of Criminal Intelligence has reported drug arrest and seizure statistics since 1992, in relation to drugs such as cannabis, heroin (and other opioids), amphetamines, cocaine, and other drugs (not defined elsewhere). In the period 1995–96 to 2001–02, the majority of drug arrests involved cannabis. However, for both cannabis and heroin a declining trend in arrests was evident, whereas there was an increase in amphetamine arrests.

The majority of people arrested for drug offences are **consumers** rather than **providers**, irrespective of drug type (AIC 2002a: 81). For example, 87 per cent of persons arrested for cannabis offences in 2000–01 were consumers. Most of those arrested for drugs consumption have been cannabis users, although the proportion of such users decreased from 82 per cent to 65 per cent of all drug-related consumer offences between 1995–96 and 2001–02 (AIC 2003: 97).

In the case of providers, while the largest offence category relates to cannabis this has declined greatly over recent years. In 1995–96, 82 per cent of arrests against providers were for cannabis offences compared with 56 per cent in 2000–01. Meanwhile, the percentage of total provider arrests accounted for by amphetamine offences increased from 4 per cent in 1995–96 to 16 per cent in 2000–01 (AIC 2002a: 83).

There is an interesting age dynamic between drugs as a productive activity for making money, and drugs as illegal consumption activity. Research into patterns of drug use among people under 25 years of age found that 23.7 per cent of 400 people aged under 18 who were interviewed in Melbourne engaged in drug use. This compared with 28.5 per cent of 150 young people between the ages of 18 and 25. Each age group felt that young people engage in these kinds of activities due to boredom and the need for excitement (White et al. 1997). When it came to drug dealing, however, there were even more remarkable differences in participation. While the biggest category of criminal activity identified by the teenagers was drug dealing (33.8 per cent), the figure was much higher for the young adult group (49.1 per cent). The young adults described drug dealing as a prevalent type of illegal activity that young people engage in for money. Drug dealing was closely identified with activity at the local neighbourhood level. Knowing people in the area meant knowing the local market. Also, many of the young people in this particular study were from disadvantaged backgrounds, and looked to the criminal economy, including drug dealing, as an important alternative source of income (White et al. 1997).

## THE CAUSAL RELATIONSHIP BETWEEN DRUG USE AND CRIME

The issue of the relationship between drugs and crime is clearly a complex one. Media reports frequently suggest that involvement in drugs is associated with other types of crimes, such as burglary and assault. There is certainly evidence of high levels of drug use among offenders. The Drug Use Monitoring in Australia (DUMA) project run by the Australian Institute of Criminology (AIC) monitors illicit drug use among police detainees in several sites across Australia (AIC 2002a: 89). Between 1999 and 2001, the DUMA project found that around 70 per cent of the young people in these sites routinely tested positive to drugs of some kind, such as cannabis, opiate, amphetamines, or cocaine. Other studies have also found high levels of drug use among young offenders (in South Australia, for example; Putnins 2001: 7). There is also evidence that young offenders in secure care facilities engage in problem drinking at a higher rate than other young people (Howard & Zibert 1990).

While drug use is certainly associated with offending behaviour, the exact nature of the relationship is unclear. Public perceptions are that drugs lead to crime because of the need to fund an expensive drug habit. But this is not the only possible relationship. It could be that the physiological effects of drugs such as alcohol or marijuana reduce inhibitions and so increase risk-taking behaviour, especially violence. Alternatively the causal relationship may be in the opposite direction with engagement in crime leading to increased substance use, because, for example, people engaged in crime take drugs and encourage newcomers to do the same. Or perhaps it is just that those who take drugs and those who engage in crime have a number of characteristics in common and they are not causally related.

Studies investigating these hypotheses have produced contradictory findings. For example, while there is evidence that heroin users are more likely to develop a criminal career than non-heroin users (Dobinson & Ward 1986) most offenders who are also drug users commence their offending prior to their involvement in crime (Makkai & Payne 2003). Evidence that violent crime is not caused by the psychopharmacological effects of drug use (Fagan 1990: 241) is also contradicted by offenders who report that drugs have a psychopharmacological effect on their behaviour, which leads to crime (Makkai and Payne 2003).

The most recent study of the relationship between drugs and crime was conducted by Makkai and Payne (2003). Their study of male offenders found little evidence to support the view that offenders are forced into crime by their illegal drug use. However, they did find that drug use increased involvement in crime. Not only was drug addiction associated with increased property offending, but 51 per cent of those who reported drug use attributed all or most of their offending to illegal drugs and alcohol. They also suggest that there are a number of pathways into involvement in drugs and crime, with offenders of different crime types starting offending and drug use at different ages. This suggests that there are multiple paths linking the relationship between drug use and crime. It is also probable that the factors that influence drug use overlap with those that are linked with involvement in street crimes, such as poor social support, difficulties in school, and low income (AIC 2004).

## ALCOHOL AND CRIME

Alcohol use represents a special case when it comes to legal issues and criminal offences. The consumption of alcohol is regulated through a range of age-related laws and licensing arrangements, as well as prohibitions on drinking and driving. There are a number of offences that tend to accompany excessive alcohol consumption, ranging from making too much noise through to serious assaults. Research has examined the different types of drinkers and the probability of committing offences depending upon how one drinks. How much and the way in which one consumes alcohol is directly related to the probability of committing disorder across a number of dimensions: drink drive; verbal abuse; creating a public disturbance; stealing property; damaging property; and physical abuse (Makkai 1998). Moreover, as indicated in table 5.4, the frequency of engagement in social disorder increases according to propensity to drink heavily, to binge drink, and to drink in harmful ways.

**Table 5.4** Alcohol consumption and propensity for alcohol-related disorder

| Propensity for disorder | Non-drinker % | Moderate % | Heavy % | Binge % | Harmful/hazardous % |
|---|---|---|---|---|---|
| None | 94 | 86 | 63 | 45 | 57 |
| Single | 2 | 6 | 13 | 12 | 7 |
| Repeat | 1 | 4 | 9 | 9 | 12 |
| Multiple repeat | 2 | 3 | 10 | 17 | 14 |
| Chronic | 2 | 2 | 5 | 17 | 10 |

Source: 1993 and 1995 NDS National Household Surveys, pooled file weighted sample in Makkai (1998: 6).

## DRUG CULTURES AND SOCIAL CONTEXTS

It is important to locate drug use within the context of very specific sorts of drug cultures. For instance, we might consider how alcohol is consumed in different ways depending upon the social context. In some families alcohol may be incorporated into the rituals of the household and the family. In some Jewish communities, for example, the drinking of wine from a very early age is an ingrained part of the religious life of the household. In a different framework, some people are socialised into the idea of 'getting off your face' and, in essence, binge drinking. For a number of years at a broad-based cultural level there was an Australian cultural stereotype that suggested 'real' men 'drink heaps'. In other cultures or societies, or for other sections of the population (such as women), the drug in question may be something like prescription drugs. In the United States it is not uncommon for popular sitcom television programs to make fun of the way in which varying social problems can be solved by taking all manner of prescription or over-the-counter drugs. Advertising in North America is replete with drug messages of this kind. Taking antidepressants is portrayed as just good commonsense and a 'natural' way to deal with life's pressures and strains.

The high profile given to illegal drugs in the mass media has been accompanied by moral panics over drug use among teenagers (see case study 5.1). Headlines about deaths linked to the taking of ecstasy and lurid details about deaths due to heroin overdoses have further reinforced public concern over how best to tackle the presumed 'war on drugs'. A closer look at the problem reveals that as a proportion of all crimes committed by juveniles, as formally processed in the criminal justice system, drug offences are not especially significant (Freeman 1996). Furthermore, most prosecutions for drug offences are for minor offences. For example, at least 87 per cent of all cannabis-related offences (reported or becoming known to police) relate to the personal possession and cultivation of cannabis, its use, and the possession of related implements such as 'bongs' (Atkinson & McDonald 1995). There are also significant age-related differences in drug use. At a younger age, people tend to experiment with individual drugs, including alcohol; as they get older, into the late teens and early twenties, there is a greater tendency to start mixing different kinds of drugs.

## CASE STUDY 5.1

Andrew Johnson was 'the boy in the alleyway'. In January 1999 he was photographed by a journalist being injected with heroin by a friend in Caroline Lane, Redfern, Sydney's most notorious drug alley. A few days later the *Sun Herald* ran the story under the headlines 'Shooting up on easy street' and 'A picture which shames us all'. They described Andrew as aged 12 to 13, and said he had collected his injection kit from the needle exchange van, and was undisturbed by Redfern police stationed 50m away (Sutton & Walker 1999).

A companion article described the use of drugs in the state as an 'epidemic' that was wasting young people's lives, and argued that as a country we had made the leap from 'outrage' to 'dumb acceptance' when 'children as young as 12 blatantly inject each other with illegal opiates in a grim inner-city back lane' (*Sun Herald* 1999: 46). It went on to say that: 'It would be easy to suggest the NSW Health Department, which operates 319 needle exchange outlets and hands out nine million syringes at a cost of some $9 million a year is partly to blame. Some might say supplying a needle, spoon and instructions on how to use them is aiding the distribution chain' (*Sun Herald* 1999: 46).

> In response the Health Minister immediately suspended the Caroline Lane needle exchange program and the Premier, Bob Carr, announced that a five-day Parliamentary Drug Summit would be held to assess the 'drug crisis'.
>
> Weeks later, an investigation revealed that the boy was actually aged 16 or 17, he had not received the needles from the exchange, and it was the first time he had been to Caroline Lane. In fact, he was from Whalan, a suburb some distance away from Redfern.

There is some evidence that drug use, and drug dealing, among teenagers is widespread (White et al. 1997). A national survey of illegal drug use among young people in the 14 to 19-year-old age group found that 38 per cent of the people in this group had used an illegal drug in 1998 (NSW Law Reform Commission 2001: 29). Alcohol consumption appears especially widespread. Putnins' study found that the level of alcohol consumption by offenders in South Australia was only slightly higher than that of male 16-year-old secondary school students (Putnins 2001: 7).

In general, however, the patterns of use vary considerably and appear to be closely related to socio-economic circumstances, particularly among 'street kids', unemployed youth, and the young homeless (Lennings 1996; Tressider et al. 1997; White et al. 1997). Notably, drug use among some sections of youth from higher socio-economic backgrounds, especially heroin use, has occasionally made headlines, indicating the problematic nature of drug use for this population as well as for their less advantaged peers.

Drug use connected to youth dance cultures continues to generate controversy. However, this, too, requires closer scrutiny if we are to understand the influence of specific drug cultures on drug-taking practices. For example, the use of drugs in association with rave parties has changed and evolved over time. When the rave scene commenced it was an informal, self-generated, sub-cultural leisure activity. Those in the 'scene' were also in the 'know' when it came to appropriate and safe drug use. Entrants into the culture were socialised into this kind of drug use. The drugs may have been illegal, but the drug taking was done under internally regulated guidelines. Over time, however, rave parties became more commercialised and increasingly found a home in clubs. Rave culture was radically altered, as was the clientele who attended the rave parties (Chan 1999). In this scenario, many new young people were introduced to raving, but without the subcultural training in suitable drug-use precautions. This diminishment of informal mechanisms of drug regulation increased the likelihood of problems occurring, especially among first-time and naïve drug takers. Recent discussions about the nature of teenage drug use are also pointing to the 'normalisation' of young people's drug use. Specifically, in the light of documented significant increases in the prevalence and frequency of teenage drug use in recent decades in places such as England and Western Europe, as well as Australia, it is suggested that young people are viewing and using drugs very differently today than previously (see Parker et al. 1998; Gatto 1999; Duff 2003). Whereas drug use was typically associated with 'deviancy' and law-breaking behaviour, contemporary youth now regard it as a normal and an uncontroversial aspect of the young person's life experience. Duff (2003) suggests far from being pathological, mentally ill, or irresponsible, as constructed by the popular discourse, many drug users are 'well-adjusted, responsible and outgoing'. Their use of drugs is a deliberate and strategic recreational activity. For example, rave dance parties and ecstasy use represent a conscious connection between particular pleasure pursuits and the drug that best suits the occasion. The consumption of different substances is used strategically to express one's allegiances to particular youth cultures and scenes, and thus to reinforce a particular social identity (see Duff 2003).

Further analysis of youth drug use refines this understanding. Shildrick (2002: 36), for example, argues that 'a concept of "differentiated normalization", which allows for the ways in which different types of drugs and different types of drug use may be normalised for different groups of young people, may be a more appropriate tool for understanding contemporary youthful drug use' than perspectives that see normalisation in more generalist terms.

A complicating factor in the debate over drugs is the associated public concern over offences relating to the use of legal substances, in particular alcohol, among young people. The issues are twofold. On the one hand, there has been considerable media coverage in recent years related to underage drinking, both as a status offence and as a health matter. Concern has been expressed over issues such as 'binge' drinking and the overall patterns of alcohol consumption by young people, which show extensive, and often inappropriate, use of alcohol by young people (see AIHW 1996).

On the other hand, the effects of alcohol on youth behaviour have also been the cause of worry. It is notable, for instance, that young offenders in secure care facilities engage in problem drinking and the use of various psychoactive substances at a higher rate than other young people (Howard & Zibert 1990). This appears to indicate a significant relationship between alcohol use and criminal activity. Moreover, it has been noted by young people themselves that alcohol worsens violence and makes it more likely to occur, whereas other drugs, such as marijuana, do not create the same kinds of problems (Daniel & Cornwall 1993). Another dimension of alcohol use by young people is that very often the consumption and behavioural effects of alcohol are more publicly apparent because young people, due to their age, are more likely to be in public spaces rather than in licensed premises or family homes.

Particular crime trends associated with specific ethnic groups, as with the links between Vietnamese young people and injecting drug use, creates something of a paradox for those wishing to adopt progressive measures in dealing with drug-related issues. On the one hand, acknowledgment of the problem among this community may well feed populist attacks on Vietnamese people in general and unduly stigmatise individuals and community members. On the other hand, close analysis of why some Vietnamese young people use these drugs reveals the social inequalities and social injustices underpinning their lives, and the difficulties they face in fostering a sense of social belonging (see Beyer et al. 2001). As noted in a Victorian report dealing with drug use (Parliament of Victoria 1997: 182):

> In the context of the general social disadvantages that many ethnic communities face, the consequences of drug problems tend to be magnified, and become less amenable to the sorts of solutions and strategies that suffice for mainstream cultural communities. Some ethnic communities will have the social and economic capacity to tackle their drug problems, but other communities will not be as well positioned to do this, and will stand in need of additional resources and extra efforts.

Again, crime statistics, accompanied by qualitative evaluation of actual circumstances (such as the dynamics of the immigration settlement process), are essential to understanding and acting in the best interests of these young people.

## RESPONDING TO DRUG USE AND ABUSE

The usual public debate over drugs tends to focus on (1) the use and abuse of illicit drugs; and (2) how best to respond to illicit drug use. Less concern is usually expressed over the consumption of legal substances, although from a public health perspective greater attention is now being directed at substances such as cigarettes and on the 'responsible' consumption of alcohol.

With respect to illegal substances, responses are frequently posed in terms of a tension between **'prohibition'** and **'harm minimisation'**. According to a prohibitionist, the best way to deal with substance abuse is to ban its use completely. Contrary to this, most people working in the fields of drug law enforcement and public health acknowledge that what is needed is to have many diverse strategies and a constellation of programs that together will reduce the harms to the society at large and to the individual who is the user.

Recent evaluations of cannabis laws and anti-trafficking law enforcement (Atkinson & McDonald 1995; Sutton & James 1996) have stressed the need to adopt harm minimisation approaches, rather than coercive criminal justice strategies, to deal with drug issues. For example, it has been pointed out that: 'it appears that the criminal justice system responses themselves to the prohibition options practised in Australia have less adverse impact on people's educational and employment opportunities than the knowledge of use of the drug which the criminal justice process brings into the public arena' (Atkinson & McDonald 1995: 3). In other words, the stigma associated with criminalisation for even minor drug offences may be the source of non-criminal sanctions such as suspension from school and termination of employment.

In recognition of the multidimensional nature of drug issues, and of the adverse impact of some forms of criminal justice intervention, most jurisdictions around Australia have now put into place varying kinds of harm minimisation strategies. These often include, for example, police cannabis cautioning programs, in which trivial or less serious instances of possession and use are diverted from the formal court process. The response might be an on-the-spot fine in the first instance, and recording of contact but not prosecution. In many cases, such programs are based upon multi-agency partnerships. For example, in Tasmania, the drug diversion strategy involves members of the police service (who need to have information for the referral of offenders to assessment and treatment), health workers (who engage in assessment, treatment, and education of illicit drug users), justice workers (who need to be conscious of ways to deal with offenders who default on initial diversions), and educational workers (who may have a significant role in devising educational programs). These kinds of initiatives are integral to the national drug strategy, a strategy broadly based upon harm minimisation principles and practices (see Ministerial Council on Drug Strategy 1998).

## Elements of the National Drug Strategy

The aims of the National Drug Strategy are to reduce the use of drugs in the community and minimise the harm that they cause to individual users and the community at large (Ministerial Council on Drug Strategy 1998, 2001). It involves a multi-pronged strategy aimed at:

- reducing demand
- reducing supply
- reducing drug-related harm
- providing treatment options
- developing a skilled workforce to respond to drug use.

### Demand reduction

The objective is to reduce demand through the promotion of opportunities, settings, and values that foster resilience and reduce the uptake and use of drugs and the risks of drug use. Specific aims are to:

- prevent and/or delay the uptake of illicit drug use
- increase community understanding of drug-related harm, and increase community capacity to participate in informed debate about drugs and drug policy options
- promote accessible positive alternatives to drug use that are acceptable, attractive, and meaningful to those most at risk of drug use, and those from socially, educationally, and culturally diverse backgrounds
- foster a community supportive of the family and positive parenting
- promote school and community environments safe from drug use and related harm.

## Supply reduction

Through interventions to reduce availability and supply, the aims are to:

- stabilise and ultimately reduce street-level dealing in drugs
- effectively disrupt illicit drug production, supply, and distribution networks at local, national, and international levels.

## Treatment

Through providing treatment, the aims are to:

- increase capacity to provide the full range of evidence-based treatment options for illicit drug users
- increase capacity to provide support to the families of drug users and to include them in treatment where appropriate
- provide an integrated treatment system able to provide continuity of care across relapse episodes, and across the criminal justice and the health sectors
- maintain an illicit-drug-treatment system with strong links to mainstream health and welfare systems
- increase capacity in the treatment system to undertake systematic needs analysis, including the capacity to respond to emerging drug problems and institute new services
- provide a comprehensive, relevant treatment system that is culturally appropriate and integrated with other services (including mental health), and attracts and retains drug users early in the course of harmful use.

## Reducing drug-related harm

Here the aims are to:

- reduce the harm for individuals who use drugs, their families, and the community, in particular:
  - decrease drug-related overdose deaths, illnesses, and injuries
  - decrease the spread of infectious diseases through injecting drug use (IDU) and unsafe sexual practices as a result of intoxication
  - decrease suicides and attempted suicides associated with illicit drug use
  - decrease the incidence of drug-related crime.
- improve community amenities in areas of high public drug use, drug-related crime, and disruption
- give law enforcement an increased capacity to contribute to the reduction of harm caused by illicit drugs.

## Workforce development

Through workforce development, the aims are to:

- further develop the capacity to attract and retain an effective workforce in health, welfare, education, and law enforcement sectors, with an emphasis on:
    - a generalist health and welfare workforce with increased capacity to identify drug problems and related harm and apply evidence-based interventions
    - a health, education, and law enforcement workforce educated in the principles that support the reduction of harm caused by illicit drug use
    - highly skilled law enforcement investigators who can be deployed flexibly
    - a skilled and supported health promotion workforce familiar with evidence-based health promotion and the antecedents of drug use
- increase capacity to attract and retain a highly skilled and specialist drug and alcohol workforce in the wider health system.

In addition, the strategy aims to undertake research to improve intervention and control as well as the monitoring of drug trends.

The very comprehensive approach to the strategy highlights the work that needs to be done if harm reduction and harm minimisation is to occur. Within each of the target areas for action, many different actions can be taken to achieve the stated outcomes. For example, in the case of demand reduction, specific actions include everything from enhancing retention in the educational process through to job creation opportunities for young people. Supply reduction will require things such as a national commitment to joint operations and enhanced intelligence sharing. For treatment, it is important that the police and judiciary be well briefed on the nature of drug dependence and extent of treatment options. In each intervention area, there is, therefore, a wide range of concrete measures that can be taken to address drug-related issues.

One measure that has gained prominence in recent years is that of the 'drug court'. The essential features of a drug court are that it:

- deals with a specified class of offenders
- integrates drug treatment services within a criminal justice case processing system
- provides early intervention

- uses a non-adversarial approach
- has a dominant and continuing role of the drug court judge
- uses frequent substance abuse testing
- involves frequent contacts with the court
- provides a comprehensive treatment and supervision program and a system of graduated sanctions and incentives (United States Department of Justice, cited in Freiberg 2002: 12).

There are drug courts in every state except Tasmania, and the two territories (Indermaur & Roberts 2003). The various drug courts vary in terms of legislative foundations and operational practices (Indemaur & Roberts 2003; Freiberg 2002), although they share the feature of bringing together a team of professionals who work with the drug court judge. While it may be too early to make definitive statements regarding the effectiveness of Australian drug courts (Indermaur & Roberts 2003: 150), it is nevertheless generally acknowledged that: 'The courts represent only one tool in the state's repertoire of responses of what appears to be an intractable social and legal problem' (Freiberg 2002: 15).

## CONCLUSION

This chapter has provided a brief introduction to the complex social dynamics and issues surrounding drug use in Australian society, and the response of the state to illicit drugs in particular. It points out that how drugs are classified as legal or illegal is closely related to political processes as well as changing moral values. For many years the term 'drug' was closely associated with the idea of illegal substances, but today there is a broader understanding that there are many legal drugs used by the community that are just as harmful, including prescription drugs and alcohol. From this perspective, then, drug use is part of everyday behaviour rather than one that is limited to specific, deviant groups.

This is not to suggest that drug use is not associated with social harm. The problem is not simply one of consumption, production, and supply of prohibited substances. A major issue is the effect of psychoactive drugs on people's behaviour in ways that make them a danger to others. Although the relationship between drug use and antisocial behaviour is not direct, it is clear that it is closely associated with damaging effects, from violence outside pubs and clubs to dangerous driving. Nor is the harm limited to victims, since many drugs also have serious health consequences for users. For these reasons, any consideration of drug use necessarily crosses the boundaries between criminal justice, health and welfare, and education. Responding to drug use and abuse requires both a sensitivity to social context and an appreciation of adopting holistic and multifaceted approaches.

## DISCUSSION QUESTIONS

1 Why can it be argued that drug use is an everyday activity?
2 What evidence is there that drug use is associated with involvement in criminal behaviour? What is the nature of the relationship?
3 Should drug use among young people be regarded as a social problem?
4 What are the main features of a 'harm minimisation' approach to drug use? How is this approach reflected in the National Drug Strategy?

## GLOSSARY OF TERMS

**drug consumers**
persons charged with user-type offences (for example, possessing or administering drugs for own personal use; AIC 2002a: 79)
**drug providers**
persons charged with supply-type offences (for example, importation, trafficking, selling, cultivation, and manufacture; AIC 2002a: 79)
**harm minimisation strategies**
programs for controlling drug use that focus on reducing the harms associated with drug taking at the level of both the individual and society
**illicit drug offences**
offences that include the possession, sale, dealing or trafficking, importing or exporting, manufacture, or cultivation of drugs or other substances prohibited under legislation (ABS 2003d: 75)
**prohibition strategies**
programs for controlling drug use that focus on banning the availability of illegal substances.

## FURTHER READING

Bennett, T. (1998) *Drugs and Crime: the Results of Research on Drug testing and Interviewing Arrestees*, Home Office Research Studies No. 183, Home Office, London.

Collins, D.J. & Lapsley, H.M. (2002) *Counting the cost: estimates of the social costs of drug abuse in Australia in 1998–9*, National Drug Strategy Monograph Series No. 49, Commonwealth Department of Health and Ageing, Canberra.

Goode, E. (1997) *Between Politics and Reason: The Drug Legislation Debate*, St Martins Press, New York.

Loxley, W. (2001) 'Drug use, intoxication and offence type in two groups of alleged offenders in Perth: a pilot study', *Australian and New Zealand Journal of Criminology*, 34: 91–104.

Makkai, T. & Payne, J. (2003) *Drugs and Crime: A Study of Incarcerated Male Offenders*, Australian Institute of Criminology Research and Public Policy Series No. 52, Canberra.

Measham, F., Aldridge, J. & Parker, H. (2001) *Dancing on Drugs. Risk, Health and Hedonism in the British Club Scene*, Free Association Books, London.

Nurco, D.N., Kinlock, T.W. & Hanlon, T.E. (1995) 'The Drugs–Crime Connection', in J. Inciardi & K. McElrath (eds) *The American Drug Scene: an Anthology*, Roxbury, Los Angeles.

## WEBSITES

**www.aic.gov.au/research/duma**
Australian Institute of Criminology—Provides links to various publications of the Drug Use Monitoring in Australia (DUMA) project, which seeks to measure drug use among those people who have been recently apprehended by police.

**www.ncjrs.org**
National Criminal Justice Reference Service (NCJRS)—The clearinghouse for the US National Institute of Justice, it contains summaries and full-text publications on the criminal justice system. The site includes research on federal, state, and local government reports, books, research reports, journal articles, and unpublished research. Subject areas include corrections, drugs and crime, law enforcement, juvenile justice, statistics, and victims of crime.

**www.parliament.vic.gov.au/dcpc**
Victorian Government's Drug Prevention Web Site—Has access to various prevention programs and reports on drug and crime prevention strategies.

CHAPTER 6

# White Collar and Corporate Crime

## INTRODUCTION

Although official crime data suggest that offenders are predominantly drawn from the lower ranks of society, it is widely acknowledged that **white collar crime** is extensive. Writing in the city of Chicago in the 1930s the influential American criminologist, Sutherland, described the phenomenon of white collar crime as 'a crime committed by a person of respectability and high social status in the course of his occupation' (1949: 9). Sutherland was one of the first criminologists to point out that crime in the business sector is just as real and damaging as crime among the disadvantaged. In many ways it is more serious because the sums involved are staggeringly high—far higher than the conventional crimes associated with the working class.

Today this is widely recognised, especially following the spectacular collapses of companies such as HIH and Enron. The prosecution of high-profile figures accused of white collar crimes, such as Alan Bond and Rene Rivkin, reflect an intolerance of such crimes in Australian society, particularly when the crimes become so great as to come to public notice and to generate private concern among the ranks of the powerful.

Despite this, the public attention paid to these crimes tends to be limited to the serious print and electronic media. It is often short-lived and focused on spectacular corporate collapses rather than everyday events such as violations of industrial health and safety regulations. Public debate about 'law and order' continues to focus on traditional rather than white collar crimes. This is partly explained by the ability of the wealthy to normalise their activities, so that their crimes are not recognised as 'real' crimes but are instead seen as acceptable, even necessary, business practices.

This chapter explores the concept of white collar crime before focusing more specifically on corporate crime. The range of corporate crimes is considered, as well as attempts to explain their occurrence. The chapter points out the various harms caused by white collar crime including the economic, social, and moral costs to the community, as well as physical damage to the individual and the environment. The chapter concludes with a consideration of the law enforcement issues raised by corporate crime, such as the legal difficulties of prosecution.

## DEFINING WHITE COLLAR AND CORPORATE CRIME

The phrase 'white collar crime' is a general term that is sometimes used to describe all crimes committed by non-manual workers in the course of their occupation. This particular definition can encompass:

- petty crimes by office workers and shop assistants involving no physical contact with victims and money or goods of little value, such as pilfering from employers and fiddling cash registers
- the crimes of the rich and powerful, such as 'bottom of the harbour tax schemes'
- environmental crimes, such as the dumping of toxic waste
- over-servicing by professionals, such as doctors and dentists.

The usefulness of the concept of white collar crime has been challenged for a number of reasons:

- The concept is too broad to be of investigative value.
- It focuses on individuals rather than on the more significant illegalities associated with organisations. Critics argue it is more important to understand the structural causes of white collar and corporate crime than to understand the psychological characteristics of individual offenders.
- While many of the acts described as 'criminal' may be morally reprehensible and may break civil and administrative law, they are often not legally criminal and (it is argued) therefore should not be a legitimate area of investigation for criminologists (Tappan 1947).

The argument that criminologists should only concern themselves with acts that break the criminal law has been widely challenged. Instead it is argued that it is essential for criminologists to challenge conventional social norms about what is and is not a crime. Clinard and Yaeger (1980) argue that drawing attention to the different moral judgments that are applied to the activities of the rich, compared with those of the poor, is a central part of the criminologist's role of questioning everyday assumptions about why some acts are defined as criminal and subject to close scrutiny by law enforcement agents, while others are ignored or treated much more lightly.

This argument is important for a number of analytical and political reasons. Consider for example, the following accounts of crime:

> White collar crime, although technically classified under property crime, needs to be distinguished because of its considerable impact on society. White collar crimes originally covered acts committed by business people and professionals, but today includes theft by employees, corruption, cheating on taxes, social security fraud, medi-fraud (billing by physicians for services not performed), as well as stock market swindles, consumer fraud, and price-fixing. It also includes various crimes committed with the aid of, or against, telecommunications systems and computers (Mukherjee & Graycar 1997: 10).

This definition is too restrictive in one sense, and too expansive in another. First, it is premised upon a strictly legal definition of crime and, as such, ignores a key thrust of white collar crime analysis; that is, its insistence upon going beyond official criminal definitions. Second, it disregards the centrality of class and social status in the construction of this crime category. The whole point of its introduction was to focus greater attention on crimes of the powerful as distinct from crimes of the less powerful (see Rosoff et al. 1998). This was so even in the light of certain ambiguities concerning whether or not to include some types of blue collar activity (such as cheating by tradespeople).

Alternatively, we might consider the perspective of Snider (2000), who analyses the process of re-defining activity as non-criminal and as not problematic from a regulatory point of view. Snider likewise considers white collar and corporate crime—in this case including both financial crimes, such as anti-trust and insider trading, and social crimes, such as health and safety violations and offences against the environment.

She argues that:

> Because its survival as an object of study is contingent on the passage and enforcement of 'command and control' legislation, corporate crime can 'disappear' through decriminalization (the repeal of criminal law), through deregulation (the repeal of all state law, criminal, civil and administrative) and through downsizing (the destruction of the state's enforcement capability) (Snider 2000: 172).

The issue here, then, is the re-casting of the concept of white collar crime away from questions of power (that is, the social status of the offender) and towards matters of form (for example, 'paper' crime that is classless in that it involves welfare fraud as well as corporate fraud). How crime and social harm is socially constructed, of course, has major implications for how institutional responses will be framed.

The criticism that 'white collar crime' is too ill-defined a concept has led to the emergence of a number of other terms to refer to more specific types of illegalities:

- **Organisational illegalities** are 'individual or collective illegalities that are perceived as helping to achieve, or are congruent with, the organisational goals set by the dominant coalition within an organisation' (Slapper & Tombs 1999: 14).
- **Occupational crime** refers to criminal acts committed by employees in the course of their work for personal gain. The term 'employee crime' is also sometimes used. However, in the context of white collar crime it is perhaps more appropriate to distinguish between crimes committed by persons of respectability and high social status (such as managers and professionals), and those committed by ordinary workers (those not in key decision-making or status positions).
- **Entrepreneurial crime** refers to punishable acts 'committed by individuals in controlling positions within corporations, using the resources and power deriving from the corporate form as a vehicle to achieve ends which benefit the entrepreneur personally' (Halstead 1992).
- **Corporate crime** refers to the illegal activities of businesses against members of the public, the environment, creditors, investors, or corporate competitors (Wilson 1987: 1). It includes crimes committed by corporate officials for their corporation, as well as the offences of the corporation itself.

Many scholars draw a distinction between crimes that benefit the corporation (organisational illegalities, corporate crime) and those that benefit the individual working within an organisation (employee crime, occupational crime). Nonetheless, although this is useful, the line between the two can be blurred. Some corporate crimes may benefit both the organisation and the individual, through such things as bonuses, promotions, and stock option offers, as is the case with price fixing. Conversely, some occupational crimes may benefit the corporation. The huge losses incurred by derivatives trader Nick Leeson were only possible because of his employers' willingness to put profits before risk and allow their 'star trader' unregulated access to huge sums of money (see case study 6.1).

## CASE STUDY 6.1

### NICK LEESON AND THE COLLAPSE OF BARINGS BANK

Barings Bank was Britain's oldest merchant bank, having been founded in 1762. Nick Leeson was a derivatives trader working in the Singapore branch of one of its subsidiaries, Barings Securities. Until things began to go wrong, Leeson had enjoyed a charmed life. The son of a plasterer from a public housing estate in London who failed his first maths exam, he began his working life as a clerk at the royal family's bank, Coutts, before working on the trading floor at Barings. In 1992 he became general manager of Barings' subsidiary in Singapore, Barings Securities, setting up its futures trading operation on the Singapore Monetary Exchange. Already distant from the regulation of senior managers, Barings made the fatal mistake of allowing him to be Chief Trader while also settling his own trades. As soon as Leeson arrived he began to make unauthorised speculative positions in futures linked to the Nikkei 225 stock index. When these lost money he covered up the losses in an unused error account numbered 88888. The number eight is regarded as a lucky number in Asia, but it didn't work for Nick Leeson. The more he speculated the more he lost. He dealt with this by falsely making claims on funds from other Barings subsidiaries and by falsifying client accounts.

Despite the huge sums involved, Barings failed to discover the losses or to question the unrealistic profits that Leeson claimed to be making. But, by 1995, the losses amounted to US$1.3 billion—far more than Leeson could ever hope to recover. He fled to Borneo and then boarded a plane for

Frankfurt, leaving a note saying 'I'm sorry' on his desk. At Frankfurt airport he was arrested and extradited to Singapore where he was charged with fraud and sentenced to six-and-a-half years in Changi prison. In 1999 he was released and made large sums of money writing about his experiences and becoming a hot property on the conference circuit.

As for Barings, it was forced into liquidation and was sold to ING Bank for £1. Its investors lost their savings and 1200 employees lost their jobs (Rawnsley 1995).

## CORPORATE CRIME

As noted above, the defining characteristic of corporate crime is that it involves criminal or otherwise illegal acts that benefit the corporation. Its key feature is that it occurs not because of the individual characteristics of managers or directors, but because of *organisational* imperatives relating to businesses and the environment in which they operate.

Krammer defines corporate crime as: 'Criminal acts (of omission or commission), which are the result of deliberate decision-making (or culpable negligence) by persons who occupy structural positions within the organisation as corporate executives or managers...and are intended to benefit the corporation itself' (1984: 18).

Krammer's definition highlights another feature of corporate crime: unlike traditional crime, which normally involves a positive action, corporate crime may involve *inaction*; for example, the failure to take appropriate health and safety measures or to provide accurate information about the side effects of a pharmaceutical product.

It includes illegalities that are covered by administrative and civil law, not just criminal law. For example, failure to comply with health and safety regulations is generally treated as an administrative rather than criminal offence. Hence the phrase 'illegal but not criminal' is often applied (Conklin 1977).

Some industries are more likely to engage in corporate crime than others. The pharmaceutical, motor vehicle, and oil industries are often identified as prone to corporate crime. Large corporations have a disproportionate number of violations compared with small ones (Braithwaite 1984; Clinard & Yeager 1980: 119–22), although smaller firms are often pressured by competitive and cost considerations to operate with less regard to regulations than bigger firms (Haines 1997).

## Types of corporate crime

There have been many attempts to categorise corporate crime. Wilson, for example, identifies ten main types (1987: 2), while Clinard and Yeager describe six (1980: 113–16). One widely used typology (Wilson 1987) focuses on who the victims are. Adding the category of financial offences to Wilson's list produces the following typology:

### 1 Financial and prudential offences

This type includes offences that violate state and Commonwealth statutes in relation to financial matters, including financial and trading regulation of business and the maintenance of standards for financial institutions such as banks and insurance companies. It includes:

- *Companies and securities offences*—This includes irregularities in the formation and structure of a company, inaccurate reporting to authorities, and improper procedures in company takeovers. Restrictive trade practices that break the law also fall within this type. This includes price fixing, in which rival companies conspire together to 'fix' the price of products at a level that guarantees their profits rather than competing on the open market. Other types of anti-competitive actions include resale price maintenance and monopolisation of a product or service. Some of the most widely reported companies and securities offences relate to negligent or fraudulent management practices because they are so often associated with the collapse of a company. The spectacular failure of companies such as HIH in Australia, or Enron in the USA, generate widespread media coverage, not only because of the huge sums involved, but also because of the widespread public fallout in terms of financial losses to creditors, shareholders, and employees, as well as the loss of public trust.
- *Taxation offences*—This includes tax evasion in its various forms, such as failure to pay GST, false declarations of profits, and customs duties offences.
- *Violations of prudential regulations*—Prudential regulations are designed to ensure that financial and insurance companies adhere to standards designed to ensure the safety of consumers' funds and the financial system as a whole. They cover such things as auditing, liquidity requirements, public liability insurance, and restrictions on investments.

## 2 Offences against consumers

Commonwealth and state governments have laws designed to protect consumers from false information, illegal sales practices, and the sale of unfit or unsafe products. Violations of these laws can result in death or disablement of consumers; for example, if food production standards are inadequate and contain the bacteria *E-Coli*, thus putting the health of consumers at risk.

## 3 Offences against employees

These offences involve violation of occupational health and safety regulations, sexual or racial discrimination, violation of wage laws, or of rights relating to industrial disputes. They include:

- *Occupational health and safety offences*—These include offences relating to fire precautions; the proper design and use of equipment, including building site materials, industrial plants and machinery; the use of harmful substances in the workplace; and the provision of information and training to employees.
- *Economic offences against employees*—This includes violations of industrial awards or non-payment of wages, and violations against employee rights to organise or to take other forms of industrial action.
- *Discriminatory practices*—Commonwealth and state governments have a range of laws designed to ensure that businesses operate without discrimination, particularly in relation to sex, ethnicity, or disablement.

## 4 Environmental offences

Environmental offences include: release of toxic or otherwise offensive products into the air, land, and waterways, and the control of dangerous substances in general; breaches of zoning regulations or other planning requirements; provision of false information; and illegal manufacturing practices (Wilson 1987: 2; Slapper & Tombs 1999: 43–7).

## Measuring corporate crime

There have been several attempts to estimate the extent of corporate crime. Sutherland calculated how often 70 of the largest corporations in the USA had been found to be violating legal and administrative codes in areas including trade practices, advertising, labour practices, and copyright in the period from 1890, when the oldest of the companies investigated was first established, to the late 1940s. Sutherland found that the figure varied from one to 50 and that, on average, the companies had been found to have 14 violations each, with the total number of violations equalling 980. Sutherland observed that this figure was certainly an underestimate since the study had not attempted to include all the subsidiaries of the companies and the analysis was limited to criminal offences only. Even so, on average, each corporation had been found guilty on four occasions. Sutherland observed that: 'In many states persons with four convictions are defined by statute to be "habitual criminals"' (Sutherland 1949: 25). If mandatory sentence applied to corporate crime in the way it can apply to conventional crimes, such organisations would be closed down.

Nearly thirty years later Clinard and Yaeger found that, over a two-year period, 60 per cent of the 582 American corporations investigated had at least one Federal court action brought against them and that the average was 4.4 cases. The real figure would have been significantly higher if company subsidiaries and violations of state and local government law had also been included. Violations ranged from non compliance with a federal order to act or not act in a certain way, environmental offences, financial violations such as tax evasion, unfair labour practices such as unfair dismissal and health and safety violations, manufacturing violations such as the production of unsafe or defective products, and unfair trade practices such as false advertising (1980: 113–6).

More recently, Bilimoria (1995) examined 91 of the Fortune 500 list of companies to see how many had been found guilty of violations or had proceedings taken against them between 1984 and 1986. He found that 58.2 per cent had had at least one filing made against them and 25.3 per cent had had at least one violation proven. These studies suggest that, far from being exceptional, corporate crime is pervasive and persistent throughout the business world (Braithwaite 1995).

## EXPLAINING CORPORATE CRIME

Compared with the amount of theorising that has occurred in relation to crimes committed by young, working class males, there have been relatively few attempts to explain corporate crime. One critical observation, however, is that the existence and extent of white collar and corporate crime challenges any simplistic explanation of crime in terms of poverty or psychological pathology.

Sutherland (1949) argued that the same factors that caused working class crime also caused white collar crime, and could be explained by his theory of differential association. According to this theory, people commit crimes not because of any physical, social, or psychological pathology but because of an excess of norms favouring law violation. In other words, criminal behaviour is learned through participation in a sub-culture that normalises the illegal behaviour so that breaking the law is not seen as 'real crime'.

Sutherland (1949) also argued that white collar and corporate crime flourished as a result of three structural factors:

- features inherent in capitalism as an economic system
- the existence of opportunities for illegal behaviour
- the low likelihood of getting caught.

Since Sutherland, many theories have acknowledged the importance of these factors in their explanation of corporate crime. Chambliss's study of organised crime in the city of Seattle (USA) found strong links between organised crime and the leaders of business and politics (1978). Writing from a Marxist perspective, he argued that capitalist societies promote greed and individual self-interest at the expense of altruism and community spirit. Crimes by the powerful are an inevitable outcome of this, since looking after 'number one' is all that matters.

Box's analysis is also influenced by Marxism. He points out that the survival of corporations—and the individuals within them, especially managers—depends on the achievement of profits. Where the capacity to make profits is blocked by environmental factors, such as government regulations or the price structure of competitors, companies will face considerable pressure to use illegal means to overcome the blockage. This, together with opportunities for illegal behaviour, weak law enforcement, and an ideological blurring between 'entrepreneuralism' and illegal behaviour, leads to engagement in illegal acts. Crime is there-fore a rational response to a rational objective. From this perspective, cor-porations are inherently 'criminogenic' (Box 1987: 34–67).

More recently, Reichman (1998) has used Starr's concept of 'cultural authority' (1982: 13) to explain how businesses are able both to shape the law in their interests and defend themselves against accusations of violations. Cultural authority is 'the authority to construct reality through definitions of fact and value' and includes the capacity to assign legal significance to business activities (Reichman 1998: 326). Reichman observes that many of the activities of business have an inherent potential for serious harm. Nonetheless, communities are dependent on them for the production of goods and services, as well as employment and the generation of wealth. Consequently, companies are able to use their cultural authority to ensure that the economic constraints under which they operate are recognised by the law so that, rather than seeking to eliminate their potential for harm, the state attempts to control them through regulations; for example, through guidelines about maximum levels of pollutant that can be released. In this way, companies influence the regulatory framework within which they operate, with large companies having greater regulatory authority than smaller ones. Reichman suggests that for this reason smaller companies will have most difficulty in complying with the law and will also be most likely to be prosecuted, a hypothesis supported by Australian research (Haines 1997: 223).

## THE COSTS OF CORPORATE CRIME

The costs of corporate crime are enormous and certainly outweigh the costs of traditional crime (see Friedrichs 1996; Shover & Wright 2001). These costs are both financial and physical in terms of damage to individuals and the environment. There are also serious social costs as a result of the violation of community standards and the creation of an atmosphere of cynicism and mistrust towards business in the community (Rosoff et al. 1998).

### Economic costs

While it is not possible to assess with accuracy the economic costs of corporate crime, they are acknowledged to be extremely high. The financial cost of one corporate crime can outweigh all the conventional crimes that occur in a given year (Box 1987: 35; Meier & Short 1995: 8):

- Overall, the economic costs of white collar crime have been estimated to be between 10 and 35 times as expensive as the costs of conventional crimes (Helmskamp et al. 1997 cited in Slapper & Tombs 1999: 67).

- In Australia, fraud has been estimated to cost $5.88 billion each year (Mayhew 2003). This represents 31 per cent of the total costs of crime and is more than double the cost of the next largest category, violent crime.
- In the USA, the National White Collar Crime Center estimates that economic crime costs over $500 billion annually (Oates 2003). Health-care fraud alone, which includes billing for services that were never pro-vided as well as over-servicing, is estimated by the FBI to cost US$44 billion per annum (National White Collar Crime Centre 2003).
- An Australian Tax Office audit of the top 100 Australian companies found that when only about half of them had been completed, tax adjustments arising from the audits had already exceeded $1 billion (Potas 1993: 1). In America, the US General Accounting Office estimates that 42.4 per cent of corporations fail to report all their interest earnings, and that the total amounts to about US$7 billion a year in untaxed income (National White Collar Crime Centre 2003: 2).
- In the UK, the Health and Safety Executive estimates that the over-all cost of ill-health and injuries at work to British employers was between $8.25 and $16.25 billion (£3.3 and £6.5 billion; 1995–96 figures; Health and Safety Executive 2003b).

## Physical costs

Although corporate crime is often perceived as a 'victimless' crime, the reality is quite different. The release of toxic chemicals into waterways, the inadequate testing of products, failure to acknowledge or release research results, and poor industrial safety standards, can affect literally millions of people as well as whole communities and the surrounding environment:

- The hurried release of the drug Thalidomide resulted in the birth of an estimated 10,000 tragically deformed babies in at least 20 coun-tries. The harm was not just the physical damage to the babies, but extended to the social fabric of the families (Clinard & Yeager 1980: 266; Braithwaite 1984: 65–75).
- Environmental lead pollution from Pasminco's lead smelter at Port Pirie in South Australia has been implicated in higher than normal

blood lead levels of children living in the region. Elevated levels of blood lead are associated with intellectual impairment, impaired motor development, and general emotional and behavioural problems (Fowler & Grabosky 1989: 146; Burns et al. 1999).

- Attempts by tobacco companies to deny the link between smoking and cancer affects an inestimable number of individuals (Chapman 1997: 1569).
- It is estimated that about a quarter of a million people will die from mesothelioma in Europe in the 34-year period between 1995 and 2029 as a result of exposure to asbestos (Peto et al. 1999).
- Each year, the number of avoidable deaths resulting from inadequate health and safety provisions exceed the number of deaths from homicide. In 1997 the 'at-work' death toll across the nation was 2900 people, compared with 2029 deaths on the road, 2367 suicides, and 333 homicides (Catanzariti 1997). Some scholars have argued that the organisations responsible for workplace deaths should be prosecuted for industrial homicide or manslaughter (Quinlan 1994).
- The United Carbide factory in Bhopal, India exploded in 1984 as a result of the release of toxic gases into the air. Five thousand people died in the first three days with an estimated 16,000 to 30,000 dying from the after-effects. Investigators found that the disaster stemmed from the decision to disconnect the firms' expensive safety equipment to reduce costs.
- In 1989 the oil tanker, the *Exxon Valdez* ran aground on a reef in Alaska, pouring 11 million gallons of oil into Prince William Sound. Thirteen thousand miles of shoreline was affected with huge loss of wildlife, including fish, seabirds, and seals. The local fishing community lost their livelihood. The jury is still out on how permanent the environmental damage has been (Mitchell 1999).
- In January 2000, cyanide and heavy metals poured from an Australian–Romanian gold mining operation in Romania polluting waterways in Hungary and Serbia, and eventually reaching the Danube. All life was eradicated from local rivers and an estimated 150 tons of fish died. Scientists described it as a 'tragedy' as the area was recognised as one of high biodiversity and included many protected species. The lives of the local community were disrupted and scientists fear the cyanide could remain for decades (*Sydney Morning Herald* 2000).

## Social and moral costs

A further cost of corporate crime is the violation of public trust. When a bank collapses causing thousands of innocent victims to lose their savings, it has a demoralising effect on public confidence in both business corporations and the regulatory powers of government. This, in turn, impacts on the willingness of people to place their savings in the corporate sector, which the community is dependent upon for the creation of jobs. Misrepresentation in advertising also leads to widespread cynicism about the values of our business leaders and can have a similar effect.

## CONFRONTING CORPORATE CRIME

Far from being victimless, white collar and corporate crime is certainly as destructive as traditional crime. The victims of white collar and corporate crime are as numerous and wide-ranging as the crimes themselves. The effects of such things as price fixing, the collapse of a major insurance company, or tax evasion result in higher prices for goods and services, higher insurance premiums, or denial of government services, which affect everyone. The economic viability of other organisations is also threatened by acts such as these, and this, in turn, has an effect on levels of unemployment. Whole communities are affected by environmental pollution, while investors and consumers are affected by illegal share dealing or unsafe food products. Health and safety crimes affect not just the individual, but also their families and the welfare system as a whole.

However, it is those at the bottom of the socio-economic ladder who are most adversely affected. Crimes such as bribery and corruption represent a transfer of wealth from the poor to the rich, even though it may not be a visible one. The faulty product or defective piece of equipment is most likely to be sold in a discount shop and bought by someone who is not wealthy and who is vulnerable to this form of exploitation. Women are much more likely than men to be affected by crimes committed by pharmaceutical companies. Their secondary status in the employment market also makes them vulnerable to employee crimes such as hazardous workplaces or wage exploitation, especially if they are migrants or people of colour. In this sense the costs of white collar and corporate crime go beyond the economic and social costs described above. Their uneven distribution has a profound affect on the social structure itself by exacerbating pre-existing social inequalities.

Most of the issues raised by corporate crime relate to its treatment by the criminal justice system. The working class bias of official data on who commits crimes reflects the extent to which corporate criminals are rarely caught. When it comes to the middle and upper classes, it seems that crime really does pay. There are three main reasons why corporate criminals 'get away with it': the invisibility of corporate crime, the practical difficulties of proving guilt, and the legal difficulties stemming from the organisational nature of corporate crime.

## The invisibility of corporate crime

Corporate crimes rarely come within the purview of the criminal justice system for a number of reasons:

- Most corporate crimes are not publicly observable in the way that many traditional crimes are. They are the results of conversations held behind closed doors, or of transactions in cyberspace, so it is often difficult to prove anything illegal has taken place.
- The gap between victim and offender, in terms of both time and place, means that proving the link between the two can be challenging. Victims may even be unaware that an injury was caused by a particular product or that regulations exist about safety standards. Many corporate crimes take years to discover, and even then the link between the act and the victim may have to be proved. For example, in the case of assault or burglary, the victim knows immediately, or within a short time, that a crime has occurred. In contrast, the link between exposure to a chemical and the birth of a child with a physical disability may take years to discover and even then the link between victim and perpetrator often has to be established through a drawn-out legal process.
- There can be an ideological smokescreen about corporate criminality that suggests that it is not 'real' crime and therefore should not be treated as harshly as traditional crime. This may take the form of a perception that 'everyone is doing it' or that it is the law rather than the practice that is wrong. The shared social background between corporate criminals and judges may result in sympathy for the perpetrator who is then not deemed to be morally reprehensible (Levi 1981).

- Many corporate activities that the public may consider to be reprehensible and immoral are covered by administrative rather than criminal law, and are often administered by special bodies rather than the police. Violations of occupational health and safety regulations cause serious injury or death, but are treated as accidents rather than crimes. In this way the culpability of individuals and organisations is denied.

Slapper and Tombs describe the way in which corporate crimes somehow escape the crime and justice agenda:

> At every stage of the legal process, law tends to operate quite differently with respect to corporate crimes than in the context of 'conventional' crimes. Thus an examination of the very framing of the substance and parameters of legal regulation, its enforcement, the ways in which potential offences and offenders are investigated, the prosecution of offences, and the use of sanctions following successful prosecution, point consistently towards the conclusion that most forms of corporate and organisational offences are relatively decriminalised (1999: 86).

## Practical problems of prosecution

As well as problems with the way the law has been formulated, the difficulties and expense of mounting a case and prosecuting corporate criminals also explains why they are less likely than traditional criminals to face the law (Clough & Mulhern 2002). Large companies normally have the resources to hire expensive lawyers to defend their executives. Prosecuting authorities often face extreme difficulties in locating and analysing the necessary documents to prove an event has occurred. It is not just that files can be shredded or deleted and computers 'lost' (Shapiro 1990: 354); the sheer volume of material for investigation also presents an enormous problem. The complex structure of companies is also a challenge to any investigation, especially when they belong to a global network. It is often unclear in which jurisdiction a crime took place and prosecutors must frequently negotiate with the criminal justice systems of other nations and jurisdictions. This problem is one of the main impediments to the control of corporate crime today (Fisse & Braithwaite 1993: 213–15).

The law enforcement agencies established to regulate corporations, such as the Australian Securities and Investments Commission, are very limited in terms of resources and staffing. Consequently they are only able to investigate a tiny number of companies at any one time.

## Legal difficulties of prosecution

One of the main impediments to prosecution of violations of criminal law by corporations is that they are legal fictions that exist independently of the individuals who work within them. In criminal law the concept of *mens rea*—a guilty mind—is predicated on the assumption of a conscious being with a will and intention of his or her own. Such consciousness cannot be attributed to an organisation. Crimes such as murder have been designed to deal with individual guilt, making it difficult to apply to corporations. Although the capacity of companies to commit crimes is gradually being acknowledged by the law, there remain serious problems, such as deciding which individuals should carry responsibility for an act that may not clearly be the result of individual actions (see Clough & Mulhern 2002).

Legal difficulties also arise when serious social harm results from an action that is not covered by criminal law. A survey of white collar crime conducted in the USA found that while 41 per cent of respondents who reported being a victim of a white collar crime said they had reported it, less than one in ten victimisations were reported to the police or a consumer protection agency (Rebovich & Layne 2000). While regulatory bodies can recommend the prosecution of a company, their primary objective is inspection and regulation of the organisation. Consequently, they often focus on adherence to regulations rather than the consequences of failing to do so. Their penalties usually take the form of fines, which are often so small that it can be cheaper for a company to flout the law rather than change its practices.

There can also be disputes as to whether state, federal, or even local regulatory authorities have responsibility for regulating an area. Food quality, for example, is regulated in some states by local authorities, and state authorities in others, while the Commonwealth is responsible for controlling the import and export of food (Wilson 1987: 3).

## CONCLUSION

Every day the business pages of the *Australian* contains articles about companies and individuals that have broken the law. The widespread nature of corporate crime is acknowledged by our legal and regulatory system. Laws designed to regulate and monitor corporations are regularly modified and enacted. Numerous regulatory bodies exist at all levels of government. Despite this, there is no evidence that corporate crime is on the decline. Each time a large corporation collapses or is accused of engaging in serious irregularities there is a public outcry about the need to control greedy businesses. Yet the number of businesspeople in prison is tiny. The few high-profile business leaders that go to prison often appear to be prosecuted in order to placate public opinion that 'something is being done'. Their time in prison is generally short, despite the damage caused by their actions. Often they eventually return to well-paid positions in the business sector.

One of the problems facing government in their attempt to regulate and control business is the contradiction between this need to regulate and the principles of capital accumulation in a global environment. The absence of regulation and control is a central tenet of a free-market economy. A law enforcement approach to business is met with claims from business leaders that this harms the competitiveness essential for success in a global economy. And a successful business sector is deemed to be essential for the economic health of the country as a whole.

Yet it is also true that the absence of control is just as dangerous to the community as over-regulation because it can lead to unrestrained economic activity and eventual corporate collapse. Undisciplined corporate governance, poor farming practice, and unbridled exploitation of fisheries are examples of practices that eventually rebound on business and the wider community (Grabosky et al. 1993: 1). The challenge for the future, therefore, is to create a regulatory environment in which the 'irrational exuberance' inherent in business is contained within a framework that prevents damage to the community. Issues of public accountability are nevertheless simultaneously connected to issues of public ownership, democratic decision-making, and notions of the public interest.

It is important to note, as well, that the standard sympathetic approach to the 'needs' of business finds no parallel in relation to conventional crime. The ideological framework surrounding the two types of law breaking is quite different. Although the particular circumstances of a working class offender might be brought to the attention of the court, there is no institutionalised recognition of the 'needs' of disadvantaged offenders. Nor is there any parallel to the public scrutiny that surrounds conventional crime.

The detailed statistics on trends in conventional crime are not available for the business sector. Instead, criminal behaviour by business is buried in the 'fraud' section of the seven categories of serious crime collected by the Australian Institute of Criminology. Other forms of illegality are lost in the annual reports of regulatory bodies. Despite the enormous public concern surrounding corporate collapses and tales of corporate fraud, there has yet to be a front-page headline in the popular press that screams 'Corporate Criminals Out of Control!'. Nor has corporate crime been an election issue, even though ordinary citizens are more likely to be harmed by an older man in a suit than by a young man in shorts and singlet.

## DISCUSSION QUESTIONS

1  Why are the concepts of both corporate crime and white collar crime difficult to define?
2  In what ways does the existence of corporate crime challenge conventional explanations of crime?
3  Why do you think that some sectors of industry seem especially prone to corporate crime?
4  How do you explain the fact that corporate criminals rarely face prosecution?

## GLOSSARY OF TERMS

**corporate crime**
the illegal activities of businesses against members of the public, the environment, creditors, investors, or corporate competitors (Wilson 1987: 1); it includes crimes committed by corporate officials for their corporation, as well as the offences of the corporation itself

**entrepreneurial crime**
punishable acts committed by individuals in controlling positions within corporations, using the resources and power deriving from the corporate form as a vehicle to achieve ends that benefit the entrepreneur personally (Halstead 1992)

**organisational illegalities**
individual or collective illegalities that are perceived as helping to achieve, or are congruent with, the organisational goals set by the dominant coalition within an organisation (Slapper & Tombs 1999: 14).

**occupational crime**
criminal acts committed by employees in the course of their work for personal gain

**white collar crime**
a general term used to describe all crimes committed by non-manual workers in the course of their occupation.

## FURTHER READING

Clough, J. & Mulhern, C. (2002) *The Prosecution of Corporations*, Oxford University Press, Melbourne.

HIH Royal Commission (2003) *The Failure of HIH Insurance*, 1–3, Commonwealth of Australia, Canberra.

Rosoff, S., Pontell, H. & Tillman, R. (1998) *Profit Without Honor: White-Collar Crime and the Looting of America*, Prentice Hall, Upper Saddle River.

Shover, N. & Wright, J. (eds) (2001) *Crimes of Privilege: Readings in White-Collar Crime*, Oxford University Press, New York.

Slapper, G. & Tombs, S. (1999) *Corporate Crime*, Pearson Education, London.

## WEBSITES

**www.aic.gov.au**
Australian Institute of Criminology—Provides links to various publications from Australia's leading criminologists, including research, conference papers, publications, and statistics, many of which are full text.

**www.asic.gov.au/asic/asic.nsf**
Australian Securities and Investments Commission—Provides access to reports and findings of enforcement of company and financial services laws, including full-text reports.

**www.cas.usf.edu/criminology/ccjcorpcrime.htm**
University of South Florida—Provides links to the major agencies in the USA responsible for corporate behaviour in a number of fields, including the environment, occupational health and safety, consumer protection, and food and health.

**www.corpwatch.org**
Corpwatch—Has links to various reports and documents on corporate crime in the USA and overseas.

# CHAPTER 7

# Environmental Crime

## INTRODUCTION

This chapter provides an introduction and overview of issues and trends relating to environmental crime. This area has generated considerable interest in recent years, as criminologists and other social scientists turn their attention to how best to define and respond to environmental harm. As major changes appear on the global scale, with significant impacts at the local level, so, too, greater urgency and critical analysis about environmental matters has grown.

The development of a green or environmental criminology as a field of sustained research and scholarship will by its very nature incorporate many different perspectives and strategic emphases. After all, it deals with concerns across a wide range of environments (for example, land, air, water) and issues (for example, fishing, pollution, toxic waste). It involves conceptual analysis as well as practical intervention on many fronts, and includes multidisciplinary strategic assessment (for example, economic, legal, social, and ecological evaluations). It involves the undertaking of organisational analysis, as well as investigation of 'best practice' methods of monitoring, assessment, enforcement, and education regarding environmental protection and regulation. Analysis needs to be conscious of local, regional, national, and global domains and how activities in each of these overlap. It likewise requires cognisance of the direct and indirect, and immediate and long-term, impacts and consequences of environmentally sensitive social practices.

# DEFINING ENVIRONMENTAL CRIME

Any attempt to address environmental issues from a criminological perspective must be conscious of the complexities and ambiguities of the subject matter. In recent years, two broad areas of debate are discernable when it comes to defining the nature of the problem: environmental harm and environmental victims.

## Environmental harm

First, there are issues surrounding scale, activities, and legalities as these pertain to environmental harm. To define what constitutes environmental harm implies a particular philosophical stance on the relationship between human beings and nature. What is 'wrong' or 'right' environmental practice very much depends upon the criteria used to conceptualise the values and interests represented in this relationship, as reflected for instance in anthropocentric, biocentric, and ecocentric perspectives (see Halsey & White 1998). In more discipline-specific terms, debate still takes place as to the proper object of criminological attention, and how and under what conditions an act or omission might be conceived as an environmental 'crime' as such. A strict legalist approach tends to focus on the central place of criminal law in the definition of criminality. Thus, as Situ and Emmons (2000: 3) see it: 'An **environmental crime** is an unauthorised act or omission that violates the law and is therefore subject to criminal prosecution and criminal sanctions.' However, other writers argue that, as with criminology in general, the concept of 'harm' ought to encapsulate those activities that may be legal and 'legitimate', but which nevertheless negatively impact on people and environments (Sutherland 1949; Schwendinger & Schwendinger 1975).

In the specific area of environmental criminology, this broader conceptualisation of crime or harm is deemed to be essential in evaluating the systemic, as well as particularistic, nature of environmental harm. That is, current regulatory apparatus, informed by the ideology of 'sustainable development', is largely directed at bringing ecological sustainability to the present mode of producing and consuming—one based upon the logic of growth, expanded consumption of resources, and the commodification of more and more aspects of nature.

To put it differently, it is important to distinguish (and make the connection between) specific instances of harm arising from imperfect operation (such as pollution spills) and systemic harm that is created by normatively sanctioned forms of activity (clear-felling of Tasmanian forests). The first is deemed to be 'criminal' or 'harmful', and thus subject to social control. The second is not. The overall consequence of this is for the global environmental problem to get worse, in the very midst of the proliferation of a greater range of regulatory mechanisms, agencies, and laws. This is partly an outcome of the way in which environmental risk is compartmentalised: specific events or incidents attract sanction, while wider legislative frameworks may set parameters on, but nevertheless still allow, other ecologically harmful practices to continue.

For example, Halsey (1997a, 1997b) identifies a number of social practices that are legal, but environmentally disastrous, such as clear-felling of old-growth forests. A broader conception of the problem is also vital in developing a critique of existing regulatory measures designed to manage (or, as some argue, to facilitate) such harm. For example, Seis (1993) argues that US legislation that is meant to protect air quality is based upon counter-ecological principles. As such, the legislation necessarily fails to protect and enhance air quality. The problem is not with the lack of criminal or civil law or enforcement powers: it is the anthropocentric assumptions built into the legislation.

## Environmental victims

**Environmental victimisation** can be defined as specific forms of harm that are caused by acts (for example, dumping of toxic waste) or omissions (for example, failure to provide safe drinking water) leading to the presence or absence of environmental agents (for example, poisons, nutrients) that are associated with human injury (see Williams 1996). The management of these forms of victimisation is generally retrospective (after the fact), and involves a variety of legal and social responses.

The response of the state to these kinds of harm is guided by a concern with environmental protection, which is generally framed in terms of ensuring future resource exploitation, and dealing with specific instances of victimisation that have been socially defined as a problem. Risk management in this case is directed at preventing or minimising certain destructive or injurious practices into the future, based upon analysis and responses to harms identified in the present. The ways in which the state reacts to such harms are based upon classifications of harm and wrongdoing as defined in legislation, including criminal law. The target of such legislation is specific acts and events, usually relating to pollution (see Gunningham et al. 1995; Heine et al. 1997).

Analysis of environmental issues proceeds on the basis that someone or something is indeed being harmed. In this regard, a distinction is sometimes made between 'environmental justice' and 'ecological justice'. **Environmental justice** refers to fair distribution of environmental quality among peoples (Low & Gleeson 1998) and the impacts of particular social practices on specific populations. The focus of analysis therefore is on human health and well-being and how these are affected by particular types of production and consumption. Here we can distinguish between environmental issues that affect everyone, and those that disproportionately affect specific individuals and groups (see Williams 1996). On the one hand there is a basic 'equality of victims', in that some environmental problems threaten everyone in the same way, as in the cases, for example, of ozone depletion, global warming, air pollution, and acid rain (Beck 1996).

On the other hand, as extensive work on specific incidents and patterns of victimisation demonstrates, some people are more likely to be disadvantaged by environmental problems than others (Julian 2004). For instance, American studies have identified disparities involving many different types of environmental hazards that adversely affect people of colour throughout the United States (Bullard 1994). Other work in Canada and Australia has focused on the struggles of Indigenous people to either prevent the environmental degradation of their lands, or to institute their own methods of environmental protection (see Rush 2002; Langton 1998). It is clear that environmental racism manifests itself in a number of different guises and is directly related to social inequalities that are, in turn, reflected in particular forms of environmental victimisation (Stephens 1996). The specificity of those placed at greater or disproportionate risk from environmental harm is also reflected in literature that acknowledges the importance of class, occupation, gender, and, more recently, age, in the construction of special environmental interest groups (Stephens 1996; Chunn et al. 2002; Williams 1996). There are thus patterns of 'differential victimisation' that are evident with respect to the siting of toxic waste dumps, extreme air pollution, access to safe clean drinking water, and so on.

**Ecological justice** refers to the relationship of human beings generally to the rest of the natural world. The focus of analysis therefore is on the health of the biosphere, and more specifically plants and creatures that also inhabit the biosphere (see Benton 1998; Franklin 1999; Munro 2004). The main concern is with the quality of the planetary environment (that is frequently seen to possess its own intrinsic value) and the rights of other species (particularly animals) to life free from torture, abuse, and destruction of habitat. For example, insofar as poor quality drinking water and diminished clean water resources are attributable to social practices such as disposal of agricultural, urban, and industrial effluents into water catchments and river systems, then it is not only humans who are affected. It is notable that some of Australia's largest waste-disposal companies are owned by French transnational water companies. Moreover, in Sydney, approval has been granted to locate a 'megatip'—a large waste-management facility—in the city water catchment area (Archer 2001: 34–6). The same companies that promise to supply clean water, therefore, are the same companies most likely to contaminate it. Local natural environments, and non-human inhabitants of both wilderness and built environments, are negatively impacted upon by human practices that destroy, re-channel, or pollute existing freshwater systems. Who does so, and why, are important questions to answer.

## THE EXTENT OF ENVIRONMENTAL CRIME

We have already seen that analysis of the extent of environmental crime requires acknowledgement of fundamental issues of definition. Different conceptualisations of social harm and legal distinctions between criminal, civil, and regulatory law play a critical role in public discourse on the issue. Regardless of academic and community debates over how best to define environmental harm and conceptualise environmental victimisation, the response of the state to environmental crime is informed by legally defined categories of offence (that is, as spelled out in specific Acts) and procedural pathways (that is, specific means by which to enforce compliance with the Acts). By and large, environmental crime is defined in terms of offences against the environment that fall into three broad categories: land, air, and water pollution.

Compilation of adequate statistics on environmental prosecutions and convictions is still in its infancy in many jurisdictions around Australia.

Part of the difficulty lies in determining which offences will be dealt with via regulatory agencies, such as licensing bodies and local government authorities, and which through formal courts or specific environmental protection tribunals. Moreover, depending upon how cases are proceeded against, different agencies will keep different records, have different types of follow-up procedures, and will vary in whether or not the information is easily and publicly accessible.

National court data on environmental crime incorporates property damage and environmental pollution. This data is presented in tables 7.1 and 7.2, which includes number of offences, and the proportion of these offences relative to the total number of offences with which the courts deal. While too expansive in one sense because it includes property damage, and too restrictive in another because it only includes pollution and not other types of environmental harm, the tables do provide some indication of the extent to which the state is intervening in such matters. Compared with other crimes discussed in this book, relatively little court attention is given to environmental crimes. Where there is a central investigative agency—usually in the form of an environmental protection agency—it is probable that prosecutions will be more frequent. For instance, in Tasmania, where there is not such a specialist agency, formal prosecutions are relatively small in number.

**Table 7.1** Property damage and environmental pollution offences by age and sex
Total higher courts adjudicated defendants; principal offence by age and sex

|  | Under 20 | 20–24 | 25–34 | 35–44 | 45+ | Unknown | Total | Mean age (years) | Median age (years) |
|---|---|---|---|---|---|---|---|---|---|
| **MALES** | | | | | | | | | |
| Number | 69 | 90 | 87 | 40 | 15 | 22 | 323 | 27.2 | 24.1 |
| Proportion (%) | 4.5 | 2.9 | 2.1 | 1.7 | 0.9 | 4.0 | 2.4 | – | – |
| **FEMALES** | | | | | | | | | |
| Number | 4 | 12 | 13 | 9 | 4 | 2 | 44 | 31.1 | 30.6 |
| Proportion (%) | 2.2 | 2.8 | 2.0 | 2.6 | 2.3 | 1.9 | 2.3 | – | – |
| **PERSONS** | | | | | | | | | |
| Number | 73 | 102 | 100 | 49 | 19 | 24 | 367 | 27.7 | 24.8 |
| Proportion (%) | 4.2 | 2.9 | 2.1 | 1.9 | 1.0 | 3.7 | 2.4 | – | – |

Source: ABS (2003c).

**Table 7.2** Property damage and environmental pollution offences by jurisdiction
Experimental Magistrates' Courts data; adjudicated defendants, principal offence

|  | NSW | Vic | Qld | SA | WA | Tas[a] | NT | ACT | Aust |
|---|---|---|---|---|---|---|---|---|---|
| Number | na | 3048 | 2924 | 1027 | 1612 | 55 | 214 | na | na |
| Proportion (%) | na | 3.0 | 2.6 | 3.1 | 2.8 | 1.2 | 2.9 | na | na |

a Restricted to Southern Tasmanian Magistrates' Courts for the reference period 1 March 2002 to
30 June 2002

Source: ABS (2003b).

Data that separates out property damage and environmental pollution is quite revealing. For instance, in 1998 in New South Wales Local Courts there were 6898 charges for property damage, while only 129 for environmental pollution. The figures for 2002 are 9499 and 595 respectively (NSW Bureau of Crime Statistics 2003b). While the number of pollution offences has grown from 1998 to 2002, these remain small compared with other types of offences, including property damage. Moreover, no person was imprisoned for pollution offences over the years 2000–02. In Victoria, there were only 34 major prosecutions in 2002–03, down from a previous high of 46 in 2000–01 (for examples, see below). Most of the work of the agency takes the form of infringement notices, vehicle enforcement actions, and provision of information (Victorian EPA 2003).

It is evident, therefore, that detailed study of specific offences and particular agency responses is required in order to both obtain a better picture of environmental harm, and to monitor how institutionally the state and community is responding to this type of harm.

Box 7.1 outlines a series of areas that might assist in guiding the process of gathering more data on environmental offences. The collection of this data would enable the construction of a baseline model from which the nature, extent, and dynamics of environmental harm over time can be gauged.

## PROSECUTING ENVIRONMENTAL CRIME

The primary regulatory authority for the control of environmental crime is the Environmental Protection Authority (or Agency; EPA) or equivalent. These operate at state level and their mandate includes:

- *regulating* environmental crime through administration of environmental protection legislation

Box 7.1

## STRATEGY FOR EXPLORATORY RESEARCH ON 'ENVIRONMENTAL OFFENCES'

- Define the scope of the research area (harm to the natural environment, to human beings, to non-human animals, etc.).
- Identify:
  - ▾ relevant legislation
  - ▾ relevant penal provisions
  - ▾ relevant civil enforcement proceedings
  - ▾ the responsible government agencies.
- Ascertain whether each relevant agency collates data in relation to the following:
  1 number of prosecutions or other enforcement proceedings undertaken by the agency
  2 data on conferences, mediation, and agreements undertaken by the parties under the various Acts
  3 extent to which (1) and (2) above are recorded, monitored, and/or followed up by agency
  4 number and nature of enforcement proceedings undertaken by third parties in relation to relevant legislation
  5 identification of the enforcing parties (if not the agency itself).
- Obtain data/statistics where available.
- Compile an analysis identifying:
  - ▾ existing statistical data bases
  - ▾ who maintains the above and on what basis (statutory obligation, departmental policy, voluntary)
  - ▾ areas where it is desirable that such data bases should be established.

- *educating* the community about environmental issues
- *monitoring and researching* environmental quality
- *reporting* on the state of the environment to State Parliament and other relevant bodies.

Implementation of this mandate includes protecting and conserving the natural environment, promoting the sustainable use of natural capital, ensuring a clean environment, and reducing risks to human health.

Case study 7.1 provides some illustrations of the kinds of matters that come before the courts under the *Environmental Protection Act* 1970 in Victoria (see Jackson 2003):

## CASE STUDY 7.1

### Case 1

On 5 August 2002, at the Geelong Magistrate's Court, Shell Refining (Australia) Pty Ltd pleaded guilty to one charge of breach of licence for the discharge of offensive odour beyond the boundary of its premises, contrary to section 27(2) of the *Environmental Protection Act*. The charge related to odours investigated by EPA officers in the Corio residential area. The odours emanated from a waste-water treatment plant and waste pits operated by the defendant at its Corio premises, and was described by the two investigating officers as the strongest they had ever detected. The defendant was convicted, and ordered to pay $36,500 to the City of Greater Geelong for the completion of an environmental project, and the EPA's costs of $16,620 (maximum penalty—a fine of $240,000).

### Case 2

On 9 September 2002, at the Melbourne Magistrate's Court, Walter Construction Group Limited pleaded guilty to two charges under section 27A(2)(a) of the *Environmental Protection Act*. The prosecution arose from the dumping of construction waste that came from works undertaken during the Docklands Infrastructure Project. The waste was dumped alongside, and to some extent into, the Moonee Ponds Creek in the Docklands precinct. Although the dumping activity occurred as a single, continuing course of conduct over nearly four months, two charges were laid because the offence period spanned the date on which the charge become an indictable offence, and the maximum penalty increased from $40,000 to $500,000. The Court was told that about 90 per cent of the dumping occurred during the summary period. Charges were also pending against two other parties allegedly involved in the incident and, as part of its plea in mitigation, the defendant undertook to assist the EPA in those proceedings. No conviction was imposed, and the defendant was fined $10,000, was ordered to pay $10,000 to the Docklands Authority for an environmental project, and to pay EPA's costs of $9229.75 (maximum penalty—a fine of $20,000 for the first charge and a fine of $500,000 for the second charge).

## Case 3

On 4 December 2002, at the Dandenong Magistrates' Court, Miatech Pty Limited pleaded guilty to the charge of contravening a Notifiable Chemical Order, which prohibited the storing, handling, transporting, and use of polychlorinated biphenyls (PCBs) without an Environmental Improvement Plan (EIP) approved by the EPA. The charge arose after the discovery of PCBs in approximately 4000 litres of waste oil at the premises of Master Waste Pty Ltd. Miatech was identified as having provided the contaminated waste oil, which had formerly been used in electrical transformers. No conviction was imposed, and the company was placed on an undertaking to be of good behaviour for twelve months with a special condition to pay $1000 into the Court Fund. It was also ordered to pay EPA's costs of $4100 (maximum penalty—a fine of $240,000).

An EPA usually has a range of mechanisms at its disposal to deal with environmental issues. For example, the EPA in South Australia is responsible for the protection of air and water quality, and control of pollution, waste, noise, and radiation. The EPA administers the *Environmental Protection Act* through various regulatory tools (see table 7.3).

**Table 7.3**   Regulatory tools under the *Environmental Protection Act*, South Australia

| Legal instruments | Explanation |
| --- | --- |
| Environment Protection Policy (EPP) | Established under section 28 of the Act with accompanying consultation requirements, an EPP: <br>• has the force of a standard imposed by Parliament <br>• may impose mandatory provisions with penalties <br>• is developed for a specific area, e.g. waste, water, air, noise. |
| Code of Practice (Code) | A Code regulates a specific activity and: <br>• is enforceable, via an Environment Protection Order (EPO) or mandatory provisions of an EPP <br>• provides direction and control over an industry <br>• sets measurable outcomes, e.g. 'you must achieve certain defined levels/limits' <br>• requires extensive consultation in development and alteration <br>• can incorporate specific industry elements of umbrella policies (e.g. 'Piggeries' Code may incorporate air, water, waste, and noise provisions) |

**Table 7.3** Regulatory tools under the *Environmental Protection Act*, South Australia (continued)

| Legal instruments | Explanation |
| --- | --- |
| Code of Practice (Code) (continued) | • may link to and operate under legislation other than the *Environment Protection Act*.<br>Compliance with a Code would be a defence to an alleged offence under the Act if the EPA deems that this constitutes compliance with the General Environmental Duty in section 25(3) of the Act. This would also provide a defence against third-party prosecution. |
| Regulations | As subordinate legislation made under section 140 of the Act, regulations:<br>• may give effect to administrative arrangements (e.g. container approvals under the beverage container provisions)<br>• may provide details of issues broadly established under the Act<br>• may be made for any purpose: 'such regulations as are contemplated by, or as are necessary and expedient for the purposes of, this Act' (section 140(1)). |

| Other tools | |
| --- | --- |
| Guideline | An EPA Guideline provides guidance to industry or the community concerning specific issues, and:<br>• is primarily advisory<br>• includes technical information and recommends ways of undertaking an activity: ideas for 'how to'<br>• prescribes an environmental outcome, but is not normally prescriptive about the mechanisms by which an outcome would be achieved, as it seeks to encourage rather than stifle innovation<br>• is intended for internal and external use<br>• is not directly enforceable; however, may be used to help the EPA interpret the General Environment Duty for a particular situation(s), and may be enforced through issuing an EPO or condition of licence. |
| Policy Position Paper (PPP) | A statement of the EPA's broad policy position and principles on an issue, a PPP is linked to international conventions and national policy. Consultation is at the discretion of the Board. |

The mandate of most environmental protection agencies today is not only to enforce compliance through use of criminal prosecutions, but also to forge strategic alliances and working partnerships with industries, local governments, and communities in support of environmental objectives. Often these are framed in terms of economic, and perhaps, social, objectives as well.

The multiple demands on EPAs from different sections of government, business, and community, and the varied tasks in which they participate, may lead to a dilution of their enforcement capacities and activities. A recent review of the enforcement and prosecution guidelines of the Department of Environmental Protection of Western Australia, for example, made a series of interesting and provocative observations (Robinson 2003):

> In summary, the Guidelines were found to be largely similar to those published in other states, but the language and tone could lead to an interpretation that the role of enforcement was de-emphasised in the Department's overall approach and that, in particular, the barriers to prosecution were overemphasized compared to the benefits (p. 3).
>
> While simple comparisons with other states can be misleading, the population based pro rata prosecution rate under the *Environmental Protection Act* 1986 (and indeed the rate of other punitive enforcement measures) appears to be below that which could be expected, drawing on the experience in the larger states, of what constitutes effective enforcement (p. 4).
>
> Scarcity of resources are recognized by all parties as providing a particular challenge to achieving significant improvement and this has been borne in mind in conducting the review (p. 4).

The review acknowledges the complexities of environmental regulation, including the central place of 'ecologically sustainable development' as a guiding philosophy for intervention. Regulation must be based upon cooperation, as well as use of coercive measures. Nevertheless, the review highlights the importance of a 'bottom line' when it comes to compliance with environmental laws and rules:

> 'Speak softly and carry a big stick' is an appropriate aphorism for today's environmental regulator, but to be effective there must be certainty that the big stick can and will be used and the how, why and where of its

use. It is the anticipation of enforcement action that confers the ability to deter (Robinson 2003: 11).

Accordingly, Robinson (2003: 23) argues that prosecution ought to be an equal partner in the enforcement toolbox, and should be neither the first nor the last resort, but the appropriate response to a particular set of circumstances. How regulation is constructed by governments, and how enforcement in particular is carried out in practice, is contingent upon what is occurring in the wider political economic context.

## GOVERNMENT AUTHORITIES AND ENVIRONMENTAL CONTROLS

The role of the state in the case of environmental protection tends to be fairly circumscribed. Historically, the tendency has been to emphasise efficiency and facilitation, rather than control. At a practical level the costs of monitoring and enforcement and compliance, in relation to traditional regulatory standard setting and role of government, are seen as problematic. The complexity of procedures and issues has also been accompanied by efforts to streamline processes and to rely on expert-based advice, rather than seeking full community discussion. This fits neo-liberalist government policies because the state can support economic development while also cutting costs and encouraging business growth by narrowing the scope of its purview and involvement in regulation. This can take several different forms, such as cuts in state resources allocated to environmental audits (for example, botany mapping) and the censoring of scientific information that may be publicly sensitive for specific industries (for example, fishing, forestry, mining) or for private contract partners of government (for example, water treatment plants, power station operators).

The state nevertheless has a formal role and commitment to protect citizens from the worst excesses or worst instances of environmental victimisation. Extensive legislation and regulatory procedures give the appearance of active intervention, and demonstrate that laws exist that do deter such harms. The existence of such laws may be encouraging in that they reflect historical and ongoing struggles over certain types of destructive activity. However, questions about how or whether they are used raises issues of the relationship between the state and the corporate sector, and the capacity of business to defend its interests through legal and extra-legal means.

Many businesses, for example, can gain protection from close public or state surveillance through the very processes of commercial negotiation and transaction. These range from appeals to 'commercial confidentiality' through to constraints associated with the technical nature of evidence required. For example, there is often difficulty in law of assigning 'cause' in many cases of environmental harm due to the diffuse nature of responsibility for particular effects, such as pollution in an area of multiple producers (for example, mining companies). Furthermore, it has been pointed out that: 'Evidence frequently can only be collected through the use of powers of entry, the ability to take, analyse and interpret appropriate samples and a good knowledge of the processes or activities giving rise to the offence' (Robinson 1995: 13). Such powers impinge upon the 'private' property rights and commercial interests that are at the heart of the capitalist political economy.

There are clear social differences in the ability of the powerful, in relation to the less powerful, to protect and defend their interests. This is evident in how the powerful are able to manipulate rules of evidence, frustrate investigatory processes, confuse notions of accountability, and forestall potential prosecution by ostensibly abiding by and complying with record-keeping procedures (see Gunningham et al. 1995). The expense of legal remedies in dealing with environmental harm is further complicated by the ways in which companies contest the domains of contractual and legal responsibility, and by the notions of 'privileged information' as a means to restrict access to needed evidence. In contrast with the rights of working class offenders, privacy is more likely to be assured.

Strong arguments have been put forward against the use of criminal law, in particular, in dealing with specific incidents and corporate practices. This is because of the limits inherent in the use of criminal sanctions against the more powerful groups in society (see Haines 1997). For example, corporations have considerable financial and legal resources to contest prosecution, making such prosecutions enormously expensive to run. Technical difficulties of prosecution (such as rules of evidence, multiple offenders, etc.) and the financial and human resource constraints of state legal machinery (for example, regulatory bodies such as the police, environmental protection agencies, and corporate watchdogs) preclude the use of criminal prosecution except in the most extreme or 'winnable' cases. There is, therefore, considerable discretion in prosecution and sentencing decisions.

Acknowledgement of these kinds of difficulties has fostered the development of new legal concepts relating to corporate liability and compensation (see Gunningham et al. 1995). Be this as it may, there are nevertheless persistent difficulties in prosecution of the powerful, whose use of the law is intrinsic to the maintenance of their dominant class position. The complexity of legal argument, and a political environment which sees environmental protection in the context of economic development, means that generally speaking the state is reluctant to proceed too far in either scrutinising or criminalising those sectors directly involved in productive economic activity.

Alternatively, given the limitations of criminal prosecution, it has been argued that the best way to regulate corporate misbehaviour in relation to the environment is through the use of civil and other remedies (Gunningham et al. 1995; Grabosky 1994). These may involve various forms of 'self-regulation', educational programs, and the use of tort law in dealing with, and preventing, harmful activity. The idea is that persuasion, rather than coercion, is the best way to regulate harmful practices affecting the environment, and that criminal law should only be used as a means of last resort. This approach is sustained by theoretical work that speaks about the importance of encouraging trustworthiness by individual companies and by industry associations (see Grabosky 1994). This perspective on corporate regulation rests on the idea of enlisting 'private interests' in regulatory activity via 'inducements' (by such mechanisms as creating new commercial opportunities, such as alternative energy sources, air pollution technology, earning a good reputation among consumers for environmental responsibility, and adopting waste-minimisation programs that mean more efficient production). The difficulty with this, however, is that it tends to ignore the size and market power of firms and the role this plays in the setting of and compliance with regulatory standards and norms (Haines 1997).

A further hindrance on environmental regulation is the relatively recent phenomenon of the use by companies of lawsuits against environmentalists, individual citizens, and community groups. The use of civil court action in this way has been described as 'Strategic Lawsuits Against Public Participation' or SLAPPs. The point of such suits is not to 'win' in the conventional legal sense but to intimidate those who might be critical of existing or proposed developments. Beder observes that while 'the cost to a developer is part of the cost of doing business, but a court case could well bankrupt an individual or environmental group. In this way the legal system best serves those who have large financial resources at their disposal, particularly corporations' (Beder 1997: 65). This kind of pre-emptive action has already been taken as a means to limit public participation around issues of urban development and environmental regulation in Australia (for case studies, see Walters 2003). Claims of defamation, and for damages to company reputation and potential profits, associated with campaigns against certain developments on environmental or social grounds have started to feature more prominently in the corporate arsenal. Public discussion and attempts to more strictly regulate corporate activity becomes even more difficult than normally might be the case in such an intimidating atmosphere.

## Risk management

One of the key issues of environmental '**risk management**' in relation to existing harmful practices is the matter of **benchmark information**. That is, what criteria are to be used to evaluate whether or not environmental harm has occurred, whether or not a particular body is responsible for this harm, and whether or not this can be remedied using existing technologies or whether it is something we have to 'live with' given certain economic imperatives? This raises the issues of role of 'expert opinion', and public advocacy, in assessing the nature and dynamics of environmental harm and victimisation. It also raises issues of class interests and environmental philosophy (that is, the values and analyses that should drive the assessment process), and the place of third-party public-interest groups in determination of what is harmful and what ought to be done about it.

The ways in which risk is construed and responded to with respect to environmental harm is socially patterned in ways that reflect and protect the interests of business in general. For example, the basic assumption underlying regulation is that its aim is the reduction of the impact that development is having on specific environments (for example, via Environmental Impact Assessment procedures), rather than to challenge the nature of development itself (that is, issues of material class interests).

There are strong pressures to render the issue of 'risk' in the field of environmental law and regulation to a matter of specialist expertise and legal–technical knowledge, although this varies from jurisdiction to jurisdiction (Hannigan 1995). The emphasis is not on the generic causes of environmental harm (since this immediately raises the issue of control and ownership over the means of production/destruction), but on how to regulate specific instances of actual or potential harm. The implication is that such issues can only be dealt with within the framework of 'sustainable development' and that control ought to be exercised on a rational, scientific basis, which calculates cost-benefit in economic, rather than ecological, terms.

Given this, the question of resource allocation to environmental assessment and management, and issues pertaining to public accountability, tend to be skewed in the direction of less intervention and less transparent processes of regulation. The latter are thus conceived as impediments to the exploitation of the environment, although it is conceded that specific instances of harmful activity do warrant curtailment, since they can undermine public confidence, as well as limit the availability of resources (for economic purposes) into the future.

## Environmental crime as a global issue

From the point of view of international law enforcement agencies, the major issues relating to environmental crime are:

- the trans-border movement and dumping of waste products
- the illegal traffic in real or purported radioactive or nuclear substances
- the illegal traffic in species of wild flora and fauna.

These areas have been identified by agencies such as Interpol as key subjects in relation to environmental crime. It is worth exploring the first of these in greater depth, given that much of the transfer of waste has been from advanced industrialised countries to 'third world' countries.

The biggest exporter of toxic waste is the United States of America. Hazardous residues and contaminated sludge are most likely to find a foreign home in a developing country. The pressures for this are twofold. On the one hand, the US has seen the closing of many domestic landfills due to public health problems, and increasing public consciousness of the dangers posed by toxic waste. On the other hand, poor countries (and corrupt state officials) may find it financially attractive to offer their land as sites for US waste:

When the cost of legitimately disposing of toxic waste in the United States was about $2500 per ton, some impoverished countries, burdened by massive foreign debts, were accepting as little as $3 per ton to dispose of toxins within their borders. In 1987, for example, it actually was cheaper to ship waste by barge to the Caribbean than to move it overland just forty miles (Rosoff et al. 1998:97).

The problem is not only the transfer of toxic waste, but also the generation of toxic waste in other countries by companies based in advanced, industrialised nations. The classic case of this is the *maquiladoras*, American-owned factories set up across the border in Mexico. Here, environmental regulation is lax, with resulting high levels of chemical pollution, contamination, and exposure to toxic materials. Closer to home for Australians, is the huge environmental damage caused to the Ok Tedi River in Papua New Guinea by the activities of the Australian mining corporation BHP (see Low & Gleeson 1998). Because the PNG government was dependent on the earnings from the Ok Tedi copper mine, it actively cooperated with BHP in the destruction of local rain forest and much of the river system. Many villagers have lost the entire environment that supported their way of life (Low & Gleeson 1998: 8).

These examples highlight the fact that to understand the overall direction of environmental issues demands analysis of the strategic location and activities of transnational capital, as supported by hegemonic nation–states on a world scale. Capitalist globalisation, bolstered via neo-liberal state policy, means that there is great scope to increase environmentally destructive activity. Nevertheless, different businesses may have divergent orientations to the environment depending upon their market focus (for example, public relations firms, newly emerging environmental protection industries, forestry companies).

International competition among capitalist sectors (and among communities) for access to healthy resources, including clean water, is also intensifying due to the overall shrinking of the natural resource base. The dominance of Western capital in this competition is sustained in part because 'environmental regulation' itself is being utilised as an entry card to new international markets. Markets can be protected through universalising environmental regulation in ways that advantage the high technology companies of the advanced industrialised countries (Goldman 1998a, 1998b). The largest companies are most likely to be capable of being environmentally 'virtuous', as well as having the most input into redesigning the rules of international standardisation vis-à-vis environmental management (see also Haines 2000).

Further to this, it has been argued that the cleaning up of old, dirty industries and the rewriting of property laws (particularly in developing countries and Russia) in accordance with new international standards of environmental management and trade liberalisation, is a precursor to capitalist penetration and exploitation of nature (Goldman 1998a). To see environmental regulation in this light is to acknowledge the economic rather than ecological rationale behind the actions of global regulatory bodies such as the World Trade Organization, the International Monetary Fund, and the World Bank. The undemocratic character of these institutions stems in part from the fact that 'regulation', in this instance, is about facilitation of the exploitation of nature and human beings, not about human interests and needs. Ultimately, the appeal of 'smart regulation', and its corporate expressions in various forms of environmental management systems and voluntary codes of conduct, lies in its adherence to the 'ecological modernisation' ideological framework, which sees economic interests and environmental interests as compatible (Harvey 1996). But, in practice, the emphasis remains that of efficiency and effectiveness, and the outcome ensures corporate sector 'ownership' of environmental responses.

## CONCLUSION

The study of environmental crime is in its infancy in Australia. Most critical attention to date has tended to be on matters relating to environmental regulation and issues of environmental and ecological justice. However, this analysis has highlighted the need for an approach that focuses on broader issues such as how 'harm' is defined, and the philosophies, processes, and practices that influence the regulatory environment. Investigation therefore has to be directed at political and economic developments, especially in regard to appropriation of natural resources and specific market opportunities, as well as the systemic consequences of neo-liberal policies and practices for environmental protection and preservation. At the same time, a specific firm, industry, or event can be examined in relation to the various proactive and reactive measures that exist to either forestall environmental harm or to minimise negative publicity in relation to such harm.

We also need to be cognisant of how the disappearance of criminality and coercion in regard to environmental regulation (in favour of persuasion, self regulation, and cooperative strategies) shifts the locus of the problem from one of environmental and social harm to one of enhanced 'environmentally friendly' production. Such enhancements collectively degrade the global ecological commons.

On another front, it is important to publicly expose the track record of environmental vandals as part of a public accountability process. This can be done in relation to specific environmentally related practices, as in the case of companies supplying poor or contaminated water. It can also be achieved by highlighting the overall negative practices and reputation of a company. The targets of risk assessment and management in the case of 'environmental harm' have tended to be *activities and events*. Greater focus needs to be placed on the *companies and individuals* who perpetrate the harm.

The concentration of economic power at a global level, as manifest in the large transnational corporations, will obviously have an impact on the determination of what is deemed to be harmful or criminal, and what will not. It also means that, particularly in the case of environmental issues, the international character of capital and the trans-border nature of the harm make prosecution and regulation extremely difficult. This is the case even where national legal mechanisms have been put into place to minimise environmental harm and to protect specific environments. Not only do the powerful have greater scope to shape laws in their collective interest, they also have greater capacity to defend themselves individually if they do break and bend the existing rules and regulations.

It is vital, therefore, that any decisions regarding environmental regulation be open to public scrutiny. The importance of independent audits of specific projects, specific businesses and specific government agencies cannot be underestimated. Adoption of 'whistleblower' legislation designed to protect those who reveal 'confidential' and 'sensitive' information in the public interest is also important. These can act as both a sanction for non-compliance and an incentive to be more environmentally responsible (see Edmonds 1995). Work is needed to critically evaluate the actions of companies engaged in environmentally sensitive activities (for example, Ok Tedi in Papua New Guinea), government departments that engage in production-related activities (public utilities), and government departments that have the legal brief to monitor compliance and enforce laws (such as endangered species, fisheries, and parks and wildlife).

## DISCUSSION QUESTIONS

1 Why are definitional issues of concepts such as 'environmental harm' so critical to the regulation and control of environmental crime?
2 What are the regulatory implications of locating environmental protection in the context of economic development? What should be done about this?
3 Explain the paradox that those who are most likely to commit environmental crime are also most likely to dominate new markets in developing countries?

## GLOSSARY OF TERMS

**benchmark information**
the criteria used to evaluate whether or not environmental harm has occurred, whether or not a particular body is responsible for this harm, and whether or not this can be remedied using existing technologies

**ecological justice**
the relationship of human beings generally to the rest of the natural world in a way that maintains the quality of the planetary environment and protects the rights of all species, not just humans (Benton 1998; Franklin 1999; Munro 2004)

**environmental crime**
an unauthorised act or omission that violates the law and is therefore subject to criminal prosecution and criminal sanctions (Situ & Emmons 2000: 3); more broadly, it includes those activities that may be legal and 'legitimate' but which nevertheless negatively impact on people and environments (Sutherland 1949; Schwendinger & Schwendinger 1975)

**environmental justice**
the fair distribution of environmental quality among peoples (Low & Gleeson 1998) and the impacts of particular social practices on specific populations

**environmental victimisation**
specific forms of harm that are caused by acts (for example, dumping of toxic waste) or omissions (for example, failure to provide safe drinking water) leading to the presence or absence of environmental

agents (for example, poisons, nutrients) that are associated with human injury (see Williams 1996)

**risk management**

the prevention or minimisation of certain destructive or injurious practices in the future, based upon analysis and responses to harms identified in the present.


## FURTHER READING

Boyd, S., Chunn, D. & Menzies, R. (eds) (2002) *Toxic Criminology: Environment, Law and the State in Canada*, Fernwood Publishing, Halifax.

Gunningham, N., Norberry, J. & McKillop, S. (eds) (1995) *Environmental Crime, Conference Proceedings*, Australian Institute of Criminology, Canberra.

Robinson, B. (2003) *Review of the Enforcement and Prosecution Guidelines of the Department of Environmental Protection of Western Australia*, Communication Edge, Perth.

Situ, Y. & Emmons, D. (2000) *Environmental Crime: The Criminal Justice System's Role in Protecting the Environment*, Sage Publications, Thousand Oaks.

Walters, B. (2003) *Slapping on the Writs: Defamation, Developers and Community Activism*, UNSW Press, Sydney.

## WEBSITES

**www.aic.gov.au**

Australian Institute of Criminology—Has links to various publications from Australia's leading criminologists, including research, conference papers, publications, and statistics, many of which are full text.

**www.cmc.qld.gov.au/pubscrime.html**

Queensland Crime and Misconduct Commission—Provides assess to a range of publications from this organisation, including the area of environmental crime.

**www.e-b-i.net/ebi/about_us.html**

Environmental Bureau of Investigation—A Canadian-based community group committed to the investigation and prosecuting of environmental offenders and to the protection of public resources through the application and enforcement of environmental laws.

**www.epa.gov**

US Environmental Protection Agency—Provides detailed reports on the environmental crimes and regulatory activities of this agency.

**www.epa.vic.gov.au**

Victorian Environmental Protection Authority—The official web site for the Victorian Government's environmental protection plans.

# CHAPTER 8

# State Crime

## INTRODUCTION

This chapter provides an introduction and overview of state crime. Weber's classic definition of **the state** is that it is the institution that has a monopoly on the means of coercion within a specific territory or region. As such, it exercises power through the ultimate sanction of violence. It is the state that has control of the military and police, and it determines who is allowed to carry arms and under what circumstances. While it may act on behalf of powerful interests, it is also a site of struggle between a wide range of groups. The authority vested in the state means that it has an intrinsic capacity to do harm. The question of **the legitimacy of the state**—the extent to which its actions are perceived as within its political mandate and receive the approval of the citizenship—is therefore central to how any harms associated with the state are interpreted.

Any discussion of '**state crime**' requires consideration of what is meant by 'the state'. This is a complicated matter, since the state can be analysed in many different ways. At one level we can refer to the 'state' in terms of the various institutions that make up a nation's political and administrative bodies. But such an interpretation is limited and tells us little about how the state actually works and what is the basis of its authority. In other words, it is necessary to theorise the meaning of the term 'state'. There are many different types of state. For example, the Australian state is normally characterised as a liberal democratic state, but some theorists would argue that it is better understood as a post-capitalist state or perhaps a postmodern one. The different terminology suggests a different understanding of what the basis of political power and authority are within a nation, and how this is distributed. Any analysis of the state implicitly or explicitly carries with it assumptions about what kind of state it is, such as whether or not it provides welfare and education, how independent it is from other powerful groups such as business or the military, and the extent to which civil liberties such as freedom of political expression are supported.

Understanding the state requires understanding of its complexity. Any state (or perhaps more precisely, state system) is comprised of a multitude of different agencies and institutions, from elected members of parliament through to appointed civil servants, of military commanders to schoolroom teachers. Many diverse people perform myriad different functions, roles, and tasks under the broad umbrella of the state. A large part of investigation of state crime is spent on determining issues of public accountability (that is, who is responsible for which decisions), public interests (that is, what is legitimate or not legitimate action or non-action), and who benefits and who suffers from particular state interventions.

## DEFINING STATE CRIME

Broadly speaking, **state crime** refers to crimes involving the state acting against its own citizens, or against the citizens of another state as part of inter-state conflict. Definitions of state crime are varied. This is mainly because descriptions of state crime cannot rely upon strict legal definitions insofar as such definitions derive from the state itself. In other words, who does the defining and what is defined as a crime are intrinsically linked to issues of legitimacy and to the scope of analysis.

It has been suggested that there should be a deviance-based definition of state crime, one that involves some degree of subjectivity. Green and Ward (2000), for example, argue that state crime should be defined as 'state organisational deviance involving the violation of human rights'. To determine whether or not a state has committed a crime requires the involvement of citizens as witness (or audience) in cases of acts or omissions that violate human rights.

Alternatively, Kauzlarich et al. (2003) argue that a holistic account and definition of state crime would include the following key elements. State crime:

- generates harm to individuals, groups and property
- is a product of action or inaction on behalf of the state or state agencies

extent to which civil liberties such as freedom of political expression are supported.

Understanding the state requires understanding of its complexity. Any state (or perhaps more precisely, state system) is comprised of a multitude of different agencies and institutions, from elected members of parliament through to appointed civil servants, of military commanders to schoolroom teachers. Many diverse people perform myriad different functions, roles, and tasks under the broad umbrella of the state. A large part of investigation of state crime is spent on determining issues of public accountability (that is, who is responsible for which decisions), public interests (that is, what is legitimate or not legitimate action or non-action), and who benefits and who suffers from particular state interventions.

## DEFINING STATE CRIME

Broadly speaking, **state crime** refers to crimes involving the state acting against its own citizens, or against the citizens of another state as part of inter-state conflict. Definitions of state crime are varied. This is mainly because descriptions of state crime cannot rely upon strict legal definitions insofar as such definitions derive from the state itself. In other words, who does the defining and what is defined as a crime are intrinsically linked to issues of legitimacy and to the scope of analysis.

**Table 8.1** A complicity continuum of state crime

| Omission-Implicit | Omission-Explicit | Commission-Implicit | Commission-Explicit |
|---|---|---|---|
| • Inequality | • Bureaucratic failure | • Funding unethical experiments | • Genocide |
| • Extraction of surplus value | • Regulatory dysfunction | • Funding corporate destruction of cultures and communities | • Nuclear weapons threats |
| • Avoidable human suffering | • Archetype: Crash of Valujet 592 | | • War |
| • Archetype: Social stratification and inequality | | • Archetype: US human radiation experiments | • Imperialism |
| | | | • Archetype: The Holocaust |

Source: Kauzlarich et al. (2003).

gross violations of human rights. Each spiral makes reference to the dynamic ways in which norms about the institutionalisation of human rights are reinforced or abandoned, depending upon the particular political context. The virtuous spiral, for example, may involve a process whereby 'human rights violations are labelled as deviant by domestic and later by transnational civil society in a mutually reinforcing process and, as a result, human rights norms are gradually adopted as criteria of the state's legitimacy. Human rights violations become illegitimate, in the process, because they are successfully labelled as state crimes' (Ward and Green 2000: 86). Such an analytical approach provides insight into how and why particular nation states change their practices over time, either away from human rights violations or towards more intense ones.

## CRIMES BY THE STATE

A summary of the kinds of crime typically described as **crimes by the state** is presented in table 8.2 (for elaboration, see Rosoff et al. 1998). These crimes might be defined as harms that are deliberate and involve

**Table 8.2**  Crimes by the state

| Crime | Example | State Justification |
|---|---|---|
| Use of human guinea pigs | Sterilisation of developmentally disabled citizens<br><br>Military germ or radiation warfare tests | ▪ Such actions are wrong, but understandable in the pursuit of public policy. |
| Violation of sovereignty | Bribery of government officials to obtain business contracts overseas<br><br>Illegal participation in the overthrow of other sovereign regimes | ▪ Protection by the nation–state of particular sectoral interests requires the violation of human rights and citizenship entitlements. |
| Abuse of power | Internment of 'ethnic minority' citizens in times of war/terrorism<br><br>Dissemination of false or misleading information by state agencies | ▪ Some people may have to suffer in order that the majority enjoy the benefits of the whole. |

conscious intervention by the state to achieve certain military or national security ends, or national interests. In the course of ostensibly protecting or promoting the 'national interest', the state engages in conduct that violates human rights and the rights of other sovereign nations.

The use of human guinea pigs encompasses a number of dimensions. It generally refers to governments' gross invasion of personal bodily integrity. This may take the form of enforced sterilisation of developmentally disabled citizens, or it could involve the testing of new drugs on an unsuspecting population by government authorities. Alternatively, it could relate to the conscious withholding of treatment or drugs from certain population groups, in order to gauge the nature and effect of particular diseases, viruses, or illness.

A notable aspect of the use of human guinea pigs is that it usually applies to people who are socially vulnerable or who are located within a particular institution that demands obedience of a particular type. In the first instance, subjects might include infants, pregnant women, terminally ill patients, poor people, and people with disabilities. In the second case, the targets are usually soldiers, and prisoners. Issues of what kinds of injections and other treatments soldiers are ordered to receive (on pain of being returned home in disgrace) surfaced in both the recent Gulf wars involving Iraq. The American Civil Liberties Union estimates that approximately 10 per cent of the United States prison population participates in medical and drug experiments (see Rosoff et al. 1998). Given that over two million US residents are currently under some kind of custody order, this translates into a potentially huge number of people who could be affected.

Another form of crime by the state is the violation of sovereignty. This includes bribery on the part of governments seeking business contracts for overseas markets. More dramatically, violation of sovereignty can involve varying degrees of interference in the affairs of another country. For example, the United States government, often via the Central Intelligence Agency (the CIA), has a long history of participation in attempts to overthrow foreign governments (Rosoff et al. 1998). Conversely, some regimes are maintained in power due primarily, and sometimes solely, to the military assistance provided by other countries, such as the USA's support of the Shah of Iran in the 1970s. The net result is that the citizens of the other country are deprived of basic human and civil rights.

The abuse of power by states involves actions such as the forced internment of ethnic minority citizens in times of war or in times of widespread concern about threats such as terrorism. During World War II, for example, ethnic Japanese people were imprisoned in Canada and the United States, while in Australia the main targets were ethnic Italians. Such internments represent gross violations of human rights, and are based solely upon 'ethnic' characteristics rather than assessment of actual attitudes, experiences, contributions, and community relationships. Much the same still occurs today, particularly in relation to police and state authorities' treatment of people with 'Middle Eastern' appearance. Ethnic profiling refers to state intervention on the basis of presumed ethnic background. Such profiling is based upon stereotypes, such as the assumption that all Muslims act in a certain way, and are antagonistic to the West, and involve taking pre-emptive action such as controlling whole ethnic groups to stop possible future offending. It does not matter that no crime has been committed, or that the vast majority of citizens (regardless of specific ethnic background) uphold the country's laws.

Another key aspect of state abuse of power relates to the gathering and dissemination of information. It is well known that state security services such as the Australian Security Intelligence Organisation (ASIO) in Australia, or the Federal Bureau of Investigation (FBI) in the United States, have kept secret dossiers on citizens, and periodically used this (sometimes inaccurate) information to block job opportunities on the part of unsuspecting citizens. The main issues here relate to the kind of information that is collected, about whom, why, and to what purpose. From the point of view of natural justice, it is problematic that some people are targeted for surveillance and intervention when no crime has been committed. Political dissent is not the same as subversion. Such actions raise the critical question of who is to guard the guardians, to ensure that agency power is not abused for personal or political purposes?

The way information is fed to the public by state agencies and politicians has a major bearing on the ebbs and flows of the democratic process. The US, British, and Australian intelligence organisations and, more generally, national leaders, were criticised for 'sexing up' claims about weapons of mass destruction in the months prior to the invasion of Iraq in 2003. In Australia in 2001 persistent claims by government officials that asylum seekers threw their children overboard when approached by Australian naval personnel were used to vilify refugees, and provide a political platform for the government to win the next election. In both of these examples, information and images were manipulated to the advantage of sectoral interests within government.

These violations of human rights are justified by the state in a number of ways. One of the most common is that they are in the 'national interest' and that, while some people may have to suffer, the net result will be for the benefit of the majority. This type of ideological smokescreen is used frequently as a means to justify the unjustifiable—namely, the systemic and intensive violation of human rights and democratic processes. Those who expose such violations are often accused of being disloyal, treasonous, and ignorant of the 'real threat'. In such ways, a form of 'prescriptive patriotism' may be enforced as a means to stifle alternative viewpoints (O'Leary & Platt 2001).

## CRIMES WITHIN THE STATE

**Crimes within the state** refer to harms that result from the action or inaction on the part of state agencies or their officers acting in the course of their employment. Again, this type of crime has a number of different dimensions and aspects (see table 8.3).

Corruption and doing things to one's financial advantage are typical criminal activities associated with crimes within the state. A member of the Australian Senate who uses the work phone account or travel account solely for personal purposes, or for the use of family members, is misusing their public office. Similarly, a politician who hires their lover as part of their office staff without an open employment hiring process is hardly doing the right thing by the electorate. Jobs for family members and friends violate democratic procedures for allocating goods, services, and opportunities. Diversion of political donations into a politician's own pocket is another form of corruption. If funds are stored in brown paper bags in the politician's office, then it is unlikely they will be accounted for using conventional audit methods.

One of the most common forms of corruption is when state bureaucrats or political leaders direct government money to favoured contractors in return for a kickback of some kind. The reward may be financial or the gaining of influence or support of existing business and friendship networks. State personnel may gain a financial advantage by overlooking code violations in an industry in which they have an interest, such as

**Table 8.3**   Crimes within the state

| Crime | Example | State Justification |
|---|---|---|
| Corruption | Misuse of public office for private purposes<br><br>Illicit gain, usually through bribes, to promote certain outside agendas or direct government money to particular contractors | Breaches of civil, criminal, and administrative law are wrong, but the problem is not the system but rogue individuals and organisational malfunctions. They need to be responded to by the state apparatus because they represent an attack on the rule of law and the status of the state as ultimate moral exemplar. When the state breaks the law, the legitimacy of the whole legal order is threatened. |
| Financial Advantage | 'Jobs for the boys'<br><br>Ignoring code violations in building, forestry, and fishing industries | |
| Inadequate Regulation | Failing to regulate the safety of imported medical devices<br><br>Lack of response to environmental pollution and/or harms | |
| Covering Up | Perjury<br><br>Systematic denial of harms caused by state agencies | |

financial markets or direct ownership of businesses in the building, fishing, forestry, or real estate industries. The term **graft** refers to these instances in which state officials make deals with businesses in return for money or favours. Rosoff et al. (1998: 295) argue that 'graft has always been the "common cold" of American politics'. Much of this graft occurs at the local government level. To date, little research on graft has been done in Australia although there is no suggestion that the nation is immune from this illness.

The failure of governments to do their job adequately can also be seen as a form of crime that involves both omission as well as commission (see table 8.1). In *Wayward Governance: Illegality and its Control in the Public Sector*, Grabosky (1989) presents a series of case studies that outline ways in which government institutions in Australia have failed to provide adequate regulation of harmful products and activities, and thus failed a wide range of citizens. Governments have been criticised for allowing illegal telephone tapping, fostering the abuse of prisoners, falsely accusing families and whole communities of social security fraud, failing to take responsibility in cases of obvious water pollution, and purposefully allowing nuclear testing in the knowledge of the radiation hazard to local populations, especially Indigenous Australians. Grabosky (1989) writes about gross waste and inefficiency in the expenditure of public funds as an area requiring further regulation, and greater scrutiny of government action in cases such as dealing with environmental pollution or other kinds of environmental harm.

Another problem related to inadequate regulation is the covering up of abuses and crimes by government officials. If something is exposed as a problem or as wrong, it threatens government and state officials with a loss of power. The response, in some cases, is to engage in perjury— that is, to lie or pervert the course of justice, for example, by shredding records. Other responses are to deny any wrongdoing has occurred or to hide behind secrecy provisions. Serious harms were caused by the British government as a result of nuclear testing at Maralinga in South Australia (see case study 8.1). The nuclear fallout threatened the health of personnel at the site and damaged local Indigenous people, as well as their culture and environment. However, information about the tests was classified as top secret and it was decades before the full extent of the safety issues came to light and the inadequacy of information provision by the British to the Australian government was revealed (Grabosky 1989).

## CASE STUDY 8.1

At the edge of the Great Victoria Desert in South Australia a town sprang up, seemingly overnight. The British government gave it a name that meant 'Thunder Fields' in the language of its Indigenous owners, the Tjarutja people. It was called Maralinga.

The story behind Maralinga was the British government's determination to possess nuclear power. Against the backdrop of the cold war the British planned to create a massive arsenal of 1000 bombs, sufficient to 'knock out' the Soviet Union. Between 1955 and 1963 the British government, with the consent and active participation of the Australian government, exploded seven nuclear bombs at Maralinga and conducted 550 other experiments and trials. The result was the contamination of a site that stretched for thousands of kilometres and the exposure of an estimated 17,000 to 37,000 civilians and defence personnel to life threatening levels of radiation.

Maralinga had been chosen on the grounds that it was uninhabited and provided excellent security conditions. In reality it was criss-crossed with dreamtime tracks used by the Tjarutja people. The British and Australians attempted to forcibly remove them, but it is clear that they did travel through contaminated lands. But the harm extended beyond the Tjarutja and their lands. Thousands of British and Australian servicemen were exposed to radiation, some being required to strip and service radioactive aircraft without protective clothing, to walk through the radioactive bush only hours after an explosion, and to engage in experiments in which 'accidents' took place. Nor was the damage limited to Maralinga. In 1958 a cloud from the third major bomb drifted south, passing over the city of Adelaide. Far from declaring the incident a national disaster, the bodies of deceased Australians were secretly taken away for analysis.

The events at Maralinga violated numerous national and international codes, including the code of ethics drawn up at Nuremberg after World War II relating to health experimentation, and the memorandum of agreement on the Discontinuance of Nuclear Weapons signed in Geneva in 1958. Other offences included the non-reporting of dumping of radioactive waste into urban sewerage systems.

The land at Maralinga was forcibly taken from the Tjarutja people. Since then they have demanded its return—cleaned and safe—as well as compensation. Veterans of Maralinga have also demanded compensation for the wide range of radiation induced illnesses and health problems they and their offspring have suffered. Hundreds contracted radiation-linked terminal illnesses. While the British government has systematically denied responsibility, in recent years the Australian government has accepted responsibility for the clean-up of Maralinga and recommended that Maralinga veterans should lodge claims for compensation.

Source: Debelle (2003); Keane (2003).

## UNDERSTANDING STATE CRIME

Attempts to explain state crime range from explanations in terms of situational and organisational factors to arguments that it is caused by structural factors endemic to the political and economic system. The argument that state crime is caused by organisational factors assumes that the 'normal' state and legal system is morally exemplary, but from time to time state agencies and the individuals working within them become corrupt or act inappropriately due to pressures arising out of a particular set of circumstances. From this perspective, state crime is the result of organisational pathology that can be identified and corrected.

Grabosky (1989) identifies the following organisational weaknesses that lead to state crime:

- weak arrangements for external oversight
- powerlessness of prospective victims
- poor leadership by senior management
- inadequate direction by senior management
- inadequate supervision by middle management
- rapid organisational expansion
- strong goal orientation.

In this view, the reasons behind inadequate regulation or persistent abuse of people by state officials lie in weak institutions of external oversight. If prisoners, for example, are being abused, then we need to ask what the Police, or Ombudsman, or Prison Visitor, or Prison Inspector are doing to rectify the situation.

Issues of corruption, lack of regulation, and protecting one's back often reflect organisational features and the activities of particular individuals and groups within the state system. However, they fail to explain state-sanctioned activity that systematically violates the most fundamental human rights—including the right to life. In contrast, structural explanations argue that the state can, and often does, support fundamentally unjust, abusive, unequal, and immoral social relations and practices. From this perspective, 'normal' state activity can encompass active engagement in systematic social injury or harm. Such an argument rests on the assumption that the state is a site of political struggle and is dominated by powerful groups who will use it as a tool of oppression if they feel their interests are under threat.

## STATE-SPONSORED VIOLENCE

**State-sponsored violence** is a form of state crime that involves harms associated with gross violation of human rights and commission of serious criminal offences such as murder, rape, espionage, kidnapping, and

**Table 8.4**   State-sponsored violence

| Type of Violence | Example | State Justification |
|---|---|---|
| Genocide | 'Ethnic cleansing' such as the Holocaust<br><br>The 'stolen generation' | ▪ State action of this kind is wrong, but past atrocities cannot be dealt with by present governments. |
| Torture | Special procedures that allow illegal confinement<br><br>Special laws and conditions that sanction torture | ▪ Some actions can be justified by circumstantial necessities. |
| Massacres | The justification of the killing of citizens with the concept of 'collateral damage'<br><br>The killing of prisoners or other vulnerable enemies | ▪ War and the war on terrorism dictates that human rights may have to be diminished in some cases. |
| Targeted state killing and group sanctions | Assassination of foreign opponents or enemies<br><br>Forced migration of people into settlement areas or camps | |
| State-sponsored terrorism | Support for groups that undertake acts of violence against selected targets<br><br>Support of religious-based communal violence | |
| Responses to dissent | Arrest and imprisonment of protesters<br><br>Banning of public assemblies and distribution of literature | |

assault (see table 8.4). These forms of state crime involve crimes against humanity and the systematic deprivation of rights through use of repressive measures (see Friedrichs 1996).

What is remarkable about this kind of state crime is that it is so widespread and yet has received so little attention from criminologists until very recently (Cohen 1993). Yet, the harm created through state action of this nature can far exceed that generated by conventional crime. State sanctioned genocide provides one of the most vivid examples of this.

## Genocide

The UN Convention on the Punishment and Prevention of Genocide of 1948 defines genocide as a specific form of crime under international law that applies in both war and peace. The UN convention contains two key elements—the definitions of *protected groups* and *prohibited acts*. It stipulates that genocide means:

Any of the following acts committed with intent to destroy, in whole or in part, a national, ethnical, racial or religious group, as such:

(a) killing members of the group;

(b) causing serious bodily or mental harm to members of the group;

(c) deliberately inflicting on the group conditions of life calculated to bring about its physical destruction in whole or in part;

(d) imposing measures intended to prevent births within the group;

(e) forcibly transferring children of the group to another group.

What is important to recognise about genocide is that while it often involves extreme forms of violence, in some cases it may not. The forced removal of children may not involve extreme, overt violence, but is still genocide. In an extended discussion of genocide and the forced removal of Indigenous children from their families by colonialist governments, Cunneen (1999: 131) observes: 'In summary, genocide can occur without physical killing, it can occur with mixed motives (some of which may be perceived to be beneficial), and it can occur without the complete destruction of the group.'

What distinguishes genocide from other forms of group violence is not so much the degree of violence but the fact that the action is consciously designed to destroy another group. How this is to be achieved will vary, and can involve a range of different measures—from massacres through to the break up of families and communities.

Examples of genocide include the massacre of hundreds of thousands of Armenians by Turkey in 1915, the Holocaust against Jewish people in Europe perpetrated by the Nazi German state in the 1930s and 1940s, the episodes of 'ethnic cleansing' in Bosnia in the 1980s, and mass killings in Rwanda in the 1990s. Each of these instances of genocide involved conscious political choices and the engagement of state officials at some level of government. Contemporary analyses of genocide examine it as a form of social exclusion ultimately linked to the elimination of the threatening 'other' (see Jamieson 1999).

## Torture

Torture likewise is a state crime, if crime is understood in terms of a general world consensus against certain actions. According to the United Nations, the act of torture is an offence to human dignity and deserves to be condemned. In the Convention Against Torture and Other Cruel, Inhuman or Degrading Treatment or Punishment passed in 1984, torture is defined as:

> ...any act by which severe pain or suffering, whether physical or mental, is intentionally inflicted on a person for such purposes as obtaining from him (sic) or a third person information or a confession, punishing him for an act he or a third person has committed or is suspected of having committed, or intimidating or coercing him or a third person, or for any reason based on discrimination of any kind, when such pain or suffering is inflicted by or at the instigation of or with the consent or acquiescence of a public official or other person acting in an official capacity. It does not include pain or suffering arising only from, inherent in or incidental to, lawful sanctions.

Not every country signs these types of Conventions, but nevertheless they do point to a world standard that says 'torture is wrong'. Yet, there are a number of countries that use torture or have recently and routinely used torture, and which persist in such conduct. In some cases, the use of torture is explicitly legitimated in law, as in the case of Israel, which allows it under certain specified circumstances. Other countries have used torture covertly, including the British army against members of the IRA in Northern Ireland. In 2004 the United States army was also accused of using torture against insurgents in Iraq.

## Special procedures

The use of special holding tanks and special procedures in dealing with alleged war criminals, illegal immigrants, and terrorists opens the door to all kinds of human rights violations. Such is the case, for example, of the

American government's action in penning prisoners up at Guantanamo Bay in Cuba, an action that the US government deemed to be outside the jurisdiction of both domestic American law and the international community. The Australian government's immigration policy locks up asylum seekers in remote and poorly resourced detention camps and has been criticised as, in essence, constituting a form of torture for many detainees, especially children (see Weber 2002; Pickering & Lambert 2002).

## Massacres

Massacres occur both in peacetime and in war, and target a wide range of groups. The massacre of Indigenous peoples took place in select spots in Australia well into the twentieth century. In war the main targets can include soldiers as well as civilians. For instance, in the first Gulf War in the early 1990s retreating Iraqi conscripts were deliberately killed by the victorious United States army. The use of cluster bombs, the planting of mines, and the use of radioactive munitions in war have devastating and long-term consequences for combatants and non-combatants alike. The concept of 'collateral damage' reflects state acceptance that civilians will be killed in bombing raids and artillery barrages—no 'smart bomb' has yet been devised to kill only enemy soldiers. Liberation thus begets annihilation. In fact, reliance upon high technology, especially that which allows distance from the battlefront, opens the door for even greater killing of enemies and civilians.

It is not uncommon for whole groups or populations to pay for the actions of a dictator or other individuals who may pose a threat to citizens or businesses of another country. This can occur during wartime conflicts as indicated above. It can also occur when group sanctions are used as punishment for the actions of an individual. For example, bulldozing the house of a suicide bomber or razing a block of houses near a border crossing point penalises the innocent (who, in some cases, may not have even known about the activities of their housemate or family member). According to most legal conventions and criminal laws, only the guilty ought to be punished for a crime. When the state intervenes beyond this, critical questions can be asked concerning justice and human rights, quite apart from the distrust and resentment caused by group sanctions.

Another form of collective punishment is the forced migration of people into settlement camps and restricted areas. The emphasis here is on containment and denial of basic freedoms (of movement, of association, of speech, etc.). Such was the lot of many Indigenous communities in colonial Australia (Johnston 1991). It is a process that has its contemporary counterparts in the world today, as in the case of refugee camps.

## Assassination

Occasionally states do engage in more targeted and selective criminal acts. The use of assassination to kill particular enemies is regularly practiced against Palestinians by the Israeli government. Shortly after the events of 11 September 2001 there was talk in Washington about re-constituting a body within the US State Department that used to assassinate people in other countries (including numerous attempts to kill the President of Cuba, Fidel Castro). What was interesting about this discussion was that in talking about re-constituting the unit, government officials were actually admitting that there was an organisation within the US government that did illegally kill people.

## The death penalty

The death penalty is also a form of state killing. Many nations have abolished the death penalty over the last 50 years, but there are notable exceptions. Each year, the United States, Russia, and China collectively condemn thousands of people to die at the hands of the state each year. According to human rights organisations such as Amnesty International, this is a fundamental violation against humanity and cannot be justified on any grounds.

## State-sponsored terrorism

The issue of state-sponsored terrorism presents one of the greatest challenges to human rights today. **State-sponsored terrorism** refers to the support by states for groups that undertake acts of violence against its enemies. In some cases, the acts of violence are random in nature. The Taliban regime in Afghanistan hosted and supported terrorist organisations that embarked upon activities designed to kill and maim people in the most devastating and spectacular fashion.

But what do we mean by terrorist and terrorism, and how should these labels be applied? In what circumstances is the terrorist a 'freedom-fighter' and the 'freedom fighter' a terrorist? Most of the anti-colonial and liberation struggles of the twentieth century involved movements whose members were branded terrorists and lawbreakers, but who became legitimate political leaders after winning the struggle. Israeli leaders such as Golda Meir and Moshe Dayan engaged in terrorist acts in British-occupied Palestine. Nelson Mandela was accused of the same in apartheid South Africa. From this perspective it seems that 'their' terrorism is terrorism, but 'our' terrorism is not something to be worried about. In the 1980s the Sandinista government of Nicaragua took the United States to the World Court where it was found guilty of illegal acts of war involving the mining of Nicaraguan territorial waters, but the US refused to subject itself to this judgment (see also Dixon 1985).

State terrorism is not only about supporting groups that create terror, or engaging in actions that are lethal and illegal, in other countries. It also has an internal dimension, in the sense that some states may foster groups to enforce a particular type of order domestically, such as the notorious militias who terrorised opponents of Indonesian rule in East Timor prior to independence. Another example is the use of thuggery in Zimbabwe as a means to influence the electoral process in favour of the Mugabe regime. Or, in some states, major communal violence has occurred. In some instances, it is the *inaction* of the state that is the problem when it allows the 'right' ethnic or religious group to commit acts of violence. It is now known that in the months prior to the massacre of almost one million Tutsi people by the Hutu in Rwanda in 1994, both the United Nations and the French government were aware of what was taking place but did not intervene. Similarly, when East Timor was invaded by Indonesia in 1975 Western governments, including the USA and Australia, were aware that this violence was likely to occur but did nothing to prevent it.

## Oppression of dissenters

**State repression** refers to the coercive control of individuals and groups who criticise the government. There are many forms of state repression including:

- arrest and imprisonment
- banning of investigatory reporting

- banning of foreign critics
- the use of violence against demonstrators
- paramilitarisation of public order policing
- restrictive permit conditions
- withholding of permits to distribute political literature
- anti-terrorism laws that violate human rights and democratic principles.

The question of how states deal with dissent is increasingly central to the issue of state crime—its definition, and how best to respond to it.

## STATES IN DENIAL

One of the key problems in dealing with and discussing state crime is that it is not only governments and perpetrators who deny its existence, but citizens, too. Cohen (1993: 102) argues that: 'We have to remember (perhaps by inscribing this on our consciousness each morning) that state crimes are not just the unlicensed terror of totalitarian or fascist regimes, police states, dictatorships or military juntas.'

The point Cohen is making is that state crime is 'our' problem, too. Consider for a moment the issue of torture. The conflicts in the Middle East are well known worldwide. The terrorism experienced by the Israeli people at the hands of Palestinian suicide bombers parallels the terror of armed occupation experienced by the Palestinian people at the hands of the Israeli state. From an Israeli point of view, torture may in some circumstances be justified if it is related to the seeking of information about, for example, a potential bomb attack. However, the UN Convention against Torture makes it clear that human rights are not negotiable:

Article 2

1   Each State Party shall take effective legislative, administrative, judicial or other measures to prevent acts of torture in a territory under its jurisdiction.

2   No exceptional circumstances whatsoever, whether a state of war or a threat of war, internal political instability or any other public emergency, may be invoked as a justification of torture.

3   An order from a superior officer or a public authority may not be invoked as a justification of torture.

In an important and path-breaking book, *States of Denial: Knowing about Atrocities and Suffering*, Cohen (2001) provides a sustained analysis of how it is that, contrary to UN Conventions and everyday moral standards, governments deny their responsibility for acts such as genocide, torture, and massacres—and how so often ordinary people allow this denial to occur. Appeals to national loyalties, ethnic identifications, and simply following orders are only some of a wide range of explanations put forward to justify the unjustifiable.

Crelinsten (2003) has further developed the analytical framework developed by Cohen to analyse the phenomenon of torture. He argues that torture is made possible, despite almost universal condemnation in legal codes, by the construction of a closed world that permits the use of torture against specific members of society defined as enemies. In a complex analysis of the causes of torture, Crelinsten (2003: 296) explores the factors permitting torture by exploring domestic and international dimensions that impact upon perpetrators, victims, and bystanders. He argues that torture is explained by the construction of a reality whose central feature is the creation of a powerful and dangerous enemy that threatens the social fabric:

> Laws are directed against this enemy, labels to describe this enemy are promulgated and disseminated via the mass media, people are divided into us and them, for us or against us. To imbue this purported enemy with sufficient substance, to render the presumed threat credible, the police or the military target groups most likely to be perceived by the general population as enemies, such as ethnic or religious minorities or political dissidents. If such groups happen to include violent insurgents or separatists at their radical fringe, so much the better, since the threat will be more easily depicted as real.

For torture to happen, there needs to be some form of torture training. This usually includes 'techniques designed to supplant normal moral restraints about harming (innocent) others and to replace them with cognitive and ideological constructs that justify torture and victimisation and neutralise any factors that might lead to pangs of conscience or disobedience to authority' (Crelinsten 2003: 295). This type of analysis is also applied to how a torture-sustaining reality is maintained and institutionalised, how it can be dismantled or deconstructed, and how it can be prevented from forming in the first place.

## The role of criminology and criminologists

The analysis of the 'culture of denial' (Cohen 2001) is one of the important tasks for a criminology that wishes to unpack and expose the nature of state crime. Along the way there are bound to be uncomfortable moments. This is because criminologists themselves are implicated in this very culture. For example, consider the issue of genocide as this pertains to Indigenous people in Australia. In 1997, a major report on the forced separation of Aboriginal and Torres Strait Islander children from their families was released. The 'Bringing Them Home' report provided a powerful and damning indictment of the actions of the Australian state over a long period of time. In response, the government of the day refused to acknowledge the problem. As Cunneen (1999: 136) observed: 'In summary, the Australian Government has denied that genocide took place. Flowing from this is the denial of specific recommendations such as the need for an apology, the need for compensation, and the need for guarantees against repetition. In particular the requirement that action be taken against the contemporary removal of Indigenous children has been ignored.'

Cunneen's work on this issue is relevant on two counts. First, it represents a sustained attempt to bring the government to book for actions that historically, and today, it has responsibility for. It is an attempt to break through the culture of denial relating to the state, Indigenous people and genocide. Second, it also represents a sharp rebuff to criminology and the role of criminology in genocide. Cunneen (1999: 137) asks the question: 'What did criminology do while the genocide was taking place?'

> Was criminology as a discipline merely accidentally involved in genocide or were the discursive foundations of criminology part of the same knowledges which legitimised the removal of Indigenous children? To what extent was criminology actually complicit in providing a scientific foundation for taking Indigenous children from their families and institutionalising them, and to what extent does it continue to do so today? In other words, we need to consider whether criminology had and has a stake in genocide.

State crime rarely occurs in a social vacuum. A critical question for contemporary criminology is to what extent and in what ways it sustains this sort of crime, as well as how best it might contribute to addressing it.

## CONCLUSION

This chapter has provided an introduction and overview to various kinds of state crime. In particular, it has considered state crime in terms of crimes by the state, crimes within the state, and state-sponsored violence. In addition to exposing the variety of criminal activities perpetrated by states, the chapter has also raised the issue of denial. How states cover up illegal and criminal acts, how they deny wrongdoing, and how they absolve themselves of responsibility for harming others are important topics for research and further investigation. So, too, the 'culture of denial' pertaining to state crime and associated harms also has implications for the role and activities of criminology—as handmaiden of the state, or critic and agent of change.

## DISCUSSION QUESTIONS

1 Think of two state crimes that have involved acts of omission rather than commission.
2 What are the main weaknesses of the argument that state crime is due to organisational weakness?
3 What contribution can sociology make to our understanding of why recognition of the existence and extent of state crime has taken so long to be acknowledged?
4 Why does Cohen call his book *States of Denial*?
5 How relevant is the study of state crime to political actions undertaken by the contemporary Australian state?

## GLOSSARY OF TERMS

**crimes by the state**
    those harms that are deliberate and involve conscious intervention by the state to achieve certain military or national security ends, or national interests
**crimes within the state**
    those harms that result from the action or inaction on the part of state agencies or their officers acting in the course of their employment
**graft**
    those instances in which state officials make deals with businesses in return for money or favours

**legitimacy of the state**
the extent to which the actions of the state are perceived as within its political mandate and receive the approval of the citizenship

**the state**
the institution that (successfully) claims the monopoly of the legitimate use of physical force within a given territory (Gerth & Mills 1948: 78)

**state crime**
crimes involving the state acting against its citizens or against the citizens of another state as part of inter-state conflict

**state repression**
the coercive control of individuals and groups who criticise the government

**state-sponsored terrorism**
the support by states for groups that undertake acts of violence against its enemies

**state-sponsored violence**
those harms associated with the gross violation of human rights and commission of serious criminal offences such as murder, rape, espionage, kidnapping, and assault.

## FURTHER READING

Cohen, S. (2001) *States of Denial: Knowing About Atrocities and Suffering*, Polity, Cambridge.

Grabosky, P. (1989) *Wayward Governance: Illegality and its Control in the Public Sector*, Australian Institute of Criminology, Canberra.

Green, P. & Ward, T. (2000) 'State Crime, Human Rights, and the Limits of Criminology', *Social Justice*, 27(1): 101–15.

Kauzlarich, D., Mullins, C. & Matthews, R. (2003) 'A Complicity Continuum of State Crime', *Contemporary Justice Review*, 6(3): 241–54.

Rosoff, S., Pontell, H. & Tillman, R. (1998) *Profit Without Honor: White-Collar Crime and the Looting of America*, Prentice Hall, Upper Saddle River.

## WEBSITES

**http://212.153.43.18/icjwww/icj002.htm**
International Court of Justice—English-language web page of the court, including access publications and decisions made by the court.

**www.aic.gov.au**
Australian Institute of Criminology—Provides links to various publications from Australia's leading criminologists, including research, conference papers, publications and statistics, many of which are full text.

**www.corpwatch.org**

Corpwatch—Provides links to various reports and documents on corporate crime in the USA and overseas.

**www.un.org/english**

United Nations—Official web site of the United Nations with search facilities and access to reports on the activities of special investigations into state crime.

# PART 2

# Criminality and Social Division

# CHAPTER 9

# Class and Crime

## INTRODUCTION

At first glance, there would seem to be an obvious connection between crime and class. Official data on crime suggests that criminal behaviour is concentrated among the working class, and sections of Indigenous people, some of which can be seen as forming a racialised underclass. Implicit in this argument is the 'common sense' assumption that poverty causes crime. The involvement of working class and disadvantaged groups in crime is assumed to arise out of unmet needs that can only be met through illegal means. The suggestion is that the pressure on them to commit crimes must be greater than on more wealthy members of society. The link between involvement in crime and factors such as welfare dependence, unemployment, and low educational attainment also seems to fit well with a view that criminal involvement is a logical outcome of disadvantage (see White & Haines 2004).

Closer inspection of this assumed relationship between class, poverty, and crime reveals serious flaws. One of the most obvious weaknesses is the existence of white collar crime. If poverty causes crime, why is it that some of the most destructive crimes are perpetrated by middle class people with well-paid jobs and comfortable lifestyles? Simplistic notions of 'need' clearly do not apply. Why is it also that so many people who are unemployed or living in difficult circumstances are nonetheless law-abiding? The argument also assumes the accuracy of official data on crime that certainly does not reflect the real extent of crime.

The problematic nature of the link between poverty and crime can be easily demonstrated. If there is a straightforward link, then the crime rate should increase during periods of economic recession and decrease in periods of affluence. However, a study of crime in the USA in the 1960s found the opposite to be true (Wilson 1975). While economic factors are clearly implicated in involvement in crime they interact in complex ways with a wide range of variables. Instead of a simplistic and reductionist argument that 'poverty causes crime' what is required is a more nuanced understanding of the relationship between economic need and the multiplicity of factors implicated in patterns of crime.

## UNDERSTANDING CLASS

The concept of class is often used as a shorthand way of referring to the role of economic factors on the relationship between different social groups and patterns of crime. While its meaning varies according to different theories and empirical uses, it is most simply understood as referring to the economic position of different groups within a particular social formation. Its classic definition is a Marxist one and refers to the relationship of a group of people to the means of production—who owns and controls factories, banks, retail businesses, farms, and so on has major structural implications with regard to the allocation of communal resources and the exercise of social power. From this perspective, class is concerned with how a group of people earn their living, and implies an assumption that people who share a similar economic situation will have other characteristics in common, such as levels of education or political outlook.

**Class** is a useful way of understanding both the distribution of economic resources such as wealth, property, and income, and the relationships between different groups. Despite the economic, social, and cultural changes that have taken place in countries like Australia in the last fifty years, the idea that Australia is divided into an **'upper-class'**, **'middle-class'** and **'working-class'** still has relevance and captures the reality that very different levels of wealth and power continue to exist.

Suggesting that there is a link between crime and the working class is to imply that there is something about the economic position of this group that is associated with crime (much the same can be said about crimes of the powerful as well). For example, it suggests that changes in the labour market, especially in relationship to employment, are linked to patterns of crime. Since the state plays such a critical role in shaping the economy of a nation, its activities are also implicated. Government economic and social policies—especially in relation to the labour market, welfare, education, and taxation—are likely to have an impact on criminal activity. Understanding crime therefore requires an understanding of the role played by structural forces in the form of political and economic factors.

## Class patterns of criminality

Typical patterns of crime are linked with specific classes and particular motivational factors. Class situation is a prime influence in type of criminality. Certain behaviours emerge out of very specific class circumstances and are subject to particular limits and pressures associated with class location (see White & van der Velden 1995; Reiman 1998).

As a structural relation, class reflects the different positions and capacity of people to marshal economic and political resources as dictated by their relationship to the means of production (White & van der Velden 1995). In a society such as Australia, the ruling or dominant class is the capitalist class; that is, the owners of capitalist enterprises and those who manage the capital accumulation process on their behalf. It is the dominant class economically, but the smallest numerically. Not surprisingly, criminality in this instance aids the accumulation process from a business point of view or augments one's personal wealth.

Accumulative and augmentative forms of criminality are closely linked aspects of class position. Accumulative criminality refers to corporate or organisational crime—as a direct link and natural flow-on of the capital accumulation process (that is, profit enhancement and cost minimisation). Augmentative criminality refers to the closely connected but distinct personal wealth-enhancement component in the criminality process that flows from access to and advantage gained from the ownership and control of the capital accumulation process. In the case of owners of capital, the personal augmentation of wealth through criminality may be the basis for accumulating capital, or for hiding accumulated capital (and vice versa). In the case of managers of capital, accumulative criminality (as a necessary feature of corporate business success or to stave off failure) may be the basis for expanded personal wealth (for example, bonuses) or a calculated necessity in job retention.

The **middle class or petty bourgeoisie** (defined as including new middle layers of employment) is made up of small-scale owners of capital (for example, family farmers, small landlords, small-business owners), self-employed professionals (for example, doctors, lawyers), and middle management levels of capitalist enterprises and various apparatus of the state. The petty bourgeoisie forms an intermediate layer poised between the capitalist and the working class proper. It constitutes a relatively privileged class grouping compared with the working class, but does not hold decisive social or economic power. The petty bourgeoisie has an ambiguous character and location between capital and wage-labour. Criminality within this class grouping frequently consists of both accumulative and augmentative forms of criminality.

In the case of petty bourgeois criminality, however, while generally incorporating features indicative of capitalist criminality, their diversity of circumstances reflect that of their structural position in the class structure. As such, petty bourgeois criminality would in some sectors or circumstances shade to that resembling the subsistence-level criminality of the working class or underclass (that is, poor farmers, struggling small shopkeepers, and independent tradespeople) while others would be more indicative of the criminality of the capitalist sectors, albeit on a reduced scale (that is, doctors, lawyers, engineers, real estate agents, and small to medium businesses). With the latter, for example, one might think of fraud and over-servicing in relation to Medicare and the Pharmaceutical Benefits Scheme on the part of some doctors.

The working class (wage labour) is comprised of those who live by the sale of their labour power to those who own capital, including high and low waged, skilled and unskilled, full and part-time workers (this category also includes the majority of state workers). Some sections of the working class are, relatively speaking, affluent; other sections decidedly poor.

Unemployment, and the threat of unemployment, is one of the conditions of the working class, given the importance of the wage for economic survival and a general dependency on the capitalist to provide work in return for a wage or salary. The working class includes unemployed workers who constitute the 'reserve army of labour'. The theoretical core of the **'reserve army of labour'** is that it forms an available pool of surplus labour that capital can draw upon according to expansionary requirements. The effect of this pool upon the labour market is to lower the price of labour power, to enforce the political discipline of labour, and to cushion the effects of cyclical changes in the capitalist labour market.

The **'underclass'** (marginalised individuals) comprises those people who are non-working, and whose source of income lies effectively permanently outside the capital–wage labour relationship and whose economic conditions of life lie generally at or below relative subsistence. The 'underclass' or 'lumpenproletariat' is essentially a residual class, closely related to, but distinct from, the working class proper. The underclass is an ambiguous location insofar as it both emerges out of the residual effects of the working class condition (for example, unemployment), yet remains outside the basic capitalist labour market framework. The 'underclass' is more akin to 'surplus population' (see Spitzer 1975). Members of the underclass lie outside the boundaries of the labour market as permanently discarded, obsolete, or unusable labour power, or (as a consequence of not having any foreseeable labour power to commodify) because they have socially and culturally removed themselves from the parameters of capitalist production relations (White 1996). The extent to which the underclass is growing depends upon movements and transitions in the class structure involving the long-term unemployed, the 'never likely to be employed', and the part-time working poor.

In the case of working class and underclass criminality, the generating force for much of this crime is subsistence or to supplement one's income relative to subsistence levels. With regard to underclass criminality specifically, crime has more of a survival component and plays a greater part in basic economic subsistence. The extreme marginalisation and disconnection experienced by members of the underclass translates into a greater dependency upon alternative survival measures—and this often means a greater chance that this will include 'serious' crime linked to a 'criminal career' and the 'criminal economy'. Working class economic crime is more supplementary in character, and includes such things as stealing from job sites, avoiding tax through payment by cash-in-hand, and low-level social security fraud.

Within the context of institutional definitions of crime, there are substantively different patterns and experiences of criminality associated with different class circumstances (see table 9.1). Particular forms of criminality, however, may be class-specific (solely linked to one particular class), class-related (predominantly linked to one particular class), and cross-class (universal) in nature. Nevertheless, in general, there are major differences in the motivations behind working class criminality (for example, theft of money for purposes of immediate consumption) and capitalist criminality (for example, theft of money linked to start-up capital for investment). Moreover, the alienations experienced by members of the working class resurface in antisocial behaviour and crimes of violence that often reflect the economic and social tensions associated with class situation.

There is a close relationship between power, crime, and the criminal justice system. The amount of power possessed by an individual or group is closely related to how much wealth or prestige they have. Class position is therefore an indicator of power. Other factors such as gender and

**Table 9.1** Crime, class, and power

| CRIMES OF THE POWERFUL | |
| --- | --- |
| *Typical crimes* | *Examples* |
| Economic | Breaches of corporate law, environmental degradation, inadequate industrial health and safety provisions, pollution, violation of labour laws, fraud |
| State | Police brutality, government corruption, bribery, violation of civil rights, misuse of public funds |
| *Motivations* | *Examples* |
| Maximisation of profit | Structural imperative to minimise costs and maximise economic return in a competitive capitalist market environment |
| Augmentation of wealth | Attempts to bolster one's own personal position in the economic and social hierarchy |

| CRIMES OF THE LESS POWERFUL | |
| --- | --- |
| *Typical crimes* | *Examples* |
| Economic | Street crimes, workplace theft, low-level fraud, breach of welfare regulations, prostitution |
| Socio-cultural | Vandalism, assault, rape, murder, resistance via strikes and demonstrations, public order offences, workplace sabotage |
| *Motivations* | *Examples* |
| Subsistence | Gaining illegal income to meet basic income needs, attempting to supplement low wages and one's income relative to subsistence levels |
| Alienation | Separation of people from mainstream social institutions such as education and work, and structural and emotional sense of powerlessness |

Source: adapted from Cunneen & White (1995) and White & van der Velden (1995).

age are also implicated in the distribution of power. For example, a young, unemployed woman has far less power than a wealthy, middle-aged businessman. This impacts on the capacity of each person to deal with the criminal justice system. For example, if the young woman is accused of fraud she might be able to draw on her social networks for practical and moral support, but she would have limited financial and educational resources with which to respond. In contrast, if the wealthy businessman is accused of fraud he is likely to have strong informal networks to advise him and can also pay for expert advice and defence.

The vulnerability of different groups to criminalisation is therefore closely related to issues of class, power, and inequality. In the next section we explore in greater depth the classed nature of criminality by examining the specific ways in which disadvantaged class situations shape behaviour, including criminal activity.

## DISADVANTAGE AND CRIME

In a wage-based economy, subsistence is wrapped around having a paid job. If this is not available, then a number of social problems are bound to present themselves, including crime. For example, there is strong evidence that demonstrates a positive relationship between long-term unemployment and criminal activity (Chapman et al. 2002), and where communities are embroiled in high levels of unemployment, social disorganisation is likely to be highly prominent (Wilson 1996).

Hagan (1996) reviewed the literature on the relationship between class and crime in the USA. He found that class is linked to crime, but emphasised that the link was an indirect one and was mediated through other factors such as family relationships and community structures. In a similar vein, work by Weatherburn and Lind (2001) in Australia found that the crucial variable in explaining youth crime was parental neglect. However, this variable only had critical effect in the context of wider economic and social stresses at the neighbourhood level, such as unemployment. The role of parenting and delinquent peers are presented as intermediary factors in the relationship between economic stress and youthful criminality.

Hagan (1996) also inverts the relationship suggested by others that unemployment causes crime, arguing instead that involvement in crime can be a cause of unemployment. This is not necessarily an either/or proposition. For example, Braithwaite and Chappell (1994) point out that unemployment can indeed be linked causally to crime; but, simultaneously, for some people crime is the principal reason why they cannot get jobs. In other words, there is a dynamic and mutually impacting relationship between crime and unemployment.

In fact, the connection between disadvantage and crime has been the subject of considerable research. In exploring it, social researchers have stressed the need to distinguish between the range of factors that require investigation. In particular, it is necessary to consider the separate effects of:

- unemployment
- absolute poverty (that is, basic physical needs for survival, such as food, warmth, and shelter)
- relative poverty (that is, subjective feelings of being relatively worse off)
- inequality (that is, the distance between those at the top of the social hierarchy and those at the bottom)
- class position and movement within the class structure.

Although these factors are related to one another, they are different phenomena and require separate analysis.

Other points that should be acknowledged in the study of disadvantage and crime include the need to:

- be sensitive to the way terms such as unemployment, poverty and crime are socially constructed. These terms are not 'objective facts' but are concepts that require definition. For example, the meaning of 'unemployment' requires specification in terms of type and amount of labour, as well as the relevant period of time.
- distinguish between different types of crime, especially property crime, violent crime, and white collar crime. The effect of unemployment on property crime, for example, is different from its effect on violence.
- take into account the multidimensional nature of factors influencing patterns of crime, and their interrelationship with one another. For example, the effect of unemployment on a young, white girl will be different from its effect on a middle-aged NESB male; demographic changes, such as the distribution of age in the population, have a separate influence on patterns of crime and also interact with changing distributions of resources.

- acknowledge the complex relationship between patterns of crime and the political economy. For example, property crime tends to increase during periods of affluence because of the increase in the availability of consumer goods, which generates increased opportunities for crime. At the same time, a countervailing tendency may result from the state's introduction of tougher eligibility requirements for welfare.

## Unemployment and crime

Since the 1970s there has been considerable investigation of the relationship between unemployment and crime. Many of these studies are quantitative in nature and seek to examine the relationship between levels of unemployment and crime rates. The findings are not straightforward and often contradict one another, with some studies finding no relationship between crime and unemployment (Weatherburn et al. 2001; Field 1990; 1999), while others suggest there is a positive relationship.

However, an influential review of the research literature by Chiricos (1987) found that overall the evidence favoured the argument for a significant, positive relationship between unemployment and crime. Box's review of over sixty studies on the relationship between crime and economic recession concluded that there was sufficient evidence to assert that increases in inequality result in increases in traditional crime. He found the evidence on the relationship between unemployment and crime to be tenuous, but still argued that higher levels of unemployment probably led to increases in crime (1987: 96–7). Studies in the USA (Land et al. 1995) and Australia (Kapuscinski et al. 1998; Weatherburn 1992) also suggest there is a link.

One suggestion for explaining the contradictory findings is that they are due to methodological problems, such as the failure to distinguish between participation in crime and frequency of offending, and flawed indicators of unemployment (Weatherburn 1992; Chapman et al. 2002). Chapman et al. found that the period of unemployment is an important variable (2002). Long-term unemployment appears to increase the likelihood of involvement in crime because of its association with reduced labour market chances. The longer a person is unemployed the more difficulty they have in finding stable work. Consequently, illegal means of earning a livelihood become more attractive. This is exacerbated by their subjective sense of reduced opportunity in the formal economy. Poor expectations of finding legitimate work enhances willingness to turn to crime (Chapman et al. 2002). Conversely, involvement in education increases expectations of return to the labour force and therefore diminishes the relative attractiveness of criminal activity.

Box also identifies the role played by subjective feelings in the relationship between unemployment and crime. He observes that:

> Unemployment and income inequality only appear to lead to crime when they occur within a cultural context which infuses them with an acute sense of 'failure' and rejection and these in turn produce a sense of 'relative deprivation' or 'thwarted ambition'. Without these subjective states, the motivation towards crime would be absent (1987: 199).

Box's argument is supported by other work that suggests that young working class males are most vulnerable to these feelings of relative deprivation. Subcultural theorists such as Cohen (1955) and Cloward and Ohlin (1961), as well as radical criminologists such as Lea and Young (1984), have also used this concept to explain some of the motives behind engagement in crime. Lea and Young, for example, argue that if a group of individuals share a sense of relative deprivation, they will develop lifestyles that help them to deal with this problem. This may involve engagement in criminal behaviour, especially if they face restricted opportunities for legitimate employment.

## Inequality and crime

The argument that inequality causes crime is often expressed, but is difficult to prove empirically because both crime and inequality are very general concepts. Gaining insight into the relationship requires more specific identification of the factors involved. For example, the relationship is supported by research on homicide that consistently shows a link between higher rates of homicide and higher rates of economic inequality (Void et al. 2002; Kapuscinski et al. 1998). As well, it is hard not to locate the high levels of violence among some Indigenous communities within the context of their location as an underclass within Australian society—with little hope for the future and serious problems of ill health and social deprivation.

Yet lack of economic resources in itself is not a cause of crime. Many cultures, including pre-colonial Indigenous cultures, lacked economic resources yet had low rates of crime. For this reason, it is often argued that it is the sense of relative deprivation that is linked with crime rather than objective need. **Relative deprivation** is the idea that people's experience of need is relative to their perception of the lifestyles of other groups in society. This concept, rather than absolute poverty, is used to explain why crime rates tend to rise during periods of economic recession when only some areas of the economy are depressed, but may actually decline in periods of economic depression when the economy as a whole is in decline (Wilson & Lincoln 1992). In the specific case of Indigenous people, relative deprivation is only part of the story. The oppressions associated with colonialism, including the fragmenting of communities and entrenchment of racist practices and social images, do great damage to how people perceive themselves and the world around them.

The concept of relative deprivation is also used to explain crime among the middle and upper classes. Braithwaite is one of a number of researchers who argue that inequality leads to crime not only because of need but also because of greed (Braithwaite 1979, 1991; Box 1987). While need may contribute towards crime among underprivileged social groups, greed and the sense of relative deprivation is an important explanation of crimes of the wealthy. This argument implies that because the unequal distribution of resources is inherent to capitalist economies, crime is also inevitable. The materialism and consumerism that are central to the capitalist economy, together with the existence of high levels of inequality, combine to make such economies '**criminogenic**'.

In addition, some theorists argue that fear of crime is sometimes used by politicians as an instrument of social control, especially in times of economic recession. Box suggests that while these concerns are partly fuelled by public fears, they also result from anxiety that the most marginalised members of society will be a source of rebellion and political unrest. Rather than dealing with these concerns by pursuing full employment or increasing welfare benefits, governments tend to become more punitive in their dealings with these groups. Funding for crime control is increased, which, in turn, increases arrest and prosecution rates as well as the more punitive forms of punishment, such as imprisonment. This therefore creates the false impression that crime rates increase during economic recession. A similar argument was presented by Hall et al. in their classic study of violence in England in the 1970s (1978).

## YOUNG PEOPLE, UNEMPLOYMENT, AND CRIME

In his analysis of the link between unemployment and crime, Weatherburn (2002) suggests there are two major explanations for the engagement of young, unemployed people in crime. The first argument suggests that young unemployed people are bored because their lack of work and limited resources mean they have few legitimate activities available to them. This, together with other situational factors, creates opportunities for crime and increases the likelihood that they will engage in it. The second argument presented by Weatherburn is that it is the poverty associated with unemployment that leads to crime. Unable to meet either their basic or relative needs, they turn to crime.

These arguments are supported by a number of studies that also shed light on the social context in which the criminal activities of young people occur (see Cunneen & White 2002). Since the 1980s unemployment has become a serious problem for young people. In 1993 Australia had the fifth-highest youth unemployment rate among thirteen OECD countries, and ten years later still fares badly (Muir et al. 2003). This problem has arisen out of a major restructuring of the labour market, so that even during periods of prosperity and economic growth the labour market for young people has been depressed. In the 1950s and 1960s most early school leavers went into apprenticeships and on to a lifetime of labour. From the late 1970s the number of apprenticeships available to young people has been declining, leaving this group with poor employment prospects. There has also been a casualisation of the labour force so that permanent full-time jobs have declined in favour of casual, part-time work, often in the informal as well as formal economy (White & Wyn 2004). The entrance of women into the workforce has also impacted negatively on the availability of employment for early school leavers.

Changes in the labour market have been exacerbated by a shift in the provision of the government's welfare net that is designed to cushion the effects of unemployment and financial hardship. Between the 1950s and 1970s social policy in most developed countries favoured direct state involvement in the redistribution of economic resources. Welfare provision was one of the major mechanisms by which this was achieved. From the late 1970s this situation was reversed. Many services, such as employment services, have been privatised, welfare provision has been reduced, and services such as education and health increasingly operate on user-pays principles. The introduction of stringent eligibility requirements for welfare services also mean that those caught within the welfare net are subject to increasing levels of regulation and control (see Australian Council of Social Services 2001). The combined effect of these changes has been to subject young, disadvantaged people to a regime of regulation and control, and severely restricted resources.

These restrictions are compounded by the effects of living in a society in which identity formation among young people is closely tied to involvement in commercialised leisure activities. Young people are targeted by the media as a major site of consumption. There is intense pressure to have knowledge of, and participate in, the latest cultural scene. Style serves as a shorthand for identity. Going clubbing, buying the latest CDs, or wearing the coolest clothes are symbols that define membership of a social group. Image is everything and it costs money. The minimal resources available to young, unemployed people marginalises them from activities that form an essential part of growing up in a capitalist economy, leaving them with only a restricted space in which to express who they are. It is against this background that the involvement of some young people in crime must be placed.

## Young people, economic adversity, and violence

With the exception of homicide, most of the discussion on the relationship between disadvantage and crime relates to types of property crime. Polk (2000), however, argues that rising levels of unemployment, together with the winding back of the welfare state, are contributory factors in rising levels of violence among young males. Polk points out that levels of violence in Australia since 1995 have been trending upwards and that young, working class males are probably responsible for most of this rise. His hypothesis of 'youth abandonment' suggests that a combination of structural and cultural factors are implicated in this development.

The structural factors identified by Polk (2000) as impacting on young people include:

- the overall growth in inequality that has occurred since the late 1970s
- the declining labour market prospects of young, working class males, including the growth in unemployment and the corresponding growth in precarious, casualised part-time work
- the decline in welfare provision.

These combine to create a winners–losers culture in Australian society, with losers caught in a 'dreadful development trap'. Young people who choose to leave school early find the traditional path to adulthood through full-time employment blocked. Without a wage and with minimal government support they face a bleak future. Their ability to form stable relationships is diminished as a result of poverty and often they are forced to live with their parents well beyond the age when they would expect to start their own family. Polk writes:

> Such individuals become stuck in a social and economic no-man's land where a central feature of their existence is that normal supports for identity as a 'man' or 'woman' are not available. This developmental trap then, forces such young people to engage in complicated and innovative ways to struggle with their central identities as males or females (Polk 2000: 97).

This impacts particularly on young males for whom the breadwinner role continues to be central to their sense of masculinity. Bereft of this role, Polk argues that engagement in violence presents an alternative means for the negotiation of masculine identity. It costs nothing, is immediately available, and offers a means for the establishment of prestige among peers. In this sense, it is one pathway for marginalised young men to become a 'winner'. Such a route to manhood is only possible in a culture that is ambiguous about the use of violence, exonerating it in some contexts while condemning it in others. This explains why the violence takes place in particular social contexts such as pubs, and public spaces such as parks and shopping malls.

## CLASS AND BEYOND

### Gender, inequality, and crime

One of the problems with the 'inequality causes crime' thesis is that it all too often ignores gender. Since all people are affected by inequality, why is it that males rather than females are predominantly offenders? Arguments that women are protected from involvement in crime because of their dependence on a male breadwinner cannot be supported in an era in which most women work and increasing numbers of women are single. Nor has this argument ever been true for black women in the

USA, most of whom have never been able to rely on a man's income. While women who become offenders are most likely to be drawn from disadvantaged sections of the social hierarchy, this does not explain why so few turn to crime.

Arguments that suggest a link between violence and disadvantage are also challenged when gender is brought into the picture. Although crimes such as assault and homicide are more prevalent among the working class, domestic violence occurs across all social classes, including the wealthy. Violence in the home cannot, therefore, be reduced to problems associated with poverty and inequality. In other words, while there is a close association between different forms of criminality and class situation, not all crime can be attributed simply or solely to class factors. Having said this, the prevalence of economic and social tensions among members of the working class and underclass increases the likelihood of family violence relative to other class situations. Moreover, even when violence occurs 'in the best of families', there is greater capacity among the rich to evade detection and prosecution due to their financial resources and social connections.

Nevertheless these examples highlight the role played by gender in any analysis of crime. Polk's (2000) explanation of violence among young, unemployed men explores the interplay between cultural forces around working class conceptions of masculinity and economic factors influencing involvement in crime. Similarly, Carlen's study of women, crime, and poverty (1988) argues that although the women she interviewed identified poverty as the primary motive for their criminal activity, this needed to be located within the wider range of social forces affecting their lives. Their poverty was an outcome of the combined effects of gender and class that shaped the opportunities available to them. Again the issue is not so much class *or* gender, as one of class *and* gender (and, we might add, ethnicity and 'race').

## Regional inequality

According to various social indicators, people living in rural areas tend be less well off than their urban counterparts. People living in rural areas tend to have lower levels of household income and higher levels of unemployment (White & Wyn 2004). Population loss and economic shifts in the rural sector, resulting in a declining level of employment, have affected the structure of many rural communities. At the same time, rural education and other services are increasingly unable to provide the necessary ingredients to service all rural populations. Governments have felt compelled to reduce public spending, the consequence of which is the withdrawal of health, social welfare, and educational services to rural communities across Australia.

The main economic activity of Australia has shifted to the cities, as have employment opportunities. This is where essential services, such as hospitals, are concentrated as well. Meanwhile, the application of new technologies and greater concentration of production in the hands of large corporate giants have been associated with an overall decline in the number of rural workers across diverse industries (such as farming and forestry) and the demise of rural community (Lawrence et al. 1992; 1996). As a direct consequence, many rural and some regional areas of Australia are going through dramatic economic and social changes. Not all communities are being affected the same way by these changes, and there is considerable diversity among Australia's rural, regional, and remote populations. Nevertheless, the issue of regional inequality clearly deserves greater attention than hitherto has been the case within criminology.

Consistent with the theme of this chapter, analysis of regional issues must take into account the immediate and longer-term political economic context. Basically, class counts, whether it be in the country or in the city. But how it counts varies depending upon the population group and the issue in question. For example, we might consider the nature of youth offending in a rural context, and in particular how young people's social standing in a local community, and the community's perception of the crime problem, impact upon the criminalisation process (Mounsey 1997). A Victorian study found that specific families and neighbourhoods were subject to constant stigmatisation. Families of low socio-economic status were highly susceptible to social exclusion and isolation, with major consequences for the young people if offending did occur. Thus, 'if such young people did offend, not only was the community's response extremely punitive, but the expectation was transformed into a reputation which served to reinforce their own social exclusion and isolation within that community' (Mounsey 1997: 31). The social and economic marginalisation of young people by way of labelling, stigmatisation, and refusal of employment was a contributing factor in their offending behaviour. Simultaneously, some communities, especially the smaller ones, reinforced this marginalisation once the young person had committed an offence.

Social and economic factors also play a major role in shaping the perceptions and experiences of family violence in rural areas (see case study 9.1). For instance, recent research points to chronic levels of violence within some Aboriginal communities, at least some of which can be explained in terms of rural economic decline (Hogg & Carrington 2003). Such violence is also linked to the continuing legacy and present practices of colonial rule that disempower and diminish, thus contributing to alienated existence. Less visible, but certainly a major and growing problem, is the 'hidden' violence among white rural residents and families (Hogg & Carrington 2003). In this case, violence can be at least partly attributed to specific cultural and institutional factors linked to patriarchy, as well as pressures relating to the economic environment.

## CASE STUDY 9.1

A Wyong Council report released in 2003 revealed that the New South Wales shire has the second-highest level of child abuse in New South Wales and the highest for the number of children put into care after the reporting of the incident. Levels of domestic violence are also among the worst in New South Wales, with Wyong police attending more than 1300 calls to domestic violence incidents per year. The number of requests for apprehended violence orders is the third highest in New South Wales.

The report describes a bleak cycle of rising levels of unemployment, welfare dependency, and weak infrastructure, such as poor social services and few transport facilities. Families wait up to ten years for public housing, while 48 per cent of teenagers are early school leavers, compared with the state average of 36.5 per cent. According to the 2001 census a fifth of Wyong's 15 to 19 year olds cannot find a job.

The report blames the failure of government-funded services and job opportunities to keep up with the community's needs: 'Much of the shire's growth and development has occurred at the expense of the social fabric and social infrastructure, including jobs, education, family support and public transport'.

The report explained that the population expansion experienced by the region included many young families from Western Sydney who had come to the region, leaving their support networks behind in Sydney. According to the president of the Toukley St Vincent de Paul Society, the number of families the branch had helped had increased by 25 per cent since the previous year.

The report stressed that the key to overcoming the problems was the provision of additional government funding.

Source: Kelly (2003).

From the point of view of class and criminality, the question of geography and regional inequality also brings with it consideration of new types of crime and social harm. For example, the quality of plant and animal products may be influenced by things such as the (illegal) use of pesticides and herbicides; the proliferation of Genetically Modified Organisms (GMOs), whether intended or unintended; pollution of waterways and landmasses; and diseases directly stemming from mass production processes (for example, feeding practices and mad cow disease). What is produced and how it is produced reflects the pressures and demands of those who stand at the commanding heights of the economy—in the case of rural Australia this very often means the big agribusiness companies, forestry transnationals, and mining groups. Those living in disadvantaged regions can ill afford not to do what the bosses demand of them.

## CONCLUSION

An analysis of the relationship between class and crime is concerned with unravelling the links between economic factors—such as class position, wealth, or unemployment—and engagement in crime. This chapter has highlighted the complexity of the relationship, pointing out the need to acknowledge the multidimensional connections between class and crime.

In the past the link between class and crime was understood to be relatively straightforward. Crime was a working class phenomenon and its roots lay either in the character of the working class or in the social deprivations associated with their position. Today there is an understanding that crime occurs in all social classes, and also that there are important differences in the types of crimes engaged in by the different socio-economic groups, as well as different motivations. For wealthy people the motives for engagement in property crime relate to greed (the desire to accumulate more and to augment their wealth), while for the poor they relate to survival. Yet this is still a gross oversimplification. Notions such as risk, relative deprivation, and gender also need to be taken into account.

When it comes to violent crime the picture is different again. Domestic violence occurs across all social classes, but is also exacerbated by factors relating to economic scarcity and marginalisation. The intersection of class and culture is also important; for example, Polk suggests that violent crime is linked to particular types of class-related masculinities (Polk 2000).

Understanding the relationship between class and crime therefore requires understanding of the role of numerous intermediary factors, such as where you live, cultural values, social policy, and levels of affluence within the community. These forces impact differently on different social groups. The socio-economic context is also profoundly influential on both the crimes of the rich and the crimes of the poor. As an economic system, capitalism creates structural inequalities that are undeniably linked to both property and violent crime, even though the precise nature of those links has still to be unravelled. Cultural values linked to capitalism—such as materialism and 'looking after number one', as well as the acceptance of some forms of violence—are also important. Understanding the interplay of these forces is especially important in a climate of growing inequality. The last thirty years have seen increasing polarisation between the rich and the poor. Rising housing costs, increased barriers to higher education, cuts to welfare, and the casualisation of labour create a climate in which there is a real possibility that those at the bottom of the ladder will become a permanent underclass. The likelihood that the poor will be stigmatised as the cause of the crime 'problem' is reduced by an understanding of the complexity of forces linking class and crime.

## DISCUSSION QUESTIONS

1 Identify three ways in which class and crime are linked.
2 What role does the experience of 'relative deprivation' play in the incidence of crime?
3 What are some of the pressures on young people that might be associated with involvement in crime?

4 Why can violence in the home not be reduced to problems associated with poverty and inequality?

5 Identify some of the ways in which geographical region, inequality, and crime intersect.

## GLOSSARY OF TERMS

**class**
> the distribution of economic resources, such as wealth, property, and income, and the relationships between different groups within social formations

**criminogenic**
> refers to the idea that some processes and institutions within social formations encourage or endorse criminal behaviour, including the criminal justice system itself

**middle class or petty bourgeoisie**
> the individuals and groups who lie between the working and upper classes; they are small-scale owners of capital (for example family farmers, small landlords, small business people) or self-employed professionals such as doctors and middle managers of capitalist enterprises

**relative deprivation**
> the idea that people's sense of deprivation is determined subjectively in terms of whether they see themselves as unfairly disadvantaged over others whom they believe have similar attributes, or deserve similar rewards, as themselves

**reserve army of labour**
> an available pool of surplus labour that capital can draw upon according to expansionary requirements

**underclass**
> those people who are not working and whose source of income lies permanently outside the capital–wage relationship and whose economic conditions of life are normally at or below relative subsistence

**upper class**
> those individuals and groups who own or control the means of production

**working class**
> those individuals and groups who live by the sale of their labour power to those who own capital; they include high and low-waged, skilled and unskilled, and full-time and part-time workers.

## FURTHER READING

Box, S. (1987) *Recession, Crime and Punishment*, Macmillan, London.

Reiman, J. (1998) *The Rich Get Richer and the Poor Get Prison*, Allyn & Bacon, Boston.

Spitzer, S. (1975) 'Toward a Marxian Theory of Deviance', *Social Problems*, 22: 638–51.

Weatherburn, D. (2002) 'The Impact of Unemployment on Crime', in P. Saunders & R. Taylor, *The Price of Prosperity: The Economic and Social Costs of Unemployment*, UNSW Press, Sydney: 226–48.

White, R. & van der Velden, J. (1995) 'Class and Criminality', *Social Justice*, 22(1): 51–74.

## WEBSITES

**www.aic.gov.au**

Australian Institute of Criminology—Provides links to various publications, including research, conference papers, publications, and statistics, many of which are full text.

**www.ncjrs.org**

National Criminal Justice Reference Service (NCJRS)—The Clearinghouse for the US National Institute of Justice, it contains summaries and full-text publications on the criminal justice system. The site includes research on federal, state, and local government reports, books, research reports, journal articles, and unpublished research. Subject areas include corrections, drugs and crime, law enforcement, juvenile justice, statistics, and victims of crime.

**www.uncjin.org**

United Nations Crime and Justice Information Network—An organisation of the United Nations researching crime and prevention strategies. The website provides access to investigations and reports in a number of criminal justice areas.

# CHAPTER 10

# Women and Crime

## INTRODUCTION

Issues relating to gender are integral to both why and how crime occurs. Whereas in the past the masculine nature of crime was taken for granted, feminist scholarship has thrown this issue into relief. Why is it that every aspect of crime—who commits it, who polices it, who judges it, who punishes it, who studies it—is dominated by men? Why is over 90 per cent of the prison population male? What does this tell us about how masculinity is constructed in Australia and other Western countries? Why are women who break the law often treated as if they are sick and in need of therapy while men are seen as bad and in need of punishment and control? Why are working class young men responsible for far more car theft than working class young women, when both need transport equally? Why do African-American women form gangs while white women rarely do?

To answer these questions it is necessary to understand the ways in which the social construction of gender shapes both the incidence of law breaking and the response of the criminal justice system to this. Discourses of masculinity and femininity, relationships between and within genders, and the intersection of gender with class and ethnicity are just some of the ways gender shapes patterns of crime.

Until the 1970s the way gender patterned crime was taken for granted. Men's involvement in crime and women's exclusion from it was more or less accepted without question. In the last thirty years feminist research on women and crime has rendered problematic the normality of male crime. By challenging positivist criminology's acceptance of crime as straightforward and unproblematic, feminists have opened up a rich seam of knowledge (see White & Haines 2004). Today, the issue of gender is a central theme in the study of crime.

Feminist contributions to the study of crime include:

- the development of feminist theories of crime that place issues of gender at the centre of the analysis and offer non-sexist explanations of women's involvement in crime
- removal of the silence around crimes against women such as domestic violence, sexual assault, and homicide
- demands for law reform in areas such as prostitution, women's imprisonment, rape, and domestic violence
- analyses of how gender shapes women's involvement in specific types of crime, such as prostitution and gangs
- analysis of the treatment of women by the criminal justice system, including recognition of the essentialist and stereotyped notions of the 'good', virtuous woman that have shaped the criminal justice system's treatment of female offenders and victims
- analysis of the link between poverty, ethnicity, and women's involvement in crime.

By the 1980s, feminist insights into the role of gender in shaping women's relationship with the criminal justice system led to studies that explored men as gendered subjects. Since then the concept of masculinity has emerged as a key concept in explaining men's involvement in crime (see Messerschmidt 1986, 1997; Polk 1994).

## WOMEN AND CRIME

Until feminist criminologists such as Carol Smart (1976) and Frances Heidensohn (1968) began to write about women and crime, female offenders were almost ignored by criminological theory and research. Rafter and Heidensohn (1995: 5) observe that late twentieth century mainstream criminology 'was the most masculine of all the social sciences, a speciality that wore six-shooters on its hips and strutted its machismo'. Because women did not appear to be responsible for much crime it was assumed they were not worthy of study. Attempts to explain crime took males as the universal figure of human behaviour and ignored the reality that the issues behind male and female patterns of crime are quite different.

On the rare occasions when female criminality was studied, essentialist, male stereotypes about them prevailed. Women were assumed to be 'naturally' passive and non-criminal, while men were 'naturally' aggressive and active. Male engagement in crime was understood as a logical extension of their normal behaviour. From this perspective, when women broke the law, they also broke cultural norms and expectations about what it is to be a woman. Their crimes were portrayed as an aberration best explained as the result of inadequate socialisation and maladjustment. One of the few early studies on female crime, by W.I. Thomas, was tellingly called *The Unadjusted Girl* (1923). While the sexist views expressed by writers such as Thomas can be explained as a reflection of the period in which they lived, similar views were also apparent in the 1960s (Pollack 1961). Meanwhile, even in the 1970s, it is notable that there was a complete absence of women from the work of radical criminologists such as Taylor et al. (1973).

One of the first issues feminist criminologists explored concerned the accuracy of data on patterns of female crime. Both official and unofficial crime data suggest that in every category of serious crime women are under-represented and commit fewer crimes than men (see also figure 10.1). In 2001 just over one in five offenders was female (AIC 2002a: 40).

- Men are responsible for the majority of each of the seven major serious crimes recorded by the police (see figure 10.1). For serious crimes, female participation in the offender population is highest for other theft and lowest for sexual assault.

**Figure 10.1** Female offenders as a percentage of total offenders by offence type 2000–01

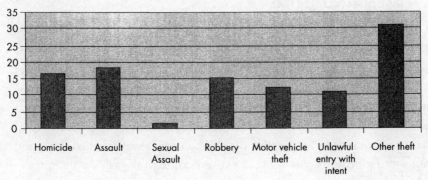

Source: AIC (2003: 40).

- When women do commit crimes they are primarily property offences such as larceny (including shoplifting), fraud and misappropriation, offences against justice procedures, and possession and the use of opiates and other drug offences (Trimboli 1995). The value of the goods involved is usually relatively small.

- The main offences for which female offenders are imprisoned include drug offences and robbery; for men the main offences are break and enter, robbery, and sex offences (AIC 2002a: 62).

- Whereas violent offences such as homicide, assault, and sex offences account for almost 50 per cent of the offences for which men were imprisoned in 2001, only one-third of women in prison were there as a result of violent offences (AIC 2002a: 62).

- Women are not only less likely to offend, they are also less likely to re-offend. Studies by Broadhurst and Maller (1990, 1991) of the length of time before re-incarceration occurred found that the median time for non-Aboriginal women was 23.4 months, compared with 17.6 months for non-Aboriginal men.

- The long-term pattern of female imprisonment is different from that of men. At times the male rate of incarceration has fallen while that of females has risen (Ross & Forster 2000).

The few areas where women's crime does exceed that of men's are shoplifting, prostitution, and 'promiscuity'. Among juveniles, girls are much more likely to be the subject of care and protection orders than boys (Alder 1997).

This data suggests that where women do predominate as offenders it is in areas that relate to their female gender role. They relate to their sexuality (prostitution, promiscuity), to their domestic role (shoplifting and social security offences), and to their roles as child-rearers (crimes against children and infants, and illegal abortion). In regard to status offences (offences based upon age prohibitions for certain types of behaviour), young women predominate in areas such as promiscuity, ungovernability, and running away from home.

The profile of female offenders is also quite different from men. For example, female homicide offenders are usually older than male offenders, and are twice as likely as male offenders to be divorced or separated at the time of the incident (16 per cent versus 8 per cent). They are also twice as likely to be outside of the labour force (25 per cent versus 11 per cent; Mouzos 2002: 15–16).

## Interpreting the statistics

One of the main questions raised by both feminist and other criminologists is whether official statistics on the pattern of female crime are accurate. Do women really commit fewer crimes than men, or are they more successful at evading detection and arrest?

In *The Criminality of Women*, Otto Pollack (1961) argues that criminal statistics disguise the true extent of female crime. The real rate of female crime is hidden by a number of factors:

- Women possess a 'natural cunning and deceitfulness' that gives them the capacity to disguise their crimes. This derives from their passive role in sexual intercourse, and their ability to fake orgasm—something a man cannot do.
- It is easy for women to disguise their crimes because most take place in the privacy of the home or other domestic settings. Women's criminal acts are therefore less visible than traditional male crimes, such as burglary, and consequently they are less easily exposed. Their victims are likely to be vulnerable social groups such as children and the elderly who are unable to draw attention to their victimisation.
- Women often do not actually commit the crime, but instead inspire a man to do the deed. They instigate but do not actually perpetrate the criminal act.
- When women do come to the attention of law enforcement agencies they are treated more leniently than men. Pollack's 'chivalry thesis' suggests that male law enforcers are reluctant to charge women who violate the law, and even more reluctant to imprison them. This is because of assumptions that women are not 'really' criminal, because women are assumed to be unable to cope with the stress of social retribution, and because as nurturers the incarceration of women would mean innocent children would suffer.

Although treated seriously at the time, today it is obvious that Pollack's arguments are based on sexist assumptions about the essential characteristics of women. They also lack empirical support. Statistical analyses of the relationship between gender and sentence have found that differences in sentencing are attributable to factors such as type of offence, prior convictions, and other legally relevant variables (Grabosky & Rizzo 1983; Douglas 1987).

Present-day scholars agree that women do commit fewer crimes than men. This does not mean that female involvement in crime is static. For example, in New South Wales the number of women found guilty in the Local Courts increased by 23.5 per cent in the five-year period between 1994 and 1998 (Fitzgerald 1999). Offences against the person by female offenders more than doubled in this period (up 51.4 per cent), as did offences against justice procedures (up 61.3 per cent). The number of women appearing for driving offences also increased significantly (up 30.8 per cent). In the Higher Courts the number of women convicted of robbery has increased from 25 individuals in 1994 to 45 in 1998.

To date there has been little attempt to explain these increases. The work that has been done suggests they are due to social and economic changes affecting women. The rise in theft may relate to the increased opportunities offered by self-service and credit purchase. The growth in the number of women living below the poverty line that has taken place in the last two decades probably partly explains the increase in offences against justice procedures, as women experience difficulties in meeting deadlines for the payment of fines (Fitzgerald 1999). The rise in poverty may also explain increases in property offences, such as larceny, as well as assaults and robberies. The rise in the number of women using illegal substances is also significant. According to household surveys, the percentage of women reporting using heroin in the past 12 months increased from 0.2 per cent in 1994 to 0.5 per cent in 1998. In 1998 there were 39,100 recent female users (AIHW 1999). The link between robbery and hard drugs, such as heroin, is well established.

Pollack (1961) has argued that one of the reasons for the low female crime rate is that women who are caught breaking the law are less likely to be charged or sentenced to prison, because of a **'chivalry factor'**. He suggests that traditional male attitudes to women as weak and in need of protection, together with their role as child-rearers, makes male law enforcers reluctant to apply the full weight of the law. A number of studies have been undertaken to discover whether such a factor exists. While there is some evidence that it does exist, it appears to apply in only a minority of cases and especially to white, middle class women. In most cases the reverse is true, especially for disadvantaged women and women of colour. Here the studies confirm the feminist hypothesis that women who fail to conform to social conventions and are different from the white norm, who behave 'badly', and demonstrate 'male' behaviour such as hanging around in the street, getting into fights, and engaging in criminal behaviour, often receive harsher treatment than males.

## UNDERSTANDING FEMALE CRIME

Until feminists began to write about women and crime, the limited work that had been done on the relationship between gender and crime focused on explaining why women were not as criminal as men. Initially, feminist work on women's involvement in crime presented a critique of these approaches, both conservative and radical (see Smart 1976; Naffine 1987).

A second wave of feminist criminology explored how and why women become involved in crime. This led to new knowledge about the role of gender in shaping social interactions with the law. These included the insight that the motives for women's involvement in crime are different from those of men. In the case of homicide, for instance, while men commit crimes for reasons directly associated with the criminal act, such as thrill seeking, or defence of honour (Polk 1994), women are more likely to engage in crime as a strategy for survival following family violence or sexual abuse. Although there is evidence that a percentage of both men and women offenders have experienced abuse of some kind, the figures are higher for women (Finkelhor & Baron 1986: 45; Campbell 1993; Chesney-Lind 1997).

Studies of girls on the streets, in court, and in prison consistently show high rates of physical and sexual abuse. In the USA, Silbert and Pines (1981: 409) found that 60 per cent of the prostitutes in their sample had been sexually abused as juveniles. Chesney-Lind and Rodriguez (1983) found that virtually all their sample of female prisoners had experienced physical and/or sexual abuse when young.

Chesney-Lind (1989) argues that many of the young women in the criminal justice system are there as a result of the criminalisation of survival strategies. Faced with unacceptable situations in the home, they run away and engage in petty crimes such as prostitution, social security fraud, and larceny in order to survive. In these stressful circumstances many also turn to drugs. It is against this background that many come to the attention of the police and appear before the courts and face imprisonment.

In the case of young girls, the line between welfare and justice can often be blurred. Young girls in the care of the state are much more likely to enter the juvenile justice system than the rest of the female juvenile population. The Australian Law Reform Commission also noted that 'children who have been made wards of state in New South Wales are fifteen times more likely to enter a juvenile justice centre than the rest of the juvenile population' (cited in Alder 1997). Girls in welfare placements or foster care are particularly vulnerable to being charged with criminal offences and being characterised as a 'serious offender' in situations where they may be acting out as a result of their difficult situation (Alder 1997).

Alder (1997) makes the point that dominant discourses of girls' sexuality have been constructed in negative terms as an area of danger and victimisation. Girls are seen as in need of protection, not only from those who would abuse them but also from their own desires. This has been the basis of a policy of control and containment that has stifled their independence and prevented them from developing their own sense of agency.

A further criticism of the treatment of women made by feminists and other writers (Fine 1992; Baines 1997; Carrington 1993) is the tendency to pathologise girls' behaviour; for example, by explaining girls' 'problems' as the result of sexual abuse. Constituting girls as victims in this way limits understanding of their behaviour to a narrow discourse as passive recipients of social arrangements. This is both morally and philosophically problematic. It not only exonerates them from responsibility for their actions but also denies them any sense of agency. Alder argues that instead of being treated as problematic, 'girls' wilfulness, their efforts to seek independence and safety, need to be considered in the context of their lives, and their strengths understood as a resource to be built upon' (1997: 8).

Alder (1997) is suggesting that the explanations for girls' law-breaking behaviour should not always be understood in negative terms but can be seen as a positive attempt to take control of their lives, to have fun, and to rebel against the confines of girlhood.

This understanding of girls as actively constructing their sense of identity, while situated within the constraints of particular social arrangements, has been developed by Messerschmidt (1995) in his work on female gangs. Utilising the concept of '**doing gender**' he explores the way men and women interact with dominant constructions of gender in an active, creative way that both challenges and transforms them. His analysis of interviews with young women who belong to female gangs in New York argues that young women 'do' gender in a way that reflects both their active choice and the realities of their social situation. He explains their involvement in violence as part of the creation of 'bad girl femininity' that takes pride in being tough and engaging in street fighting:

> But once you're in a fight, you just think—you've got to fuck that girl up before she does it to you. You've got to really blow off on her. You just play it crazy. That's when they get scared of you. It's true—you feel proud when you see a girl you fucked up. Her face is all scratched or she got a black eye, you say, 'Damn, I beat the shit out of that girl, you know' (Messerschmidt 1995: 170).

In 'bad girl femininity', feminine behaviour that is normally regarded as abnormal; that is, aggression, is normalised as appropriate within the domain of the street. At the same time, some gang girls value 'emphasised femininity' and take pride in their appearance and nurturing skills as mothers and sexual partners. Messerschmidt observes: 'Their 'bad girl femininity' therefore consists of a combination of conventional gender practices (such as cooking and childcare) and atypical gender practices (such as violence), each practice justified by appropriate circumstances' (1995: 184).

Messerschmidt (1995) argues that gender needs to be understood as a fluid category, which suggests that the interaction between gender and crime is not static. Rather, engagement in criminal activity, especially within gangs, becomes a site that provides space for the negotiation of gender. Within this framework the rigid separation of male (violent) and female (non-violent) crime breaks down, leaving room for deeper insight into the way gender is both actively accomplished and constrained by existing structures. This provides a more flexible framework for understanding criminal behaviour as well as social behaviour in general.

## WOMEN IN CRIMINAL JUSTICE

A major point made by feminist criminologists is that the invisibility of women that pervades society as a whole is especially evident within the criminal justice system. Just as women's criminality has been ignored, so, too, their treatment, needs, and experiences within the justice system have been denied. This has taken many forms, including denial that the women who come to the attention of the courts are 'really' criminals, claims that their number is too small to justify investigation (Edwards 1995), a sense that women's prisons are not 'really' prisons (Carlen 1983), and the devaluation of work with female prisoners and detainees (Alder 1997).

Feminists also argue that assumptions about how men and women should behave compromise the principle of due process, which lies at the heart of the judicial system. The law is seen as a site where dominant discourses about masculinity construct men as 'naturally' active, aggressive, and sexually promiscuous, while those about femininity construct notions of the 'good woman' as passive, gentle, and faithful. When men are unfaithful, or get into fights, their behaviour is condoned as an expression of their nature—they are 'real men'. If a woman behaves the same way the response is quite different. The sexually promiscuous or aggressive woman breaks society's norms about how women should behave and she is understood as sick, deviant, or bad and in need of punishment or treatment.

Feminists argue that these stereotypes have led to a **double standard** within the criminal justice system that disadvantages women (Smart 1976). Behaviour that is acceptable in one gender is subject to regulation and control in another. A women who violates the law as a result of sexual promiscuity or physical aggression is doubly 'offensive', firstly because of the violation of the law and secondly because she transgresses social expectations about female behaviour. Many empirical studies by feminists support these claims (Worrall 1990; Lees 1997).

Worrall's (1990) study of female offenders in the United Kingdom deconstructs the way solicitors in the UK treat their female clients. Worrall argues the legal professions operate with hidden assumptions about normal female behaviour and that women who do not conform to this are treated as deviants, even though their behaviour in legal terms may be no different from that of other people.

Carlen's (1988) analysis of female prisoners found that the key factor in determining the decision to incarcerate was not so much the gravity of their offence but whether they had stepped outside domestic discipline by not marrying or having an unconventional lifestyle. The majority of the women in her study had grown up in care and had always been poor. Very few had been able to find satisfactory employment, even when they had undergone training. Many had experienced abuse at the hands of men—fathers, stepfather, lovers, and husbands. Carlen (1988) argues that for these women the conventional offers of the 'gender deal' of marriage and children or the 'class deal' of work were not viable.

Consequently their survival strategies and rejection of society's conventions made them vulnerable to criminalisation and imprisonment.

Lees (1997) argues that the law is biased against women because of the way the principle of provocation is applied in cases of homicide (see case study 10.1). Her study of murder trials at the Old Bailey in London in the late 1980s, and her analysis of newspaper reports, led her to conclude that dominant discourses of masculinity and femininity result in men getting away with the murder of their partner, while women who kill their sexual partners are treated harshly. This results from the use of the concept of **provocation** as grounds for the commutation of murder to manslaughter. In law the concept of provocation suggests that the behaviour of the victim precipitated his or her death by causing the offender to suddenly and temporarily lose their self-control. Lees argues that in courts of law sexist assumptions and prejudices colour the use of this concept, resulting in a double standard in which men are treated more favourably than women. Grounds for provocation that have been accepted in cases where men have killed their partner have included evidence that the victim was seeking a divorce or was unfaithful. This has been accepted by the judge and jury with the result that sometimes, even in cases when the man had a history of violence towards his partner, he received no more than a suspended sentence and walked free from the court. In contrast, women perpetrators who have killed in self-defence and claimed provocation on the grounds of years of physical abuse have often faced long prison sentences.

## CASE STUDY 10.1

In February 1999, a 36-year-old woman was murdered in her home by her ex-boyfriend, a 20-year-old man. Both had been born in Fiji, had come to Australia in 1996, and had formed a relationship shortly after their arrival, although they had not previously known one another. Despite opposition from relatives on both sides of their families, they began living together in 1997. The relationship was a stormy one and the woman complained to her family on a number of occasions that her partner had assaulted her. She left him on at least two occasions but eventually reconciled with him.

In 1998 the woman laid charges of assault against her partner and was also granted a Protection Order against him. The man was found guilty and fined. At the hearing he told the magistrate that it was her fault because she had sworn at him and insulted his parents. Later that year the couple again lived together, but by the end of the year the woman had left Queensland with the intention of putting an end to the relationship. When she visited Fiji for a family wedding he phoned her family and told the woman's relatives that he was going to come and kill her and her sisters.

In December 1998 the woman moved to Melbourne, but before departing wrote to her ex-partner telling him she wanted him back but was concerned about his behaviour. The young man followed her to Melbourne and through contact with mutual friends they eventually came into contact with one another. Sometimes her behaviour towards him was friendly, but on other occasions she showed fear of him. He eventually found out where she lived and was observed standing near the unit on several occasions. He said that he had asked her to marry him but she had refused. Although he told the police that she later invited him to live with her, this was contradicted by other evidence that although she had slept with him she did not want to live with him and that she was scared of him.

On 6 February 1996 he came to his ex-partner's flat in the expectation, so he told the police, that he would receive a friendly welcome. Instead the woman refused to open the door and phoned the police requesting assistance. When the police came twenty-five minutes later the man had left. The police gave her advice about obtaining an intervention order and then left. Half an hour later her ex-partner returned and when the woman did not answer the door he picked up a metre-long pipe from the road and a knife from his car. He then smashed his way into the house. The woman's injuries included between nine and thirteen stab wounds to the body and eleven chopping injuries (probably with a meat cleaver) mainly to the head and neck. There were also nine defence injuries to her forearms.

The man was accused of murder but he pleaded not guilty, presenting the defence of provocation on the grounds that when she had refused him entry the woman had sworn at him and had insulted his family in Hindi, saying his mother was a prostitute, his father was not a man, and his brother and sister mixed with Muslims and slept with them. A Hindi interpreter provided evidence that to a person of Hindu religion such insults would have been 'pretty bad' and she could not think of anything worse.

The 'provocation' defence was rejected and he was sentenced to twenty years' imprisonment with a non-parole period of sixteen years. In 2002, he sought leave to appeal on grounds that included the complaint that the trial judge should not have withdrawn the defence of provocation from the jury. The application was dismissed.

Source: *R v Kumar* [2002].

Recent developments in Australia relating to these issues also warrant attention. We know, for example, that there is often a history of violence between the victim and the offender in homicide cases involving sexual intimates. For example, between mid 1996 and mid 1999, there was documented evidence of prior domestic violence in 30 per cent of intimate partner homicides, and in four out of five of these the victim was female. Research undertaken in New South Wales showed that in 70 per cent of the cases where women killed their husbands there was evidence of previous domestic violence, and in half of these the woman claimed that she was acting in response to an immediate threat (see Brown et al. 2001: 497).

The law's response to women who kill has been problematic in a number of different ways, particularly in instances where domestic violence is evident. The legal rules that traditionally gave shape to the doctrine of *self-defence*, for example, were designed (or interpreted) by the courts to tailor the defence to a factual paradigm involving a one-off confrontational encounter between two strangers of roughly equal size and strength (see Brown et al. 2001; Scutt 1990). This paradigm is inappropriate in the context of domestic violence and where the offender is a woman. In other words, the core concepts underpinning self-defence fail to take into account the actual experiences of women. They emphasise:

- *imminence* of attack (versus the reality of pre-emptive defensive attacks, arming themselves before attack, of killing during a lull in violence in the course of a battering incident)
- *proportionality* (versus experience of seriousness of attack)
- *serious harm* (versus foreknowledge of what is to come based upon experience)
- *duty to retreat* (versus lack of access to effective peaceful mechanisms for retreat or avoidance).

Lack of appreciation by the courts of women's defensive behaviour within its surrounding circumstances is compounded by the fact that the courts frequently minimise the deceased's violence towards the accused; and by appeal to 'standards of reasonableness' based upon the hypothetical reasonable man.

One result of the persistent criticisms of the courts' failure to take into account gender-specific experience has been increasing reliance upon the **'battered woman syndrome'** (BWS) in court. This describes a psychological condition in which the cumulative effect of surviving domestic violence for the women concerned may be a particular state of mind characterised by features such as 'learned helplessness' and 'chronic fear'. These features mean that a woman is psychologically unable to escape a violent relationship, or particular incidents of violence, even when the opportunity is ostensibly open for her to do so. However, the battered woman syndrome has been criticised on a number of grounds, such as an overemphasis on the psychology of the defendant, and consequent under-emphasis on the context in which the offence took place—reinforcing the notion that the accused's behaviour was not objectively reasonable but only to be evaluated in the light of a particular psychological state; and placing attention on the pathology of the defendant in ways which diminish the pathology of the offender or situation (Scutt 1995).

In legal terms, the danger of the BWS, in practice, is that rather than transforming self-defence (and the gender biases in the law pertaining to this), it may be used more in support of those defences that stress emotional response (provocation) or mental instability (diminished responsibility)—both of which may serve to actively reinforce particular gender stereotypes and that tend to locate the problem within individual psyches (rather than as a social problem). To put it differently, legal applications of the BWS tend not to focus directly on what it was about the circumstances of domestic violence that could produce a criminal response in reasonable women, but rather on the transient psychological state occurring in otherwise normal women as a result of surviving such abuse (Scutt 1995).

Close analysis of homicide (against women, and by women), and the defences used by men or women who kill, indicate that there are strong gender biases that run throughout the law. Recent changes in legal rules and court interpretation have in essence been generated by concerted campaigns by feminist activists, both within the legal system and outside of it, on issues such as female homicide in cases associated with domestic violence. As recent rethinking about the BWS approach indicates, however, for every step forward in defending against criminal charges in such cases, success has tended to be partial and to raise even more questions.

Gender also appears to be an important variable influencing the way police go about their work. Research suggests that the way the police respond to men is different from their treatment of women. The assumption that women are treated more gently than men has been challenged by studies that suggest a more complex picture. For example, Alder's (1994) investigation of the influence of gender stereotyping by the police found that while white women may generally benefit from this, black women and young women may experience over-policing in the form of harassment and intimidation. This may partly explain their over-representation in official statistics. This argument builds on Smart's (1976) earlier argument that a double standard exists in relation to sexuality, with young women's sexuality being subjected to social control in a way that young men's is not.

This is particularly true for juvenile girls. Until relatively recently girls held in detention were far more likely than boys to be there for non-criminal offences, often under care and protection orders. In 1990, it was observed that although fewer girls than boys were placed in juvenile corrective institutions—about 200 nationally, compared with about 1100 boys—proportionally fewer were there as the result of a criminal act. About 85 per cent of boys were held on delinquency offences compared with 50 per cent for girls (Muhkherjee et al. 1990: 27). This suggests that a paternalistic criminal justice system was placing girls in institutions in order to protect them from moral danger. The judgment that girls are in need of 'care and control' or that they are 'ungovernable' was reached far more readily than for boys.

Since that time most states in Australia have separated their handling of juvenile offending from care matters, leading to a general reduction in young people held in detention. This has particularly impacted on girls. Whereas in December 1983, 102 of the total 161 female detainees in juvenile correctional institutions were non-offenders, in December 1996 there were none. All of the 58 female detainees were alleged or proven offenders (Alder 1997). However, although this situation is better than the USA, where welfare and offender populations continue to be held in detention centres (with girls much more likely than boys to be held as status offenders), concerns remain. Alder (1997) argues that simply separating care and offender populations does not alter the often very difficult situations in which some of the girls find themselves, and that more should be done to meet their needs.

## Women in prison

The percentage of women in prison in Australia has historically been very low. In 2002 less than 7 per cent of the prison population was female with

1484 females in Australian prisons compared with 21,008 males (Gelb 2003). In the eighteen-year period between 1983 and 2001, just over 6 per cent of all prisoners were female (AIC 2001c: 64). This is typical of the pattern of female imprisonment throughout the developed world.

Although relatively small in number, female prisoners tend to be drawn from a very vulnerable population. Indigenous women are especially over-represented and their incarceration rate is even higher than that of Indigenous men. It is also estimated that as many as 80 per cent of women in prison have a dependence on drugs. Numerous studies have found a similarly high percentage have been victims of violent crime, especially incest and sexual abuse (Alder 1994). Like Chesney-Lind in the USA and Carlen in the UK, Alder (1994) found that many young female prisoners in Australia are there as a result of pursuing a survival strategy after leaving unacceptable situations at home. Like all prisoners, women in prison tend to lack education and have limited skills. In Victoria, in 1999, only 20 per cent of female prisoners had completed secondary education or above. About 80 per cent of female prisoners were unemployed or not part of the paid workforce prior to incarceration (Cameron 2001).

Many female prisoners also come from situations of homelessness or inadequate housing and have a high level of debt. Although their level of education is higher than that of their male counterparts, it is still very low. Most are sole parents so their children therefore experience a form of hidden punishment as a result of their parents' imprisonment. For these reasons, Alder (1994) argues that when it comes to female prisoners, official categories of victim and offender tend to blur.

The issues faced by female prisoners are quite different from those of male prisoners, and often relate to their role as nurturers. They include:

- concern at the appropriateness of imprisoning women at the cost of placing their children into the care of the state
- concern at the high number of women prisoners who are prescribed psychotropic prescription drugs
- concern at the high level of self-harm committed by women in prison, including high levels of suicide and attempted suicide
- the imprisonment of women who have killed their husbands after prolonged periods of domestic violence
- the relatively higher incarceration and recidivist rates of Aboriginal Australian women (Cameron 2001).

These issues have raised questions about the appropriateness of imprisoning women for what are usually minor offences that do not threaten public safety, such as breaches of community services orders.

Instead of declining, the female prison population has grown significantly over the last two decades, albeit from a low base rate (Gelb 2003; Ross & Forster 2000; Fitzgerald 1999). In the seven years between 1995 and 2002 the absolute number of male prisoners increased by 27 per cent while the absolute number of females increased by 78 per cent (see figure 10.2). For males, the rate of incarceration has increased from 245.9 per 100,000 population in 1995 to 262.4 in 2002, a rise of almost 15 per cent. For females, over the same period the rate has increased from 12.0 per 100,000 population to 19.2 per 100,000, an increase of 60 per cent. In other words, the increase in the rate per 100,000 population for women is four times that of males.

There are three possible explanations for this increase:

- Women are committing more serious offences that are likely to lead to imprisonment.
- The recidivist rate for female offending has increased.
- Changes in sentencing policy have resulted in women being treated more harshly than in the past.

In the UK, where a similar trend has occurred, the research suggests that the main reason is harsher sentencing policies (British Home Office 2002 cited in Gelb 2003). Is this also true of Australia? Research by Gelb

**Figure 10.2**   Imprisonment rates for males and females 1995–2002

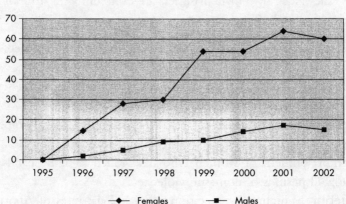

Source: Gelb (2003: 4).

(2003) suggests that the two main reasons are changes in the nature of female offending together with harsher sentencing practices. There does not appear to be an increase in recidivism among female offenders.

A number of studies have found that the proportion of female prisoners who have been sentenced for a violent crime has increased and that most of this is accounted for by a rise in the number of females imprisoned for robbery. ABS data reveals that this has increased from 6.9 per cent in 1995 to 11.9 per cent in 2002. In contrast, the number of women sentenced for non-violent crimes has declined, including deception offences and break and enter (Gelb 2003). No such changes have occurred in the type of offences for which males have been imprisoned where both violent and non-violent offences have remained fairly stable. A similar trend was found in Fitzgerald's study of court data in New South Wales for the period 1994–98 (Fizgerald 1999). While the number of women appearing before the Higher Courts declined by 31.5 per cent, from 355 persons to 243, the number of women appearing for robbery rose from 26 individuals to 46 individuals. Fitzgerald (1999) argues that this may have contributed to the rise in female imprisonment from 87 (24.5 per cent) to 117 (48.1 per cent) over the same period. Like Gelb, Fitzgerald concludes that the change in the nature of female offences is one of the reasons for the growth in female imprisonment.

In addition, Fitzgerald (1999) argues that sentencing policy has become more severe in recent years, so that women appearing for robbery, property, and drug offences are more likely to receive a prison sentence than in the past. In 1994, 52.0 per cent of women convicted of robbery were imprisoned. By 1998 this had risen to 68.9 per cent. According to Baker (1998) this is part of a broader trend of the increasing use of custodial sentences by the courts than in the past.

Of particular concern is the fact that the number of female Aboriginal Australians being imprisoned is growing even faster than the general female trend (see figure 10.3).

Although women share the repressive regime common to men's prisons, they also experience conditions that are specific to their gender. Facilities for rehabilitation have often been limited and have tended to confirm women's traditional roles, for example, cooking and sewing (Smart 1976), although in recent years there has been a move to introduce education and training programs which are more appropriate to the labour market (Cameron 2001; Edwards 1995).

**Figure 10.3** Aboriginal and Torres Strait Islander female prisoners 1995–2001

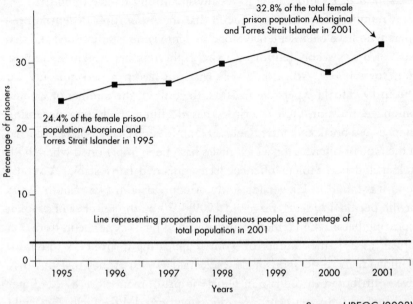

Source: HREOC (2003).

A key point made by Carlen (1988) is that the invisibility that women experience everywhere is just as powerful in prisons as it is elsewhere. When visiting prisons for interview subjects she found that prison staff often denied the existence of female prisoners. By this they meant that most of the prisoners were not 'real' because their relatively trivial offences, such as fine defaulting, did not count. Similar remarks by prison officers related to their views that the regime was 'soft' compared with that for men, while others thought that the prison was more like a hospital because of the number of respondents who appeared to have a mental illness (Carlen 1988: 17).

## CONCLUSION

This review of women as offenders has emphasised that their pattern of involvement in criminal behaviour is distinct from men's. This difference resides not only in the different level and type of female criminal activity, but also in the forces that shape their involvement in it. It seems that for a significant number of women their criminal behaviour stems from their own victimisation. Feminist analyses of women offenders has also emphasised the way in which the criminal justice system reflects patriarchal notions about how women should behave, and the consequences this carries for women who fail to conform to these ideals. Understanding female crime therefore requires an understanding of women's involvement in the criminal justice system as both victims and self-determining agents.

This emphasis on gender as a major force shaping both the involvement and treatment of those who offend against the law is now seen as having relevance for the analysis of male offenders. One of the achievements of feminist criminology has been to raise questions about the way in which cultural norms about masculinity influence men's involvement in crime. For both men and women, then, the construction of gender is now understood as central to understanding who becomes involved in crime and why this is so.

## DISCUSSION QUESTIONS

1 What evidence is there that the crime rate among women is increasing? How do you explain this?
2 Outline the argument that when women engage in crime it is often the result of strategies for survival.
3 How does the concept of 'doing gender' help to explain the involvement of young women in gangs in the USA?
4 In what ways has the criminal justice system's response to women who kill been problematic?
5 What does Alder mean when she suggests that when it comes to female prisoners, traditional categories of victim and offender tend to blur?

## GLOSSARY OF TERMS

**'battered woman syndrome'**
a psychological condition in which the cumulative effect of surviving domestic violence for the women concerned may be a particular state of mind characterised by features such as 'learned helplessness' and 'chronic fear'; these features mean that a woman is psychologically unable to escape a violent relationship, or particular incidents of violence, even when the opportunity is ostensibly open for her to do so

**chivalry factor or thesis**

the theory that one of the reasons for the apparently low female crime rate is that traditional male attitudes to women as weak and in need of protection, together with their role as child rearers, makes male law enforcers reluctant to apply the full weight of the law (Pollack 1961)

**doing gender**

the way men and women interact with dominant constructions of gender in an active, creative way which both challenges and transforms them (Messerschmidt 1995)

**double standard**

the argument that behaviour that is acceptable in men is subject to regulation and control if it is engaged in by women

**provocation**

the legal defence in cases of homicide that the behaviour of the victim precipitated his or her death by causing the offender to suddenly and temporarily lose their self-control; if this is accepted as a mitigating circumstance, the charge of murder is commuted to manslaughter.

## FURTHER READING

Alder, C. (1997) 'Young Women and Juvenile Justice: Objectives, Frameworks and Strategies', paper presented at the Australian Institute of Criminology Conference 'Towards Juvenile Crime and Juvenile Justice: Towards 2000 and Beyond', Adelaide.

Chesney-Lind, M. (1997) *The Female Offender: Girls, Women and Crime*, Sage, Thousand Oaks.

Daly, K. (1994) *Gender, Crime and Punishment*, Yale University Press, New Haven.

Miller, S. (1998) *Crime Control and Women: Feminist Implications of Criminal Justice Policy*, Sage, Thousand Oaks.

Rafter, N. (2000) *Encyclopedia of Women and Crime*, The Onyx Press, Phoenix.

## WEBSITES

**www.aic.gov.au**

Australian Institute of Criminology—Provides links to various publications from Australia's leading criminologists, including research, conference papers, publications and statistics, many of which are full text.

**www.ncp.gov.au**

National Crime Prevention Programs, Commonwealth Attorney-General's Department—Provides research on ways of reducing and preventing crime and the fear of crime. Most of the reports are available in full text.

**www.uncjin.org**

United Nations Crime and Justice Information Network—An organisation of the United Nations researching crime and prevention strategies. The website provides access to investigations and reports in a number of criminal justice areas.

# CHAPTER 11

# Ethnicity and Crime

## INTRODUCTION

This chapter explores the relationship between ethnicity and crime. While ethnically, religiously, and culturally diverse, it is nevertheless the case that Australia remains dominated by the majority Anglo-Australian population and that particular non-Anglo groups thereby have 'minority' status (Guerra & White 1995). This is reflected in a number of different ways: in terms of culture, economic patterns, and institutional arrangements (see Jamrozik et al. 1995). It is also reflected to some degree in crime patterns and in the ways in which ethnic minority groups are involved with the criminal justice system.

The concept of 'ethnicity' certainly warrants discussion. The idea that this chapter is about 'ethnicity and crime' belies the fact that everyone is part of an ethnic group. It is particular *ethnic minority* groups that tend to be the main focus of public concern over ethnicity and crime. This is so even though 'ethnicity' itself is a notoriously difficult notion to pin down in quantitative terms. For instance, it involves variations related to country of origin, ethnic identification, language, religion, and physical appearance. Similar considerations apply with regard to the category 'migrants'. After all, the leading category of migrants to this country is from British or broadly European background. Yet popular discourse equates 'migrant' with 'ethnic minority' or 'non-English speaking' person.

The contemporary media images and treatments of certain ethnic minority communities in Australia are generally negative. This is especially the case with respect to groups such as the Vietnamese, Lebanese, and Pacific Islander, although other groups have also felt singled out for negative and stereotyped media treatment (White et al. 1999; Collins et al. 2000; Foote 1993). It is frequently the case as well that particular events are seized upon by the media to reinforce the 'ethnic' character of deviancy and criminality in ways which stigmatise whole communities (Noble et al. 1999; Poynting 1999; Poynting et al. 2001).

In terms of specific targets, the presence of identifiable groups of young people in public places has been portrayed as especially disturbing by some sections of the media. Congregations of ethnically identifiable young people have frequently been publicly associated with images that are negative, dangerous, and threatening. The media have tended to emphasise the 'racial' background of youth groups, and their presumed criminality, to the extent that identification with a particular ethnic group becomes equated with 'gang membership'. The extra visibility of young ethnic minority people feeds the media's moral panics over gangs, as well as bolstering a racial stereotyping based upon physical appearance (White 1996).

This chapter provides an overview of statistical information on the distribution of crime in relation to ethnicity. It also considers the nature of so-called ethnic youth gangs—an issue that has gained special prominence in the media in recent years. As well, the chapter examines key issues that warrant further research and conceptual work if we are to appreciate fully the complexities and dynamics of the relationship between ethnicity and crime.

## ETHNICITY AND CRIME DATA

### Ethnicity as a variable

One of the difficulties of any discussion of the experiences of 'ethnic minority groups' is the dearth of statistical data and empirical material dealing specifically with 'ethnicity' as a key variable. There are a number of methodological and political reasons for this, such as problems of definition and fear of the stigmatisation of marginal groups. This makes it difficult to analyse the role of ethnicity in shaping patterns of crime.

Moreover, as a broad generalisation, Australian criminology has not really come to grips with the fact that this country is one of the most diverse and poly-ethnic societies in the world. With over 170 different nationalities, cultures, ethnic groups, and so on represented in the Australian mosaic, the area of 'criminology, race, and ethnicity' certainly warrants much more attention than has hitherto been the case. Having said this, it is also apparent that greater academic, community, and government concern is now being directed at issues relating to ethnic minorities in the criminal justice system.

The first point to note in any discussion of race and ethnicity is that there is no such thing as 'race'. **Race** is not a biological given but a social construct, based upon perceived differences between groups on the basis of physical characteristics, cultural background, and country of origin. Genetically, there are more differences within a so-called racial population than there are between it and other 'racial' groups. This explains why every attempt to group humans into racially distinct groups has failed. There is only one human species and we share the same fundamental biological characteristics.

The idea of **ethnicity** differs from that of race insofar as it refers to cultural differences between social groups. This difference becomes the basis of a shared sense of identity both within the group itself and by those outside it. These differences may be physical appearance, religious allegiance, language, custom, or attachment to an ancestral homeland, or some combination of these.

Although 'country of origin' is often used as an indication of ethnicity it is important to understand that while this may provide broad indications of criminal justice patterns, it nonetheless fails to acknowledge that there is no neat overlap between the two. Neither race nor ethnicity can be reduced to country of origin, language, or colour. For example, in Vietnam, there are a variety of 'ethnic' groups, including ethnic Chinese, Vietnamese, Montagnards, and Khmer. In Israel, the Jewish community comprises Europeans, Africans, and people from the Middle East, who vary greatly in terms of appearance, language, and spiritual expression. Furthermore, as the history of Vietnamese migration to Australia has demonstrated, there are significant class differences within communities, and differences related to time of immigration, which have major impacts in terms of the re-settlement process at any point in time (see Viviani 1996).

For present purposes, while acknowledging the heterogeneity of diverse national and 'ethnic' groups, the term **'ethnic minority'** will be used to describe those Australians whose cultural background is neither Anglo-Celtic nor Indigenous. It includes non-English speaking migrants, but is not exclusive to this group since many 'visible minorities' come from regions or families where English is spoken, such as India, Sri Lanka, and the Pacific Islands.

Visible difference is a key factor in membership of an ethnic minority. Ethnic group membership is a status conferred both by self-identification and by the dominant culture. For example, the Chinese have settled in this country since at least the mid 1800s. Their descendents may simply refer to themselves as Australian: their language is English; their home life may be typically Australian. However, they may be confronted with questions like 'where are you from?' and assumptions that they are familiar with Chinese culture and unfamiliar with Australian mores. Conversely, a white middle class Canadian may not be seen as a 'migrant' even though objectively this may be the case.

Another difficulty in collecting appropriate empirical information is the issue of first, second, and third-generation migrants. This relates back to the issue of how we can best define 'ethnicity', and how this can change over time for certain groups. For these reasons it is essential that fine-grained analysis of different ethnic minority communities be undertaken, as the experiences vary greatly between groups, and within groups over time (see White et al. 1999). For example, the Turkish have been here in Australia in significant numbers for several decades and their place and involvement in mainstream institutions has undergone distinct changes over time, according to the basis of, and perceptions about, their migration experience. In a similar vein, different sections of various communities migrated at different times under very different circumstances. For example, the Lebanese who migrated to Australia in the 1950s were predominantly Christians from areas around Beirut seeking a better life, whereas those who migrated in the 1970s were predominantly Sunni Muslims from the north escaping the Lebanese civil war (Batrouney 2002).

In considering the relationship between ethnic minority groups and the criminal justice system, questions of definition are central. On what basis should ethnicity be assigned? Should it be on the basis of language spoken, cultural heritage, physical appearance, religion, and/or migration status? Is it an objective social characteristic (you are who you are), or does it involve subjective elements (you are who you say you are)? These are important questions and how we answer them will greatly influence the type of information and statistical data that is gathered, and the analytical generalisations being made about specific social groups.

## Crime statistics and ethnic background

In the case of recent migrants, there is some evidence to suggest that the incidence of crime among migrants is significantly lower than among the general population, as measured by conviction rates and participation in prison populations (see Hazlehurst & Kerley 1989; Eastel 1994). Offences committed by migrants are mostly minor in nature, but involve crimes against the person and drug-related offences. Interestingly, the longer the period of residence, the closer offending rates of migrants parallel those of the general population.

Paradoxically, it would appear that very often the police have targeted ethnic minority groups, especially recent migrants, for special attention. Research suggests that this has been based upon certain prejudices as new groups of migrants have entered the country at different times en masse. In other words, as a new and visible minority group has immigrated to Australia in relatively large numbers, so, too, the police have tended to be ignorant of the socio-cultural attributes of the incoming group and/or to assume levels of criminality that, in most cases, simply do not show up in the official statistics (see New South Wales Ombudsman 1994; Chan 1997). It may be that this results from the influence of particular 'ethnic' stereotypes associated with certain criminal groups, such as the Mafia, the Triads, or the Yakuza. Images of criminality based upon the activities of organised crime thus may be transposed to communities as a whole, with the consequence of generating ongoing suspicion and lack of trust.

Despite these stereotypes, until recently ethnic minority youth did not feature prominently, if at all, in official crime statistics (see Cunneen 1995; Eastel 1997). The data on ethnicity and crime suggested a low incidence of criminal involvement for ethnic minority youth, and correspondingly low rates of involvement with the criminal justice system. For example, Eastel's (1989) study of young Vietnamese refugees in New South Wales in the 1980s demonstrated that these young people were likely to be under-represented in criminal statistics and behaviour.

In recent years, however, this pattern appears to be changing in some jurisdictions, if country of origin is accepted as an indicator of 'ethnicity'. Current crime data suggests a new trend in some jurisdictions in Australia in which greater numbers of ethnic minority people are being sent to prison. The overall numbers are not large, relative to the total number of inmates in the system. However, they are large enough to warrant official concern about how best to manage and design facilities and programs for specific groups.

The most sustained analysis of ethnicity and crime in Australia was carried out by Mukherjee (1999) using police data from Victoria and data from the National Prison Census. Acknowledging the limitations of data collection and statistical analysis in this area, Mukerjee (1999) looked at crime statistics in relation to country of origin of alleged offenders across the broad offence categories of Violent, Property, Drug, and Other. The data from Victoria showed that, in 1993–94, the vast bulk of alleged offenders were born in Australia (99,511), followed by those born in the United Kingdom (2968), New Zealand (2297), and Vietnam (2220). Numerically, therefore, the key offending group is comprised mainly of Australian-born people. However, the size of the population of migrant groups varies substantially, so that, for example, there was a disproportionate number of alleged offenders born in New Zealand, Lebanon, Vietnam, Turkey, and Cambodia relative to each community's population size. To put this over-representation into perspective, however, one needs to still compare absolute numbers as well as rates per 100,000 population. Thus, almost 100,000 alleged offenders were Australian-born, compared with just over 2000 Vietnamese-born.

In comparing Victorian data from 1993–94 with data from 1996–97, Mukherjee (1999) noted that the proportion of alleged offenders who were Australian-born actually grew from 75 per cent to 77 per cent. Substantial increases in the number of alleged offenders was also observed in relation to those people born in Hungary, Fiji, Vietnam, Poland, and Romania. Substantial decreases were observed for groups born in Ireland, Sri Lanka, the United Kingdom, and New Zealand. In both data sets, a majority of alleged offenders from all birthplace groups were processed for property offences.

Mukherjee (1999) also looked at prison data from the period 1983 through to 1997. The Australian-born constituted, by far, the largest category of prisoners, comprising 8213 out of 10,195 prisoners in 1983, and 14,677 out of 19,082 in 1997. According to country of origin, the next highest categories of prisoner were from the UK/Eire, New Zealand, and Vietnam, although for each of these categories the number was less than 1000 in 1997.

With regard to ethnic minority young people, data from New South Wales indicates that there has been an increase in detention figures for

Indo-Chinese, Pacific Islander, and Lebanese young people (Cain 1994; Standing Committee on Social Issues 1995). Questions have been raised as to whether the rise in Vietnamese young people in detention has been due to increased police targeting of these youths, an actual reflection of a rise in criminality, or an increase specifically in involvement with drugs (Eastel 1997; Bhathal 1998). Mukherjee (1999) found that in the specific case of Cambodian and Vietnamese-born persons there was an increase in those processed for drug offences in Victoria from 4.5 per cent and 10 per cent of all offences for these groups to 27 per cent and 33 per cent respectively. In other words, over time, while property offences remain the largest category of offence, the drug offence category had increased significantly. Given the nature of drug offences, and the seriousness with which they are taken by the Higher Courts, it is not surprising to also find that prisoners born in Vietnam displayed the largest percentage increase in number (from 18 in 1983 to 457 in 1997). About half of the Vietnamese prisoners were imprisoned for drug offences, such as dealing, trafficking, or manufacturing drugs (Mukherjee 1999: 5). Again, however, it needs to be pointed out that Australia-wide in 1997 there were 19,082 prisoners. Proportionate increases of any one population group have to be kept in perspective by locating any increase in the context of total numbers of prisoners. Changes in migration patterns will also influence these figures, for example, if there is a significant increase in migration from Vietnam.

Other research on sentencing patterns indicates that minority groups receive harsher penalties, and more control orders than Anglo-Australian young people (Gallagher & Poletti 1998). The Aboriginal and Torres Strait Islander and the Pacific Islander groups were more likely to receive significantly harsher penalties than their Anglo-Australian counterparts. The latter were also slightly favoured in relation to the other groups as well.

The evidence that levels of crime among ethnic minority groups in Australia has increased in recent years is contradicted by self-report studies. Junger-Tas found a 'striking disparity in delinquency self-reports of ethnic minorities and their over-representation in police statistics' (1994: 179). Such differences suggest a degree of bias in the criminal justice system. Although this may take a number of forms, there is evidence that problems associated with police–ethnic minority youth relations are a contributory factor, with selected groups of teenagers being more likely to be arrested, charged, and convicted of offences than others (see Cunneen & White 2002).

This pattern of the unequal representation of particular groups within the criminal justice system is not unique to Australia. A recent survey of nine Western countries found that:

> Members of *some* disadvantaged minority groups in every Western country are disproportionately likely to be arrested, convicted, and imprisoned for violent, property, and drug crimes. This is true whether the minority groups are members of different 'racial' groups from the majority population, for example, blacks or Afro-Caribbeans in Canada, England, or the United States, or of different ethnic backgrounds, for example, North African Arabs in France or the Netherlands, or—irrespective of race or ethnicity—are recent migrants from other countries, for example, Yugoslavs or Eastern Europeans in Germany and Finns in Sweden (Tonry 1997: 1).

Comparative research on Indigenous people and criminal justice in New Zealand, Canada, Australia, and the United States has also found similar patterns of over-representation (Hazlehurst 1995). The increased frequency of involvement with the criminal justice system, particularly in relation to drug offences and use of violence, means that the heightened media attention of ethnic minority young people does bear some relation to what is occurring at a grassroots level.

To understand what is happening it is necessary to consider the structural changes that have impacted on ethnic minority young people in recent years. Analysis of social indicators, such as employment and levels of education, suggests that many of these young people are being marginalised economically and socially from the mainstream institutions of school and work. In many of the working class areas where ethnic minority youth live, the manufacturing industry has collapsed or declined, affecting the livelihoods of their parents and their own employment prospects. The bleak outlook they face in relation to employment prospects is exacerbated by things such as inadequate schooling facilities and resources. The commercialisation of leisure and recreation also means that these young people may even be excluded from these areas as they lack the means to pay if they want to play. This suggests that the difficulties experienced by young ethnic minorities is inextricably linked to their class situation.

It needs to be reiterated, however, that a minority of people in any community are engaged in antisocial behaviour and serious criminal activity.

Cain (1994) estimates that only 3 per cent of Vietnamese young people commit criminal offences in New South Wales. The problem is that prejudicial stereotyping in the media often leads to the differential policing of the whole population group. This not only violates the ideals of treating all citizens and residents with the same respect and rights, but also can inadvertently lead to further law-breaking behaviour (such as carrying weapons to protect oneself from racist violence). The negative images of ethnic minority people therefore not only stigmatise the community as a whole, but, to some degree, also create a self-fulfilling prophecy, creating the very conditions they purport to fear.

## ETHNIC YOUTH GANGS

The notion of ethnic youth gangs has featured prominently in media reports of youth activities over the last few years. While media and police reports indicate that 'ethnic youth gang' activity appears to be rising, there has been little empirical information regarding the actual activities of ethnic minority young people (but see Guerra & White 1995; Pe-Pua 1996). Even less is known about those ethnic minority young people allegedly involved in drug-related activities and other kinds of offending behaviour. Despite concern about the responsibility of the states to collect data on these issues (see Cunneen 1995; Collins et al. 2000), there has been a dearth of systematic statistical material regarding welfare, criminal justice, and employment trends in relation to these young people.

Much of the public consternation regarding so-called ethnic youth gangs relates directly to the use of public space by ethnic minority young people. The presence of large groups of young people on the street, or young people dressed in particular ways or with particular group affiliations, appears to have fostered the idea that Australia, too, has a gang problem similar to that found in countries such as the United States. This not only misconstrues the nature of 'gangs' in the US (see Klein et al. 2001), which are far more diverse and complex than media images imply, but it also misrepresents the dynamics of youth group formation. There is a substantial difference between specific criminal organisations, which are usually not age-specific and that are expressly concerned with criminal activity (for example, criminal bikie gangs), and youth groups, which tend to be based upon age-based peer associations, and in which illegal activity is incidental to group membership and formation (see Perrone & White 2000).

In the specific case of 'ethnic youth gangs', the activities and perceptions by and of ethnic minority youth present a special case. The extra 'visibility' of young ethnic minority people (relative to the Anglo 'norm') feeds the moral panic over 'youth gangs'. Whole communities of young people can be affected, regardless of the fact that most young people are not systematic law-breakers nor particularly violent individuals. The result is an inordinate level of public and police suspicion and hostility being directed towards people from certain ethnic minority backgrounds.

A sustained study of ethnic minority youth, particularly in relation to the issue of gang-related behaviour, was undertaken in Sydney's western suburbs (Collins et al. 2000). The research involved Lebanese young people and other community members, as well as media and policy analysis. The authors were very critical of the media for attributing criminality to 'cultural' factors (in this case related to being Lebanese). The clear implication is that everyone associated with this particular community shared similar negative attributes. Conversely, they argued that existing research demonstrates that crime is more of a socio-economic issue than a cultural one. There is in fact very little reliable evidence that shows that 'ethnic crime' as such is a problem. Instead, its roots appear to lie in factors such as inequality rather than ethnic background.

What is a problem, however, is the 'racialised' reporting of crime in which the media uses ethnic identifiers in relation to some groups, but not others (such as Anglo-Celtic Australians). Moreover, the 'explanations' for such 'ethnic crime' tend to pathologise the group, as if there were something intrinsically bad about being Lebanese or more generally Middle Eastern (see case study 11.1). They also suggest that the origins of the criminality stem from outside Australia and are related to immigration policies and 'foreign' ideas and cultures, rather than the social and economic inequalities within this country. Such racialisation has a major impact upon public perceptions of the people and the issues, as well as on the response of state agencies such as the police.

## CASE STUDY 11.1

In late 2000 there was widespread media reporting of a horrific series of gang rapes that took place in Sydney's southwest. A number of teenage girls had been lured to places such as parks, public toilets, and industrial estates and viciously raped by a group of young men. There were a number of aspects to the rapes that inflamed the public response. The rapes were orchestrated with the rapists using mobile phones to contact one another to join in the attacks. The number of young men involved was very high with, in one case, up to fourteen men involved or looking on. The girls were held for a long time, with one of the rapes lasting six hours. Of even greater concern was the racial overtones to the rapes. During the rapes the girls were taunted with racial slurs, such as being told they were being raped because they were 'Aussies' and the men were going to 'fuck you Leb style'.

Eventually fourteen men were arrested and brought to trial. They were a group of Australian men of Lebanese descent. Their plea of 'not guilty' was rejected by the jury with most being given very long sentences, the longest being for 55 years.

Initially the media coverage of the rapes played down the racial aspects, but eventually this became the subject of intense public debate. Some writers argued that the politically correct position *not* to acknowledge the racial aspect of the rapes was misguided since 'ignoring it exacerbates it'. It amounted to 'gutless censorship' (Albrechtsten 2002). Others pointed out the double standard of both the community and media, providing examples of other horrific acts that were accompanied by none of the moral outrage applied in this instance. The media furore over the alleged rapes (no charges were laid) by the Canterbury Bulldogs in 2004 said nothing about the ethnic background of the rapists or their victims, nor did coverage of sexual assaults that took place in an exclusive Anglican all-boys school in Sydney where a group of boys were charged with 75 sexual assaults over a six-month period. Wakim, the founder of the Australian Arabic Council, pointed out that, in reality, the cultural identification of the Sydney rapists was more likely to be with American black rappers 'than some Lebanese warlord of the 1970s...yet the self-appointed high priests of moral society in Australia had already decided that the ethnicity was as guilty as the perpetrators' (2004).

Most of the convicted rapists appealed their sentences. The outcomes are still pending.

Source: Albrechsten (2002); Wakim (2004).

The Sydney study pointed out that the groups that exhibit the highest rates of imprisonment—including the Lebanese, Vietnamese, and Turkish—also have the highest unemployment rates. This association suggests that problems associated with social exclusion are likely to be central to any explanation of youth offending involving particularly disadvantaged groups. Collins et al. (2000) also identified social marginalisation as a critical factor behind the perception of widespread involvement in 'youth gangs' among Lebanese youth. There was a high level of association between young Lebanese people so that their friends were primarily drawn from the same ethnic group. The main purpose of these groups was not to engage in criminal behaviour but to defend themselves against experiences of racism and exclusion from the cultural mainstream.

A number of recent studies suggest that street violence plays an important part in the lives of young ethnic minority people, especially young men (Foote 1993; White et al. 1999; Collins et al. 2000). This can be understood as a reflection of the prevalence of certain types of aggressive physicality within marginalised and working class communities, and is explained in terms of cultural conceptions of masculinity. Being tough and engaging in acts that put one's bodily integrity at risk is generally associated with working class male culture (in its many varieties and permutations). Typically, the matters of physique and the physical have been central to working class forms of aggressive masculinity that celebrate strength, speed, agility and general physical prowess (White 1997–98). Under conditions of economic disadvantage, social stress, and group marginalisation, there is even greater recourse to 'the body' as a key site for identity construction and affirmation (see Connell 1995, 2000). Thus, a lack of institutional power and accredited social status appears to leave little alternative to physicality itself as the main form of self definition, whether this manifests itself as self-destructive behaviour or as violence directed at others.

Collins et al's (2000: 143) analysis of violence and aggression between ethnic groups suggests it has more to do with questions of status and masculinity than with inter-ethnic conflicts. Their experience of institutional racism and economic marginalisation leads them to form associations that offer them a sense of identity, community, solidarity, and protection. Group membership also provides them with what Collins et al. describe as a 'valorisation of respect in the face of marginalisation' (Collins et al. 2000: 150). Within the group, values of loyalty and toughness prevail in the face of real and perceived outside threats. In some cases the collective assertion may also take the form of contempt for 'Aussies' (as the dominant social group), as well as wariness of other ethnic minority groups, even though they are also struggling to garner respect and reputation in a hostile environment.

The effect of this is to create a negative dynamic in which the experiences of structural exclusion are reinforced by the young people's collective response to it. Institutionalised racism (restricted life chances and the dominance of monocultural norms), economic marginalisation (unemployment and poverty), and reliance upon particular notions of masculinity (reliance on physical and symbolic markers of toughness) place these young people in a particularly vulnerable and volatile social situation. Their response is the assertion of their identity and collective social power via membership of street groups and engagement in fighting. While this is a response to the experience of racism and perceived threats from outsiders, it paradoxically both reinforces their subordinate, 'outsider' position while also fuelling further negative social reaction.

In a political environment in which 'race politics' is a predominant feature, the spectre of 'ethnic criminality' is effectively bolstered by the actions of ethnic minority youth themselves, as they struggle to negotiate their masculinities, ethnicities, and class situations. In this way the activities of ethnic minority youth are open to distortion and sensationalism in ways that portray them as 'racist', 'un–Australian', and socially divisive.

## ETHNIC MINORITIES AND VICTIMISATION

### Women, economy, and domestic violence

Contemporary research has broken the silence surrounding violence involving ethnic minority women, particularly those who have immigrated recently to Australia. Why is it, for instance, that Filipino women are almost six times over-represented as victims of homicide in Australia? (Cunneen & Stubbs 1997) How do aspects of ethnicity or the migration experience contribute to the incidence and low disclosure of violence against overseas-born women in the home? In answering these kinds of questions, investigators have examined a wide range of economic, social, and cultural factors.

A study of Filipino women in Australia by Cunneen and Stubbs (1997) found that they are particularly vulnerable to homicide and domestic violence. Their research found that they were about six times more likely to be victims of homicide than the general population of women in Australia. They suggest that this can only be explained through an understanding of the way in which cultural representations of gender and ethnicity intersect in international relations. The marketing of marriage and sex, as well as the use of the internet, has meant that many Filipino women come to Australia as (e)mail-order brides. They are also constructed in the media as both passive and exotic in ways that make them vulnerable to masculine fantasies of male domination. These racialised notions of gender place them at risk of abuse and deny their capacity to act for themselves. This conclusion is reinforced by Saroca's (2002) case study of the murder of Rosalina, a Filipino woman. Her analysis of media representations of Filipino women suggests that these locate Filipino women within Orientalist discourses as 'exotic, inferior and backward' and subject to the power of the West. In this way they are defined as commodities for the consumption of Australian men in ways that set them up as victims. At the same time the media blames them for their victimisation, firstly for coming to Australia despite knowledge of the risks they face and, secondly, because they are manipulative and predatory, seeking to escape poverty by using Australian men as a passport to a better life. Such stereotypes prevailed in media coverage of Rosalina's death, although interviews with her family suggest these were far from the truth. By creating and maintaining stereotypes in this way Saroca (2002) suggests that the media actually contributes to the situations of violence it describes.

Eastel's (1996a) study of migrant survivors of domestic violence and practitioners working in the field found that the experience of migration itself was often identified as a contributory factor. The stress of migration, especially in the case of refugees, can lead to tensions that express themselves in domestic violence. Family members also may find that their education and training credentials are not accepted, and so experience unemployment or downward mobility, placing further strains on the family. Language problems and other difficulties of cultural adjustment are also common. At the same time, Eastel notes that the violence usually preceded migration.

One of the factors identified by Eastel (1996a) as contributing to violence against overseas-born women included the challenges to traditional gender roles that living in Australia often presented. Financial pressures on the family meant that women sometimes entered the workforce, especially if their partners were unable to find paid work. The assimilation of offspring into Australian culture was also a source of friction. Some women also experienced social isolation and loss of traditional support, such as extended kinship networks. They also experienced difficulties in dealing with mainstream services, including specialist services for migrants and refugees, not only because of language problems but also because they lacked knowledge about their rights.

Cultural values and beliefs derived from the women's homeland were also significant. These include attitudes towards shame, values relating to the privacy of the home, and beliefs about the woman's obligation to stay in the marriage no matter what. For some, the fact that in their homeland the police had no involvement in control of domestic violence also made it difficult for them to see them as a potential support.

Eastel (1996a, 1996b) makes a number of recommendations for the reduction of domestic violence among overseas-born women:

- Establishment of a database on men who have assaulted previous partners to be made available to immigration posts around the world.
- Public education targeted at ethnic communities focusing on increasing understanding of the nature of violence against women and its various manifestations. For example, many women had little understanding that rape could take place within marriage or that forced social isolation was a form of abuse.
- Consideration of the implementation of education campaigns about the possible correlation between domestic violence and alcohol abuse.
- Re-examination of policies which result in non-recognition of overseas education and training qualities.
- Improvements in the communication of information to women migrants of the support services that are available, including the establishment of support groups and phone services, educational videos and information booklets in the women's own language.
- An expansion of refuge accommodation which also need to tackle issues of cultural difference.
- An expansion of funding to refugees.
- The Department of Immigration also needs to make provisions for women who are sponsored as fiancées but who break the engagement because of the sponsor's violence (1996a: 176–7, 1996b: 27–30).

Patton's (2003) study of domestic violence in Tasmania also recommends that governments should ensure that the staff of interpreting services receive domestic violence training and that female interpreters are available when requested. She also suggests that all domestic violence support services and relevant key agencies train and require staff to use interpreting services and develop culturally appropriate community development strategies aimed at enhancing the women's sense of self, agency, cultural identity, and community (Patton 2003: 130).

## Racial vilification and violence

There is evidence that the level of violence and vilification against ethnic minority people has risen in recent years, partly due to the impact of the 'race debate' accompanying the emergence of the One Nation party (see Cunneen et al. 1997). Earlier investigations carried out by the Human Rights and Equal Opportunity Commission had already pointed to the prevalence of such violence directed at minority groups in Australia (HREOC 1991a). In a period of heightened political agitation around 'race' themes, it is not surprising that certain groups (especially people from South East Asia and the Middle East) have had to cope with greater levels of aggression levelled at them.

But the problem extends far wider than particular groups. A recent report on how ethnic minority people in Melbourne viewed issues of crime and safety found that:

> Nearly all groups indicated they feared some form of racial discrimination including vilification as a result of looking different from others in the local area. Some participants considered that as they were easily identified as belonging to a certain community they were treated in a negative way by members of the general community, figures of authority and service providers (Victorian Multicultural Commission 2000: 8).

What this indicates is that racial discrimination and vilification is not reducible to the actions of a few individuals who engage in hate crime. Rather, the issues are ingrained in wider community relationships, and police as well as other groups are implicated in this process.

In strict legal terms, racist violence and vilification are outlawed through specific incitement to racial hatred legislation, anti-discrimination legislation, and, more generally, criminal law (see McNamara 2002). In practice, however, there are major tensions at the street level between groups of people from different ethnic backgrounds. Stir into the equation moral panics about terrorism and Muslim fundamentalism, and the situation can become volatile. One consequence of the linking of 'difference' with 'deviance' is an increase in fear and aggression in relation to specific ethnic minority groups. Not surprisingly, it is people from Middle Eastern backgrounds or who are of 'Middle Eastern appearance' who have borne the brunt of contemporary race-based hatred and vilification in recent times (see especially Poynting et al., 2004).

## CRIME STATISTICS AND ETHNIC MINORITIES

A key issue in discussions about ethnicity and crime is how authorities construct and interpret relevant crime statistics. There are compelling arguments for a more systematic compilation of crime and criminal justice statistics that incorporate ethnic background on patterns of offending. So, too, there is a need to quantify the differential treatment of different groups within the criminal justice system, and statistics can be useful in uncovering discrimination and providing the impetus for reform. The purpose of improving data collection in these areas should be on assessing how well criminal justice agencies are dealing with issues of access and equity, as well as exposing the socio-economic reasons behind certain crime and criminal justice trends (Cunneen 1995; Collins et al. 2000).

Another issue to consider is how changes in police recording practices might influence the construction of official crime rates in relation to particular groups, as well as police attitudes towards intervention with these groups (see National Police Ethnic Advisory Bureau 1997). The definitions used in police records are directly related to the way in which ethnic identity is linked to an offender. It is the police who usually identify a person's ethnicity for record-keeping purposes and their use of categories of ethnic classification—such as Caucasian, Asian, Indigenous, or Middle Eastern—are based on their subjective appraisals using visual and verbal cues. Such classifications therefore reflect both police perceptions of ethnic background and the arbitrary nature of the system of categorisation itself. As noted earlier, defining ethnicity is not simply about place of origin, or 'ethnic' appearance. It also involves subjective assessment on the part of the people themselves. However, from a criminal justice perspective, ethnicity is often used primarily as a marker of social distinction that provides a shorthand means to identify potential offenders or troublemakers. Since the extent of ethnic-related crime is directly related to these processes of record keeping, they can serve to entrench stereotypes about the relationship between ethnicity and offending. In this way they exacerbate, rather than alleviate, tensions between police and ethnic minority youth.

This is not to deny the difficulty of collecting data on ethnicity and crime. Politically, such data can be highly sensitive and, methodologically, it is difficult to measure because of the conceptual and definitional problems. Recording facts about racism is also challenging because of the difficulty of establishing objective definitions and measures. These issues have given rise to a debate about whether or not such data should be collected in Australia. Box 11.1 outlines the arguments.

## COLLECTION AND USE OF STATISTICS ON RACE AND CRIME

**Box 11.1**

### Arguments against race-crime statistics

#### 1. The quality of crime statistics

Whether a racially motivated crime appears in official crime statistics is influenced by many factors including:

- Citizen perceptions and definitions of crime—Most police work is a response to citizen complaints so notions of what is a crime or images of 'typical' offenders (or victims) greatly influence the amount of crime that appears in official statistics.
- Law enforcement procedures and practices—This includes factors such as the effects of police training, increases in number of police personnel, the introduction of specialised police units, and specific operational campaigns against specific crimes, as well as the political environment.
- The extent of police surveillance of ethnic minority communities.
- Police recording practices, including recording of number of arrests versus number of people arrested and how victims are counted.
- Crime rates in relation to population size and under-counting of populations (for example, in the case of unregistered migrants).
- Low levels of reporting of victimisation by minority groups, apart from more serious crimes.

Box 11.1

### 2. The difficulty of conceptualising and measuring race and ethnicity
Race-crime means different things to different people.

- The categories used to record crime tend to ignore important differences; for example, the category 'white' refers to people from Italy, Russia, Africa, and South America, even though they come from totally different cultural backgrounds.
- If self-definition is used as the basis of categorisation, it makes statistics vulnerable to manipulation by various groups.
- If skin colour is used by the police, this may be dramatically different to definitions of ethnicity used by the Australian Bureau of Statistics.

### 3. The use of race-crime statistics
If race-crime statistics are collected, they are open to misinterpretation and may be used to support racist theories of crime causation:

- Despite evidence to the contrary, there continue to be theories suggesting the existence of genetically based hierarchies in which it is argued that blacks are inherently less law-abiding than whites and Asians. There are also other explanations of crime based on race that ignore the multidimensional nature of crime and criminal motivations.
- Racist theories of criminal behaviour contribute to the problem they seek to explain because they lead to differential treatment of minority groups by criminal justice personnel, and can be used to justify exclusionary immigration policies and discrimination in housing, employment, education, and other areas.

## Arguments in favour of race-crime statistics

### 1. The need to determine whether there is differential treatment of different groups within the criminal justice system

- Race-crime statistics are useful in uncovering discrimination within the criminal justice system.
- Evidence of discrimination can provide the impetus for reform of existing practices.
- Statistical data provides an ongoing check on the operation of the criminal justice system, thereby making criminal justice personnel as individuals more accountable for their actions.

Box 11.1

**2. Challenging biological explanations of crime causation**

- Race-crime data is likely to provide evidence of considerable temporal and cross-cultural variations in crime patterns among black populations. For example, African-American homicide rates are very different from black African crime rates.
- Statistical evidence is useful for comparisons with other measures such as levels of economic inequality, unemployment, poverty, and so on. They can be used to support arguments that it is inequality rather than biology that causes high levels of crime.
- The data can be used to expose particular social problems; for example, to support arguments that the high levels of homicide among African-Americans is a form of black genocide in the USA. As such the data provides the impetus for reform measures.

**3. Banning the collection of race-crime data will not necessarily prevent the spread of racist theories**

- Proponents of racist theories already have free access to other statistical collections which they use to substantiate their arguments.
- The absence of race-crime data can be seen as an attempt by minority groups to disguise the extent of the relationship between race and crime.

Source: Based on Wortley (1999).

## CONCLUSION

Research into the relationship between ethnicity and crime requires sensitivity to the volatile political atmosphere that often characterises this area (see Solomos 1988). Yet critical work is needed on important topics such as the media portrayal of asylum seekers and refugees, the actions of racist groups that target 'ethnic' businesses for firebombing, and the spread of hate literature. As well, more work is needed on the ways in which anti–racist training and cross–cultural education might be expanded within the police services and the judiciary. Each of these areas has been associated with varying degrees of prejudice, discrimination, resistance to change, and extremism of some sort. Research can provide a platform for informed progressive change and helps to push the political process in directions that enhance social justice and communal peace.

The politics of research also increases the responsibilities of the researcher in undertaking study of controversial issues in a climate of heightened 'race' or 'ethnic' tensions. For example, work with ethnic minorities with links to the Middle East or to Judaism or Islam raises questions of the researchers' relationship to the community, sponsorship of the research, confidentiality, and the potential use or misuse of any findings. It is essential, as well, to be aware of the diversity of 'voices' within a select community. Crime research can be misused to bolster control over certain target groups. How research is presented, reported, and used, therefore, has significant ramifications for the groups being investigated. These issues affect whole communities and so cannot be taken lightly.

For quality criminological research, it is essential to provide an integrated analysis of specific and wider socio-economic and political issues, and to examine critically the meanings of state policies and their consequences for particular target groups. Findings have to be contextualised or framed in terms of local law-and-order environments, social and economic factors, group dynamics and histories, and social justice issues. Crime and ethnicity research is never politically neutral. Given this, it is imperative that researchers and scholars undertake work that is affirmative and community linked. Research ought to be partial (that is, socially progressive) but objective. To engage 'without fear or prejudice' is especially meaningful in this field of endeavour.

While much of the writing about ethnicity and crime has been informed by stereotype and misrepresentations, the actions of law enforcement officers and politicians that have been influenced by such images have, in turn, impacted upon the behaviour of people from ethnic minority backgrounds. This leads to a 'catch 22' situation in which the reality starts to mould itself into the image and the outcome is social polarisation and community fragmentation.

## DISCUSSION QUESTIONS

1   What are some of the problems associated with the question of how to define and operationalise the concept of 'ethnicity'?

2 What evidence is there that levels of crime among ethnic minorities are rising?

3 What are the 'dangers' associated with the collection of race-crime statistics?

4 Why is violence in the home a particular problem among overseas-born Australian women?

5 What are the politics of research into the relationships between ethnicity and crime?

## GLOSSARY OF TERMS

**ethnicity**
cultural differences between social groups, which form the basis of a shared sense of identity both within the group itself and by those outside it; these differences may be physical appearance, religious allegiance, language, custom, attachment to an ancestral homeland, or some combination of these

**ethnic minority**
Australians whose cultural background is neither Anglo-Celtic nor Indigenous

**race**
not a biological given but a social construct, based upon perceived differences between groups on the basis of factors such as physical features, cultural background, language, religion, and country of origin.

## FURTHER READING

Collins, J., Noble, G., Poynting, S. & Tabar, P. (2000) *Kebabs, Kids, Cops & Crime: Youth, Ethnicity and Crime*, Pluto Press, Sydney.

Cunneen, C. & Stubbs, J. (1997) *Gender, 'Race' and International Relations: Violence against Filipino women in Australia*, Monograph Series No. 9, Institute of Criminology, Sydney.

Eastel, P. (1996) *Shattered Dreams: Marital Violence against Overseas-born Women in Australia*, Bureau of Immigration, Multicultural and Population Research, AGPS, Canberra.

Mukherjee, S. (1999) *Ethnicity and Crime*, Trends and Issues in Criminal Justice No. 117, Australian Institute of Criminology, Canberra.

Wortley, S. (1999) 'A Northern Taboo: Research on Race, Crime and Criminal Justice in Canada', *Canadian Journal of Criminology*, 41(2): 261–74.

## WEBSITES

**www.aic.gov.au**

Australian Institute of Criminology—Provides links to various publications from Australian and overseas criminologists, including research, conference papers, publications and statistics, many of which are full text.

**www.uncjin.org**

United Nations Crime and Justice Information Network—An organisation of the United Nations researching crime and prevention strategies. The website provides access to investigations and reports in a number of criminal justice areas.

**www.uws.edu.au/research/researchcentres/ccr/ccrresearchprojects/publications**

University of Western Sydney—Provides access to research publications on youth, ethnicity, and crime.

# CHAPTER 12

# Indigenous People and Crime

## INTRODUCTION

The relationship between Indigenous people and the criminal justice system is an issue of widespread public concern, especially since the Royal Commission into Aboriginal Deaths in Custody (RCIADIC 1991) and the 'Stolen Generations' Report (NISATSIC 1997). Even before these reports were released the study of this relationship almost amounted to an industry within criminology. At one level the reason for this is obvious—liberal democracies such as Australia are founded on the principle of fair and equitable treatment to all, and evaluation of the criminal justice system is one of the main mechanisms by which this is measured. The gross over-representation of Indigenous people at every level of this system casts a severe shadow over Australia's standing as a democratic nation.

Understanding the relationship between Indigenous people and the criminal justice system requires an examination of their status as both offenders and victims. However, just as the line between offender and victim is blurred in the case of women, so it is for Indigenous people, although for different reasons. While both groups, in general, are disadvantaged, the level of disadvantage is far greater for Indigenous people because it involves the overt attempt over 200 years to obliterate and denigrate a whole culture. The criminal justice system has been deeply involved in this process and has been in itself a major 'cause of the tearing, bleeding rift between black and white communities' (Braithwaite in Lincoln & Wilson 1994: 61). This chapter explores these issues, placing patterns of offending by Indigenous people within this broader social context.

## THE CONCEPTUALISATION OF ABORIGINALITY

Since the colonisation of Australia by white Europeans in the eighteenth century, 'whitefellas' have used the term 'Aboriginal' to describe the continent's original inhabitants. White Australians have consistently portrayed Indigenous people as a single 'race' and it is only recently that the diversity of Indigenous groups has been recognised. Even today, the term 'Aboriginal' conjures up an image of a single community or 'nation'. Yet at the time of the British invasion there were estimated to be well over 500 different tribal groups. Despite the efforts of white Australians to destroy Indigenous cultures there are still about 200 different Indigenous languages. Recognition of the diversity that exists among Indigenous people is an essential prerequisite to understanding why there is disagreement among Indigenous communities about their predicament as an oppressed group within Australia.

The construction of the concept of 'Aborigine' has come to be used in a variety of ways. Although it has been an instrument of racist domination and control by white people, the Indigenous population has reversed the negative symbolism associated with white Australia's use of the term, turning it into an important source of identity. Just as African-Americans in the 1970s coined the phrase 'black is beautiful' to express pride in their identity as blacks, so Indigenous people today have turned the term 'Aboriginal' into an expression of cultural difference and resistance to white culture. The term 'Aboriginal' is also being replaced with, or used alongside, the Indigenous names of regional tribal groups such as the Murri of Southern Queensland.

Within the media, however, the dominant construction of Aboriginality remains largely negative and tends to be associated with stereotypes such as the long-grasser, juvenile joyrider, petty thief, and drunk (Jakubowicz & Goodall 1994; Trigger 1995; Sercombe 1995). In their analysis of the images of Indigenous people in the media Jakubowicz et al. (1994) argue that positive images tend to be limited to rural and remote locations where their traditional way of life is romanticised. In contrast, images of Indigenous people in urban settings are presented in the context of criminality and disorder. Whatever the setting or the subtext, the images are largely marginal to mainstream Australian culture so that Indigenous people are presented to the white gaze as separate and 'other', who do not belong to ordinary, modern life.

These stereotyped images do little to promote understanding of the wide and varied experience of Indigenous people. For example, the stereotyped image of Indigenous people as drunks ignores the reality that, as a whole, Indigenous groups drink less than non-Indigenous people. The image derives from particular groups of Indigenous people using alcohol in particular circumstances, often in public settings. To understand the use of alcohol by Indigenous people requires understanding the processes of socialisation that led to the use of alcohol, as well as their regulation in public places by the police and other agents of social control.

## ABORIGINAL DISPOSSESSION AND COLONISATION

The relationship between Indigenous people and the criminal justice system can only be understood within the context of their dispossession from their lands and culture. The destructive treatment of Indigenous people by British and, later, Australian governments, and by white communities, was expressed in a series of policies that sought to separate or annihilate Indigenous cultures.

This began with the declaration of *terra nullius* in which the legal fiction of an unoccupied land was used to justify white settlement of the continent. After an initial period of violent confrontation, the policy of segregation was introduced. From the mid 1880s Indigenous people were removed, often forcibly, onto reserves that were under the control of missionaries and other Anglo-Celtic groups. Unable to speak their own language or to practice their own way of life, they were subjected to severe regulation and restrictions in the name of 'civilisation'. This included the imposition of white manners and ways, such as wearing European dress and practicing Christianity. They were simultaneously denied the white precepts of social justice such as liberty, citizenship, and dignity. Indigenous people were located outside the protection of white law and instead became the subject of special laws designed to regulate and control them as a separate group within Australian society. They were also exploited as a cheap source of labour in white homes, farms, and industries.

From 1869 the policy of **protectionism** was introduced. This gave the colonial powers complete authority over the lives of Indigenous populations. Implicit within this policy was an attempt to exterminate Indigenous culture. The forced removal of light-skinned children from their families was an overt attempt to achieve this goal. The 1921 Report of the New South Wales Board of Protection stated: 'The continuation of this policy of dissociating the children from camp life must eventually solve the Aboriginal problem' (cited in Read 1999: 50).

From 1937 the protectionism policy was replaced by **assimilation.** This explicitly stated that over time it was expected that all Aboriginal people, including those of 'mixed blood', would be expected to live like other white Australians do. Like protectionism, this policy was deeply racist in its presumption of the inferiority of Indigenous culture compared with European culture. It is hardly surprising, therefore, that behind the rhetoric of assimilation, the practice of segregation was widespread. Indigenous people were still excluded from citizenship, were subject to separate education, welfare, and health facilities, and were excluded from white leisure facilities. White unions, which were so powerful in support of white men, ignored their exploitation. Their labour for white men and women was repaid with subsistence wages or sometimes just basic food and lodging.

It was not until the 1960s that the racist treatment of Indigenous people was systematically and publicly questioned. This, together with the obvious failure of assimilation, led to the 1967 national referendum that resulted in Constitutional recognition of Indigenous people as citizens and the introduction of integration as the new policy. Although initially this policy shift meant little, it was the beginning of a new environment and, in conjunction with changes in immigration policy, was superseded in the early 1970s by the current policy of multiculturalism.

The systematic removal of Indigenous children from their families was a practice that continued until the early 1970s and has been a major cause of cultural dislocation among Indigenous communities. Between 1910 and 1970 it is estimated that between 10 per cent and 30 per cent of Indigenous children were removed. In some regions and at some times the figures would most certainly have been higher (NISATSIC 1997). Some were placed in institutions, and others in white foster or adoptive homes. Many children were moved from one institution or home to another and knew neither home nor family. Those in institutions were sent to work as soon as possible and told not to return. Nearly all were systematically kept apart from their families. Some were told their parents had died or that they did not want them and that their families were 'bad'. Others were reared as white children and taught to denigrate Indigenous culture. The discovery that they were Aboriginal was often profoundly challenging. While some of the 'stolen children' have reclaimed their Indigenous identify by reconnecting with their Indigenous families, others have been unable to rediscover their family or have found it a painful experience. In its analysis of the effects of forced removal, the National Inquiry into the Separation of Aboriginal and Torres Strait Islander Children from Their Families noted:

> Subsequent generations continue to suffer the effects of parents and grandparents having been forcibly removed, institutionalised, denied contact with their Aboriginality and in some cases traumatised and abused...For the majority of witnesses to the Inquiry, the effects have been multiple and profoundly disabling. An evaluation of the following material should take into account the ongoing impacts and their compounding effects causing a cycle of damage from which it is difficult to escape unaided. Psychological and emotional damage renders many people less able to learn social skills and survival skills. Their ability to operate successfully in the world is impaired causing low educational achievement, unemployment and consequent poverty. These in turn cause their own emotional distress leading some to perpetrate violence, self-harm, substance abuse or anti-social behaviour (<http://www.austlii.edu.au/au/special/rsjproject/rsjlibrary/hreoc/stolen/stolen19.html> accessed 2 August 2004).

In establishing grounds for reparation, the Inquiry concluded that the government policy of forced removal of Indigenous children amounted to:

- a denial of common law rights, such as deprivation of liberty and deprivation of parental rights
- a breach of human rights; the policy was not only racially discriminatory but in its attempt to eliminate Indigenous culture amounted to genocide in terms of international law
- a practice that involved both racial discrimination and genocide in terms of international law (1997: 249–75).

In addition, like the Royal Commission into Aboriginal Deaths in Custody (RCIADC), the Inquiry found a strong connection between early removal from home and later involvement in crime. Indigenous people continue to be severely over-represented in the welfare system, with about 20 per cent of children in care being Indigenous (Cunneen

& White 2002: 159). There is little doubt that this is partly a legacy of the policy of forced removal of Indigenous children.

The tragedy of the 'stolen children' highlights the effects of over two centuries of racist domination of Indigenous people by white Australians. These experiences, including the effects of disease, violence, and geographic dislocation, led to the collapse of many Indigenous communities—including kinship networks, customary laws, and traditional means of subsistence—and the establishment of a new pattern of welfare dependence. Throughout this history the criminal justice system has played a central role, and this has not been forgotten by many Indigenous communities. Hazlehurst observes: 'Aboriginal people still have fresh memories of pitched battles, poisoned water and flour, expropriated tribal lands and the abduction and enforced labour of Aboriginal children' (1992: 236).

From the earliest days the police assisted in the settlement of the Australian continent, and this involved sometimes brutal confrontation with the local population (see Cunneen 2001). Throughout the years of protectionism, police were involved in the regulation of Indigenous reserves and in more remote regions were sometimes appointed as guardians. Until 1963 those living on the reserves were subject to the power of the guardian to grant them the right to move freely away from the reserves. The police were also involved in the removal of children, as they often accompanied welfare officers. The police were also sometimes instrumental in identifying children who were judged to be in 'need' of removal.

The withdrawal of missionary and government agencies from direct control of Indigenous communities in the 1960s was followed by widespread welfare dependence. Stigmatised by white Australia they had limited education, no financial resources, increasingly poor health, and little hope for the future. In some communities alcoholism and violence became significant social problems and made them vulnerable to police intervention (RCIADIC 1991; Hazlehurst 1992). It is in this social context that the relationship between Indigenous people and the criminal justice system must be placed.

## PATTERNS OF OFFENCES

Indigenous people are arrested, charged, and incarcerated at rates far in excess of their number in the population. Moreover, the overrepresentation is not limited to particular states or offences, but occurs across the board, in every state, for almost every offence, and at every level of the criminal justice system, whether it be arrests, court appearances, police custody, juvenile detention centres, or prisons. The over-representation is particularly severe in some areas, notably Western Australia and Queensland.

According to the RCIADIC, Indigenous people are arrested at 29 times the rate of non-Indigenous people, although there is considerable local variation (RCIADIC 1991). In New South Wales in the five years between 1997 and 2001 about 25,000 Indigenous people appeared in a New South Wales court charged with a criminal offence. This represents 28.6 per cent of the state's Indigenous population and is 4.4 times higher than the population as a whole. In 2001 nearly 13 per cent of the total Indigenous population in New South Wales aged 10 and over appeared in court in 2001. The figure for males is much higher than for females. Nearly one in five Indigenous males in New South Wales appeared in court in 2001 charged with a criminal offence. While 40 per cent of Indigenous males aged between 20 and 24 years appeared before the New South Wales courts for a criminal offence in 2001, the corresponding figure for all males was only 8.4 per cent. For Indigenous men over 50 the figure is 4 per cent, whereas it is 0.8 per cent for all males in that age group (Weatherburn et al. 2003).

The over-representation of Indigenous women is of equal concern. In 2001 more than 6 per cent of the female Indigenous population appeared before the New South Wales courts, compared with 0.7 per cent for the female population as a whole. For Indigenous women in the 20–24 age group the rate of court appearance was eight times higher than the corresponding rate for women in the general population.

Figures for most other states are similar. In Western Australia, for example, police arrest data shows the level of over-representation of Indigenous people in 2001 was 11.1 (Loh & Ferrante 2003).

This pattern is exacerbated the deeper the level of involvement in the criminal justice system. In 2003 just over 20 per cent of the prison population in Australia was Indigenous. As a group, they are 16 times more likely to be imprisoned than the non-Indigenous population. Whereas 0.7 per cent of all males aged 25 to 29 years were in prison in 2003, the figure for Indigenous males in the same age range was nearly 6 per cent (ABS 2004). In New South Wales in 2001, 2.2 per cent of the Indigenous population was given a custodial sentence—sixteen times higher than the overall rate of contact between the total adult population and the prison system. In the five years between 1997 and 2001 about 6.8 per cent of the Indigenous population in New South Wales was given a custodial sentence. Men aged between 20 and 34 were most vulnerable, with nearly one in ten Indigenous males imprisoned. In 2001 Indigenous women were 18 times more likely than women in the general population to receive a prison sentence (Weatherburn et al. 2003).

In areas where there is a high population of Indigenous people they are up to ninety times more likely to be imprisoned than white Australians. According to Clifford, Indigenous people are 'if not the most incarcerated people in the world, then at least second to no other' (in Hayes 1996: 318).

Of equal concern is the fact that the rate of contact and imprisonment is increasing despite the widespread adoption of diversionary policies. In Western Australia the level of over-representation at the point of arrest was 7.6 in 1991, compared with 11.1 in 2003. The upward trend is particularly strong for women. Since 1990 arrest rates for Indigenous women in Western Australia have doubled (Loh & Ferrante 2003). Nationally, the proportion of Indigenous prisoners has increased from 15 per cent in 1993 to 20 per cent in 2003 (ABS 2004). While this reflects a general upward trend in rates of arrest and imprisonment, it contradicts the recommendations of the RCIADIC and remains an ongoing source of conflict between black and white communities.

The position of young Indigenous people is of particular concern. According to Gale et al., who studied data from South Australia:

> ...the degree of disadvantage suffered by [Indigenous youths] becomes more pronounced as they move deeper into the system. Over-represented in relation to their population numbers by some seven times at the point of apprehension, their relative position deteriorates until, at the final point of detention, they are over-represented by some twenty-three times (Gale et al. 1990: 116).

Similar patterns occur in other states. In Western Australia, for example, 76 per cent of young people placed in custody are Indigenous (Hayes 1996: 318–21). This is reflected in the median age of imprisonment for Indigenous people nationally, which is 2.2 years younger than the population as a whole (ABS 2004).

## Type of offences

The type of offences that bring Indigenous people into contact with the law are varied and changing. Older studies found that public order and other minor offences predominated, especially offensive behaviour, public drunkenness, vagrancy, and traffic offences (Lincoln & Wilson 1994: 65). They were also over-represented for justice offences that cover non-payment of fines and breaches of probation or other court orders. However, they were also over-represented in the broad range of offences against the person, as well as burglary (Biles 1992: 97).

More recently, the type of offences has become more serious, with assault and property crime becoming more common. Weatherburn et al's (2003) analysis of New South Wales data found that at the point of court appearance Indigenous people were most likely to appear for offences related to violence and public order, whereas the most common offences for all appearances were 'acts intended to cause injury', 'theft and related offences', and 'road traffic and motor vehicle regulatory offences'. For the prison population, the most common offences were 'acts intended to cause injury', 'unlawful entry with intent/burglary, break and enter', and 'theft and related offences'. Substantially higher proportions of

**Figure 12.1**  Sentenced prisoners by selected most serious offence

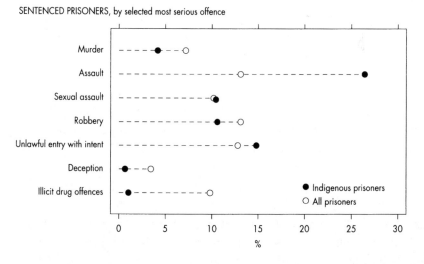

SENTENCED PRISONERS, by selected most serious offence

Source: ABS (2004: 8).

Indigenous offenders were imprisoned for 'acts intended to cause injury'. They were less likely to be imprisoned for illicit drug offences and there was little difference between the two populations for offences against justice procedures (Weatherburn et al. 2003).

Nationally, Indigenous offenders in prison are twice as likely as the overall sentenced population to have assault recorded as their most serious offence. In 2003, 26 per cent of the imprisoned Indigenous population had assault as the most serious offence (see figure 12.1). Figure 12.1 also shows that the sentenced Indigenous population has a relatively higher level of sentencing for unlawful entry with intent, but a lower level for murder and drug offences (ABS 2004).

While it is helpful to look at general patterns of offending it is important to recognise that they vary according to age, gender, and region. The pattern of Indigenous juvenile offending is also distinct from the pattern of adult Indigenous offending (see Cunneen & White 2002).

## EXPLAINING THE OVER-REPRESENTATION

There are two principal explanations for the over-representation of Indigenous people in the criminal justice system. One is that it is a straightforward reflection of their higher level of involvement in crime compared with the general population. The other is that it results from racial discrimination within the criminal justice system and the broader society. The two explanations are not contradictory and may interact in a process of mutual reinforcement.

There is certainly a relationship between poverty, unemployment, and crime rates, although the exact nature of that relationship is complex. As well, young Indigenous people often come from families under stress (in many cases associated with the impact of the 'stolen generations'), another factor associated with involvement in crime. The association between involvement in crime and factors of colour, poverty, unemployment, and unstable family arrangements also exists in the USA, which also has high levels of official crime rates for African-Americans and Hispanic Americans. Marginalisation and exclusion from mainstream society, especially through high levels of unemployment, makes young people of colour especially vulnerable to criminal behaviour (Hayes 1996: 320). In Australia, Indigenous people are almost twice as likely to be unemployed at the time of their reception into prison compared with whites (Biles 1992: 99). Poverty is also implicated in the relatively high number of justice procedures offences (which includes offences such as non-payment of fines) among Indigenous people. Clearly then, structural factors of gender, class, and 'race', and the effects of two centuries of cultural dislocation and oppression, are deeply implicated in the level of crime within the Indigenous population (Cunneen 2001; Cunneen & Kerley 1995).

The high rate of **recidivism** (that is, a repeated pattern of offending and punishment) among the Indigenous population also contributes to their over-representation. Only 17 per cent of Indigenous males and 27 per cent of females having a court appearance in New South Wales in 2001 had no previous appearance in the preceding five years. More than 25 per cent of Indigenous males and more than 15 per cent of Indigenous females had appeared in court more than five times in that period (Weatherburn et al. 2003). The figures for some parts of Australia are even higher. Nationally, 77 per cent of Indigenous offenders in prison in 2003 had been in prison before (ABS 2004).

There are also strong arguments in support of the second contention relating to the **criminogenic** influences of the system itself; that is, that the exertion of control by the criminal justice system actually causes the crimes it seeks to prevent. A pioneering study of Indigenous people by Elizabeth Eggleston in the 1970s argued that the over-representation of Indigenous people in the criminal justice system was as much to do with their treatment by the system as with their actual behaviour. She focused particularly on the over-policing of the Indigenous population by the police. **Over-policing** occurs when certain groups—such as young people, ethnic minorities, and known criminals—are regularly targeted by the police for surveillance and intervention. Eggleston suggests that this occurs in relation to Indigenous Australians in a number of ways; for example, the police accept public drunkenness and offensive language in white people but not in blacks, who are apprehended and arrested with far greater frequency (Eggleston 1976).

More recent studies support the claim that the Indigenous population is treated more harshly by the criminal justice system. Cunneen's (1990) investigation of police violence against young Indigenous people found that:

- Eighty-five per cent of respondents interviewed reported being hit, punched, kicked, or slapped by police officers.

- In New South Wales, 82 per cent of respondents reported being assaulted. The figure for Queensland was 90 per cent, while in Western Australia it was 94 per cent.
- Sixty-three per cent of respondents reported being hit with objects by the police. The most common object identified was a police baton (49 per cent), followed by telephone books (23 per cent), torches (14 per cent), and other objects such as baseball bats and chairs.
- Twenty-three per cent of respondents reported that a police officer either drew or fired a revolver.
- Young Indigenous women reported instances of sexual harassment.
- Some young Indigenous respondents reported that, while they were in police custody, criminal justice personnel made suggestions to them about suicide or threats in relation to hanging.

A study by Gale et al. (1990) found geographical variations in the over-representation of juvenile Indigenous people in South Australia, with contact with the criminal justice system varying 'dramatically from one region to another...and even from one suburb to another within the same city'. They argue that this cannot be explained by behavioural differences among Indigenous young people since there were marked differences in judicial outcome despite the similarities between districts and the lifestyles of the young people within them. Instead they suggest the differences are due to the 'attitude of the local community'. Gale et al. said juvenile Indigenous people 'appear to be treated more severely by the justice system in areas where racial discrimination is highest...justice operates differently in different locations, according to the degree of prejudice held by the white community' (1990: 116).

At the same time they point out that the high levels of detention among Indigenous juveniles also results from the 'compounding effect of discrimination (both racial and class-based) suffered at earlier steps in the criminal justice process'. The problem of differential treatment therefore begins at the point of apprehension but its effects are compounded as individuals pass further into the system (Gale et. al. 1990: 7).

Research by Luke and Cunneen (1995) and Cunneen and Luke (1995) draws similar conclusions. They compared what happened to Indigenous and non-Indigenous juveniles in New South Wales in 1990 from the point of apprehension to sentencing. Of the 670,000 non-Indigenous children aged 12–17, 15,598 or 1.7 per cent were apprehended by the police. The comparable figure for Indigenous children was 12.9 per cent of the population of 12,400 children. In other words, at the point of apprehension, Indigenous people were over-represented by a factor of 7.5. At the next stage, the decision to divert them or commit them to court, 12.9 per cent of non-Indigenous juveniles were released with a police caution, compared with 5.7 per cent of Indigenous juveniles, thereby making a mockery of policies recommending diversion away from the criminal justice system. Moreover, while 6.9 per cent of non-Indigenous people were refused bail and held in custody, the figure for Indigenous people was 10.6 per cent. Finally, of the non-Indigenous juveniles who appeared in court 520 individuals were the subject of a control order and placed in custody, compared with 168 of the 262 Indigenous juveniles. Thus, whereas 0.08 per cent of the non-Indigenous juvenile population was given a control order, the figure for the population of Indigenous juveniles was 1.4 per cent—17.5 times higher.

It has also been suggested that when it comes to sentencing the courts are harsher on Indigenous people than on the non-Indigenous population. However, a number of studies have demonstrated that, overall, the reverse is true and that the courts are lighter on Indigenous offenders than they are on their non-Indigenous counterparts (Biles 1992). However, this, too, has to be interpreted carefully. For while Indigenous offenders appear to receive lighter sentences than their non-Indigenous counterparts for the same offences, the frequency of contact and persistent recidivism means that overall Indigenous people spend more time in prison. They are also more likely to be re-apprehended once out of prison.

## DEATHS IN CUSTODY

Concern at the number of black people dying in prison or police custody eventually led to the Royal Commission into Aboriginal Deaths in Custody (RCIADIC), which investigated the 99 deaths that occurred between 1980 and 1989. The major finding of its report (RCIADIC 1991) was that the level of deaths among Indigenous people was 'comparable to those of non-Aboriginal people in custody' (House of Representatives Standing Committee on Aboriginal and Torres Strait Islander Affairs 1994: 9). This finding, however, could not hide the stark reality that there were 75 Aboriginal deaths per 100,000 of the Aboriginal population—a figure 23 times higher than the rate of **deaths**

**in custody** among the non-Aboriginal population (3.3 deaths per 100,000). To emphasise the significance of these deaths, Lincoln and Wilson point out that 'if non-Aboriginal people had been imprisoned at the same rate as Aborigines, then over 8500 non-Aboriginal people would have died in custody' (1994: 85). Although the report was strongly critical of the police, and suggested they had some responsibility for some of the deaths, it did not single out the involvement of any particular officer or police force in relation to a specific death.

Some of the concerns identified by the report include:

- the geographical distance between Indigenous prisoners and their homes. The Report suggests that the sense of separation and abandonment this engendered among Indigenous offenders contributed to the rate of suicide in custody (see case study 12.1). For example, in New South Wales all the female prisons are located in Sydney (Edwards 1995).
- the imprisonment of Indigenous people for good order offences. In particular, a high proportion of Indigenous people who had died in custody were found to have been held on charges related to alcohol use.

In its conclusions the report argues that the high rate of Aboriginal imprisonment is closely related to their structural disadvantage.

Recommendations arising from responses to the report included the following:

- Empowerment and self-determination are key elements in overcoming the structural disadvantage of Indigenous people.
- Three essential pre-requisites to empowerment and self-determination are:
  - ▼ the desire and capacity of Indigenous people to put an end to their disadvantaged situation and to take control of their own lives
  - ▼ assistance from the broader society
  - ▼ self-determination.
- The imprisonment of Indigenous people should only be used as a last resort.
- Arrest rates should be minimised.
- Public drunkenness should be decriminalised and detoxification centres staffed by Aboriginal and Torres Strait Islander people should be established (House of Representatives Standing Committee on Aboriginal and Torres Strait Islander Affairs 1994: 9–12).

The Commission's findings make deeply disturbing reading, revealing institutional racism, insensitivity at all levels of the justice system, and the terrible tragedy of unhappy, wasted lives. Equally disturbing is the limited success of the Commission in effecting positive change. Not only has the level of imprisonment of Indigenous people increased, but the number of deaths in custody remains correspondingly high (see figure 12.2).

## CASE STUDY 12.1

David Jason Barry was an Indigenous man who was brought up on Palm Island. At the age of 16 he was diagnosed as being HIV positive. On learning of this his behaviour changed. His illness made him distance himself from his friends and he became socially isolated. He lost his self-confidence, went through a period of alcoholism, and complied poorly with his medication.

In 1990 he was charged with a number of offences, including wilful exposure, assaulting a police officer, and break and enter. He had no previous offences. He pleaded guilty, expressed remorse for the offences, and claimed that he had been intoxicated at the time of the offences and suffering from severe depression. Since the offence he had sought counselling and claimed to have overcome his problems and to be in an alcohol-free environment.

Despite this, Barry was given custodial sentences for each offence and faced a total period of imprisonment of three years. He was only expected to live for two. In sentencing the judge referred to threats of the infliction of AIDS in the commission of the offences, although no evidence of this had been submitted. Barry applied for leave to appeal against the severity of the sentences, but this was rejected by the Queensland Court of Criminal Appeal. In reference to Barry's medical condition, one of the Appeal Court judge's commented: 'We understand that he had also been informed at the beginning of 1990 that he had the HIV condition and that he will die from it. He is a person of low intelligence.'

Barry was imprisoned 350km away from his family who were only able to visit him on two occasions. Alternative options of home detention or halfway houses were not considered. His illness also affected his treatment in prison. Visits took place in an isolated booth and a worker visiting him claimed that she had been required to sign a disclaimer form releasing the Corrective Services Commission from any liability in the event that she caught AIDS.

All attempts to improve Barry's treatment by the criminal justice system failed, including an application that he be granted a pardon on compassionate grounds since he was in the later stages of the AIDS virus. The application included a statement by a health worker and AIDS expert that she was concerned that 'he will inevitably take his own life'.

The application was rejected by the Queensland Government Solicitor. The Attorney General was waiting for an opinion by the Minister for Justice before handing down a final decision when Barry committed suicide and was found dead in his cell. He died eight days before his eighteenth birthday.

Source: Behrendt (1992: 26–9).

In addition, although Indigenous people are less likely to be imprisoned for public order offences, public drunkenness remains an offence on the statutes of some states, albeit sometimes in hidden guise. Consequently, Indigenous people continue to be placed in police custody for this reason. This particularly affects Indigenous women. A recent analysis of female deaths in custody found that Indigenous women were more likely than non-Indigenous women to be placed in police custody for good order offences (usually public intoxication), and that one out of two Indigenous women who died in custody were detained for such offences compared with just over a quarter of non-Indigenous women (Collins & Mouzos 2002). These findings support those of an earlier study by Kerley and Cunneen (1994) and suggest that the custody system administered by the police is a major factor in the deaths of Aboriginal and Torres Strait Islander women. Collins and Mouzos (2002) also stress the need for the decriminalisation of public drunkenness.

**Figure 12.2**  Trends in Aboriginal deaths in custody

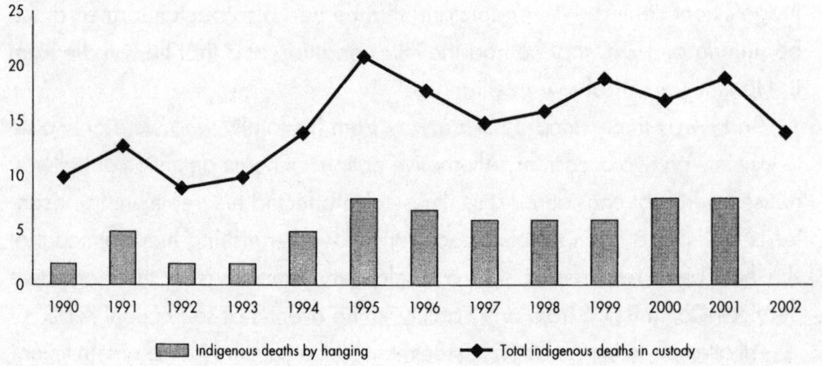

Source: Collins & Ali (2003).

Despite the limited success of the RCIADC, it has been an important instrument of reconciliation because of its role in raising awareness of the conditions in which many Indigenous people live and of the factors that lead to their imprisonment. For example, the level of violence that occurs in some Indigenous communities has become a major public issue in recent years. Although it affects both women and men, domestic violence against women appears particularly prevalent. In 2001, 18 per cent of female victims of homicide were Indigenous, even though they represent only 2 per cent of the Australian population (Mouzos 2002: 13–15).

This raises the question of what can be done to deal with the myriad issues covered in this chapter. In fact, it has been recognised for many years that the solution to the over-representation of Indigenous people in the criminal justice system lies in amelioration of the structural conditions that explain it. In their analysis of patterns of Indigenous offending in New South Wales, Weatherburn et al. (2003) suggest that:

> Given the extraordinary level of contact between Aboriginal people and the criminal justice system it is to be doubted that further contact with the system is the best means of bringing down rates of Aboriginal offending...The point is...that focusing on the factors that lie behind Indigenous offending, such as alcohol abuse, poor school performance and unemployment, is likely to do more to reduce crime in Indigenous communities than policies designed to apprehend and imprison an even higher proportion of Indigenous offenders (2003: 9).

More broadly, the answer lies in the empowerment of Indigenous people. This can only be achieved by restoring to them their sense of dignity and self-respect. Reconciliation in ways that are meaningful to Indigenous people themselves has the potential to play a vital role in this process. A blueprint and informed discussion of what self-determination can mean at a policy and practical level is provided in the *Bringing Them Home* report dealing with the 'stolen generation' (NISATSIC 1997).

## CONCLUSION

The over-representation of Indigenous people within the criminal justice system remains a powerful social issue. It can only be understood in terms of their position as a racialised minority within Australian society. Brutalised at the hands of a colonial state, the legacies and practices of an oppressive regime continue to this day. This is reflected in welfare, education, employment, crime, and other relevant social statistics that continue to show immense disadvantage and marginalisation among Indigenous peoples around the country.

At the same time, there is still some cause for hope and reconciliation. On National Sorry Day in 2000, 250,000 Australians joined the Walk for Reconciliation over the Sydney Harbour Bridge. And although the Liberal Government has resisted pressure to say 'Sorry', a number of state parliaments have done so. Yet such gestures can only have meaning if they are accompanied by a genuine willingness to return to Indigenous people a sense of power and real control over their own lives. Self-determination remains the key agenda if criminal justice issues are to be resolved and social justice obtained.

## DISCUSSION QUESTIONS

1  Why can it be argued that when it comes to the relationship between Indigenous Australians and the criminal justice system the line between victim and offender is blurred?
2  In what ways does an understanding of the history of colonialism in Australia help to explain the current relationship between Indigenous Australians and the criminal justice system?
3  Why can it be argued that the National Inquiry into Aboriginal Deaths in Custody was a failure?
4  Explain what Gale et al. (1990) mean when they say that 'the degree of disadvantage suffered by [Indigenous youths] becomes more pronounced as they move deeper into the system'.

## GLOSSARY OF TERMS

**assimilation**
the British government's policy within Australia that all Aboriginal people, including those of 'mixed blood', would be expected to live like other white Australians

**criminogenic**
the idea that the exertion of control by the criminal justice system actually causes the crimes it seeks to prevent

**deaths in custody**

a 'death in custody' is a death, wherever occurring, of a person:

- who is in prison custody or police custody or detention as a juvenile
- whose death is caused or contributed to by traumatic injuries sustained, or by lack of proper care while in custody or detention
- who is fatally injured in the process of police or prison officers attempting to detain that person
- who is fatally injured in the process of that person escaping or attempting to escape from prison custody or police custody or juvenile detention (RCIADIC 1991: 189–90)

**over-policing**

when certain groups such as young people, ethnic minorities, and known criminals are regularly targeted by the police for surveillance and intervention

**protectionism**

the British government's policy of establishing a Protector of Aborigines as the legal guardian of all Aborigines within a given territorial region of Australia

**recidivism**

a repeated pattern of offending and punishment

***terra nullius***

the legal fiction of an unoccupied land that was used to justify white settlement of the continent.


## FURTHER READING

Broadhurst, R. (1997) *Aborigines and Crime in Australia*, University of Chicago, Chicago.

Cunneen, C. (2001) *Conflict, Politics and Crime: Aboriginal Communities and the Police*, Allen & Unwin, Crows Nest.

Hazlehurst, K.M. (ed.) (1995) *Perceptions of Justice: Issues in Indigenous and Community Empowerment*, Avebury, Aldershot.

Mackay, M. & Smallacombe, S. (1996) 'Aboriginal Women as Offenders and Victims: The Case of Victoria', *Aboriginal Law Bulletin*, 3(80).

National Inquiry into the Separation of Aboriginal and Torres Strait Islander Children from their Families (Australia) (1997) *Bringing them Home: Report of the National Inquiry into the Separation of Aboriginal and Torres Strait Islander Children from their Families*, Commissioner: Ronald Wilson, Human Rights and Equal Opportunities Commission, Sydney.

Weatherburn, D., Lind, B. & Hua, J. (2003) *Contact with the New South Wales Court and Prison Systems: The Influence of Age, Indigenous Status and Gender,* Contemporary Issues in Crime and Justice No. 78, Crime and Justice Bulletin, NSW Bureau of Crime Statistics and Research, Sydney.

## WEBSITES

**www.aic.gov.au**
   Australian Institute of Criminology—Provides links to various publications from Australian criminologists, including research, conference papers, publications and statistics, many of which are full text.

**www.ainc-inac.gc.ca/pr/pub/index_e.html**
   Canadian Department of Indian and Northern Affairs—Provides publications on indigenous affairs in Canada.

**www.aiatsis.gov.au/rsrch/index.htm**
   Australian Institute of Aboriginal and Torres Strait Islander Studies—Provides access to research papers on a number of areas pertaining to Indigenous people in Australia.

**www.lawlink.nsw.gov.au/ajac.nsf/pages/index**
   Aboriginal Justice Advisory Council—The council provides advice to the New South Wales Government on law and justice issues affecting Aboriginal people. The site has access to reports, newsletters, and fact sheets.

# CHAPTER 13

# Juvenile Crime

## INTRODUCTION

The killing of a university lecturer by two boys dropping a boulder from a bridge onto his car as it travelled along a freeway in Victoria, football hooliganism, the brutal murder of two-year-old Jamie Bulger by two young boys in the UK, vandalism in our shopping malls, gang violence in Cabramatta, riots in Redfern—these are all crimes which have involved young people and have been accompanied by widespread media coverage and public expressions of concern. Talk to business people in the CBD or pick up the local paper and it would seem that crimes by young people are one of society's most serious problems.

This chapter provides an overview of perceptions and engagements of young people in criminal and delinquent activity. It explores issues relating to the way in which the law constructs young people and points out that the notion of a generation gap has been present throughout history. In considering patterns of juvenile offending, it points out the differential treatment of the criminal law in relation to specific social groups. Not only are disadvantaged groups such as young Indigenous people more likely to be criminalised, but the law also responds to rule-breaking behaviours differently. For example, young women are treated differently from young men. The chapter also explores the issue of gangs, as well as some explanations of juvenile crime. Throughout the chapter there runs the theme of the links between crime and disadvantage. The chapter points out that while the identification of 'risk factors' for involvement in crime has become prominent in recent years, in reality all this does is paint the profile of what is already known—that underlying patterns of crime are structural factors in which inequality and social exclusion are profoundly linked.

## DEFINING JUVENILE CRIME

'Juvenile', 'youth', 'young person', 'delinquent'—these terms are loaded with associations, many of which are negative. Think 'juvenile' and the word 'delinquency' is not far behind. Think 'young person' or 'youth' and words like 'out of control', 'underage drinking', and 'drugs' may come to mind. Other associations might be 'suicide', 'unemployment', and 'troubled'. It seems that to be young today is to be designated to an inferior and unenviable position in society.

Although words like 'juvenile' and 'youth' are used loosely to describe people whose age falls within a range somewhere between 8 and 24, in criminal law the term 'juvenile' has a specific meaning based on biological age. That is, childhood and adolescence is bounded by consideration of the idea that young people have varying stages of development and varying levels of understanding. The vulnerability and developmental aspects of youth are legally protected through a range of criminal and civil legal measures designed to take into account their overall level of maturity (see Schetzer 2000; Western Australia Office of Youth Affairs 2000). These measures involve elements of prescription and compulsion (as with the imposition of compulsory schooling), and elements of proscription and prohibition (as with the banning of alcohol sales to people under a certain age; see box 13.1). A partial list of how the law positions young people would include such things as:

- *Criminal law*—International instruments (such as the United Nations Convention on the Rights of the Child) hold that criminal responsibility should not be fixed at too low an age, bearing in mind the facts of emotional and intellectual maturity. In the Australian context, this generally means 10 years of age as the minimum age of criminal responsibility, with the doctrine of **doli incapax** also applying to young people up to the age of 14 (a rebuttable presumption that children who have turned 10 and not yet reached the age of 14 are incapable of knowing that their criminal conduct was wrong).
- *Contracts and leases*—As a general rule, people under the age of 18 are not bound by contracts, leases, and other transactions unless they are

for their benefit. Opening a bank account or borrowing money is possible at age 18, although the former is possible at any age as long as there is parental/guardian consent.

- *Driving*—Gaining a driver's license is generally possible at 16 years (a learner's permit) with provisional license available at 17 years.
- *Alcohol and cigarettes*—Generally a young person under the age of 18 is not permitted to buy alcohol or cigarettes, or to possess or consume alcohol in a public place. Drinking alcohol at a private residence may not be covered by law.
- *Medical treatment*—Generally at 14 years or over, young people can legally give consent to their own general medical or dental treatment.

The law thus shapes the eligibility and responsibility of children and young people around distinct age markers. Variations will occur between jurisdictions, but generally speaking there are similar key transition ages in most places. In some cases there may be variation in what a child or young person may or may not do, depending upon permission being granted by the parent or guardian, a court, or relevant government department.

One implication of having such age-based parameters on activity is that juveniles, in particular, are subject to additional legal control measures called **status offences**. These refer to those offences that only apply to

---

## EXAMPLES OF KEY TRANSITION AGES FOR ACTIVITIES

**Box 13.1**

**Under 10**—no criminal responsibility; compulsory schooling

**10 to 15**—criminal responsibility (but rebuttable presumption of *doli incapax*), compulsory schooling

**15 to 18**—eligible to leave school, gain a driver's license, take up full-time job, engage in sexual activity (although different age provisions may apply for same sex relationships), qualify for social security payments if satisfy various eligibility criteria, and consent to medical and dental treatment

**18 to 21**—can drink and buy alcohol and buy cigarettes, live independently, rent a house, borrow money, open a bank account, marriage, vote, watch R-rated movies

**21 to 25**—Adult rather than youth wages, movement towards full adult social security entitlements

young people, such as 'uncontrollability', 'running away from home', and 'in need of care and protection'. The idea here is that, until they reach a suitable age (as determined by legislators and courts), young people should be subject to particular types of social controls.

Underlying the distinctions between child, juvenile, and adult are assumptions about the biological and psychological development of a 'normal' human being. Childhood is seen as an age of innocence in which physiological foundations for moral categories of 'right' and 'wrong' are believed to be absent or undeveloped, making the notion of *mens rea*—the intention to commit a wrongful act—inappropriate. A child that violates legal expressions of morality by, for example, killing their parent, is seen as in need of psychological help rather than punishment or moral correction. In some cases, where the behaviour has been exceptionally shocking and especially when it has attracted widespread media coverage, there may be prolonged debate about how the law should be applied (see case study 13.1).

## CASE STUDY 13.1

Corey Davis was six when he was picked up by another boy and thrown off a sheer drop into Georges River at Macquarie Fields in Sydney's south-west and left to drown. The boy who threw him in was 10 years old at the time. In court he was described as slow, intellectually backward, and socially inept, although his mother described him as 'just a normal kid'.

The case created a legal quandary because the age of criminal responsibility in Australia is 10. This means that children under 10 cannot be charged with a criminal offence. Between 10 and 14 they are presumed to be *doli incapax*, which means they are incapable of understanding wrong. The chief magistrate of the Children's Court ruled that a jury would be unlikely to convict and released the boy, declaring it an 'act of bullying that went horribly wrong'. However, in the face of strong pressure from the media, the Director of Public Prosecutions in New South Wales ordered that the boy face trial for manslaughter in the Supreme Court. The boy's grandmother, whom he lived with, welcomed the decision.

The facts of the case were not in dispute, but for the act to be a crime the jury had to prove intent and understanding. In the Court the first jury was dismissed when one juror stepped down, saying he was overwhelmed by the task. Another jury was sworn in. In the opening address the Crown Prosecutor told the court he would not be pushing for an 'all-out conviction' and the accused boy, too small to see over the dock, sat with his lawyers at the Bar table. Throughout the trial he was described as sitting expressionless, sometimes falling asleep. Four young children gave evidence by video of an event that occurred 18 months ago. The father of one refused permission although he was under subpoena, saying it was 'too stressful'. One witness stuck his tongue out at the prosecutor.

The trial lasted three weeks and reached a 'not guilty' verdict. One reporter commented: 'It may be a long time before another 10-year-old in this State is charged with such a serious criminal offence'.

Source: Phelan (1999: 43).

## VIEWS OF YOUNG PEOPLE THROUGH TIME

The sense of crisis that often accompanies talk about street crime and violence often gives the impression that the incidence of these crimes—which are widely assumed to have been committed by young people—is growing. There is a feeling that the nation is somehow in decline from a 'golden age' of the past in which young people were well behaved and respectful. However, closer investigation reveals that, far from being a new phenomenon, this sense of crisis has accompanied most generations as they compare their young people with those of past times (Sanders 1970; Pearson 1983).

Concern with hooliganism and vandalism in shopping malls, for example, has been mirrored in previous ages when 'respectable' people were too frightened to go out onto the streets for fear of violence. In *Hooligan: A History of Respectable Fears* (1983) Pearson analyses documents dating back to seventeenth-century Europe and finds similar themes have echoed down the centuries. Each generation deplores the unruly behaviour of its offspring and harks back to a previous age—usually the generation just before their own—as one in which peace and harmony prevailed.

Although it is impossible accurately to assess whether young people today are more disorderly than their peers of previous generations, there is little doubt that complaints and fears about young people have been expressed regularly and predictably. Nonetheless, there are three aspects of delinquency that differentiate the contemporary situation from that prevailing in the past: the recognition of adolescence as a stage of growth; the shift from the family to the state as agent of punishment; and the growth in influence of the mass media.

- The notion of adolescence as a separate stage in the lifespan is a modern one. In his classic work *Centuries of Childhood*, Aries (1973) points out that until about the middle of the nineteenth century childhood was not regarded as an age of innocence and children were unprotected from the often-harsh realities of existence. Although there were class differences, in general children wore the same clothes as adults and were expected to both work and play beside them. They worked down mines and in mills and went to taverns alongside adults. Nor did the law make any formal distinction between adults and children. Children as young as eight were hung on the gallows, incarcerated in gaols, and transported (Morris & Giller 1987: 6; Seymour 1988: 8–9), although there were occasions when childhood was recognised as a mitigating factor (Platt cited in Morris & Giller 1987: 8). It was only in the middle of the nineteenth century that the legal changes associated with the establishment of the modern system of juvenile justice began to be put in place (Cunneen & White 2002: 1–31).
- Until the nineteenth century the state's involvement in controlling and punishing delinquency was rather limited. Instead the family was the main site of both containment and retribution. This was just as true of Australia prior to white settlement as it was of pre-industrial Europe and America. Industrialisation and urbanisation weakened the strength of family and community ties, and the state took on many of their roles. Today the state is the main player in the identification, containment, and response to juvenile crime. The problem of 'youth offending' as we understand it today can therefore be understood as a consequence of industrialisation and urbanisation. At the same time the shrinking of the welfare state that has occurred from the 1980s has seen a reversal of this trend, as the state seeks once again to shift responsibility for controlling the behaviour of young people back onto the family. This can be seen in a wide range of measures, from restorative justice to legislation that punishes parents for failing to control their children (White & Wyn 2004).

- The mass media now play a significant role in shaping public knowledge and therefore indirectly influence the formation of juvenile justice policies. This includes popular culture in the form of films, videos, TV shows, and books about young people and crime, as well as documentaries and reporting of crime in electronic and print media. It has been noted that very often 'crime news' is for all intents and purposes 'youth news'. That is, the media is saturated with stories about 'young thugs', 'youth gangs', ' school vandals', the (youth) 'drug problem', and so on. Young people are portrayed as deviant, and as threats to the moral fabric and social order. The pervasiveness of the media, and the negativity of their coverage of crime and youth, generates a political climate in which youth crime is seen to be out of control, and an ever-growing problem. Media-generated 'moral panics' can and do have major consequences for perceptions of, and policy responses to, youth offending (see Cohen 1973; Goode & Ben-Yehuda 1994).

## PATTERNS OF YOUTH OFFENDING

Sources of information on juvenile offending include incidents reported to the police, cases decided by the courts, victim surveys, self-report offender surveys, and research into specific groups, such as juveniles held in detention. The usual warnings about the use of this data apply vis-à-vis reliance upon official statistics and the limitations of different data collection methods. In addition, enforcement patterns in relation to juveniles vary over time. For example, the willingness of police to use cautions instead of charging a juvenile is subject to changes in policy at both the local and state level, and can have a significant effect on court records of the number of appearances before the Children's Court. Many juvenile crimes may go unreported, especially when young people themselves are victims. This is particularly the case for vulnerable young people who experience a sense of powerlessness and resignation, such as homeless youth, Indigenous Australians, and young women (Underwood et al. 1993: 14).

According to official data, most juveniles do not engage in crime. Court records for July 1994 to June 1995 show that only 2 per cent of young people aged from 10 to 17 years came into contact with the New South Wales Children's Court (Freeman 1996). However, juveniles are certainly over-represented in offender statistics of all kinds. In 2000–01 young people aged between 10 and 17 years accounted for about one quarter of the offender population (AIC 2003: 41). While juveniles were three times more likely than adults to be identified as offenders (AIC 2003: 41), the age groups above them have a higher rate of offending. In addition, there is considerable evidence that the over-representation of juveniles is partly explained by the distinctive pattern of their engagement in crime, which makes them more likely to be identified as offenders than adults (see Cunneen & White 2002):

- They are more likely than adults to commit offences in the company of others. This not only increases their chances of being caught but also means that a number of offenders are charged with the same offence. Both these factors inflate the extent to which juveniles are responsible for offences compared with adults.
- Juveniles tend to commit offences such as shoplifting, motor vehicle theft, and burglary that have a high level of visibility.
- Juveniles are relatively inexperienced in crime and the often opportunistic, sometimes attention-seeking nature of their behaviour increases the likelihood of detection.
- Juveniles tend to commit crimes in their own neighbourhood making it more likely they will be identified and reported.

Although there is no way of knowing for certain, criminologists agree that the 'dark figure' of crime (that is, unreported crime) is smaller for juveniles than for adults. Official criminal records suggest that juveniles are responsible for the majority of motor vehicle thefts (Higgins 1997: 3). However, since the clearance rate for motor vehicle theft is only just over 10 per cent, we know very little about who is responsible for most motor vehicle theft. The group most likely to have a low rate of apprehension is professional thieves, some of whom may belong to organised gangs. This means juveniles are likely to be responsible for a significantly smaller amount of motor vehicle theft than official data suggest.

The argument here is that the official processing of juveniles does not necessarily mean that they are more criminal than other groups, but simply that they come to the attention of the criminal justice system is particular ways. Wundersitz, for example, says that: 'Where there is a high clear up rate (such as murder, rape and fraud) juveniles account for a comparatively small percentage of apprehensions. By contrast, where there is

**Figure 13.1** Ratio of juvenile to adult offenders by offence type 2000–01

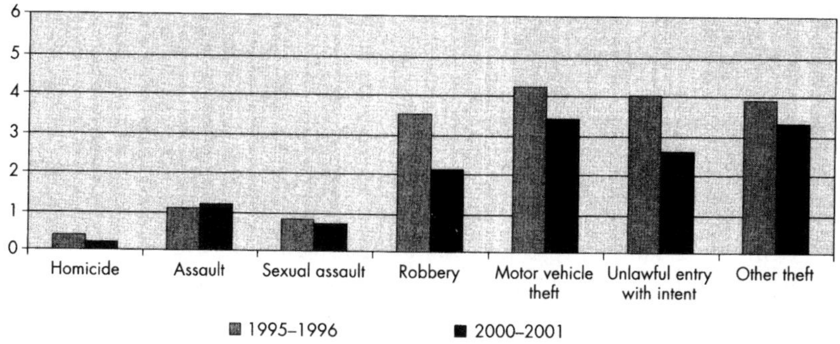

Source: AIC (2002a: 42).

a low clear up rate (for example, break and enter) juveniles account for a disproportionately large proportion of crimes solved' (1996: 130).

This observation implies that young people are apprehended at a greater rate than adults for certain types of crimes, but in the case of more serious offences they do not constitute a high proportion of all offenders.

Despite the media focus on violent offences committed by juveniles, most of their offences involve theft and other types of property crime. Often the goods involved have little value, especially when compared with other categories of crime, such as fraud (Mayhew 2003). Figure 13.1 provides data on the ratio of juvenile to adult offending for specific offences. Whereas adults are much more likely to be identified as offenders when it comes to crimes of homicide, sexual assault, assault, and robbery, the adult–juvenile ratio is reversed for motor vehicle theft, unlawful entry with intent, and other theft. When juveniles do engage in violent crime, the majority involve assault rather than crimes such as homicide, sexual assault, or robbery. Juveniles are also less likely to use a weapon than adults.

## Indigenous young people and the law

Any consideration of juvenile crime must necessarily draw attention to the severe over-representation of young Indigenous people in the juvenile justice system. In 2002, Indigenous juveniles were over-represented at a rate of 18.9 (Bareja & Charlton 2003). The detention rate for Indigenous girls is particularly severe. In 2002 the rate was 58.2 per

100,000 population compared with an overall rate of 5.1 for girls (2.6 for non-Indigenous girls; Bareja & Charlton 2003). The previous year the figure was a staggering 79.8 per 100,000 (Cahill & Marshall 2002).

The extreme over-representation of young Indigenous Australians is one of the most urgent issues within the juvenile justice system. It is associated with alcohol abuse, long-term unemployment, future incarceration, and involvement in violence, both as offenders and as victims. It stems from longstanding processes and relationships forged in the crucible of colonialism, which continue to the present day.

The question of whether the over-representation results from higher levels of offending or covert institutionalised racism is worth considering. In a sense, however, this question is irrelevant since even if Indigenous Australians do commit more offences than non-Indigenous Australians the underlying causes relate to the demoralisation and disempowerment of Indigenous Australian communities. For this reason responses that focus on the individual or that seek to ameliorate the problem through state aid are incapable of addressing the underlying issues. Instead, both Aboriginal leaders and many academics argue that the most important response is to return to Indigenous Australians their capacity for self-determination (see Cunneen 2001).

## Young women and juvenile justice

Most juveniles who engage in crime are male. While this may be partly because police officers target males more than females, numerous studies suggest that women do commit far fewer crimes than men. However, proportionally more females are involved in juvenile crime than in adult crime. In 2000–01, females represented about 25 per cent of the juvenile offender population, compared with 20 per cent of the adult offender population. It is also noteworthy that the percentage of female juvenile offending has increased by 4 per cent in the five-year period between 1995–96 and 2000–01 (AIC 2003: 42).

As in every other area of crime, the young women who come to the attention of the criminal justice system are those drawn from the edge of society. They are predominantly from families that have experienced hardship or abuse and many are from Indigenous backgrounds. It is these situations that tend to lead them into crime rather than a desire for more money in itself or thrill seeking. Their motives are, therefore, rather different from that of young men and relate to strategies of survival. These strategies often lead to involvement in relatively minor forms of law-breaking that make them vulnerable to criminalisation.

A second area in which young women are treated differently from young men is the paternalistic role of the state in seeking to enforce dominant ideologies of femininity on young women. Many young women come to the attention of the juvenile justice system not because they represent a threat to society but because they fail to conform to conventional standards of how a young woman should behave. Young women who challenge stereotypes about female sexuality or who behave 'like a man' in engaging in adventurous behaviour are far more likely to be seen as at risk and out of control, and therefore in need of the 'protection' of the state. For the young women themselves the outcomes are subjection to a disciplinary regime that pays little attention to their real needs (Alder 1997; Chesney-Lind 1989). Although the law has changed in Australia and categories such as 'ungovernability' have been removed from the statutes, it is still the case that there is considerable difference in the way young men and women are treated by the juvenile justice system.

## Is juvenile crime increasing?

Concern about rising levels of juvenile crime appears to be a perennial social issue. Both national and local media regularly carry reports about crimes committed by young people and the dangers this represents to social order. Sometimes these reports have racist undertones, implying that certain ethnic groups are responsible for terrorising local communities. Often the reports are based on one or two incidents that become the focus of community fears about the collapse of law and order and traditional ways of life. While some of these incidents may be serious and deserving of attention, the sense of moral panic generated by the media's often sensationalist coverage is not only unjustified but serves to intensify social divisions.

Contrary to public perceptions, research by Wundersitz (1993) suggests that juvenile crime has remained relatively stable across most jurisdictions in recent years. She analysed the rate per thousand of youth population for matters processed by juvenile justice systems in each state from 1979–80 to 1990–91 and found only small variations. She concluded that the rate of offending was relatively stable. The exception to this was Western Australia. Even here, although there was a dramatic increase in the number of juveniles coming into the justice system in the late 1980s, there was an equally dramatic decline by the end of that decade, so that by 1993 it had returned to the same level that existed in 1979 (Wundersitz 1993).

More recently, official crime records indicate that juvenile crime has actually decreased, while adult crime has correspondingly increased. In the five-year period between 1995–96 and 2000–01 the proportion of juvenile crime decreased from 4545 per 100,000 to 4165 per 100,000. Most of this decrease related to property crime—that is, motor vehicle theft, other theft, and unlawful entry with intent—although robbery also increased. In the same period, for the offences of homicide, sexual assault, and assault, juvenile rates remained stable relative to adult offender rates (AIC 2003: 41–3). This suggests that, while fluctuations in the rate of juvenile offending may occur, the assumption that it is inexorably increasing is incorrect.

## YOUNG PEOPLE AND GANGS

In 2001 a series of violent rapes by a group of young men in Sydney grabbed the attention of the nation. Media reports described in graphic detail how a gang of young men, apparently from an ethnic minority, lured young women to isolated spots in Sydney before viciously sexually assaulting them, using text messaging to call other members of the gang to the scene. The nation was horrified. Newspaper editorials were written about the attacks, politicians declared their determination to get to the root of the problem and police chiefs announced they would bring the culprits to justice. While the attacks were certainly very serious and deserving of condemnation, the impression conveyed in the media was that it was the work of an organised gang. When some of the young men were caught, it turned out they were actually a close-knit network of friends and relatives who shared a common ethnic background and a common sense of alienation from mainstream Australian society. While such behaviour cannot be condoned, the critical task for the social scientist is to explicate the social factors underlying it.

Fear of youth gangs has become a commonplace feature of contemporary society, with the reproduction of American-style ethnic gangs being seen as one of the undesirable side effects of immigration. Incidents like the sexual assaults in Sydney are feared not only because the acts are so damaging to the victims but also because they suggest that Australia is on the verge of becoming 'another America' in its law and order problems.

But what do we mean by the word 'gang'? In the USA in the 1930s gangs were associated with organised crime, involving drug dealing, gambling, and bootlegging in the Prohibition era. Such groups involved older criminals for whom crime was an occupation akin to that of normal professions (Sutherland 1933). Today, the word 'gangs' is associated with young men—and some young women—who engage in often-violent street crime and other marginal activities, such as drug dealing and prostitution.

While academics are not agreed on the meaning of the word 'gang', its minimal meaning is that it is a group of people who see themselves, and are seen by others, as a gang primarily because of their illegal activities (White 2002). The key characteristic of a gang is that membership tends to revolve around some shared characteristic such as similar social interests, ethnic identity, or the need for social belonging (White et al. 1999).

Building upon work undertaken by the United States Bureau of Justice Assistance, White (2002) describes gang-related behaviour in terms of four main categories:

- *Criminal activity*—in which the motive for crime is to make money through activities such as drug dealing or theft.
- *Conflict*—in which street fighting with rival gangs is the main activity. The motive is social status and street reputation and is characterised by an emphasis on honour, personal integrity, and territoriality. Prolonged conflict between gangs is rooted in issues of self-esteem and identity, as well as social constructions of masculinity and self-protection.
- *Retreat*—in which activities are focused on heavy drug use and withdrawal from mainstream social interaction. Although drug use is the main activity, the need for drugs may lead sometimes to senseless acts of petty violence and theft.
- *Street culture*—that involves activities such as graffiti, tattooing, hand signals, body ornaments, and distinctive ways of speaking. Activities may be based on media-created images or they may be an organic expression of group membership and identity.

White (2002) makes the point that engagement in one or more of these activities is not specific to gangs, but is common behaviour among young people at some point in their lives, although the nature and extent of their engagement is influenced by factors such as social background and locality. Engagement in these activities should not be equated with gang membership. Nor does membership of a gang necessarily involve participation in these activities. Howell (2000) also suggests that the activities of youth gangs are distinct from adult gangs, with youth gangs less likely to be engaged in drugs and violence than adult gangs.

What motivates young people to join a gang? A number of factors stand out:

- People desire to be part of a close-knit social group, often similar to membership of a family or clan (Messerschmidt 1995: 175). Membership provides a sense of belonging and a source of social identity. This offers opportunities for self-expression in an environment where alternatives are limited (Collins et al. 2000).
- Membership offers an inexpensive and accessible source of social presence in the community, which is especially relevant to disempowered and impoverished young people (Messerschmidt 1997).
- Gangs provide an important way of 'doing' masculinity for marginalised young men who are cut off from mainstream sources of masculine identity through conventional work and the establishment of a family (Collins et al. 2000). The same applies to young, disadvantaged women who belong to female gangs where 'bad girl' femininity may be one of the few available ways of doing gender (Messerschmidt 1997).
- Numerous studies suggest that gang membership is important to young people as a form of mutual protection (Collins et al. 2000; Gordon & Foley 1998; White et al. 1999).

Work by a number of Australian researchers (Collins et al. 2000; McDonald 1999; White et al. 1999) suggests that these factors are particularly relevant to vulnerable young people from ethnic minorities growing up in an environment of racism. From this perspective the existence of youth gangs needs to be understood as arising from conditions of social division, marginalisation, and disadvantage. Beyond this generality, the specific form gangs take—including such factors as their lifespan and level of involvement in crime—will be dependent on the specific social conditions prevailing in particular places at particular times (White 2002).

Research by Perrone and White (2000) suggests that American-style youth gangs (at least as presented in stereotypical fashion) are not prevalent in Australia. Nonetheless, they warn that some of the social conditions that give rise to the formation of gangs among ethnic minorities are present, including negative stereotyping by the public and media, police harassment, and social exclusion, and these need to be addressed.

## EXPLAINING JUVENILE CRIME

In the first half of the twentieth century, explanations of juvenile crime tended to be psychological. Books with titles like *Wayward Youth* (Aichhorn 1935) suggested that a young person's involvement in crime was the result of some underlying abnormality, either in the family structure or in the mental health of the individual. Today, juvenile crime is understood as a multidimensional phenomenon with a wide range of psychological and sociological factors contributing to its occurrence.

### Psychological explanations

Psychological explanations of juvenile crime include theories about neuropsychological problems in childhood, personality characteristics, and the effects of abnormal developmental patterns at various points in a child's life (Farrington 1996). Some developmental criminology theories suggest that juvenile offending is influenced by the impact of exposure to risk and protective factors at different points in a child's development (Developmental Crime Prevention Consortium 1999). Loeber and Stouthaer-Loeber's (1986) review of research found that the most powerful predictors of participation in juvenile crime were lack of parental supervision, the rejection of a child by a parent, and the amount of involvement a child has with the parent.

Many studies have found that children who experience maltreatment are more likely to engage in adolescent offending than those who do not (Smith & Thornberry 1995, Weatherburn & Lind 1997, Widom & Maxfield 2001). Thornberry et al. (2001) found that children who are maltreated in adolescence are more likely to offend than those whose maltreatment is restricted to childhood. Other studies suggest that the type of maltreatment is influential, with physical abuse and neglect more likely to lead to offending than sexual or emotional abuse (Widom & Maxfield 2001).

A large, quantitative study of the effects of maltreatment on children born in Queensland in 1983 (Stewart et al. 2002) found that about 5 per cent of children who came into contact with the Department of Families had a court appearance for a proven offence. Of eleven predictive factors for youth offending, physical abuse and neglect were the most significant. Twenty-three per cent of maltreated children who were the victims of neglect subsequently offended, compared with 14 per cent of maltreated children who were not neglected. Sexual abuse and emotional abuse were not related to later offending. The study also found that placement of the child outside the home influenced the likelihood of a child offending. Twenty-six per cent of maltreated children who were placed outside the home subsequently offended at least once, compared with 13 per cent of children who were never placed outside the home. Because placement outside the home is likely to be indicative of the seriousness of the maltreatment, the authors suggest that the greater the severity of the maltreatment the greater the likelihood of subsequent criminal offending. In conclusion, the authors argue that preventing child maltreatment is likely to produce a large reduction in offending (Stewart et al. 2002).

Family structure has also been identified as a risk factor for juvenile delinquency. Numerous studies have demonstrated that children who do not live with their original parents are more likely to be involved in offences than those whose parents are together (Baker 1999). Other aspects of family relationships have also been found to be significant, especially the amount of supervision, with low supervision being associated with involvement in crime (Baker 1999). The 'parenting theme' (Gelsthorpe & Morris 1999) has long been prominent in debates surrounding youth crime and youth justice (see especially Goldson & Jamieson 2002). The usual language alludes to families in crisis, or bad parenting, or parental neglect. However, much of this research has been criticised insofar as identification of these 'risk factors' has failed to link young people's lives with broader social processes, beyond simply family dynamics of which they and their families are also a part (for critique, see White & Wyn 2004).

One of the problems of psychological theories is their implication that delinquency is caused by individual pathology. This suggests that normal, well-adjusted individuals do not engage in offending behaviour. The problem with this assumption is that deviant and criminal behaviour is widespread among young people. Self-report studies suggest that a high percentage of young people have engaged in illegal behaviour. A 1996 survey of 10,441 secondary school students in New South Wales found that in the 12 months prior to the survey just under half had participated in at least one of six criminal offences, ranging from assault outside sport (that is, attacked someone to hurt them outside of sport) to theft of a motor vehicle; 9.4 per cent had participated in break and enter at some time in their lives (Baker 1999).

A second difficulty with psychological explanations of juvenile delinquency is that the solution is usually seen in terms of some form of treatment of the individual; for example, counselling or medication. This not only places young people in the hands of 'experts', whose knowledge and understanding of the causes of their behaviour may be far more limited than they acknowledge (Cohen 1985), but it also ignores the significant role played by social factors.

Finally, research suggests that it is necessary to distinguish between factors influencing participation in juvenile crime and those that influence frequency of offending. While developmental factors such as child neglect and poor parenting are correlated with participation, lifestyle factors—such as drug use or thrill seeking—are the strongest predictors of offending frequency (Freeman 1996).

### Subjective understandings

A number of investigations into how young people themselves explain their engagement in crime have been undertaken. Salmelainen's (1995) study of juvenile offenders in detention centres in New South Wales asked them why they engaged in motor vehicle theft, shoplifting, and break and enter. For shoplifting and break and enter, the main reasons given related to economic factors; for example, to obtain money for its own sake or for drugs or alcohol. For motor vehicle theft, the main reason given—need or want of transport (49.6 per cent)—was also related to economic factors. Excitement, thrills, and fun was the second most important reason, whereas this was less important for the other two offences (Salmelainen 1995). Salmelainen concluded that lifestyle factors were the most important correlates of offending frequency, especially those relating to drug use and its associated income requirements. Like other studies, Salemainen also found that thrill seeking was associated with a higher rate of offending (Katz 1988).

Sykes and Matza (1957) described the motivational accounts provided by young people themselves as to why they engage in certain types of activity. They argued that young people use certain techniques of neutralisation as a way of denying the moral bind of law (for example, 'they started it', 'no one got hurt'). In studying the values, perceptions, and emotions of young people, Matza (1964) explored the reasons that propelled some youth into further criminal activity. Although most people at some stage engage in some form of criminal, antisocial, or deviant behaviour, not all young people experience offending and criminal justice in the same way. Matza found that juveniles generally 'drift' between the two poles of conventional and unconventional behaviour (including crime), without being fully committed to either. In the end, most young people drift towards conventional lifestyles and behaviours as their permanent pattern. However, if during the teenage years of drift there is official intervention and social reaction to specific kinds of unconventional behaviour, this may well precipitate the movement of the juvenile into a more permanent state of delinquency. The importance of these observations is that 'deviancy' among teenagers is seen as basically 'normal', rather than exceptional. It is part of the developmental processes associated with growing up. How young people engage in various activities is shaped by their subjective experiences of these activities, their understandings of the meaning of these activities, and their rationalisations for their personal engagement in the activities.

Katz (1988) was also interested in the relationship between crime and subjective experience. In particular, he wanted to consider the emotional states of offenders. He turned his attention to the seductions of crime, and found that crime, in emotional terms, can be exciting and exhilarating. It represents a transcendence of the mundane, an opportunity to creatively explore emotional worlds beyond that of 'normal' rational behaviour. As with the themes and issues raised by Matza, for Katz (1988) it is important to examine the lived experiences of criminality, to consider the emotional and interpretive qualities of crime. Emotions such as humiliation, arrogance, ridicule, pleasure, and excitement are often central to why we act as we do. This is illustrated in the work of Ferrell (1997) for example, who describes the liberating feelings and sense of power and resistance associated with graffiti. A common theme in much of this work is that deviance offers the perpetrator a means of 'self-tran-scendence', a way of overcoming the conventionality and mundanity typ-ically associated with everyday regular life (Hayward 2002).

Another area in which a focus on subjective understanding of young people's experience provides insight into patterns of crime is the obser-vation by labelling theory that subjective understandings of situations have real effects insofar as they are experienced as real (White & Haines 2004). This observation is helpful in understanding how young people respond to the negative labelling and police harassment they experience as a social group. Studies of police–youth relations, for example, point to persistent and ongoing problems and conflicts between law enforcement officials and young people (White & Alder 1994; Blagg & Wilkie 1995). The perception that they are being specifically targeted for police atten-tion can lead young people to feel resentment and anger at the situation. This, in turn, can exacerbate what may already be negative and volatile relationships on the street. When 'race' and 'racism' are stirred into the equation, major problems can arise, particularly in relation to ethnic minority youth (see Collins et al. 2000). Official reaction to certain youth group formations can thus generate further reaction on the part of the young people. In this way, any real or potential deviancy is amplified by the interaction itself.

A number of studies have argued that the creation of moral panics about the perceived threat presented by young people creates a self-ful-filling prophecy. It is the experience of being labelled that influences young people to act according to the label (Cohen 1973; Hall et al. 1978, Cunneen et al. 1989). This argument is supported by McDonald whose interviews with young men and women from non-English speaking backgrounds found that many expressed anger and resentment at the way the media identified their social group as a problem for society (McDonald 1999). This was compounded by a lack of resources. Most faced unemployment and a future with limited financial prospects. The feelings of victimisation and blame generated by negative stereotyping does little to enhance their sense of self-esteem but instead contributes further to their sense of alienation from mainstream society.

Even though subjective experiences play a major role in how young people engage in criminal and antisocial behaviour, big questions remain as to why certain young people tend to commit certain kinds of crime. In other words, why is it that there are identifiable patterns of juvenile offending, particularly given the social backgrounds of those young people caught up in the institutions of criminal justice? To answer this requires an approach that goes beyond the subjective and the psychological.

## The frequent few

An important observation, first made by Wolfgang et al. (1972) in the USA, was that while the majority of juveniles have only one contact with the justice system a very small percentage have multiple contacts. This led to the thesis of *the frequent few*—that a small number of juveniles are responsible for a disproportionately large amount of crime. This thesis has been borne out by research in Australia (Morgan 1993; Coumarelos 1994; Wundersitz 1996; Cain 1998). The 1996 survey of secondary school children in New South Wales found that while a large number of New South Wales secondary students had participated in crime, the majority did not offend very often. Among the participants in each offence, however, there was a number of frequent offenders who had an annual offending frequency of 10 or more times. Coumarelos's (1994) study of juveniles having a first appearance before the New South Wales Children's Court between 1982 and 1986 found that 69.7 per cent did not appear again, while the average time between the first and last court appearance was two years, suggesting that the majority of juveniles who become involved in crime do so for a relatively short period. However, 45.4 per cent of appearances were accounted for by only 15.4 per cent of juveniles. The three most important predictors of recidivism were number of previous appearances before the Children's Court, the seriousness of the first offence, and age at first proven appearance: the younger juveniles were at their first proven appearance, the more likely they were to reappear over a four-year period.

Wundersitz's (1996) study of juvenile crime in South Australia is especially valuable because it provides detailed information about the background of repeat offenders. She found that of all appearances of all those born in South Australia in 1972 that were finalised by Aid Panels and the Children's Court, 21.1 per cent had some contact with the justice system. Of these, 65 per cent had only one appearance, while 4.5 per cent had more than five appearances. The serious repeat offenders were twice as likely to be boys than girls, most were Aboriginal, were unemployed, and came from non nuclear families (Wundersitz 1996: 128–33).

Cain's (1998) study of recidivism among juveniles brought before the Children's Court in New South Wales from 1986 to 1994 produced similar results. The study examined the records of all juvenile offenders who were first convicted of a criminal offence in the Children's Court on or after 1 January 1986 and who had reached the age of 18 by the end of 1994. Of the 52,935 juveniles identified, 81.9 per cent were male. Just under 70 per cent of the sample had only one appearance, leading to the conclusion that the majority of juvenile offenders will not reappear after their first offence. However, while a further 15 per cent had just two proven appearances, 9 per cent of juvenile offenders were responsible for almost one-third of all criminal appearances, with less than 2 per cent responsible for almost 10 per cent of all criminal appearances.

Cain also found that 86 per cent of the offences for which juveniles appeared and reappeared at the Children's Court were property offences and that juveniles who re-offended did not escalate to more serious and violent crimes.

These studies confirm the view that most juveniles grow out of offending behaviour as they mature. They also confirm that those young people who do engage in repeat offending tend to come from disadvantaged backgrounds and marginalised social circumstances.

## Poverty, unemployment, and social exclusion

While young people as a whole might be popularly perceived as a threat to social order, it is only disadvantaged young men and women who come to the attention of the law. The juvenile justice system is not filled with middle or upper class young people but with individuals drawn from the impoverished sections of society. Indigenous Australians, state wards, and the children of families experiencing long-term financial and interpersonal instability are particularly vulnerable to involvement in crime.

Wundersitz's study of 6574 cases finalised by panels or courts in South Australia in 1992–93 identified the following profile of juvenile offenders:

- 81 per cent of offenders were males
- two-thirds of those who had left school were unemployed
- most came from non-nuclear families (single parents, foster homes, extended family relations, living independently) with only 41.8 per cent residing with both natural parents at time of arrest.

A further study of 34 of these young people who had eight or more prior convictions revealed a background of severe marginalisation. Twenty-nine of the 34 were male, 22 were unemployed, and 20 were living in non-nuclear families. Closer investigation into the background of 25 of these young people revealed that:

- more than half had experienced the death of at least one parent and a number had begun their offending soon after that death
- many came from homes with problems of substance abuse, psychiatric disorder, and family violence
- 22 of the young people had substance-abuse problems
- 20 of the young people had experienced multiple abuse (rape, emotional, physical, or sexual abuse)
- 10 had attempted suicide; one had been successful
- all had a history of truancy from school
- 22 had never had a job; none had managed to hold a position for more than a few weeks.

This study, plus consideration of the general social factors underpinning juvenile offending (see Cunneen & White 2002), demonstrates a strong connection between class situation, youth engagement in crime, and the criminalisation of marginalised young people.

For these marginalised groups, the broader social problems that impact on all young people are much more severe because of their lack of material and social resources. It is against this background that their involvement in crime must be placed.

The association between poverty and crime has led some theorists to develop the idea of a political economy of crime. This suggests that patterns of crime are intimately associated with the way a nation creates and spends its wealth. Changes in patterns of production and consumption are particularly relevant to juvenile crime because their impact on young people occurs at a critical time in the life cycle as they establish their identity as adults (see Cunneen & White 2002).

As argued at length in the chapter on class and crime, there can be no doubt that broad socio-economic conditions do have a major influence on patterns of crime. For young people, these conditions constitute an important context within which decisions are made, and future prospects developed. Perhaps the important question, in the light of high levels of youth unemployment and the further casualisation of the work-force, is how come more young people are not committing more crime?

Studies such as Wundersitz et al's have contributed to the development of an empirically based knowledge base on what the risk factors are that predict which young people are most vulnerable to becoming heavily involved in crime. They include factors such as:

- coming from a low socio-economic background
- using drugs or alcohol
- being reared in a single parent family
- wagging school
- having poor school performance
- experiencing parental neglect or rejection
- receiving little parental supervision
- having parents who are involved in crime (Baker 1999; Salmelainen 1995; Herrnstein 1995; Mak 1994; Jarjoura 1993; Barnes & Farrell 1992; Smith et al. 1991; Nagin & Smith 1990; Blumstein et al. 1986).

These characteristics basically describe the nature of the young offender; however, they do not explain young offending as such. Indeed, researchers may identify a multitude of 'risk factors' (such as drug abuse) and 'protective factors' (such as family cohesion) that influence whether or not an individual engages in criminal or antisocial behaviour (Catalano & Hawkins 1996). In the end, however, risk and protective factors are socially distributed.

To put it differently, at an immediate concrete level, why certain young people commit certain crimes is answerable by consideration of their personal life history, their immediate life circumstances, and their position in the wider social structure. For example, the decision to commit vandalism may incorporate elements of an abusive childhood, difficulties at school, unemployment, and bad experiences with authority figures, or it could be as simple as 'having a good time'. But, in theoretical terms, these distinct individual biographies can be seen to be socially patterned. As a broad generalisation, they reflect deep structural inequalities and social divisions that predispose certain classes or groups of children and youth to live, and to behave, very differently from their more privileged peers. This is why, at the end of the day, the profile of young offenders tends to look basically the same—young, marginalised people (Cunneen & White 2002).

## CONCLUSION

The problems and difficulties experienced by young people are not evenly spread but are distributed through the prism of class, ethnicity, and gender. The groups that engage in criminal behaviour cannot be separated from their background of social, economic, and political exclusion. While the social harm caused by criminal acts cannot be ignored or justified, they need to be located within a social environment that provides some social groups with little hope for achieving the level of material wealth and lifestyle that is widely regarded as normal.

The last twenty-five years have seen a deepening of the structural disadvantage experienced by young, working class people, especially young men. Against a backdrop of rising expectations of consumption, and the growth in the precariousness of paid work, some sectors of youth have been left behind. Lacking a future, and carrying some sense of injustice, it is not surprising if some feel they have little to lose by engaging in crime. The challenge faced by politicians and policy makers is to acknowledge that responsibility for both the 'problem' and the solution to juvenile crime lies not just with the young person but also with wider community relationships and social structures.

## DISCUSSION QUESTIONS

1 In what ways can it be said that categories such as 'juvenile' and 'youth' are socially constructed?
2 What social factors seem most influential in shaping patterns of crime? How do you explain this?
3 What contribution can subjective understandings of crime offer to the analysis of juvenile crime?
4 What are the strengths and limitations of the identification of 'risk factors' for involvement in crime?

## GLOSSARY OF TERMS

*doli incapax*
    the common law presumption that children are incapable of wrongdoing because they are unable to understand the concepts of right and wrong

**status offences**
offences that only apply to young people, such as 'uncontrollability', 'running away from home', and 'in need of care and protection'; the assumption is that until they reach a suitable age (as determined by legislators and courts), young people should be subject to particular types of social controls

## FURTHER READING

Collins, J., Noble, G., Poynting, S. & Tabar, P. (2000) *Kebabs, Kids, Cops and Crime: Youth, Ethnicity and Crime*, Pluto Press, Sydney.
Cunneen, C. & White, R. (2002) *Juvenile Justice: Youth and Crime in Australia*, Oxford University Press, Melbourne.
Stewart, A., Dennison, S. & Waterson, E. (2002) *Pathways from Child Maltreatment to Juvenile Offending*, Trends & Issues in Criminal Justice No. 241, Australian Institute of Criminology, Canberra.
White, R. & Alder, C. (eds) (1994) *The Police and Young People in Australia*, Cambridge University Press, Melbourne.
White, R. & Wyn, J. (2004) *Youth and Society: Exploring the Social Dynamics of Youth Experience*, Oxford University Press, Melbourne.
Wundersitz, J. (1993) 'Some Statistics on Youth Offending', in F. Gale, N. Naffine & J. Wundersitz (eds) *Juvenile Justice: Debating the Issues*, Allen & Unwin, North Sydney.

## WEBSITES

**www.aic.gov.au**
Australian Institute of Criminology—Provides links to various publications from Australia's leading criminologists, including research, conference papers, publications and statistics, many of which are full text.
**www.ncjrs.org**
The National Criminal Justice Reference Service (NCJRS)—The Clearinghouse for the US National Institute of Justice, it contains summaries and full text publications on the criminal justice system. The site includes research on federal, state, and local government reports, books, research reports, journal articles, and unpublished research. Subject areas include corrections, drugs and crime, law enforcement, juvenile justice, statistics, and victims of crime.
**http://ojjdp.ncjrs.org**
The Office of Juvenile Justice and Delinquency Prevention—Provides access to research publications on the prevention strategies and responses to juvenile delinquency and victimisation in the USA.

**www.uncjin.org**
United Nations Crime and Justice Information Network—An organisation of the United Nations researching crime and prevention strategies. The website provides access to investigations and reports in a number of criminal justice areas.

# CHAPTER 14

# Victims of Crime

## INTRODUCTION

This chapter examines the nature of victimisation in Australia, and how 'victims' are defined and statistically constructed within the criminal justice system. The intention is not to discuss issues surrounding victim services and victim needs (instead, see Cook et al. 1999; White & Perrone 1997). Rather, the aim of the chapter is to explore the nature and dynamics of victimhood from the point of view of specific events and activities in the lives of people and communities. It is thus an exploration of how victimisation occurs, and the social contexts that frame who a **victim** is.

An important part of the chapter is to present an overview of the main strands within 'victimology' and to illustrate the complex ways in which a 'victim' is conceptualised in the criminological research. Issues relating to the social processes underpinning the 'making of victims', and the manner in which the status of victim itself carries certain connotations and policy implications will also be explored.

## WHO IS A VICTIM?

'"Victims" means persons who, individually or collectively, have suffered harm, including physical or mental injury, emotional suffering, economic loss or substantial impairment of their fundamental rights, through acts or omissions that are in violation of criminal laws operative within Member States, including those laws proscribing criminal abuse of power' (United Nations Office for Drug Control and Crime Prevention (1999).

Victims can be divided into two categories (see Cook et al. 1999):

- **Primary victims**—those who suffer directly as a result of a crime
- **Secondary victims**—which can include people who are witnesses to a crime, family members, friends, neighbours, and whole communities, who may also suffer trauma.

The extent and seriousness of the issue of victimisation is indicated in the following observation (Cook et al. 1999: 3):

According to recorded crime statistics, over one million people in Australia are victimised by crime each year. In 1998, almost one in every 100 persons was a victim of crime against the person, and just over six in every 100 persons were victims of crimes against property. These figures do not include the friends and family of the victim, and the community in general, who also suffer as a result of the crime.

The figures also do not include unreported conventional crimes, and nor do they include crimes associated with white collar crime, state crime, and environmental crime. Nevertheless, even given their limitations, the figures demonstrate a strong and wide-ranging experience of victimisation in Australia. This affects people both directly (in regard to actual harm) and indirectly (in regard to fear of crime). In either case, the experience of victimisation represents a major influence on how individuals, groups, and communities carry out the day-to-day routines of living.

## STATISTICAL ACCOUNTS OF VICTIMISATION

For the purposes of crime measurement and statistical analysis, 'victim' has been defined by the Australian Bureau of Statistics in different ways depending upon the offence category (ABS 2003a: 41–2):

- For murder and attempted murder, manslaughter and driving causing death, assault, sexual assault, and kidnapping/abduction, the victim is an individual person.
- For robbery, the victim may be either an individual person or an organisation. Where the robbery involves an organisation or business, the element of property ownership is the key to determining the number and type of robbery victims.

- If the robbery only involves property belonging to an organisation, then one victim (that is, the organisation) is counted regardless of the number of employees from which the property is taken. However, if robbery of an organisation also involves personal property in an employee's custody, then both the organisation and employee(s) are counted as victims.
- For blackmail/extortion, the victim may be either an individual person or an organisation.
- For unlawful entry with intent (UEWI), the victim is the place/premise that is defined as a single connected property that is owned, rented, or occupied by the same person or group of people.
- For motor vehicle theft, the victim is the motor vehicle.
- For other theft, the victim is either an individual person or an organisation.

**Table 14.1**   Mapping of recorded crime offences to ASOC

| National Offence Category Description | ASOC Code | ASOC Offence |
|---|---|---|
| Homicide and related offences | 0111 | Murder |
| | 0122 | Attempted murder |
| | 0131 | Manslaughter |
| | 0132 | Driving Causing Death |
| Assault | 0210 | Assault |
| Sexual Assault | 0310 | Sexual Assault |
| Kidnapping/abduction | 0511 | Abduction and Kidnapping |
| Robbery | 0610 | Robbery |
| Blackmail/extortion | 0621 | Blackmail and Extortion |
| Unlawful entry with intent | 0711 | Unlawful Entry with Intent/Burglary, Break and Enter |
| Motor vehicle theft | 0811 | Theft of Motor Vehicle |
| | 0812 | Illegal Use of a Motor Vehicle |
| Other theft | 0813 | Theft of Motor Vehicle Parts or Contents |
| | 0821 | Theft from a Person (excluding by force) |
| | 0823 | Theft from Retail Premises |
| | 0829 | Theft (except motor vehicles) n.e.c. |
| | 0841 | Illegal Use of Property (except motor vehicle) |

In order to enable cross-jurisdictional comparisons of victimisation and offending patterns, the ABS has developed the Australian Standard Offence Classification (ASOC). This provides a classificatory framework for the comparison of statistics on offences across Australia. The mapping of recorded crime offences in relation to the ASOC is shown in table 14.1.

As indicated by the other types of crimes, offences, harms, and victims discussed elsewhere in this book, the particular offences chosen by the ABS and other criminal justice agencies tend to reflect a fairly narrow and conventional range of socially harmful behaviour.

## Victims as recorded by police

In snapshot, the following types and patterns of victimisation were identified by the police services nationally in the year 2002 (see ABS 2003d: 3–6, 10).

The offence categories with the largest number of victims recorded by Australian police were: theft (679,460), unlawful entry with intent (394,374), and assault (159,548). By way of contrast, there were only 318 instances of murder and 344 cases of blackmail/extortion. Property offences have consistently accounted for the bulk of the major crimes. Of these offences, the most commonly recorded is 'other theft'—which includes offences such as pickpocketing, bag snatching, and shoplifting.

The number of victims decreased between 2001 and 2002 across most offence categories. Those offence categories seeing a decrease included, for example, robbery (down 21 per cent), armed robbery (down 30 per cent), motor vehicle theft (down 19 per cent), unlawful entry with intent (down 9 per cent), kidnapping/abduction (down 9 per cent), other theft (down 3 per cent), and blackmail/extortion (down 3 per cent). In numerical terms, the biggest decreases in offences were for victims of unlawful entry with intent (down 41,380), motor vehicle theft (down 26,505), and other theft (down 20,677). To interpret the significance of these figures requires a broader time frame than a year-to-year comparison. Nevertheless, it is significant that, for example, the number of robbery offences increased by 82 per cent from 1995 to 2001 (AIC 2002a: 5), yet declined sharply in 2002 (mainly due to targeted policing strategies to deal with this particular kind of offence). Indeed, the robbery victimisation rate (106 per 100,000 population) was the lowest since 1995.

The rates for unlawful entry with intent, and for motor vehicle theft, were the lowest since the commencement of the national Recorded Crime collection in 1993.

Conversely, the offence categories for which there were increases between 2001 and 2002 in numbers of incidents recorded included sexual assault (up 6 per cent) and assault (up 5 per cent). Assault was the most commonly recorded violent crime, accounting for the vast majority of recorded violent crimes (that include homicide, assault, sexual assault, and robbery). The assault victimisation rate increased by 44 per cent from 563 to 810 per 100,000 population between 1995 and 2002. The sexual assault victimisation rate also increased, from 69 to 91 per 100,000 population between 1993 and 2002. Murder, attempted murder, and manslaughter victimisation rates tended to remain fairly stable over this period.

Victim characteristics, such as sex, age, and relationship to offender, vary according to the nature of the offence category (see ABS 2003a):

- Males are more likely than females to be victims of robbery (70 per cent of victims were male), blackmail/extortion (69 per cent), attempted murder (66 per cent), driving causing death (62 per cent), murder (60 per cent), and assault (57 per cent).
- Females were more likely than males to be victims of sexual assault (80 per cent) and kidnapping/abduction (62 per cent).
- Persons aged 24 years or less comprised the majority of recorded victims of sexual assault (72 per cent), kidnapping/abduction (64 per cent), and robbery (51 per cent). Persons aged 20 to 24 had the highest assault victimisation rate of 1729 per 100,000 population, which is over twice the recorded victimisation rate of the total population (810 per 100,000 population).
- In states and territories where data was available, at least half of the victims of murder knew the offender. For sexual assault, in those incidents where the victim knew the offender, the offender was twice as likely not to be a family member, for those state and territories for which information was available. However, most sexual assaults are committed by a person known to the victim (AIC 2002a: 23).
- According to information published by the Australian Institute of Criminology (AIC 2002a: 18), 38 per cent of male victims of assault knew the offender compared with 68 per cent of female victims. Assaults occurring against females were three times more likely to be

perpetrated by a family member than those occurring against males, and 40 per cent of male victims were assaulted by strangers compared with only 16 per cent of female victims.

The location of crime again varies according to offence category, with obvious connections between some types of crime (for example, shoplifting) and particular places (for example, retail shops). Most sexual assaults take place in a residential location, as do most homicides. Robbery tends to occur in community and retail locations (such as car parks, schools, and retail shops). Over half of the locations of unlawful entry with intent consist of private dwellings.

## Victims as recorded by victim-survey

In order to gauge trends in victimisation the ABS undertakes periodic household surveys that involve individuals identifying their experiences of crime, their perception of problems in their neighbourhoods, and their feelings of safety (ABS 2003a). The surveys involve persons aged 15 years or older and, in the specific case of sexual assault, persons aged over 18 years. The *Crime and Safety Surveys* concentrate on those categories of more serious crime that affect the largest number of people: household break-in, motor vehicle theft, assault (including sexual assault), and robbery. Highlights of the 2002 study include:

- *Household crime*—It was estimated that 4.7 per cent of households (456,300 out of a total of over 7 million households in Australia at the time of the survey) were victims of at least one break-in to their home, garage, or shed, and that there were 428,500 incidents in which there were signs of at least one attempted break-in. Over 80 per cent of victim households experienced a single break-in. Two per cent of households had at least one motor vehicle stolen.

- *Personal crime*—It was reported that of persons aged 15 years and over in Australia at the time of survey, 1 per cent (95,800) were victims of at least one robbery, and 4.7 per cent (717,900) were victims of at least one assault. It was estimated that 33,000 or 0.2 per cent of persons aged 18 years and over were victims of at least one sexual assault.

Household and personal crimes varied greatly across states and territories. For example, the lowest level of total household victimisation was Victoria (7.0 per cent) whereas the highest was the Northern Territory

(20.3 per cent). The Northern Territory also had the highest level of person victimisation in the country, where an estimated 8.1 per cent of persons aged 15 years and over experienced at least one of the selected personal crimes, compared with a rate of 4.7 per cent in Queensland.

As with officially recorded offences, victim characteristics—such as sex, age, and relationship to offender—vary according to the nature of the offence category:

- Males were more likely than females to be victims of robbery (68 per cent), especially young males aged 15 to 19 years (22 per cent of all persons who were victims of robbery). Just over half of the assault victims were male (55 per cent).
- Females were more likely than males to be victims of sexual assault (86 per cent). Furthermore, in cases of assault, it is notable that 47 per cent of females reported that the most recent incident had occurred in the victim's home, compared with 24 per cent of males.
- The highest incidence rate for assault was for both males and females in the 25 to 34 year age group. By way of contrast, persons aged 65 years and over were least likely to be victims of assault, with this age group making up approximately 3 per cent of male victims and 2 per cent of female victims of assault.

While this survey of statistical data on patterns of victimisation provides an indication of how people are victimised for different kinds of offence, it is important to bear in mind that they are not definitive. For instance, data on sexual assault might usefully be bolstered by interviews with staff at women's refuges and centres dealing with sexual assault, as well as perusal of hospital emergency room records. A range of data sources and empirical studies are needed to gauge fully the 'dark figure' of crime, especially in cases involving interpersonal violence among family members.

There is also a growing recognition of the extent to which small businesses are victims of crime. The Small Business Crime Safety found that for every 100 businesses surveyed 62 incidents of burglary occurred, with liquor outlets being particularly vulnerable. Just under half of the businesses surveyed had experienced at least one incident of crime. The study also found that just as a small number of offenders are responsible for a disproportionate number of crimes, so a small number of businesses are repeatedly targeted and account for a large proportion of all crimes measured in the survey (Taylor & Mayhew 2002).

## THE PAINS AND PROCESSES OF VICTIMISATION

Statistical analysis can be useful in highlighting general patterns of victimisation, and general processes that are associated with being a victim and allow for social differences to be acknowledged across several different dimensions.

### Distributions of risk and impact

An important issue for consideration is the way in which the response to both the incidence of crime and its consequences, as well as the fear of crime, is differentially distributed among social groups. One significant distinction is between groups that are at 'high risk' of crime and groups that have a 'high impact' of crime. For example, older people are statistically less likely to be a victim of assault than young people in the 20–24 year age category. They are not at 'high risk'. However, if subjected to assault, the impact is likely to be greater than in the case of a younger victim. The nature of the impact plays an important role in how victims perceive and fear the possibilities of crime victimisation.

### Geographies of victimisation

It has been observed that one of the crucial factors affecting risk of crime, fear of crime, and geographical mobility in urban areas is gender (Painter 1992). Other factors include such things as age, ethnicity, class, and lifestyle. Spatial and temporal analysis of who gets victimised where, by whom, and why, provides important insights into the social dynamics and power structures of the society as a whole. Women are more likely to be subjected to specific kinds of harassment and harm depending upon the time of day, the nature of public space, and the company they are in. In fact, research in the UK suggests that women experience higher levels, and a wider spectrum of crime, than men (Painter 1992), and that this is directly related to the organisation of physical environments and public spaces.

### The pains of victimisation

Being a victim can have physical, emotional, financial, and psychological effects not only on individuals but also on groups and communities.

Its effects may also be long-lasting (see Cook et al. 1999). Depending on the nature of the harm, victims may suffer from post-crime trauma, they may be fearful for their lives, and they may change their behaviour by restricting their activities and friendship networks. They may be incapacitated through physical injuries or psychological and emotional wounds. They may suffer financial loss or property damage. The impacts of crime vary depending upon the nature of the person, the type of harm, the social networks of the victim, the community context, and so on. In some cases, the pain is not 'realised' until well after the event.

## Repeat victimisation

Crime does not occur uniformly across the population, nor does it happen the same way in every location. It tends to be concentrated on particular people, and found in particular places. The re-occurrence of crime is known as **repeat victimisation**. This is where certain people or places are victimised more than once. It is a phenomenon common to many crimes, including, for example, domestic or family violence, incest and paedophilia, burglary and wilful entry with intent, hate crimes, and bank robberies. Repeat victimisation of personal crimes can be especially traumatising and have profound and long-lasting negative effects.

Repeat victimisations account for a disproportionately large amount of crime. While the annual prevalence rate of repeat victimisation is low (2.4 per cent of households and 1.4 per cent of persons aged 15 and over), these households or individuals account for more than half the incidents of crime occurring during the year. In the case of property crimes, half the incidents occur in just over one quarter of all households with 10 per cent of all victimised households experiencing three or more incidents. Together these accounted for 25 per cent of all incidents. In the case of violent crime, two-thirds of the incidents are experienced by 41 per cent of victims (Mukherjee & Carcach 1998).

## Double victimisation

The concept of **double victimisation** is also important. This refers to the idea that the ways in which the state responds to victimisation can add further burdens to a victim. For instance, rape victims can be described as doubly victimised because of the way in which courtroom processes put women 'on trial' by suggesting they invited the incident in some way. Sex workers can also be seen as doubly victimised in the sense that they are sexually exploited by men and victimised by the courts, which operate with a double standard that criminalises them but not their male clients (Scutt 1990; Graycar & Morgan 1990; Brown et al. 2001).

## Reporting of victimisation

How individuals and households respond to victimisation varies with the nature of the offence and the victim's view of the incident. This is reflected in large differences in rates of reporting. The Australian Bureau of Statistics (ABS 2003a: 8) data reveals that reporting rates for different offence types range from:

- 95 per cent for household victims of motor vehicle theft
- 75 per cent for household victims of break-in
- 50 per cent for victims of robbery
- 31 per cent for victims of assault
- 20 per cent for female victims of sexual assault.

The reasons for not reporting include feeling that the incident is a personal matter and that victims will take care of themselves (in cases of assault) and feeling there is nothing the police can do (in cases of household victimisation as well as robbery).

## VICTIM–OFFENDER RELATIONSHIPS

Victimisation is rarely a one-off event. Being a victim can have repercussions far beyond the direct and immediate consequences of harm. For example, anticipating the release of an offender who has harmed a person, group, or community can have ongoing consequences:

> For many violent victims, the thought of living in the same community as the person who caused them such terrible harm and deep psychological trauma is foreboding. Re-entry partnership professionals and volunteers must accept this factor and find ways, to the degree possible, to honor the victim's wishes. This may mean establishing a geographic 'safe zone' perimeter around the victim (for example, in

California it is 30 miles from the victim's place of residence), and developing strict conditions of supervision that center on the victim's need for safety (Seymour 2001: 8).

Responding to these concerns has recently been acknowledged in research literature and government policy. In particular, the main concern is with ensuring victim safety and personal security, while simultaneously addressing the need for offender re-integration back into the community.

Table 14.2 provides information on the concerns that victims express when considering the re-entry of imprisoned offenders back into the community—and potentially into their lives. The table illustrates that victimisation is not over once an offender has been caught, prosecuted, sentenced, and 'done their time'. Victims often have to confront their victimisation over and over again, as they come to grips with the possibilities of seeing their offender again.

**Table 14.2** Concerns and needs of victims when their offenders re-enter the community

| Need or Concern | Percentage |
| --- | --- |
| Information about whom to contact if victim has concerns | 75% |
| Notification of offender location | 75% |
| Notification of offender status | 65% |
| Protective or 'no contact' orders | 64% |
| Input into conditions of release (Victim Impact Statement) | 33% |
| Financial/legal obligations | 29% |
| Information about referrals | 22% |
| Offender programming that creates awareness | 19% |
| Input into interstate compact | 16% |
| Input into conditions of community service | 15% |
| Victim/offender programming (mediation) | 12% |

Source: Seymour (2001: 4).

In New South Wales, victims have two kinds of rights in relation to the issue of impending release (Garkawe 2002: 261):

- *The right to information*—Victims have the right to be kept informed of the offender's impending release or escape from custody, or of any change in security classification that results in the offender being eligible for unescorted absence from custody. This right has implications for system management, but does not present any civil liberty concerns as such in relation to the inmate.

- *The right to participation*—Victims have the right to make submissions with respect to decisions on whether 'serious offenders' are eligible for unescorted leave of absence. This right can have an impact on prisoner rights, in that victim submissions may influence the relevant authority (for example, parole board, prison officials) to disallow, defer, or place more stringent conditions on any external leave granted to the prisoner.

Given the impact that the exercise of different rights may have, it is essential to explore the rationale behind how such rights ought to be implemented in practice (see case study 14.1). Garkawe (2002) discusses the specific contexts within which different rights ought to be exercised. It is acknowledged by most commentators that the 'right to information' concerning criminal justice decision-making processes and outcomes is desirable and should be encouraged. However, the use of the 'right to participate' does require certain qualifications. For example, the right of victims to present a submission to a parole hearing needs to be based upon the requirement that any evidence so presented must be legally relevant and factually verifiable. In other words, participation by victims is bounded by consideration of whether the evidence is 'legally relevant' to the decision-making task at hand (for example, documented threats or negative behaviour directed towards the victim on the part of the prisoner).

## CASE STUDY 14.1

Kelley-Anne Laws was brutally stabbed to death in 1995 by her fiancé's brother, Kevin Presland. He was an electrician who, hours before, had been taken by the police to Newcastle's James Fletcher Hospital covered in blood due to a fight he had just had with a workmate, Blake, at Blake's home. According to newspaper reports, Presland believed that Blake was in league with the devil and was inciting one of his pet rats to attack him. When Presland allegedly attempted to strangle a child, Blake hit him on the head with a cricket bat.

In the days before Kelley-Anne Laws' death Presland had drunk up to ten schooners of beer and smoked six doses of marijuana daily. Apparently this had precipitated a psychosis. Although the psychiatrist at the hospital had assessed Presland as 'suffering a bizarre and violent episode' he was not detained.

Presland was charged with the murder of Laws but pleaded not guilty by reason of insanity. He served two-and-a-half years in jail and a psychiatric unit at Long Bay.

Preston subsequently sued the hospital for negligently discharging him. The Supreme Court ruled that he was entitled to be compensated because he needed care and if the hospital had not released him he wouldn't have killed Kelley-Anne. He was awarded $225,000 damages for the pain and suffering he experienced as a result of killing the woman plus $85,000 for lost earnings during his detention as a forensic patient. The family of the victim had received $50,000 in victim compensation. The decision to compensate Presland devastated the Laws family.

*The family said:* It was his choice to take marijuana, his choice to drink—nobody else's. No one made him do it, yet the system sees fit to pay him. I can't understand the law.

*The executive director of the Victims of Crime Assistance said:* The victims of these acts enter a never-never land where they have to explain their lack of status and ask somewhat ironically: 'Well, if he's innocent, who killed Kelley-Anne?'

*The judge said:* 'Mr Presland was alienated from his family and there is a heavy load of guilt. His time in prison on remand was a terrifying nightmare. His incarceration as a forensic patient only slightly less so.

*The head of the Mental Health Association of New South Wales said:* People have a right to treatment...He is a victim as well because he was ill at the time...It's very hard for all of them. It's a system that failed everybody.

Somewhat more contentiously, there is a range of subjective matters of concern to victims that also needs to be evaluated. Victims may be fearful of the offender, perceive them to be untrustworthy, or they may not have forgiven the prisoner. This raises the question of how or if the criminal justice system ought to respond to the emotional responses of victims. Garkawe (2002: 271) suggests that the victim's views may be of some relevance in a small minority of cases where the conditions of parole (or day release) are being determined. In other words, conditions relating to contact with victims or members of the victim's family, and place of residence or movement, might be subject to imposed special conditions as a result of victim submissions.

Victims have an interest in the re-entry process of offenders across several domains (see Seymour 2001). These include:

- *victim notification*—information about rights, processes, resources, options, and services
- *victim protection*—personal safety and security concerns, feelings of safety, actual fear, and perceived fear
- *victim impact*—harms or hurt suffered by the victim, physically, emotionally, and financially
- *victim restitution*—financial compensation from offender, government compensation, dialogue with offender.

The official position of the Probation and Community Corrections Officers Association of Australia (PACCOA) is that notification of victims is important and needs to be formally recognised (2003). However, it is also acknowledged that any notification system has to balance several competing interests:

> A primary victim's right to information about the status of an offender's progress through the criminal justice process should be balanced with that offender's right to privacy of personal information. In general, on victim request, offers of status and other information should be made pro-actively to the primary victim....
>
> Unless legislation provides for otherwise, PACCOA will only support the release of information on the proviso that:
>
> - it will not be publicly disseminated in any way, including through the media, the internet or any other form,
> - it will not be used for any unlawful purpose that could cause harm or detriment to any person,
> - such information will not enable unwanted contact between offender or victim, and
> - information divulged by victims to other third parties be restricted to the purposes of:
>   - ▾ self protective measures to minimise risk of harm to themselves or immediate family,
>   - ▾ enhancing their healing within the confidentiality of treatment environments, or
>   - ▾ disclosure to statutory authorities for legitimate business.

In general, PACCOA does not support the concept of issuing release notifications to communities, only to primary victims or their personal representatives (or statutory authorities where there is perceived risk to any individual in the community). PACCOA believes that victim services and probation/community corrections share the responsibility of both protecting their clients and assisting them to deal with the fear and mistrust that each may hold for the other.

Garkawe (2002) points out that information about things such as the prisoner's place of detention, where the prisoner will reside after being released, and details of their treatment or participation in prison programs may breach the prisoner's privacy and may be used by some victims or their families to harass the prisoner or the prisoner's family. In the light of this, it is suggested that the privacy rights of prisoners should prevail in the absence of victims' genuine security needs.

The PACCOA Statement on Victims (2003) also makes comments relevant to the issue of victim safety, security, and protection. For example, it is pointed out that:

> One of the most effective ways to encourage victim participation in the entire criminal justice process is to ensure their safety from intimidation or harm by offenders or those associated by offenders. Correctional agencies have an important obligation to protect victims from intimidation and harassment and/or harm from offenders under their supervision. A combination of sound policies, supervision procedures and modern technology may offer many innovative approaches to increasing and enforcing victim protection measures.

From a victim perspective, the interest in what happens to offenders is immediately relevant. It is thus important that victims' needs be fully considered when assessing offenders' risk. This involves knowing as much as possible about the circumstances of the victimisation, including the personal relationship between the victim and offender.

## VICTIMS AND VICTIMOLOGY

The criminological study of victims and victimisation not only centres on crime and safety statistics, the dynamics of victim events and geography, and the impacts and fears of victims over time—it also includes theories about what causes victimisation and the relationship between victim and

Box 14.1

# APPROACHES TO VICTIMOLOGY

## Realist or positivist victimology

This approach is informed by the notion that crime is 'out there', and that, likewise, victims are 'out there'. That is, there is the idea that crime, and victims, exist in an 'objective' sense, so victimisation can be measured simply by observation and/or scientific methods. The main method of investigation adopted is the victimisation survey.

The main orientations and findings of positivist criminology include:

- an identification of factors relating to the potential *risk of victimisation* (for example, work is done to examine people, situations, and places that are associated with the risk of crime)
- investigation that tends to concentrate on *interpersonal crimes of violence and certain types of property crimes*, rather than crimes of the powerful, including crimes of the state
- a tendency to regard victims themselves as being implicated in their own victimisation (for example, victim precipitation is said to occur in the situation where a young woman is hitchhiking, for she is said to have willingly gone into an 'at-risk' situation).

## Institutionalist or critical victimology

Rather than taking victims as a given, this perspective looks at victimisation as a social process. In particular, it examines how victims are made by the operation of institutions and particular forms of interaction. Victimhood is contingent upon who is doing the labelling, and on the manner in which official labels are conferred.

The main orientations of the institutionalist perspective include:

- how the label comes into being, who applies the label, and under what circumstances (for example, gay and lesbian bashings, and the *denial of victim status* when the police choose not to respond)
- a concern to uncover the *power relations* that underpin how institutions confer victim status, and that ignore other sorts of actual social harm
- an interest in moving beyond simple descriptive categories such as 'victim' and 'offender' to view human behaviour in the light of *situational and structural contexts* (for example, who suffers from so-called victimless crimes such as prostitution and drug taking).

Box 14.1

**Left realist victimology**

This approach builds upon and provides a critique of aspects of both the previous perspectives. Concerned to deal with the gaps in mainstream victim surveys, the left realist approach does not wish to only concentrate on victimisation as a social process and issues of bias in definition, but also to document particular types of victimisation.

The major contributions and propositions of left realist victimology include:

- placing crime victims at the centre of the research gaze, and doing so in a manner which, *methodologically*, will provide better and more precise information about the nature and processes of victimisation (for example, undertaking geographically focused local surveys that generally involve interviews and in-depth discussion about the issues)
- undertaking victim research in a way that provides an adequate *representation* of women, ethnic minority groups, young people, and the poor
- attempting to broaden the scope of questions asked about crime, by tapping into issues such as the private sphere of child abuse, corporate crime, environmental crime, and safety regulations at work.

Source: drawn from White & Perrone (1997: 233–6).

offender. There are three main approaches to the study of victims: realist, institutionalist, and left realist (see Walklate 1990; Mawby & Walklate 1994). These are summarised in box 14.1 (see also White & Perrone 1997).

While the diverse approaches to victimology, taken together, provide us with a more precise sense of the level of victimisation in the community, more needs to be said about the criminal victimisation process as a whole. For example, too often victimisation is seen in terms of a snapshot in time, as simply an 'event'. Analysis of the processual aspects of victimisation suggest a more complex and ambiguous process.

## VICTIM STATUS

**Victimisation** is a process in which people learn to be a victim. How this occurs and under what circumstances it occurs has a major bearing on how victim status is socially constructed. For example, victims are generally pictured as passive, not active, which denies the idea that humans make their own world, if not always as they like it. The application of victim status tends to be loaded with negative connotations, such as weakness, passivity, and other such terms.

This is particularly so in crimes associated with women, and it can have the effect of disempowering them. For instance, it has been argued that traditionally women were trained to be potential rape victims from an early age—they were taught to cry, plead, look for a male protector, but never to fight and win (Brownmiller 1976). In response, it has been suggested that we should be talking about *survivors* of rape and/or incest, rather than victims. In this manner, it is argued, those subjected to the harm will be better able to regain control and power over their lives. The new terminology implies that the status of victim is not fixed, but can be changed.

In a similar vein, it has been argued that certain conceptions of the 'ideal victim' are a culturally ingrained part of male-dominated society. This builds into certain definitions of crime notions of who a true or worthy victim really is. For example, rape victims tend to be judged against a stereotype of the virginal chaste woman. This means that when certain women (such as sex workers) attempt to utilise the law and law enforcement agencies, they may be denied full victim status and/or not be treated seriously by police or judges. Similarly, how a rape victim reacts to the assault (for example, struggle or not struggle), her personal sexual history (for example, active or not), and her marital status (for example, single or married) all tend to have implications for whether or not she 'achieves' victim status or not (McCarthy 1993).

Analysis of the politics and disempowering aspects of 'victimhood' can also be applied to groups such as Indigenous people, who are frequently referred to as victims (of colonialism, of poverty, of racism, etc.). Again, this can imply passive acceptance of circumstance. What about the notion of active struggle? Until recently, most non-Aboriginal writers treated Aboriginal history in generally, and often exclusively, negative terms, ignoring the strength and courage that exemplifies active struggle against repression and genocide. In fact, the Aboriginal experience is a heterogeneous one, marked by achievements and disasters, but fundamentally by the active participation of Indigenous people in fighting against enforced victimisation (Palmer & Collard 1993).

One of the issues here is the way in which victim status is *universalised*, so that for example all Aborigines are seen as being the same. This master status is untrue, because it cannot apply equally to all in the same way. The diversity of experience from group to group, and from region to region, makes it difficult to ascribe to a whole people a uniform experience. Certainly when it comes to issues surrounding victim status, and the connotations of passivity and helplessness, such a view does more damage than good. It reflects a patronising attitude that contributes to the making of victims, rather than acceptance of rights, dignity, and respect.

## VICTIMISATION AND FEAR OF CRIME

Fear of crime is an important issue for the community, affecting quality of life and the social capital of communities. Its roots are multidimensional and include factors such as perceptions of levels of physical and social incivility in the neighbourhood (Taylor & Hale 1986), social and economic disadvantage, type of crime, isolation, and feelings of vulnerability (Hale 1996). Just as victimisation is not evenly spread in the community, so fear of crime affects some groups disproportionately. Some populations are much more fearful than the objective likelihood of their victimisation suggests (Attorney-General's Department 1995). This is especially true of older people. The 2002 *Crime and Safety Survey* (ABS 2003a) found that only 23 per cent of people over the age of 65 felt very safe at home during the day, compared with 42 per cent of people aged between 15 and 19. Yet it is younger people, especially young males, who are most likely to be victims. Other research suggests that when it comes to fear of violence in general, young people are actually more fearful than older people, presumably because of their lifestyle (Kelley 1992 cited in Grabosky 1995b).

Women are another group that is fearful of violent crime. Whereas 78 per cent of men feel very safe at home alone after dark, only 61 per cent of women do (ABS 2003a). Women are also more fearful than men of walking in their neighbourhood at night (Grabosky 1995b). This suggests that fear of 'stranger danger' is prevalent among women and older people, but this fear is misplaced in both groups for different reasons. For women, violence is more likely to occur from intimates, while older people in general experience far less violence than other social groups.

As well as gender and age, the presence of disorder and incivility in the neighbourhood is also linked to fear of crime (Grabosky 1995b).

The media is often cited as contributing to the disproportionately high level of fear of crime in the community. Newspapers, magazines, films, and TV stories feed the public a daily diet of crime stories. While these certainly appear to increase sales, they do little to generate a sense of trust in the community. Often these stories have little relationship to real levels of crime or actual events, or else the 'facts' are conveyed in a sensationalist way that creates a sense of crisis and alarm in the audience.

There have been three main attempts to explain fear of crime:

- *community concern perspective*—argues that fears are rooted in people's perceptions about local problems based on objective factors such as levels of crime, socio-economic factors, and physical conditions
- *perceived disorder perspective*—argues that fear is derived from the inter-action between low socio-economic status and perceptions about a neighbourhood's level of physical and social incivility
- *indirect victimisation perspective*—argues that vulnerability is a key factor in generating fear of crime and this will be conveyed through local social networks. Consequently, people who have been previously victimised and those with local ties are most likely to be fearful (Mukherjee & Carcach 1998: 26).

Any analysis of victimisation has to also consider the wider impact of victimisation on members of the community who, although perhaps not directly subjected to harm, may be fearful of crime because of stories about those who have been.

## VICTIMISATION AS A PROCESS

If we wish to see victimisation in a more dynamic way, we must view it as a process. For example, we might consider the Bhopal Union Carbide plant explosion in India. At one level, this event was tragic and produced numerous victims. But if we examine the incident more closely, we find that the process of victimisation continued well beyond the immediate incident (see Walklate 1990). On the fifth anniversary of the explosion, for instance, over 200 environmental groups met to discuss the continu-ing ecological impact of the explosion, and to acknowledge that deaths were still continuing as a consequence of the explosion. The incident, and the response to the victimisation, reverberated worldwide. People in the United States who had Union Carbide factories in their neighbourhoods demonstrated their concerns over the prospect of a similar occurrence, and their action led to changes in legislation and a closer monitoring of the process.

Another example of victimisation as a social process is that of child abuse (Walklate 1990; see also Harding 1994; Egger 1994). Several decades ago this was a 'hidden' problem, concealed by a persistent wall of denial. However, social momentum built up and ignorance and reluctance to 'interfere' in the private domain of the family and home were eventually overcome. Child abuse was finally acknowledged as a real problem, much public anger was vented over its occurrence, and the campaign momentum was translated into numerous changes in legislation and in law enforcement practices (for example, mandatory reporting of child abuse).

We also need to consider the issue of time in discussions of issues such as child abuse. That is, such abuse can occur over a number of years, but the manifestation of pain and trauma may not occur instantly but only emerge later on in a person's life. This may be so for at least two reasons. In some cases, people will block out of their mind particularly stressful and painful incidents. As they get older, or if they receive counselling, they may begin to remember what their mind had put to rest. In other cases, it might be that people have always remembered, but were afraid to publicly speak about or tell anyone about their ordeals. For example, many of the boys brought to Australia as 'orphans' (although in many cases they were not) at the end of World War II were to suffer abuse in their new institutional settings. The boys are now men, and only now, after media publicity, are they admitting their experiences of abuse.

It is important to view victimology as a process. Otherwise, we may end up with fear and the disempowerment of people at a community level. This fear can then generate moral panics that emphasise crime control rather than causation. Furthermore, a processual account can also appreciate better the dilemmas of victimisation. For instance, everyday approaches to victimisation tend to fix on exclusive categories of 'victim' and 'offender', failing to recognise that the victim can also be the offender. For example, the woman who beats her child may herself be suffering abuse. Similarly, members of the 'underclass' who engage in criminal activities are also arguably its most vulnerable victims. Ultimately, we need to question what it is about our social system that makes both victims and offenders.

## CONCLUSION

While the definition of 'victim' is straightforward, as an indication of status the term is fundamentally ambiguous. It is positively associated with a recognition of the violation of human rights but also negatively associated with passivity and powerlessness. To be recognised as a victim carries with it claims to recompense and social justice, but also images of a loss of control over one's life. For this reason, the status of victim is something that individuals and groups have strived to achieve while rejecting its negative connotations.

These issues reflect the fact that being recognised as a victim is not something that is given automatically, but results from a social process in which relations of power are central. As well as the relationship between victim and offender, this includes all those individuals and institutions involved in the definition of the act that led to the label 'victim' being applied. The term 'victim' is, therefore, fundamentally a political concept, and one that is socially constructed, contested, and open to different interpretations.

Much more can be said, therefore, about the social construction of crime within victimology itself—and, in particular, the continuing prominence given to 'street crime' and interpersonal crime over and above that of crimes of the powerful. How these emphases might in turn reinforce the fear of crime, due to the subject matter, is an issue of some policy and political relevance. The nature of the victim–offender categorisation also needs further critical scrutiny. For example, on the one hand, the dichotomy between victim and offender can obfuscate the fact that very often the same person can be both simultaneously (for example, battered women who kill their abusing partners).

## DISCUSSION QUESTIONS

1 What factors influence the distribution of risks of victimisation?
2 What are the dilemmas faced by the criminal justice system in balancing the rights of victims with those of offenders?

**3** How does the left realist victimology differ from critical victimology?

**4** What are the advantages of a processual understanding of victimisation?

## GLOSSARY OF TERMS

**double victimisation**
the way in which the state's response to victimisation can add further burdens to the victim

**primary victims**
those who suffer directly as a result of a crime

**repeat victimisation**
one of two categories of victimisation, it occurs when a crime occurs in the same location or to the same individual on more than one occasion

**secondary victims**
the other category of victimisation, covering those who are not directly affected by a crime but who suffer trauma as a result of it; such people include witnesses to a crime, family members, friends, neighbours, and whole communities

**victim**
persons who, individually or collectively, have suffered harm, including physical or mental injury, emotional suffering, economic loss, or substantial impairment of their fundamental rights, through acts or omissions that are in violation of criminal laws operative within Member States, including those laws proscribing criminal abuse of power (United Nations Office for Drug Control and Crime Prevention 1999)

**victimisation**
the process in which a person learns to be a victim.

## FURTHER READING

Cook, B., David, F. & Grant, A. (1999) *Victims' Needs, Victims' Rights: Policies and Programs for Victims of Crime in Australia*, Australian Institute of Criminology Research and Public Policy Series No. 19, Canberra.

Garkawe, S. (2002) 'Crime Victims and Prisoners' Rights', in D. Brown & M. Wilkie (eds) *Prisoners As Citizens: Human Rights in Australian Prisons*, The Federation Press, Sydney.

Probation and Community Corrections Officers' Association (2003) *The Foundations of Corrections Based Services for Victims of Crime: A PACCOA Position Paper*, PACCOA Papers, 1(1).

Seymour, A. (2001) *The Victim's Role in Offender Reentry: A Community Response Manual*, Office for Victims of Crime, US Department of Justice, Washington DC.

## WEBSITES

**www.aic.gov.au**
Australian Institute of Criminology—Provides links to various publications from Australia's leading criminologists, including research, conference papers, publications, and statistics, many of which are full text.

**www.lawlink.nsw.gov.au/voc**
New South Wales Government Victims of Crime Unit—Provides information for victims of crime and links to other research activities.

**www.ncjrs.org**
National Criminal Justice Reference Service (NCJRS)—The Clearinghouse for the US National Institute of Justice, it contains summaries and full-text publications on the criminal justice system. The site includes research on federal, state, and local government reports, books, research reports, journal articles, and unpublished research. Subject areas include corrections, drugs and crime, law enforcement, juvenile justice, statistics, and victims of crime.

# Bibliography

ABS *see* Australian Bureau of Statistics.

AIC *see* Australian Institute of Criminology.

Aichorn, A. (1935) *Wayward Youth*, Viking Press, New York (reissued in 1965).

AIHW *see* Australian Institute of Health and Welfare.

Albrechsten, J. (2002) 'Talking Race not Racism', *The Australian*, 17 July <www.theaustralian.news.com.au/printpage/0,5942,4718201,00.html> (accessed 2 June 2004).

Alder, C. (1997) 'Young Women and Juvenile Justice: Objectives, Frameworks and Strategies', paper presented at the Australian Institute of Criminology Conference 'Towards Juvenile Crime and Juvenile Justice: Towards 2000 and Beyond', Adelaide.

Alder, C. (1994) 'The Policing of Young Women', in R. White & C. Alder (eds) *The Police and Young People in Australia*, Cambridge University Press, Melbourne.

Allas, R. & James, S. (1997) *Justice Gone Walkabout: A Study of Victorian Aboriginal Offending 1989–90 to 1993–94*, Victorian Aboriginal Legal Service Cooperative, Melbourne.

Archer, J. (2001) *Australia's Drinking Water: The Coming Crisis*, Pure Water Press, Sydney.

Aries (1973) *Centuries of Childhood*, Cape, London.

Atkinson, L. & McDonald, D. (1995) *Cannabis, the Law and Social Impacts in Australia*, Trends and Issues No. 48, Australian Institute of Criminology, Canberra.

Attorney-General's Department (1995) *The Justice Statement*, Office of Legal Information and Publishing, Attorney-General's Department, Canberra.

Aumair, M. & Warren, I. (1994) 'Characteristics of Juvenile Gangs in Melbourne', *Youth Studies Australia*, 13(2): 40–44.

Australian Bureau of Statistics (2004) *Prisoners in Australia* (Cat. No. 4517.0), ABS, Canberra.

Australian Bureau of Statistics (2003a) *Crime and Safety: Australia April 2002* (Cat. No. 4509.0), ABS, Canberra.

Australian Bureau of Statistics (2003b) *Criminal Courts* (Cat No. 4513.0), ABS, Canberra.

Australian Bureau of Statistics (2003c) 'Labour Market Transitions of Teenagers', *Australian Labour Market Statistics* (Cat. No. 6105.0), ABS, Canberra.

Australian Bureau of Statistics (2003d) *Recorded Crime: Victims* (Cat. No. 4510.0), ABS, Canberra.

Australian Bureau of Statistics (2002a) *Crime and Safety*, (Cat. No. 4509.0), ABS, Canberra.

Australian Bureau of Statistics (2002b) *Recorded Crime: Australia* (Cat. No. 4510.0), ABS, Canberra.

Australian Council of Social Services (2001) 'Breaching the Safety Net: The Harsh Impact of Social Security Penalties', *ACOSS INFO*, 305, 13 August.

Australian Institute of Criminology (2004) *Does Drug Use Cause Crime? Understanding the Drugs–Crime Link*', AIC Crime Reduction Matters, 22, <www.aic.gov.au/publications/crm> (accessed 25 May 2004).

Australian Institute of Criminology (2003) *Australian Crime: Facts & Figures 2003*, Australian Institute of Criminology, Canberra.

Australian Institute of Criminology (2002a) *Australian Crime: Facts & Figures 2002*, Australian Institute of Criminology, Canberra.

Australian Institute of Criminology (2002b) 'Organised Crime', *Crime Fact Info*, Australian Institute of Criminology, Canberra.

Australian Institute of Criminology (2002c) 'The Illegal Market in Australian Abalone', *Crime Fact Info*, Australian Institute of Criminology, Canberra.

Australian Institute of Criminology (2002d) 'The Trade in Stolen Antiquities', *Crime Fact Info*, Australian Institute of Criminology, Canberra.

Australian Institute of Criminology (2001a) 'People Smuggling Facts', *Crime Fact Info*, Australian Institute of Criminology, Canberra.

Australian Institute of Criminology (2001b) 'Sea Cargo Accounts for the Majority of Heroin Detected in Australia', *Crime Fact Info*, Australian Institute of Criminology, Canberra.

Australian Institute of Criminology (2001c) *Australian Crime: Facts & Figures 2001*, Australian Institute of Criminology, Canberra.

Australian Institute of Criminology (2000) *Crimes against Small Business in Australia: A Preliminary Analysis*, Trends & Issues in Crime and Criminal Justice No. 184, Australian Institute of Criminology, Canberra.

Australian Institute of Health and Welfare (1999) *1998 National Drug Strategy Household Survey: First Results*, AIHW, Canberra.

Australian Institute of Health and Welfare (1996) *Australia's Health*, AIHW, Canberra.

Baines, M. (1997) 'Mad, Bad or Angry?', *Youth Studies Australia*, 16: 19–23.

Baker, J. (1999) *Juveniles in Crime: Part 1: Participation Rates and Risk Factors*, NSW Bureau of Crime Statistics and Research, Sydney, <www.lawlink.nsw.gov.au/bocsar1.nsf/pages/r45textlink> (accessed 29 November 2003).

Baker, J. (1998) *Are the Courts Becoming More Lenient? Recent Trends in Convictions and Penalties in NSW Higher and Local Courts* Crime and Justice Bulletin No. 40, NSW Bureau of Crime Statistics and Research, Sydney.

Bandaranaike, S. (2001) *Graffiti: a culture of aggression or assertion*, paper presented at the Character, Impact and Prevention of Crime in Regional Australia Conference, Australian Institute of Criminology, Townsville, 2–3 August 22.

Barclay, G. & Tavares, C. (2003) *International Comparisons of Criminal Justice Statistics 2001*, Research, Development and Statistics Directorate, Home Office, London.

Bareja, M. & Charlton, K. (2003) *Statistics on Juvenile Detention in Australia*, Technical and Background Paper Series No. 5, Australian Institute of Criminology, Canberra.

Barnes, G.M. & Farrell, M.P. (1992) 'Parental Support and Control as Predictors of Adolescent Drinking, Delinquency and Related Problem Behaviours', *Journal of Marriage and the Family*, 54: 763–76.

Batrouney, T. (2002) 'From White Australia to Multiculturalism: Citizenship and Identity', in G. Hage (ed.) *Arab Australians Today: Citizenship and Belonging*, Melbourne University Press, Melbourne.

Beatty, A. (1995) 'Prosecuting the crown for environmental offences' in N. Gunningham, J. Norberry & S. McKillop (eds) (1995) *Environmental crime*, Australian Institute of Criminology, Canberra, proceedings of a conference held 1–3 September 1993, Hobart.

Beck, U. (1996) 'World Risk Society as Cosmopolitan Society? Ecological Questions in a Framework of Manufactured Uncertainties', *Theory, Culture, Society*, 13(4): 1–32.

Becker, H. (1963) *Outsiders: Studies in the Sociology of Deviance*, Free Press, New York.

Beder, S. (1997) *Global Spin: The Corporate Assault on Environmentalism*, Scribe Publications, Melbourne.

Behrendt, J. (1992) *Aboriginal Perspectives on Criminal Justice*, Institute of Criminology Monograph Series No. 1, Sydney: 26–9.

Benton, T. (1998) 'Rights and Justice on a Shared Planet: More Rights or New Relations?', *Theoretical Criminology*, 2(2): 149–75.

Bessant, J., Carrington, C. & Cook, J. (eds) (1995) *Cultures of Crime and Violence: The Australian Experience*, La Trobe University Press in association with the Victorian Law Foundation, Bundoora.

Beyer, L., Reid, G. & Crofts, N. (2001) 'Ethnic Based Differences in Drug Offending', *Australian and New Zealand Journal of Criminology*, 34(2): 169–81.

Bhathal, A. (1998) 'Culturally Accessible Justice Or Cultural Curse? Family Group Conferencing and Vietnamese Juvenile Offending', MA Thesis, School of Law and Legal Studies, La Trobe University, Melbourne.

Biles, D. (1992) 'Aboriginal Imprisonment—A Statistical Analysis', in D. Biles & D. McDonald (eds) *Deaths in Custody Australia, 1980–1989*, Australian Institute of Criminology, Canberra: 85–105.

Bilimoria, D. (1995) 'Corporate Control, Crime and Compensation: An Empirical Examination of Large Corporations', *Human Relations*, 48(8): 891–908.

Blagg, H. & Wilkie, M. (1995) *Young People and Police Powers*, The Australian Youth Foundation, Sydney.

Blumstein, A., Cohen, J., Roth, J.A. & Visher, C.A. (1986) *Criminal Careers and 'Career Criminals'*, Vol. 1, National Academy Press, Washington DC.

Bonney, R. & Kery, L. (1991) *Police Reports of Non-Aggravated Assault in New South Wales*, General Report Series, New South Wales Bureau of Crime Statistics and Research, Sydney.

Borzycki, M. (2003) *Bank Robbery in Australia*, Trends & Issues in Crime and Criminal Justice No. 253, Australian Institute of Criminology, Canberra.

Bourdieu, P. (1986) 'The Forms of Capital', in J.G. Richardson (ed.) *Handbook of Theory and Research for the Sociology of Education*, Greenwood Press, New York: 241–58.

Box, S. (1987) *Recession, Crime and Punishment*, Macmillan, London.

Box, S. (1983) *Power, Crime and Mystification*, Tavistock, London.

Boyd, S., Chunn, D. & Menzies, R. (eds) (2002) *Toxic Criminology: Environment, Law and the State in Canada*, Fernwood Publishing, Halifax.

Brady, M. (1992) *The Health of Young Aborigines*, National Clearinghouse for Youth Studies, Hobart.

Braithwaite, J. (1995) 'White collar crime', in G. Geis et al. (eds) *White Collar Crime: Classic & Contemporary Views* (3rd edn): 12–30.

Braithwaite, J. (1993) 'Responsive Business Regulatory Institutions', in C.A.J. Coady & C. Sampford (eds) *Business Ethics and the Law*, Federation Press, Sydney.

Braithwaite, J. (1991) 'Poverty, Power, White-Collar Crime and the Paradoxes of Criminological Theory', *Australian and New Zealand Journal of Criminology*, 24: 40–58.

Braithwaite, J. (1984) *Corporate Crime in the Pharmaceutical Industry*, Routledge & Kegan Paul, London.

Braithwaite, J. (1979) *Inequality, Crime and Public Policy*, Routledge and Kegan Paul, London.

Braithwaite, J. & Chappell, D. (1994) 'The Job Compact and Crime: Submission to the Committee on Employment Opportunities', *Current Issues in Criminal Justice*, 5(3): 295–300.

Brantingham, P.J. & Brantingham, P.L. (1981) 'Notes on the geometry of crime', in P.J. Brantingham & P.L. Brantingham (eds) *Environmental Criminology*, Sage, Beverly Hills.

Briscoe, S. & Donnelly, N. (2001) *Assaults on Licensed Premises in Inner-Urban Areas*, NSW Bureau of Crime Statistics and Research, Sydney.

Broadhurst, R. (1997) *Aborigines and Crime in Australia*, University of Chicago, Chicago.

Broadhurst, R.G. & Maller, R.A. (1991a) 'Sex Offending and Recidivism', *Crime Research Centre*, University of Western Australia, Perth.

Broadhurst, R.G. & Maller, R.A (1991b) 'Estimating the numbers of prison terms in criminal careers from one-step probabilities of recidivism', *Journal of Quantitative Criminology* 23: 275–90.

Broadhurst, R.G. & Maller, R.A. (1990) 'The Recidivism of Prisoners Released for the First Time: Reconsidering the Effectiveness Question', *Australian and New Zealand Journal of Criminology*, 23: 88–103.

Brown, D., Farrier, D., Egger, S. & McNamara, L. (2001) *Criminal Laws: Materials and Commentary on Criminal Law and Process in New South Wales*, The Federation Press, Sydney.

Brownmiller, S. (1976) *Against Our Will*, Penguin, Harmondsworth.

Bullard, R. (1994) *Unequal Protection: Environmental Justice and Communities of Color*, Sierra Club Books, San Francisco.

Burns J.M., Baghurst, P.A., Sawyer, M.G., McMichael, A.J. & Tong, S. (1999) 'Lifetime low-level exposure to environmental lead and children's emotional and behavioural development at ages 11–13 years. The Port Pirie Cohort Study', *American Journal of Epidemiology*, 149(8): 740–9.

Cahill, L. & Marshall, P. (2002) *Statistics of Juvenile Detention in Australia: 1981–2001*, Technical and Background Paper Series No. 1, Australian Institute of Criminology, Canberra.

Cain, M. (1998) 'An analysis of juvenile recidivism', in C. Alder (ed.) *Juvenile Crime and Juvenile Justice*, Australian Institute of Criminology Research & Public Policy Series No. 14, Australian Institute of Criminology, Canberra.

Cain, M. (1994) 'Juveniles in Detention. Special Needs Groups: Young women, Aboriginal and Indo-Chinese Detainees', *Information and Evaluation Series No.3*, Department of Juvenile Justice, Sydney.

Cameron, M. (2001) *Women Prisoners and Correctional Programs*, Trends & Issues in Crime and Criminal Justice No. 194, Australian Institute of Criminology, Canberra.

Cameron, M. (2000) *Young Men and Violence Prevention*, Trends & Issues in Crime and Criminal Justice No. 154, Australian Institute of Criminology, Canberra.

Campbell, A. (1993) *The Girls in the Gang*, Blackwell, Oxford.

Carlen, (1988) *Women, Crime and Poverty*, Open University Press, Milton Keynes.

Carlen, P. (1983) *Women's Imprisonment: A Study in Social Control*, Routledge & Kegan Paul, London.

Carrington, K. (1983) *Offending Girls*, Allen & Unwin, Sydney.

Carrington, K. (1989) 'Girls and Graffiti', *Cultural Studies*, 3(1): 89–100.

Catalano, R. & Hawkins, J. (1996) 'The Social Development Model: A Theory of Antisocial Behaviour', in J. Hawkins (ed.) *Delinquency and Crime: Current Theories*, Cambridge University Press, New York.

Catanzariti, J. (1997) 'Corporate Liability for Manslaughter Firmly Established', *Law Society Journal*, 35(2): 26–8.

Chambliss, R. (1978) *On the Take*, Indiana Press, London.

Chambliss, W. (1970) 'A Sociological Analysis of the Law of Vagrancy', in C. Bersani (ed.), *Crime and Delinquency: A Reader*, Macmillan, New York.

Chan, C. & Cunneen, C. (2000) *Evaluation of the Implementation of the New South Wales Police Service Aboriginal Strategic Plan*, Institute of Criminology, Sydney.

Chan, J. (1997) *Changing Police Culture: Policing in a Multicultural Society*, Cambridge University Press, Melbourne.

Chan, J. (1994) 'Policing Youth in "Ethnic" Communities: Is community policing the answer?', in R. White & C. Alder (eds) *The Police and Young People in Australia*, Cambridge University Press, Melbourne.

Chan, S. (1999) 'Bubbling Acid: Sydney's techno underground', in R. White (ed.) *Australian Youth Subcultures: On the Margins and In the Mainstream*, Australian Clearinghouse for Youth Studies, Hobart.

Chapman, B., Weatherburn, D., Kapuscinski, C.A., Chilvers, M. & Roussel, S. (2002) *Unemployment Duration, Schooling and Property Crime*, Contemporary Issues in Crime and Justice No. 74, Crime and Justice Bulletin, NSW Bureau of Crime Statistics and Research, Sydney.

Chapman, S. (1997) 'Tobacco Industry Memo reveals Passive Smoking Strategy', *British Medical Association*, 314: 1569.

Chappel, D. & Egger, S. (eds) (1995) *Australian Violence: Contemporary Perspectives II*, Australian Institute of Criminology, Canberra.

Chatterton, P. & Hollands, R. (2003) *Urban Nightscapes: Youth Cultures, Pleasure Spaces and Corporate Power*, Routledge, London.

Chesney-Lind, M. (1997) *The Female Offender: Girls, Women and Crime*, Sage, Thousand Oaks.

Chesney-Lind, M. (1989) 'Girls' Crime and Woman's Place: Towards a feminist model of female delinquency', *Crime and Delinquency*, 35(1), 5–29.

Chesney-Lind, M. & Rodriquez, N. (1983) 'Women under Lock and Key', *Prison Journal*, 63: 47–65.

*Christine Ann Scott v. SA Police* [1993] 61 SASR 589.

Chunn, D., Boyd, S. & Menzies, R. (2002) '"We all live in Bhopal": Criminology Discovers Environmental Crime', in S. Boyd, D. Chunn & R. Menzies (eds) *Toxic Criminology: Environment, Law and the State in Canada*, Fernwood Publishing, Halifax.

Clinard, M.B. & Yeager, P.C. (1980) *Corporate Crime*, The Free Press, New York.

Chiricos, T. (1987) 'Rates of Crime and Unemployment: An Analysis of Aggregate Research Evidence', *Social Problems*, 34: 187–212.

Churchman, F. (2003) *Drinking time's over, it's time to go home*, Australian Broadcasting Corporation, Darwin, <www.abc.net.au/darwin/stories/s1005505.htm> (accessed 4 June 2004).

Clough, J. & Mulhern, C. (2002) *The Prosecution of Corporations*, Oxford University Press, Melbourne.

Cloward, R.A. & Ohlin, L.E. (1961) *Delinquency and Opportunity*, Free Press, Glencoe.

Cohen, A. (1955) *Delinquent Boys*, Free Press, Glencoe.

Cohen, S. (2001) *States of Denial: Knowing About Atrocities and Suffering*, Polity, Cambridge.

Cohen, S. (1993) 'Human Rights and Crimes of the State: The Culture of Denial', *Australian and New Zealand Journal of Criminology*, 26(2): 97–115.

Cohen, S. (1985) *Visions of Social Control Crime, Punishment and Classification*, Polity Press, Cambridge.

Cohen, S. (1973) *Folk Devils and Moral Panics*, Paladin, London.

Coleman, J.C. (1988) 'Social capital in the creation of human capital', *American Journal of Sociology*, 94: 95–120.

Colgan, P. (2004) *Bio-Security Plan 'Years Away'*, <http://news.com.au/common/story_page/0,4057,8347410%255E2,00.html> (accessed 2 February 2004).

Collier, R. (1998) *Masculinities, Crime and Criminology: Men, Heterosexuality and the Criminal(ised) Other*, Sage, London.

Collins, A. (1998) 'Hip Hop Graffiti Culture', *Alternative Law Journal*, 23(1): 19–21.

Collins, L. & Ali, M. (2003) *Deaths in Custody in Australia: 2002 National Deaths in Custody Program Annual Report*, Research and Public Policy Series No. 50, Australian Institute of Criminology, Canberra.

Collins, J., Noble, G., Poynting, S. & Tabar, P. (2000) *Kebabs, Kids, Cops & Crime: Youth, Ethnicity and Crime*, Pluto Press, Sydney.

Collins, L. & Mouzos, J. (2002) *Deaths in Custody: A Gender-Specific Analysis*, Trends & Issues in Crime and Criminal Justice No. 238, Australian Institute of Criminology, Canberra.

Conklin, J.E. (1977) *Illegal but not Criminal: Business Crime in America*, Prentice Hall, Englewood Cliffs, NJ.

Connell, R. (2000) *The Men and The Boys*, Allen & Unwin, Sydney.

Connell, R. (1995) *Masculinities*, Allen & Unwin, Sydney.

Cook, B., David, F. & Grant, A. (1999) *Victims' Needs, Victims' Rights: Policies and Programs for Victims of Crime in Australia*, Research and Public Policy Series No. 19, Australian Institute of Criminology, Canberra.

Cook, S. & Bessant, J. (eds) (1997) *Women's Encounters with Violence*, Sage, Thousand Oaks.

Coumarelos, C. (1994) *Juvenile Offending: Predicting Persistence and Determining the Cost-Effectiveness of Interventions*, NSW Bureau of Crime Statistics and Research, Sydney.

Crawford, A. (1998) *Crime Prevention and Community Safety: Politics, Policies and Practices*, Longman, Harlow.

Crelinsten, R. (2003) 'The World of Torture: A constructed reality', *Theoretical Criminology*, 7(3): 293–318.

Cunneen, C. (2001) *Conflict, Politics and Crime: Aboriginal Communities and the Police*, Allen & Unwin, Crows Nest.

Cunneen, C. (1999) 'Criminology, Genocide and the Forced Removal of Indigenous Children from their Families', *Australian and New Zealand Journal of Criminology*, 32(2): 124–38.

Cunneen, C. (1995) 'Ethnic Minority Youth & Juvenile Justice: Beyond the stereotype of ethnic gangs', in C. Guerra & R. White (eds) *Ethnic Minority*

*Youth in Australia: Challenges & Myths*, National Clearinghouse for Youth Studies, Hobart.

Cunneen, C. (1990) *A Study of Aboriginal Juveniles and Police Violence*, Human Rights and Equal Opportunity Commission, Sydney.

Cunneen, C., Findlay, M., Lynch, R. & Tupper, V. (1989) *Dynamics of Collective Conflict. Riots at the Bathurst Motorcycle Races*, Law Book Company, North Ryde.

Cunneen, C., Fraser, D. & Tomsen, S. (1997) 'Introduction: Defining the Issues', in C. Cunneen et al. (eds) *Faces of Hate: Hate Crime in Australia*, Hawkins Press, Sydney.

Cunneen, C. & Kerley, K. (1995) 'Indigenous Women and Criminal Justice', in Hazlehurst, K.M. (ed.) *Perceptions of Justice*, Aldershot, Avebury: 71–90.

Cunneen, C. & Luke, G. (1995) 'Discretionary Decisions in Juvenile Justice and the Criminalisation of Indigenous Young People: A NSW Study', *Youth Studies Australia*, 14(4): 38–46.

Cunneen, C. & Stubbs, J. (1997) *Gender, 'Race' and International Relations: Violence against Filipino women in Australia*, Monograph Series No.9, Institute of Criminology, Sydney.

Cunneen, C. & White, R. (2002) *Juvenile Justice: Youth and Crime in Australia*, Oxford University Press, Melbourne.

Cunneen, C. & White, R. (1995) *Juvenile Justice: An Australian Perspective*, Oxford University Press, Melbourne.

Daly, K. (1994) *Gender, Crime and Punishment*, Yale University Press, New Haven.

Daly, M. & Wilson, M. (1988) *Homicide*, Aldine de Gruyter, New York.

Daniel, A. & Cornwall, J. (1993) *A Lost Generation?*, Australian Youth Foundation, Sydney.

Das, A.D. (2004) 'The Big Bang Theory for Holi', *Times of India*, 7 March, <timesofindia.indiatimes.com/articleshow/543840.cms> (accessed 25 May 2004).

Debelle, P. (2003) 'Liability Snag over Maralinga Clean-up', *The Sunday Age*, 11 May: 4.

Developmental Crime Prevention Consortium (1999) *Pathways to Prevention: Developmental and Early Intervention Approaches to Crime in Australia*, National Crime Prevention, Attorney General's Department, Canberra.

Devery, C. (1991) *Disadvantage and Crime*, NSW Bureau of Crime Statistics and Research, Sydney.

Dixon, M. (ed.) (1985) *On Trial: Reagan's War Against Nicaragua, Testimony of the Permanent People's Tribunal*, Zed Books, London.

Dobinson, I. & Ward, P. (1986) 'Heroin and Property Crime: An Australian Perspective', *The Journal of Drug Issues*, 16: 249–62.

Dodd, A. (2003) 'Giants pair off as net pirates stop the music', *Weekend Australian: Weekend Money*, 8–9 November: 29.

Douglas, R. (1987) 'Is Chivalry Dead? Gender and Sentencing in the Victorian Courts', *Australian and New Zealand Journal of Sociology* 23: 343–57.

Drugs and Crime Prevention Committee (2001) *Inquiry into Crime Trends: Second Report*, Government Printer, Victoria.

Duff, C. (2003) 'Drugs and Youth Cultures: Is Australia Experiencing the "Normalisation" of Adolescent Drug Use?', *Journal of Youth Studies*, 6(1): 433–46.

Eastel, P. (1997) 'Migrant Youth and Juvenile Crime', in A. Borowski & I. O'Connor (eds) *Juvenile Crime, Justice & Corrections*, Longman, Melbourne.

Eastel, P. (1996a) *Shattered Dreams: Marital violence against Overseas-born women in Australia*, Bureau of Immigration, Multicultural and Population Research, AGPS, Canberra.

Eastel, P. (1996b) 'Violence against Immigrant Women in the Home', *Family Matters*, 45, Australian Institute of Family Studies, Melbourne.

Eastel, P. (1994) 'Ethnicity and Crime', in D. Chappel & P. Wilson (eds) *The Australian Criminal Justice System: The Mid 1990s*, Butterworths, Sydney.

Eastel, P. (1989) *Vietnamese Refugees: Crime Rates of Minors and Youths in NSW*, Australian Institute of Criminology, Canberra.

Edmonds, S. (1995) 'The Environmental Audit as a "Sanction" or Incentive under the Victorian Environment Protection Act 1970', in N. Gunningham, J. Norberry & S. McKillop (eds) *Environmental Crime*, AIC conference proceedings No. 26, Australian Institute of Criminology, Canberra.

Edwards, A. (1995) *Women in Prison*, Contemporary Issues in Crime and Justice No. 26, Crime and Justice Bulletin, NSW Bureau of Crime Statistics and Research.

Egger, S. (1994) 'Victimisation, Moral Panics...A Reply to Richard Harding', *Current Issues in Criminal Justice*, 6(1): 43–53.

Eggleston, E.M. (1976) *Fear, favour or affection: Aborigines and the criminal law in Victoria, South Australia and Western Australia*, Australian National University Press, Canberra.

Ekberg, C.J. (1998) *French Roots in the Illinois Country: The Mississippi Frontier in Colonial Times*, University of Illinois Press, Chicago.

Ekdahl, J. (1998) *International Police Cooperation: Presentation of the ICPO–Interpol and its activities in preventing and combating environmental crime*, paper presented to the Fifth International Conference on Environmental Compliance and Enforcement, Monterey, November.

Fagan, J.E. (1990) 'Social Processes of Delinquency and Drug Use Among Urban Gangs', in C.E. Huff (ed.) *Gangs in America*, Sage, Newbury Park: 183–219.

Farley, F.H. & Sewell, T. (1976) 'Test of an arousal theory of delinquency', *Criminal Justice and Behaviour*, 31(3): 5–20.

Farrington, D. (1996) 'The Development of Offending and Antisocial Behaviour from Childhood to Adulthood', in P. Cordella & L. Siegeol (eds) *Readings in Contemporary Criminological Theory*, Northeastern University Press, Boston.

Farrington, D.P. (1999) 'Measuring, explaining and preventing shoplifting: a review of British research', *Security Journal*, 12(1): 9–27.

Felson, M. (1998) *Crime and Everyday Life* (3rd edn), Sage, Thousand Oaks.

Ferrell, J. (1997) 'Youth, Crime and Cultural Space', *Social Justice*, 24(4): 21–38.

Ferrell, J. (1996) *Crimes of Style: Urban Graffiti and the Politics of Criminality*, Northeastern University Press, Boston.

Field, S. (1999) 'Trends in Crime Revisited', *Home Office Research Study*, 195, HMSO, London.

Field, S. (1990) 'Trends in Crime and their Interpretation: A Study of Recorded Crime in Post-War England and Wales', *Home Office Research Study*, 119, HMSO, London.

Financial Action Task Force on Money Laundering (2003) 'Basic Facts about Money Laundering', <www1.oecd.org/fatf/MLaundering_en.htm> (accessed 7 October 2003).

Findlay, M., Odgers, S. & Yeo, S. (1994) *Australian Criminal Justice*, Oxford University Press, Melbourne.

Fine, M. (1992) 'Sexuality, Schooling and Adolescent Females: The Missing Discourses of Desire', in M. Fine (ed.) *Disruptive Voices: The Possibilities of Feminist Research*, University of Michigan Press, Ann Arbor: 31–61.

Finkelhor, D. & Baron, L. (1986) 'High-risk children', in D. Finkelhor, *A Sourcebook on Child Sexual Abuse,* Sage Publications, Beverly Hills.

Fisse, B. & Braithwaite, J. (1993) *Corporations, Crime and Accountability*, Cambridge University Press, Melbourne.

Fitzgerald, J. (2000) *Graffiti in NSW,* Crime & Justice Statistics Bureau Brief, NSW Bureau of Crime Statistics & Research, Sydney.

Fitzgerald, J. (1999) *Women in Prison: The Criminal Court Perspective*, Crime and Justice Statistics Bureau Brief, NSW Bureau of Crime Statistics and Research, Sydney.

Fitzgerald, J., Briscoe, S. & Weatherburn, D. (2001) *Firearms and Violent Crime in New South Wales*, Contemporary Issues in Crime and Justice No. 57, Crime and Justice Bulletin, NSW Bureau of Crime Statistics and Research.

Foote, P. (1993) 'Like, I'll tell you what happened from experience…Perspectives on Italo-Australian youth gangs in Adelaide', in R. White (ed.) *Youth Subcultures: Theory, History and the Australian Experience*, National Clearinghouse for Youth Studies, Hobart.

Forrest, R. & Kearns, A. (2001) 'Social Cohesion, Social Capital and the Neighborhood', *Urban Studies*, 38(12): 2125–43.

Forrester, L. (1999) 'Street Machiners and "showing off"', in R. White (ed.) *Australian Youth Subcultures: On the Margins and in the Mainstream*, Australian Clearinghouse for Youth Studies, Hobart.

Forrester, L. (1993) 'Youth-generated cultures in Western Sydney', in R. White (ed.) *Youth Subcultures: Theory, History and the Australian Experience*, National Clearinghouse for Youth Studies, Hobart.

Fowler, R. & Grabosky, P. (1989) 'Lead Pollution and the Children of Port Pirie', in P.N. Grabosky & A. Sutton (eds) *Stains on a White Collar: Fourteen Studies of Corporate Crime or Corporate Harm*, Federation Press, Sydney: 143–59.

Franklin, A. (1999) *Animals and Modern Cultures: A Sociology of Human–Animal Relations in Modernity*, Sage, London.

Frederico, M., Cooper, B. & Picton, C. (1996) *The Experience of Homelessness among Young People from Cambodia, Laos and Vietnam*, Bureau of Immigration, Multicultural and Population Research, Melbourne.

Freeman, K. (1996) *Young People and Crime*, Crime and Justice Bulletin No. 32, NSW Bureau of Crime Statistics and Research, Sydney.

Freiberg, A. (2002) 'Drug Courts: Sentencing responses to drug use and drug-related crime', *Alternative Law Journal*, 27(6).

Friedrichs, D. (1996) *Trusted Criminals: White Collar Crime in Contemporary Society*, Wadsworth, Belmont.

Gale, F., Bailey-Harris, R. & Wundersitz, J. (1990) *Aboriginal Youth and the Criminal Justice System: The Injustice of Justice?*, Cambridge University Press, Melbourne.

Gallagher, P. & Poletti, P. (1998) *Sentencing Disparity and the Ethnicity of Juvenile Offenders*, Judicial Commission of New South Wales, Sydney.

Garkawe, S. (2002) 'Crime Victims and Prisoners' Rights', in D. Brown & M. Wilkie (eds) *Prisoners As Citizens: Human Rights in Australian Prisons*, The Federation Press, Sydney.

Gatto, C. (1999) *European Drug Policy: Analysis and Case Studies*, NORML Foundation, San Francisco.

Geason, S. & Wilson, P. (1992) *Preventing Retail Crime*, Australian Institute of Criminology, Canberra.

Geason, S. & Wilson, P. (1989) *Designing Out Crime: Crime Prevention Through Environmental Design*, Australian Institute of Criminology, Canberra.

Gelb, K. (2003) 'Women in Prison—Why the Rate of Incarceration is Increasing', paper presented at the *Evaluation in Crime and Justice: Trends and Methods Conference*, Australian Institute of Criminology and Australian Bureau of Statistics, Canberra, 24–25 March.

Gelsthorpe, L. & Morris, A. (1999) 'Much Ado about Nothing—a Critical Comment on Key Provisions Relating to Children in the Crime and Disorder Act 1998', *Child and Family Law Quarterly*, 11: 209–22.

Gerth, H. H. & Mills, C. W. (1948) *From Max Weber: Essays in Sociology*, Routledge & Kegan Paul, London.

Golden, C.J., Jackson, M.L. & Crum, T.A. (1999) 'Hate Crimes: Etiology and Intervention', in H.V. Hall & L.C. Whittaker (eds) *Collective Violence— Effective Strategies for Assessing and Interviewing in Fatal Group and Institutional Aggression*, CRC Press, Boca Raton.

Goldie, C. (2004) *Why government is treating us like animals? We are not animal, we are family*, <www.parity.infoxchange.net.au/group/noticeboard/items/20041227023h.shtml> (accessed 4 June 2004).

Goldman, M. (1998a) 'Introduction: The Political Resurgence of the Commons', in M. Goldman (ed.) *Privatizing Nature: Political Struggles for the Global Commons*, Pluto Press in association with Transnational Institute, London.

Goldman, M. (1998b) 'Inventing the Commons: Theories and Practices of the Commons' Professional', in M. Goldman (ed.) *Privatizing Nature: Political Struggles for the Global Commons*, Pluto Press in association with Transnational Institute, London.

Goldson, B. & Jamieson, J. (2002) 'Youth Crime, the "Parenting Deficit" and State Intervention: A Contextual Critique', *Youth Justice* 2(2): 82–99.

Goode, E. & Ben-Yehuda, N. (1994) *Moral Panics: The social construction of deviance*, Blackwell, Oxford.

Gordon, R. & Foley, S. (1998) *Criminal Business Organizations, Street Gangs and Related Groups in Vancouver: The Report of the Greater Vancouver Gang Study*, Ministry of Attorney-General, Vancouver.

Grabosky, P. (1998) *Zero Tolerance Policing*, Trends & Issues in Crime and Criminal Justice No. 102, Australian Institute of Criminology, Canberra.

Grabosky, P. (1995a) *Burglary Prevention*, Trends & Issues in Crime and Criminal Justice No. 49, Australian Institute of Criminology, Canberra.

Grabosky, P. (1995b) *Fear of Crime and Fear Reduction Strategies*, Trends & Issues in Crime and Criminal Justice No. 44, Australian Institute of Criminology, Canberra.

Grabosky, P. (1995c) 'Regulation by Reward: On the Use of Incentives as Regulatory Instruments', *Law & Policy*, 17(3): 256–79.

Grabosky, P. (1994) 'Green Markets: Environmental Regulation by the Private Sector', *Law and Policy*, 16(4): 419–48.

Grabosky, P. (1989) *Wayward Governance: Illegality and its Control in the Public Sector*, Australian Institute of Criminology, Canberra.

Grabosky, P. & Rizzo, C. (1983) 'Dispositional Disparities in Courts of Summary Jurisdiction: the Conviction and Sentencing of Shoplifters in SA and NSW, 1980', *Australian and New Zealand Journal of Criminology*, 16: 146–62.

Grabosky, P., Shearing, C. & Braithwaite, J. (1993) 'Introduction', in P. Grabosky & J. Braithwaite (eds) *Business Regulation and Australia's Future*, Australian Institute of Criminology, Canberra, <www.aic.gov.au/publications/lcj/business/#chap1> (accessed 3 January 2004).

Grabosky, P., Smith, R. & Dempsey, G. (2001) *Electronic Theft: Crimes of Acquisition in Cyberspace*, Cambridge University Press, Cambridge.

Grant, B. & Gillis, C. (1999) *Day Parole Outcomes, Criminal History and other Predictors of Successful Sentence Completion*, Research Branch, Corporate Development, Correctional Services of Canada.

Graycar, R. & Morgan, J. (1990) *The Hidden Gender of Law*, Federation Press, Sydney.

Green, P. & Ward, T. (2000) 'State Crime, Human Rights, and the Limits of Criminology', *Social Justice*, 27(1): 101–15.

Guerra, C. & White, R. (eds) (1995) *Ethnic Minority Youth in Australia: Challenges and Myths*, National Clearinghouse for Youth Studies, Hobart.

Gunningham, N., Norberry, J. & McKillop, S. (eds) (1995) *Environmental Crime: Conference Proceedings*, Australian Institute of Criminology, Canberra.

Hagan, J. (1996) 'The Class and Crime Controversy', in J. Hagan, A. Gillis & D. Brownfield (1996) *Criminological Controversies: A Methodological Primer*, Westview Press, Boulder.

Haines, F. (2000) 'Towards Understanding Globalisation and Control of Corporate Harm: a Preliminary Criminological Analysis', *Current Issues in Criminal Justice*, 12(2): 166–80.

Haines, F. (1997) *Corporate Regulation: Beyond 'Punish or Persuade'*, Clarendon Press, Oxford.

Hale, C. (1996) 'Fear of crime: a review of the literature', *International Review of Victimology*, 4: 79–150.

Hall, J. (1952) *Theft, Law and Society* (2nd edn), Bobbs-Merrill, Indianapolis (first published in 1935).

Hall, S., Jefferson, T., Critcher, C. & Roberts, R. (1978) *Policing the Crisis: Mugging, the State and Law and Order*, Macmillan, London.

Halsey, M. (1997a) 'Environmental Crime: Towards an Eco-Human Rights Approach', *Current Issues in Criminal Justice*, 8(3): 217–42.

Halsey, M. (1997b) 'The Wood for the Paper: Old-Growth Forest, Hemp and Environmental Harm', *Australian and New Zealand Journal of Criminology*, 30(2): 121–48.

Halsey, M. & White, R. (1998) 'Crime, Ecophilosophy and Environmental Harm', *Theoretical Criminology*, 2(3): 345–71.

Halstead, B. (1992) *Entrepreneurial Crime: Impact, Detection and Regulation*, Trends & Issues in Crime and Criminal Justice No. 34, Australian Institute of Criminology, Canberra.

Hannigan, J. (1995), *Environmental Sociology*, London, Routledge.

Hanson, P. (1996) 'Maiden Speech', Parliament House, 10 September.

Harding, R. (1994) 'Victimisation, Moral Panics, and the Distortion of Criminal Justice Policy: A Review Essay of Ezzat Fattah's "Toward a Critical Victimology"', *Current Issues in Criminal Justice*, 6(1): 27–42.

Harvey, D. (1996) *Justice, Nature and the Geography of Difference*, Blackwell, Oxford.

Hayes, S. (1996) 'Minorities as Victims and Offenders', in K. Hazlehurst (ed.) *Crime and Justice*, Law Book Company, North Ryde: 317–48.

Hayward, K. (2002) 'The Vilification and Pleasures of Youthful Transgression', in J. Muncie, G. Hughes & E. McLaughlin (eds) *Youth Justice: Critical Readings*, Sage, London.

Hazlehurst, K. (ed.) (1995) *Perceptions of Justice: Issues in Indigenous and Community Empowerment*, Avebury, Aldershot.

Hazlehurst, K. (1992) 'Aboriginal and Police Relations', in P. Moir & H. Eijkman (eds) *Policing Australia: Old Issues and New Perspectives*, Macmillan, Melbourne: 236–65.

Hazlehurst, K. & Kerley, M. (1989) 'Migrants and the Criminal Justice System', in J. Jupp (ed.) *The Challenge of Diversity: Policy Options for a Multicultural Australia*, Office of Multicultural Affairs, AGPS, Canberra.

Heilpern, D. (1999) 'Judgement: Police v Shannon Thomas DUNN, Dubbo Local Court', *Alternative Law Journal*, 24(5): 238-42.

Health and Safety Executive (2003a) *Annual Report*, <refit.hse.gov.uk/asp/ Highlight.asp?Source=http://www.hse.gov.uk/aboutus/reports/annre-port0203.htm&SearchText=annual%20report> (accessed 4 June 2004).

Health and Safety Executive (2003b) *Costs Overview*, <www.hse.gov.uk/costs/ costs_overview/costs_overview.asp> (accessed 28 October 2003).

Heidensohn, F. (1995) *Women and Crime*, Macmillan, Basingstoke.

Heidensohn, F. (1968) 'The Deviance of Women: a Critique and an Enquiry', *British Journal of Sociology* 19: 160–75.

Heine, G., Prabhu, M. & del Frate, A. (eds) (1997) *Environmental Protection: Potentials and Limits of Criminal Justice*, UNICJRI, Rome.

Herrnstein, R.J. (1995) 'Criminogenic Traits', in J.Q. Wilson & J. Petersilia (eds) *Crime*, Institute for Contemporary Studies, San Francisco.

Higgins, K. (1997) *Exploring Motor Vehicle Theft in Australia*, Trends & Issues in Crime and Criminal Justice, No. 67, Australian Institute of Criminology, Canberra.

HIH Royal Commission (2003) *The failure of HIH Insurance*, 1–3, Commonwealth of Australia, Canberra.

Hogg, R. & Carrington, K. (2003) 'Violence, Spatiality and Other Rurals', *Australian and New Zealand Journal of Criminology*, 36(3): 293–319.

Hollands, R. (1995) *Friday Night, Saturday Night: Youth cultural identification in the post-industrial city*, Department of Social Policy, University of Newcastle, Newcastle Upon Tyne.

House of Representatives Standing Committee on Aboriginal and Torres Strait Islander Affairs (1994), *Justice Under Scrutiny*, AGPS, Canberra.

Howard, J. & Zibert, E. (1990) 'Curious, Bored and Wanting to Feel Good: the drug use of detained young offenders', *Drug and Alcohol Review*, 9: 225-31.

Howell, J. (2000) *Youth Gang Programs and Strategies: Summary*, Office of Juvenile Justice and Delinquency Prevention, US Department of Justice, Washington DC, <www.ncjrs.org/html/ojjdp/summary_2000_8/home.html> (accessed 2 August 2002).

HREOC *see* Human Rights and Equal Opportunity Commission.

Human Rights and Equal Opportunity Commission (2003) *Social Justice Report 2003*, <www.hreoc.gov.au/social_justice/sjreport03/data/append1.html#aboriginal> (accessed 20 June 2004).

Human Rights and Equal Opportunity Commission (1991a) *Racist Violence*, Report of the National Inquiry into Racist Violence, AGPS, Canberra.

Human Rights and Equal Opportunity Commission (1991b) *State of the Nation: Report on People of Non-English Speaking Background*, AGPS, Canberra.

Indermaur, D. (2000) 'Violent Crime in Australia: Patterns and Politics', *Australian and New Zealand Journal of Criminology* 33(3): 287–99.

Indermaur, D. (1996) *Violent Crime in Australia: Interpreting the Trends*, Trends & Issues in Crime and Criminal Justice No. 61, Australian Institute of Criminology, Canberra.

Indermaur, D. & Roberts, L. (2003) 'Drug Courts in Australia: The First Generation', *Current Issues in Criminal Justice*, 15(2).

Iveson, K. (2000) 'Beyond Designer Diversity: Planners, Public Space and a Critical Politics of Difference', *Urban Policy and Research*, 18(2): 219–38.

Institute for the Advanced Study of Information Warfare (2003), <www.psycom.net/iwar.1.html> (accessed 3 March 2004).

Jackson, H. (2003) 'Prosecutions under the Environmental Protection Act 1970', *National Environmental Law Review* (2): 22–30.

Jakubowicz, A. & Goodall, H. (1994) *Racism, Ethnicity and the Media*, Allen & Unwin, St Leonards.

James, M. & Carcach, C. (1998) *Homicide between Intimate Partners in Australia*, Trends & Issues in Crime and Criminal Justice No. 90, Australian Institute of Criminology, Canberra.

James, M.L. & Murray, B.E. (2003) *Computer Crime and Compromised Commerce*, Research Note, Dept of the Parliamentary Library (6), 11 August, Commonwealth of Australia, <www.aph.gov.au/library/pubs/rn/2003-04/04rn06.pdf> (accessed 2 February 2004).

James, S. & Sutton, A. (1998) 'Policing Drugs in the Third Millennium: The Dilemmas of Community-based Philosophies', *Current Issues in Criminal Justice*, 9(3): 217–27.

Jamieson, R. (1999) 'Genocide and the Social Production of Immorality', *Theoretical Criminology*, 3(2): 131–46.

Jamrozik, A., Boland, C. & Urquhart, R. (1995) *Social Change and Cultural Transformation in Australia*, Cambridge University Press, Melbourne.

Jarjoura, G.R. (1993) 'Does Dropping out of School Enhance Delinquent Involvement? Results from a Large Scale National Probability Scale', *Criminology*, 31(2): 175–85.

Jochelson, R. (1997) *Aborigines and Public Order Legislation in New South Wales*, Crime and Justice Bulletin No. 34, NSW Bureau of Crime Statistics and Research, Sydney.

Johnston, E. (1991) *Report of the Royal Commission into Aboriginal Deaths in Custody* (5 vols), AGPS, Canberra.

Jones, D. (1982) *Crime, Protest, Community and Police in Nineteenth Century Britain*, Routledge & Kegan Paul, London.

Julian, R. (2004) 'Inequality, Social Differences and Environmental Resources', in R. White (ed.) *Controversies in Environmental Sociology*, Cambridge University Press, Melbourne

Junger-Tas, J. (1994) 'Delinquency in Thirteen Western Countries: Some Preliminary Conclusions', in J. Junger-Tas, G.J. Terlouw & M. Klein (eds) *Delinquency Behavior Among Young People in the Western World: First Results of the International Self-Report Delinquency Study*, Kugler Publications, Amsterdam.

Jupp, V. (1989) *Methods of Criminological Research*, Routledge, London.

Jupp, V., Davies, P. & Francis, P. (eds) (2000) *Doing Criminological Research*, Sage, London.

Kapuscinski, C.A., Braithwaite, J. & Chapman, B. (1998) 'Unemployment and Crime: Toward Resolving the Paradox', *Journal of Quantitative Criminology*, 14: 215–41.

Katz, J. (1988) *Seductions of Crime: Moral and Sensual Attractions of Doing Evil*, Basic Books, New York.

Kauzlarich, D., Mullins, C. & Matthews, R. (2003) 'A Complicity Continuum of State Crime', *Contemporary Justice Review*, 6(3): 241–54.

Keane, J. (2003) 'Maralinga's Afterlife', *The Sunday Age*, 11 May: 1.

Kelly, A. (2003) 'Shire Victim of its Own Success', *Central Coast Herald*, 5 July: 45.

Kerley, K. & Cunneen, C. (1994) 'Deaths in Custody in Australia: The Untold Story of Aboriginal and Torres Strait Islander Women', *The Canadian Journal of Women and the Law*, 9(1): 531–51.

Klein, M., Kerner, H.J., Maxson, C. & Weitekamp, E. (2001) *The Eurogang Paradox: Street Gangs and Youth Groups in the U.S. and Europe*, Kluwer Academic Publishers, Dordrecht.

Klemke, L.W. (1982) 'Exploring juvenile shoplifting', *Sociology and Social Research*, 67: 59–75.

KPMG (1999) *1999 Fraud Survey*, KMPG, Sydney.

Krammer, R.C. (1984) 'Corporations Criminality: The Development of an Idea', in E. Hochstedler (ed.) *Corporations as Criminals*, Sage, Beverley Hills.

La Grange, T. (1996) 'Marking Up the City: The Problem of Urban Vandalism', in O'Bireck, G. (ed.) *Not a Kid Anymore: Canadian youth, crime and subcultures*, Nelson, Toronto.

Land, K., Cantor, D. & Russell, S. (1995) 'Unemployment and Crime Rate Fluctuations in Post-World War II United States: Statistical Time-Series Properties and Alternative Models', in J. Hagan and R.D. Peterson (eds) *Crime and Inequality*, Stanford University Press, Stanford.

Langton, M. (1998) *Burning Questions: Emerging environmental issues for indigenous peoples in northern Australia*, Centre for Indigenous Natural and Cultural Resource Management, Darwin.

Langton, M. (1988) 'Medicine Square', in I. Keen (ed.) *Being Black: Aboriginal Culture in 'Settled' Australia*, Aboriginal Studies Press, Canberra.

Lawrence, G., Lyons, K. & Momtaz, S. (eds) (1996) *Social Change in Rural Australia*, Rural Social and Economic Research Centre, Central Queensland University, Rockhampton.

Lawrence, G., Vanclay, F. & Furze, B. (1992) *Agriculture, Environment and Society: Contemporary Issues for Australia*, Macmillan, Melbourne.

Lea, J. & Young, J. (1984), *What is to be Done about Law and Order?*, Penguin, Harmondsworth.

Lees, S. (1997) *Ruling Passions: Sexual Violence, Reputation and the Law*, Open University Press, Buckingham.

Lennings, C. (1996) 'Adolescents at Risk: Drug use and risk behaviour: Queensland and National data', *Youth Studies Australia*, 15(2): 29–36.

Levi, M. (1981) *The Phantom Capitalists: the Organisation and Control of Long-Term Fraud*, Gower, Aldershot.

Lincoln, R. & Wilson, P. (1994), 'Aboriginal Offending: Patterns and Causes', in D. Chappell & P. Wilson (eds) *The Australian Criminal Justice System: the Mid-1990s*, Butterworths, Sydney: 61–86.

Loeber, R. & Stouthaer-Loeber, M. (1986), 'Family Factors as Correlates and Predictors of Juvenile Conduct Problems and Delinquency', in M. Tonry & N. Morris (eds) *Crime and Justice: An Annual Review of Research*, University of Chicago Press, Chicago.

Loh, N. & Ferrante, A. (2003) *Aboriginal Involvement in the Western Australian Criminal Justice System: A Statistical Review, 2001*, The University of Western Australia, for the Department of Indigenous Affairs, Perth.

Low, N. & Gleeson, B. (1998) *Justice, Society and Nature: an exploration of political ecology*, Routledge, London.

Luke, G. & Cunneen, C. (1995) *Aboriginal Over-Representation and Discretionary Decisions in the NSW Juvenile Justice System*, Juvenile Justice Advisory Council of NSW, Sydney.

Mackay, M. & Munro, T. (1996) *Aborigines and Good-Order Offences: The Case of Victoria*, Discussion Paper No.3, Koori Research Centre, Monash University, Melbourne.

Mackay, M. & Smallcombe, S. (1996) 'Aboriginal Women as Offenders and Victims: The Case of Victoria', *Aboriginal Law Bulletin*, 3(80).

Mak, A.S. (1994), 'Parental Neglect and Overprotection as Risk Factors in Delinquency', *Australian Journal of Psychology*, 46(2): 107–11.

Makkai, T. (1998) *Alcohol & Disorder in the Australian Community: Part II – Perpetrators*, Trends & Issues in Crime and Criminal Justice No. 77, Australian Institute of Criminology, Canberra.

Makkai, T. & Payne, J. (2003) *Drugs and Crime: A Study of Incarcerated Male Offenders*, Australian Institute of Criminology Research and Public Policy Series No. 52, Canberra.

Makkai, T., McAllister, I. & Moore, R. (1994) 'Illicit Drug Use in Australia: Trends, Policies and Options', in D. Chappell & P. Wilson (eds) *The Australian Criminal Justice System: The Mid 1990s*, Butterworths, Sydney.

Manderson, D. (1993) *From Mr Sin to Mr Big: A History of Australian Drug Laws*, Oxford University Press, Melbourne.

Martin, S. (1996) 'Investigating Hate Crimes: Case Characteristics and Law Enforcement Responses', *Justice Quarterly*, 13(3): 455–80.

Mason, G. & Tomsen, S. (eds) (1997) *Homophobic Violence*, Hawkins Press, Sydney.

Matza, D. (1964) *Delinquency and Drift*, John Wiley & Sons, New York.

Mawby, R. & Walklate, S. (1994) *Critical Victimology: International Perspectives*, Sage, London.

May, D. & Headley, J. (2003) *Identity Theft*, Studies in Crime and Punishment No. 13, Peter Lang, New York.

Mayhew, P. (2003) *Counting the costs of crime in Australia*, Trends & Issues in Crime and Criminal Justice No. 247, Australian Institute of Criminology, Canberra.

McCarthy, T. (1993) *Victim Impact Statements—A Problematic Remedy*, position paper prepared by the Project for Legal Action Against Sexual Assault, endorsed by Victorian Services Against Sexual Assault.

McCulloch, J. (2002) '"Either you are with Us or You are with the Terrorists": The War's Home Front', in P. Scraton (ed.) *Beyond September 11: An Anthology of Dissent*, Pluto Press, London: 54–9.

McCulloch, J. (2001a) *Blue Army: Paramilitary Policing in Australia*, Melbourne University Press, Melbourne.

McCulloch, J. (2001b) 'Paramilitary Surveillance: S11, Globalisation, Terrorist & Counter-Terrorists', *Current Issues in Criminal Justice*, 13(1): 23–35.

McDonald, K. (1999) *Struggles for Subjectivity: Identity, Action and Youth Experience*, Cambridge University Press, Cambridge.

McNamara, L. (2002) *Regulating Racism: Racial Vilification Laws in Australia*, Monograph Series No. 16, Sydney Institute of Criminology, Sydney.

Meier, R.F. & Short, J.F. Jnr (1995) 'The consequences of white-collar crime', in G. Geis, R. Meier & L. Salinger (eds) *White Collar Crime: Classic and Contemporary Views* (3rd edn), The Free Press, New York: 80–104.

Messerschmidt, J. (1997) *Crime as Structured Action: Gender, Race, Class, and Crime in the Making*, Sage, London.

Messerschmidt, J. (1995) 'From Patriarchy to Gender', in N.H. Rafter & F. Heidensohn (eds) *International Feminist Perspectives in Criminology*, Open University Press, Buckingham: 175–85.

Messerschmidt, J. (1986) *Capitalism, Patriarchy and Crime*, Rowman & Littlefield, New Jersey.

Miller, S. (1998) *Crime Control and Women: Feminist Implications of Criminal Justice Policy*, Sage, Thousand Oaks.

Ministerial Council on Drug Strategy (2001) *National Action Plan on Illicit Drugs 2001 to 2002–03*, Commonwealth of Australia, Canberra.

Ministerial Council on Drug Strategy (1998) *National Drug Strategic Framework 1998-99 to 2002-03: Building Partnerships, A strategy to reduce the harm caused by drugs in our community*, Commonwealth of Australia, Canberra.

Mirlees-Black, C., Budd, T., Partridge, S. & Mayhew, P. (1998) *The 1998 British Crime Survey*, HMSO, London.

Mitchell, J. (1999) 'In the wake of the spill', *National Geographic*, March.

Morgan, F. (1993) 'Contact with the Justice System over the Juvenile Years', in L. Atkinson & S.A. Gerull (eds) *National Conference on Juvenile Detention: Conference Proceedings*, Australian Institute of Criminology, Canberra.

Morris, A. & Giller, H. (1987) *Understanding Juvenile Justice*, Croom Helm, London.

Mounsey, S. (1997) 'Youth Offending in the Loddon Campaspe Region of Rural Victoria: A Case Study of the Effect of "Locality" upon Juvenile Crime and Juvenile Justice in "the Country"', Honours Thesis, Department of Criminology, University of Melbourne.

Mouzos, J. (2002) *Homicide in Australia: 2000–2001*, National Homicide Monitoring Program annual report, Australian Institute of Criminology, Canberra.

Mouzos, J. (2000) *Homicidal Encounters: A Study of Homicide in Australia, 1989–1999*, Research and Public Policy Series No. 28, Australian Institute of Criminology, Canberra.

Mouzos, J. & Thompson, S. (2000) *Gay-Hate Related Homicide: An Overview of Major Findings in NSW*, Trends & Issues in Crime and Criminal Justice No. 155, Australian Institute of Criminology, Canberra.

Mugford, J. (1992) 'International Perspectives on the Interface of Drug Use and Criminal Behaviour', *Contemporary Drug Problems*, 19(2): 181–385.

Muir, K., Maquire, A., Slack-Smith, D. & Murray, M. (2003) *Youth Unemployment in Australia: A Contextual, Governmental and Organisational Perspective*, The Smith Family for the AMP Foundation, Sydney.

Mukherjee, S. (2000) 'Crime Trends: A National Perspective', in D. Chappell & P. Wilson (eds) *Crime and the Criminal Justice System in Australia: 2000 and Beyond*, Butterworths, Australia.

Mukherjee, S. (1999) *Ethnicity and Crime,* Trends & Issues in Crime and Criminal Justice No. 117, Australian Institute of Criminology, Canberra.

Mukherjee, S.K. (1997a) 'The Dimensions of Juvenile Crime', in A. Borowski & I. O'Connor (eds) *Juvenile Crime, Justice and Corrections*, Longman, Sydney.

Mukherjee, S.K. (1997b) 'Juvenile Crime: Overview of Changing Pattern', paper presented at the Australian Institute of Criminology Conference, *Juvenile Crime and Juvenile Justice: Towards 2000 and Beyond*, Adelaide, 26–27 June.

Mukherjee, S. (1996) 'Measuring Crime', in K.M. Hazlehurst (ed.) *Crime & Justice in Australia*, Law Book Company, Sydney: 61–89.

Mukherjee, S. (1981) *Crime Trends in Twentieth Century Australia*, George Allen & Unwin, Sydney.

Mukherjee, S. & Carcach, C. (1998) *Repeat Victimisation in Australia*, Australian Institute of Criminology Research and Public Policy Series No. 15, Canberra.

Mukherjee, S., Carcach, C. & Higgins, K. (1997) *Juvenile Crime and Justice: Australia 1997*, Australian Institute of Criminology, Canberra.

Mukherjee, S. & Dagger, D. (1990) *The Size of the Crime Problem in Australia*, Australian Institute of Criminology, Canberra.

Mukherjee, S. & Graycar, A. (1997) *Crime and Justice in Australia 1997*, Federation Press, Sydney.

Mukherjee, S., Neuhaus, D. & Walker, J. (1990) *Crime and Justice in Australia*, Australian Institute of Criminology, Canberra.

Mukherjee, S., Walker, J. & Jacobsen, E. (1986) *Crime and Punishment in the Colonies: A Statistical Profile*, History Project Inc., Kensington, NSW.

Munro, L. (2004) 'Animals, Nature and Human Interest', in R. White (ed.) *Controversies in Environmental Sociology*, Cambridge University Press.

Naffine, N. (1997) *Feminism & Criminology*, Allen & Unwin, Sydney.

Naffine, N. (1987) *Female Crime: The Construction of Women in Criminology*, Allen & Unwin, Sydney.

Nagin, D.S. & Smith, D.A. (1990) 'Participation in and Frequency of Delinquent Behaviour: A Test for Structural Differences', *Journal of Quantitative Criminology*, 6(4): 335–56.

National Committee on Violence (1990) *Violence: Directions for Australia*, Australian Institute of Criminology, Canberra.

National Inquiry into the Separation of Aboriginal and Torres Strait Islander Children from their Families (Australia) (NISATSIC), Wilson, R.D. (1997) *Bringing Them Home: Report of the National Inquiry into the Separation of Aboriginal and Torres Strait Islander Children from their Families*, Human Rights and Equal Opportunity Commission, Sydney.

National Police Ethnic Advisory Bureau (1997) *Descriptions of Persons Issued by Police to the Media: National Guidelines*, NPEAB, Melbourne.

National White Collar Crime Centre (2003) *Research Section Fact Sheet* <www.nw3c.org/research_topics.html> (accessed 20 July 2003).

Neasey, F. (1993) *Report of an Inquiry into the System of Classification of Prisoners in Tasmania and Other Related Matters*, Attorney General's Office, Hobart.

Nelson, D. & Perrone, S. (2000) *Understanding and Controlling Retail Theft*, Trends & Issues in Crime and Criminal Justice No. 152, Australian Institute of Criminology, Canberra.

Nettler, G. (1984) *Explaining Crime*, McGraw-Hill, New York.

New South Wales Bureau of Crime Statistics (2003a) *Average length of imprisonment (months), by principal offence, NSW Local Court 1998 to 2002*, <www.lawlink. nsw.gov.au/bocsar1.nsf/pages/lc_mean9802> (accessed 25 November 2003).

New South Wales Bureau of Crime Statistics (2003b) *Number of charges by offence type, NSW Local Court 1998 to 2002*, <www.lawlink/nsw.gov.au/bocsar1.nsf/pages/1c_charges9802 > (accessed 25 November 2003).

New South Wales Law Reform Commission (2001) *Sentencing Young Offenders*, Issues Paper No. 19, Law Reform Commission, Sydney.

New South Wales Office of the Ombudsman (2000) *Police and Public Safety Act*, Office of the Ombudsman, Sydney.

New South Wales Office of the Ombudsman (1994) *Race Relations and Our Police*, Office of the Ombudsman, Sydney.

New South Wales Ombudsman (1996) *Inquiry into Juvenile Detention Centres* (2 vols), NSW Ombudsman, Sydney.

Noble, G., Poynting, S. & Tabar, P. (1999) 'Lebanese Youth and Social Identity', in R. White (ed.) *Australian Youth Subcultures: On the Margins and in the Mainstream*, Australian Clearinghouse for Youth Studies, Hobart.

Nugent, S., Burns, D., Wilson, P. & Chappell, D. (1989) *Armed Robbery from an Offender's Perspective: Implications for Prevention*, Australian Institute of Criminology, Canberra.

Oates, B. (2003) *Lexis-Nexis*, cited in email communication with the National White Collar Crime Center, September 2003.

Ogilvie, E. (1996) 'Masculine Obsessions: An Examination of Criminology, Criminality and Gender', *Australian and New Zealand Journal of Criminology*, 29(3): 205–7.

O'Leary, C. & Platt, T. (2001) 'Pledging Allegiance: The Revival of Prescriptive Patriotism', *Social Justice*, 28(3): 41–4.

Painter, K. (1992) 'Different Worlds: The Spatial, Temporal and Social Dimensions of Female Victimization', in D. Evans, N. Fyfe & D. Herbert (eds) *Crime, Policing and Place: Essays in Environmental Criminology*, Routledge, London.

Palmer, D. & Collard, L. (1993) 'Aboriginal young people and youth subcultures', in R. White (ed.) *Youth Subcultures: Theory, History and the Australian Experience*, National Clearinghouse for Youth Studies, Hobart.

Parker, H., Aldridge, J. & Measham, F. (1998) *Illegal Leisure: The Normalization of Adolescent Drug Use*, Routledge, London.

Parliament of Victoria (1997) *Inquiry into the Victorian Government's Drug Reform Strategy: Turning the Tide*, Drugs and Crime Prevention Committee, Victorian Government Printer, Melbourne.

Patton, S. (2003) *Pathways: How Women Leave Violent Men*, Women Tasmania, Department of Premier and Cabinet, Government of Tasmania, Hobart.

Pearson, G. (1983) *Hooligan: A History of Respectable Fears*, Macmillan, London.

Pe-Pua, R. (1996) *'We're Just Like Other Kids!': Street-frequenting Youth of Non-English-speaking background*, Bureau of Immigration, Multicultural and Population Research, Melbourne.

Perrone, S. & White, R. (2000) *Young People and Gangs*, Trends & Issues in Crime and Criminal Justice No. 167, Australian Institute of Criminology, Canberra.

Peto, J., Decarli, A., La Vecchia, C., Levi, F. & Negri, E. (1999) 'The European mesothelioma epidemic', *British Journal of Cancer*, 79(3–4): 666–72.

Phelan, A. (1999) 'Child's Play', *Sydney Morning Herald*, 4 December: 43.

Pickering, S. & Lambert, C. (2002) 'Deterrence: Australia's Refugee Policy', *Current Issues in Criminal Justice*, 14(1): 65–86.

Polk, K. (2000) 'Changing Patterns of Violence', in D. Chappell & P. Wilson (eds) *Crime and the Criminal Justice System in Australia: 2000 and Beyond*, Butterworths, Chatswood: 87–101.

Polk, K. (1994) *When Men Kill: Scenarios of Masculine Violence*, Cambridge University Press, Cambridge.

Polk, K. & Warren, I. (1996), 'Crimes Against the Person', in K. Hazlehurst (ed.) *Crime and Justice*, Law Book Company, Sydney: 183–203.

Polk, K. & White, R. (1999) 'Economic Adversity and Criminal Behaviour: Rethinking Youth Unemployment and Crime', *Australian and New Zealand Journal of Criminology*, 32(3): 284–302.

Pollack, O. 1961, *The Criminality of Women*, University of Pennsylvania Press, Philadelphia.

Potas, I. (1993) *Thinking about Tax Avoidance*, Trends & Issues in Crime and Criminal Justice No. 43, Australian Institute of Criminology, Canberra.

Poynting, S. (1999) 'When "Zero Tolerance" Looks Like Racial Intolerance: "Lebanese Youth Gangs", Discrimination and Resistance', *Current Issues in Criminal Justice*, 11(1): 74–8.

Poynting, S., Noble, G. & Tabar, P. (2001) 'Middle Eastern Appearances: "Ethnic Gangs", Moral Panic and Media Framing', *Australian and New Zealand Journal of Criminology*, 34(1): 67–90.

Poynting, S., Noble, G., Tabar, P. & Collins, J. (2004) *Bin Laden in the suburbs: criminalising the Arab Other*, Sydney Institute of Criminology Series No. 18, Sydney.

Probation and Community Corrections Officers' Association (2003) *The Foundations of Corrections Based Services for Victims of Crime: A PACCOA Position Paper*, PACCOA Papers 1(1), August.

Putnam, R.D. (1995) 'Bowling alone: America's declining social capital', *The Journal of Democracy*, 6(1): 65–78.

Putnam, R.D. (1993) *Making Democracy Work: Civic traditions in modern Italy*, Princeton University Press, Princeton.

Putnins, A. (2001) *Substance Use By South Australian Young Offenders*, Office of Crime Statistics Information Bulletin No. 19, Attorney-General's Department, Adelaide.

Quinlan, M. (1994) 'Trends in occupational health and safety prosecutions and penalties: a comment', in R. Johnstone (ed.) *Occupational health and safety prosecutions in Australia : overviews and issues*, Centre for Employment and Labour Relations Law: 13–20.

*R v Kumar* [2002] VSCA 139 (10 September).

*R v Lander* [1999] VSC 554 (16 September).

Rafter, N. (2000) *Encyclopedia of Women and Crime*, The Onyx Press, Phoenix.

Rafter, N.H. & Heidensohn, F. (1995) 'Introduction: the Development of Feminist Perspectives on Crime', in N.H. Rafter & F. Heidensohn (eds) *International Feminist Perspectives in Criminology: Engendering a Discipline*, Open University Press, Buckingham.

Ratcliffe, J. (2001) *Policing Urban Burglary*, Trends & Issues in Crime and Criminal Justice No. 213, Australian Institute of Criminology, Canberra.

Rawnsley, J. (1995) *Total Risk: Nick Leeson and the Fall of Barings Bank*, Harper Collins, New York.

Read, P. (1999) *A Rape of the Soul so Profound*, Allen & Unwin, St Leonards.

Rebovich, D. & Layne, J.L. (2000) *The National Public Survey on White Collar Crime*, National White Collar Crime Center, Morgantown, <www.nw3c.org/ research_main.html> (accessed 20 August 2003).

Reichman, N. (1998) 'Moving backstage: Uncovering the role of compliance practices in shaping regulatory policies', in R. Baldwin, C. Scott & C. Hood (eds) *A Reader on Regulation*, Oxford University Press, Oxford.

Reiman, J. (1998) *The Rich Get Richer and the Poor Get Prison*, Allyn & Bacon, Boston.

Rengert, G.F., Piquero, A.R. & Jones, P.R. (1999) 'Distance decay re-examined', *Criminology*, 37(2): 427–45.

Robinson, B. (2003) *Review of the Enforcement and Prosecution Guidelines of the Department of Environmental Protection of Western Australia*, Communication Edge, Perth.

Robinson, B. (1995) 'The Nature of Environmental Crime', in N. Gunningham, J. Norberry & S. McKillop (eds) *Environmental Crime*, Australian Institute of Criminology, Canberra.

Rodger, J. (1992) 'The Welfare State and Social Closure: Social Division and the "Underclass"', *Critical Social Policy*, 35: 45–63.

Rosoff, S., Pontell, H. & Tillman, R. (1998) *Profit Without Honor: White-Collar Crime and the Looting of America*, Prentice Hall, Upper Saddle River.

Ross, S. & Forster, K. (2000) 'Female Prisoners: Using Imprisonment Statistics to Understand the Place of Women in the Criminal Justice System', paper presented at 'Women in Corrections: Staff and Clients Conference', Australian Institute of Criminology, Adelaide, 31 October–1 November.

Rowe, J. (2001) 'Pure Politics: A historical look at Australian drug policy', *Alternative Law Journal*, 26(3): 125–9.

Royal Commission into Aboriginal Deaths in Custody (RCIADIC) (1991) *National Report, Vol. 2* AGPS, Canberra.

Rubington, E. & Weinberg, M. (eds) (1978) *Deviance: The Interactionist Perspective*, Macmillan, New York.

Rush, S. (2002) 'Aboriginal Resistance to the Abuse of their Natural Resources: The Struggle for Trees and Water', in S. Boyd, D. Chunn & R. Menzies (eds) *Toxic Criminology: Environment, Law and the State in Canada*, Fernwood Publishing, Halifax.

Salmelainen, P. (1996) *"Home Invasions" and Robberies*, Contemporary Issues in Crime and Justice No. 31, Crime and Justice Bulletin, NSW Bureau of Crime Statistics and Research, Sydney.

Salmelainen, P. (1995), *The Correlates of Offending Frequency: A Study of Juvenile Theft Offenders in Detention*, NSW Bureau of Crime Statistics and Research, Sydney.

Salmelainen, P. (1992) *Stealing in NSW*, Contemporary Issues in Crime and Justice No. 16, NSW Bureau of Crime Statistics and Social Research, Sydney.

Sanders, W.B. (1970) *Juvenile Offenders for a Thousand Years*, University of North Carolina, Chapel Hill.

Saroca, N. (2002) 'Violence against Filipino Women in Australia: Theorising the Relationship between the Discursive and the Non-Discursive', paper presented at 'Expanding our Horizons' Conference, University of Sydney, 18–22 February.

Schetzer, L. (2000) *A Review of the Law on the Age of Criminal Responsibility of Children: Discussion Paper 3*, National Children's and Youth Law Centre, Sydney.

Schwendinger, H. & Schwendinger, J. (1975) 'Defenders of Order or Guardians of Human Rights', in I. Taylor, P. Walton & J. Young (eds) *Critical Criminology*, Routledge and Kegan Paul, London.

Scutt, J. (1995) 'Judicial Bias or Legal Bias? Battery, Women and the Law', in J. Bessant, K. Carrington & S. Cook (eds) *Cultures of Crime and Violence: The Australian Experience*, La Trobe University Press, Melbourne.

Scutt, J. (1990) *Women and the Law: Commentary and Materials*, Law Book Company, Sydney.

Seis, M. (1993) 'Ecological Blunders in US Clean Air Legislation', *Journal of Human Justice*, 5(1): 58–81.

Sercombe, H. (1995) 'The Face of the Criminal is Aboriginal', in J. Bessant, C. Carrington & J. Cook (eds) *Cultures of Crime and Violence: The Australian Experience*, Victorian Law Foundation, Bundoora.

Seymour, A. (2001) *The Victim's Role in Offender Reentry: A Community Response Manual*, Office for Victims of Crime, US Department of Justice, Washington DC.

Seymour, J. (1988) *Dealing with Young Offenders*, Law Book Company, North Ryde.

Shapiro, S. (1990) 'Collaring the crime, not the criminal: Reconsidering the concept of white collar crime', *American Sociological Review*, 55: 346–65.

Shaw, C.R. & McKay, H.D. (1942) *Juvenile Delinquency and Urban Areas*, University of Chicago Press, Chicago.

Shildrick, T. (2002) 'Young People, Illicit Drug Use and the Question of Normalization', *Journal of Youth Studies*, 5(1): 35–48.

Shover, N. & Wright, J. (eds) (2001) *Crimes of Privilege: Readings in White-Collar Crime*, Oxford University Press, New York.

Silbert, M.H. & Pines, A.M. (1981) 'Sexual Child Abuse as an Antecedent to Prostitution', *Child Abuse and Neglect*, 5: 407–11.

Situ, Y. & Emmons, D. (2000) *Environmental Crime: The Criminal Justice System's Role in Protecting the Environment*, Sage, Thousand Oaks.

Slapper, G. & Tombs, S. (1999) *Corporate Crime*, Pearson Education, London.

Smart, C. (1976) *Women, Crime and Criminology*, Routledge and Kegan Paul, London.

Smith, C. & Thornberry, T.P. (1995) 'The Relationship between Childhood Maltreatment and Adolescent Involvement in Delinquency', *Criminology*, 33(4): 451–81.

Smith, D.A., Visher, C.A. & Jarjoura, G.R. (1991) 'Dimensions of Delinquency: Exploring the Correlates of Participation, Frequency and Persistence of Delinquent Behaviour', *Journal of Research in Crime and Delinquency*, 28(1): 6–32.

Smith, R. (1999) *Identity Related Economic Crime: Risks and Countermeasures*, Trends & Issues in Crime and Criminal Justice No. 129, Australian Institute of Criminology, Canberra.

Snider, L. (2000) 'The Sociology of Corporate Crime: An Obituary (or: Whose knowledge claims have legs?)', *Theoretical Criminology*, 4(2): 169–206.

Solomos, J. (1988) *Black Youth, Racism and the State: The Politics of Ideology and Policy*, Cambridge University Press, Cambridge.

Spitzer, S. (1975) 'Toward a Marxian Theory of Deviance', *Social Problems*, 22: 638–51.

Staats, G.R. (1977) 'Changing Conceptualizations of Professional Criminals', *Criminology*, 15 (May): 49–65.

Standing Committee on Social Issues (1995) *A Report into Youth Violence in New South Wales*, Legislative Council, Parliament of New South Wales.

Stanko, E. (1985) *Intimate Intrusions: Women's Experiences of Male Violence*, Routledge and Kegan Paul, London.

Starr, P. (1982) *The Social Transformation of American Medicine*, Basic Books, New York.

Stephens, S. (1996) 'Reflections on Environmental Justice: Children as Victims and Actors', *Social Justice*, 23(4): 62–86.

Stewart, A., Dennison, S. & Waterson, E. (2002), *Pathways from child maltreatment to juvenile offending*, Trends & Issues in Crime and Criminal Justice No. 241, Australian Institute of Criminology, Canberra.

*Sun Herald* (1999) 'A Picture which Shames us all', Editorial, 31 January: 46.

Sutherland, E. (1949) *White Collar Crime*, Dryden Press, New York.

Sutherland, E. (1933) *The Professional Thief*, University of Chicago Press, Chicago.

Sutton, A. & James, S. (1996) *Evaluation of Australian Drug Anti-Trafficking Law Enforcement*, National Police Research Unit, Adelaide.

Sutton, C. & Walker, F. (1999) 'Shooting up on Easy Street', *The Sun Herald*, 31 January: 6.

*Sydney Morning Herald* (2000) 'Esmeralda Cyanide Spill', 12 February.

Sykes, G. & Matza, D. (1957) 'Techniques of Neutralization: A Theory of Delinquency', *American Sociological Review*, 22: 664–70.

Tappan, P. (1947) 'Who is the Criminal', *American Sociological Review*, 12: 96–102.

Tarling, R. (1993) *Analysing Offending*, HMSO, London.

*Tasmanian Corrections Act* 1997.

Taylor, I., Walton, P. & Young, J. (1973) *The New Criminology*, Routledge & Kegan Paul, London.

Taylor, N. (2002) *Robbery against Service Stations and Pharmacies: Recent Trends*, Trends & Issues in Crime and Criminal Justice No. 223, Australian Institute of Criminology, Canberra.

Taylor, N. & Mayhew, P. (2002) *Patterns of Victimisation among Small Retail Businesses*, Trends & Issues in Crime and Criminal Justice No. 221, Australian Institute of Criminology, Canberra.

Taylor, R.B. & Hale, C. (1986) 'Testing alternative models of fear of crime', *Journal of Criminal Law and Criminology*, 77: 151–89.

Thomas, W.I. (1923) *The Unadjusted Girl*, Little, Brown & Co., New York.

Thornberry, T.P., Ireland, T.O. & Smith, C.A. (2001) 'The importance of timing: The varying impact of childhood and adolescent maltreatment on multiple problem outcomes', *Development and Psychopathology*, 13(4): 957–79.

Tomsen, S. (2002) *Hatred, Murder and Male Honour: Anti-homosexual Homicides in New South Wales, 1980-2000*, Australian Institute of Criminology Research and Public Policy Series No. 43, Australian Institute of Criminology, Canberra.

Tomsen, S. (2001) 'Hate Crime and Masculinity: New Crimes, New Responses and Some Familiar Patterns', paper presented at the 4th National Outlook Symposium on Crime in Australia, 'New Crimes or New Responses', Australian Institute of Criminology, Canberra, 2001.

Tonry, M. (1997) 'Ethnicity, Crime, and Immigration', in M. Tonry (ed.) *Ethnicity, Crime, and Immigration: Comparative and Cross-National Perspectives*, University of Chicago Press, Chicago.

Toohey, B. (2004) 'Welcome to the 21st Century', *Weekend Australian Financial Review*, 31 December–4 January.

Tressider, J., Macaskill, P., Bennett, D. & Nutbeam, D. (1997) 'Health Risks and Behaviour of Out-of-School 16-year-olds in New South Wales', *Australian and New Zealand Journal of Public Health*, 21(2): 168–74.

Trigger, D. (1995) 'Everyone's Agreed, the West is all you Need', *Media Information Australia*, 75: 102–22.

Trimboli, L. (1995) 'Women as Victims and Offenders', *Contemporary Issues in Crime and Justice No. 22*, Crime and Justice Bulletin, NSW Bureau of Crime Statistics and Research, Sydney.

Underwood, R., White, R. & Omelczuk, S. (1993) *Young People, Youth Services and Legal Issues*, Edith Cowan University, Joondalup.

United Nations Office for Drug Control and Crime Prevention (1999) *Handbook on Justice for Victims: On the use and application of the Declaration of Basic Principles of Justice for Victims of Crime and Abuse of Power*, United Nations Office for Drug Control and Crime Prevention and the Centre for International Crime Prevention, New York.

United States Bureau of Justice Assistance (1998) *Addressing Community Gang Problems: A Practical Guide*, US Department of Justice, Washington DC.

van Kesteren, J., Mayhew, P. & Nieuwbeerta, P. (2001) *Criminal Victimisation in Seventeen Countries: Key Findings from the 2000 International Crime Victims Survey*, Research and Documentation Centre, The Hague.

Victorian Environmental Protection Authority (2003) *Annual Report 2002–2003: Compliance Report*, Victorian Government Printer.

Victorian Multicultural Commission (2000) *Multicultural Perspectives of Crime and Safety*, VMC, Melbourne.

Visher, C. & Roth, J. (1986) 'Participation in Criminal Careers', in A. Blumstein, J. Cohen, J.A. Roth & C.A. Visher (eds) *Criminal Careers and Career Criminals*, 1, National Academy Press, Washington, DC.

Viviani, N. (1996) *The Indochinese in Australia 1975–1995: From burnt boats to barbecues*, Oxford University Press, Melbourne.

Void, G., Bernard, T. & Snipes, J. (2002) *Theoretical Criminology* (5th edn), Oxford University Press, New York.

Wakim, J. (2004) 'Gang Rape, Sport, Power—and Prejudice', *The Age*, 9 March <www.theage.com.au/articles/2004/03/08/1078594295482.html> (accessed 2 June 2004).

Walker, J. (1994) 'Trends in Crime and Criminal Justice', in D. Chappell & P. Wilson (eds) *The Australian Criminal Justice System: The Mid-1990s*, Butterworths, North Ryde: 1–36.

Walker, L. (1999) 'Hydraulic sexuality and hegemonic masculinity: Young Working-Class Men and Car Culture', in R. White (ed.) *Australian Youth Subcultures: On the Margins and in the Mainstream*, Australian Clearinghouse for Youth Studies, Hobart.

Walklate, S. (1990) 'Researching Victims of Crime: Radical Victimology', *Social Justice*, 17(3): 25–42.

Walsh, T. (2004) 'Who is the "Public", in "Public Space"? A Queensland perspective on poverty, homelessness and vagrancy', *Alterative Law Journal*, 29(2): 81–6.

Walters, B. (2003) *Slapping on the Writs: Defamation, Developers and Community Activism*, UNSW Press, Sydney.

Ward, T. & Green, P. (2000) 'Legitimacy, Civil Society, and State Crime', *Social Justice*, 27(4): 76–93.

Weatherburn, D. (2002) 'The Impact of Unemployment on Crime', in P. Saunders & R. Taylor (eds) *The Price of Prosperity: The Economic and Social Costs of Unemployment*, UNSW Press, Sydney: 226–48.

Weatherburn, D. (2001) *What Causes Crime?*, Crime & Justice Bulletin No. 54, NSW Bureau of Crime Statistics & Research, Sydney.

Weatherburn, D. (1996) 'Property Crime: Linking Theory to Policy', in K. Hazlehurst (ed.) *Australian Crime & Justice*, Law Book Company, Sydney: 205–32.

Weatherburn, D. (1992) *Economic Adversity and Crime*, Trends & Issues in Crime and Criminal Justice No. 40, Australian Institute of Criminology, Canberra.

Weatherburn, D. & Lind, B. (2001) *Delinquent-Prone Communities*, Cambridge University Press, Cambridge.

Weatherburn, D. & Lind, B. (1997), *Social and Economic Stress, Child Neglect and Juvenile Delinquency*, New South Wales Bureau of Crime Statistics and Research, Sydney.

Weatherburn, D., Lind, B. & Hua, J. (2003) *Contact with the New South Wales Court and Prison Systems: The Influence of Age, Indigenous Status and Gender*, Contemporary Issues in Crime and Justice No. 78, Crime and Justice Bulletin, NSW Bureau of Crime Statistics and Research, Sydney.

Weatherburn, D., Lind, B. & Ku, S. (2001) 'The Short-Run Effects of Economic Adversity on Property Crime', *Australian and New Zealand Journal of Criminology*, 34: 134–47.

Weatherburn, D., Matka, E. & Lind, B. (1996) 'Crime Perception and Reality: Public Perception of the Risk of Criminal Victimisation in Australia', *Crime and Justice Bulletin No. 28*, Bureau of Crime Statistics and Research, Sydney.

Weber, L. (2002) 'The Detention of Asylum Seekers: 20 Reasons Why Criminologists Should Care', *Current Issues in Criminal Justice*, 14(1): 9–30.

Weeks, W. (2002) 'Towards the Prevention of Violence and the Creation of Safe and Supportive Gender Relations', in W. Weeks & M. Quinn (eds) *Issues Facing Australian Families: Human Services Respond*, Longman, Melbourne.

Western Australia Office of Youth Affairs (2000) *Youth facts WA: Young people and legal issues*, Office of Youth Affairs, Perth.

White, R. (2002) *Understanding Youth Gangs*, Trends & Issues in Crime and Criminal Justice No. 237, Australian Institute of Criminology, Canberra.

White, R. (2001) 'Graffiti, Crime Prevention & Cultural Space', *Current Issues in Criminal Justice,* 12(3): 253–68.

White, R. (1999a) *Hanging Out: Negotiating Young People's Use of Public Space*, National Crime Prevention, Attorney General's Department, Canberra.

White, R. (1999b) 'Criminality, Risk and Environmental Harm', *Griffith Law Review* 8(2): 235–57.

White, R. (1998) 'Environmental Criminology and Sydney Water', *Current Issues in Criminal Justice* 10(2): 214–19.

White, R. (1997–98) 'Violence and Masculinity: The Construction of Criminality', *Arena Magazine*, Dec–Jan: 41–4.

White, R. (1996) 'Racism, Policing and Ethnic Youth Gangs', *Current Issues in Criminal Justice* 7(3): 302–13.

White, R. (1990) *No Space of their Own: Young People and Social Control in Australia*, Cambridge University Press, Melbourne.

White, R. & Alder, C. (eds) (1994) *The Police and Young People in Australia*, Cambridge University Press, Melbourne.

White, R. & Haines, F. (2004) *Crime and Criminology* (3rd edn), Oxford University Press, Melbourne.

White, R. & Perrone, S. (2001) 'Racism, Ethnicity and Hate Crime', *Communal/Plural* 9(2): 161–81.

White, R. & Perrone, S. (1997) *Crime and Social Control*, Oxford University Press, Melbourne.

White, R., Perrone, S., Guerra, C. & Lampugnani, R. (1999), *Ethnic Youth Gangs in Australia: Do They Exist?*, Overview Report, Australian Multicultural Foundation, Melbourne.

White, R., Aumair, M., Harris, A. & McDonnell, L. (1997) *Any Which Way You Can: Youth livelihoods, community resources and crime*, Australian Youth Foundation, Sydney.

White, R. & van der Velden, J. (1995) 'Class and Criminality', *Social Justice* 22(1): 51–74.

White, R. & Wyn, J. (2004) *Youth and Society: Exploring the Social Dynamics of Youth Experience*, Oxford University Press, Melbourne.

Widom, C.S. & Maxfield, M. (2001), 'An update on the "cycle of violence"', *Research in Brief*, National Institute of Justice, Washington DC.

Williams, C. (1996) 'An Environmental Victimology', *Social Justice*, 23(4): 16–40.

Wilson, J.Q. (1975) *Thinking about Crime*, Basic Books, New York.

Wilson, J.Q. & Kelling, G. (1982) 'The Police and Neighborhood Safety: Broken Windows', *Atlantic*, 127: 29–38.

Wilson, P. (1987) *Corporate crime in Australia*, Trends & Issues in Crime and Criminal Justice No. 5, Australian Institute of Criminology, Canberra.

Wilson, P & Lincoln, R. (1992) 'Young People, Economic Crisis, Social Control and Crime', *Current Issues in Criminal Justice*, 4(2): 110–16.

Wilson, W.J. (1996) *When Work Disappears*, Knopf, New York.

Wolfgang, M.E., Figlio, R.M. & Sellin, T. (1972) *Delinquency in a Birth Cohort*, University of Chicago Press, Chicago.

Worrall, A. (1990) *Offending Women*, Routledge, London.

Wortley, Scot. (1999) 'A Northern Taboo: Research on Race, Crime and Criminal Justice in Canada', *Canadian Journal of Criminology*, 41(2): 261–74.

Wundersitz, J. (1996) 'Juvenile Justice', in K. Hazlehurst (ed.) *Crime and Justice*, Law Book Company, Sydney.

Wundersitz, J. (1993) 'Some Statistics on Youth Offending', in F. Gale, N. Naffine & J. Wundersitz (eds) *Juvenile Justice: Debating the Issues*, Allen & Unwin, North Sydney.

Youth Justice Coalition, Western Sydney Juvenile Justice Interest Group & Youth Action and Policy Association (1994) *Nobody Listens: The Experience of Contact between Young People and the Police*, Youth Justice Coalition, Sydney.

# Index